D1327876

Liberal Democrats in the Weimar Republic

The History of the German Democratic Party and the German State Party

Bruce B. Frye

Southern Illinois University Press
Carbondale and Edwardsville

Library of Congress Cataloging in Publication Data

Frye, Bruce B., 1920–
  Liberal Democrats in the Weimar Republic.

  Bibliography: p.
  Includes index.
    1. Deutsche Demokratische Partei—History.
  2. Deutsche Staatspartei—History. 3. Germany—Politics
  and government—1918–1933. 4. Liberalism—Germany—
  History. I. Title.
  JN3970.D35F78 1985   324.243'02   84-22169
  ISBN 0-8093-1207-7

  88   87   86   85   4   3   2   1

To Caroline

Contents

Contents

Preface

My interest in German history began in the events of the 1930s and my service in World War II and the German Occupation following the war. After separation from the army I completed my undergraduate work at the University of Oregon and began graduate work in history. Gordon Wright, my graduate adviser and the person who has best provided me the model of teacher and scholar, suggested a thesis on the Catholic Center party. This began my study of German political parties. Later, at Stanford University, where I continued graduate work, I wrote a political biography of Matthias Erzberger, the leader of the Center party, for my doctoral dissertation. The late Fritz Epstein suggested the topic, the late David Harris directed the dissertation, while H. Stuart Hughes was the second reader. The dissertation was completed in 1953, the same year I accepted a position at Colorado A and M College, which became Colorado State University in 1959. It was impossible for me to do research in Germany in these years, but I continued to read in the growing body of historical literature on Weimar Germany with the intent of revising the dissertation for publication. Then, in 1959, the late Klaus Epstein published his study of Erzberger, which preempted the book I had in mind. Shortly afterwards, in 1961, Agnes Peterson, curator for the Western European collection at the Hoover Institution, informed me that the collection of the NSDAP *Hauptarchiv*, which the Institution had recently microfilmed, included several reels of documents pertaining to the German Democratic party/German State party (DDP/DStP). By this time, the State Department's microfilmed edition of the Stresemann Papers could be purchased from the National Archives. These materials plus a large number of memoirs, party journals, and newspapers redirected my study of parties to the liberal parties. I received a research grant from Colorado State University in the spring of 1961 and spent the summer of 1961 at Stanford, which resulted in a professional paper and a published article on the DDP. Then, in 1963, I received a sabbatical leave for a year of research in Germany, receiving several grants which enabled me to take my family to Germany. At the time I planned a general study of Weimar middle class parties and middle class political behavior, although it soon became apparent that the best primary materials for a historical work supported a book on the Democratic party. Although several sets of private papers of DDP leaders had already been deposited in various archives, some key papers were still in the hands of relatives. I also soon discovered that my knowledge of political sociology was inadequate for the book I had in mind. Upon my return I sought to rectify my shortcomings while desperately trying to stay abreast of the flood of books and articles on twentieth-century Germany.

The chance discovery of a letter of Max Weber in the papers of Carl Petersen produced a long diversion and two articles on Max Weber and his ties to the DDP. The prominence of Jews in the DDP and my feeling that this was an area which neither the DDP members nor German historians had dealt with candidly led to another long detour. In 1973, I made a hurried trip at Christmas to Koblenz and Darmstadt to study several sets of papers which had been deposited since 1964, and, in 1975, a research trip to London to work at the Leo Baeck Institute and the Wiener Library completed my study of the DDP and the Jewish Question, which resulted in another article. By the late 1970s, a number of studies of the DDP had appeared, whereas in 1961 there had been almost none. Several works were by scholars who were most interested in liberalism as intellectual history. Others only dealt with a few years of the DDP's history or were on restricted subjects. Most of them grew out of dissertations and had utilized only a small percentage of the private papers available. Most were preoccupied with the DDP's failure and the relationship between its failure and Nazi success. I learned much from several of these studies, but the most useful books for me were Lothar Albertin's *Liberalismus und Demokratie am Anfang der Weimarer Republik* and Werner Stephan's *Aufstieg und Verfall des Linksliberalismus 1918–1933*. It seemed to me that there was still room for a scholarly political history of the party based primarily on archival sources. In 1980, I received a second sabbatical from Colorado State University, which enabled me to finish research for the book in materials deposited since 1975 and to begin the writing of the book.

During these years of research and writing, I received assistance and support from many people and institutions. Gordon Wright continued to help me in many ways. The late John L. Snell assisted me greatly in the early years of the project and more recently his successor at the University of North Carolina, Gerhard L. Weinberg, who makes his summer home near Fort Collins, has given me valuable advise and counsel. My colleagues, and especially Harry Rosenberg and Manfred J. Enssle, have read and criticized portions of the manuscript, but more importantly have given me moral support to persist. Viola Breit aided me as a research assistant in 1963–1964; Ann Allen and Larry E. Jones read the manuscript at an early stage and offered constructive advice; Theodore Hamerow and Arnold Price recently read the manuscript for Southern Illinois University Press and made many valuable corrections and comments. My daughter, Susan C. Frye, a Ph.D. candidate in English at Stanford, read the entire manuscript and made many helpful comments and corrections on style. Jean Thomas, one of my wife's colleagues in the Office of Conferences and Institutes at Colorado State University, typed two versions of the manuscript. The heirs of the DDP leaders have been unfailingly kind and supportive. I was able not only to use the papers but to microfilm portions of them. Judge Edgar Petersen, Toni Stolper, Frau Rita Dietrich-Troeltsch, Ferdinand Friedensburg Jr., Helmut Goetz, Dirk Heile, and the family of Theodor Heuss gave the necessary permission to use the papers of their relatives.

Over the years I have received, in addition to two sabbatical leaves, several research grants from Colorado State University and grants from the American Philosophical Society, the Hoover Institution, and the Social Science Foundation of Denver University. In a region where there are no first-class research libraries in European history, one must travel occasionally to the archives or research libraries and use interlibrary loans extensively. I am indebted to the William E. Morgan Library at Colorado State University and, in particular, to the Inter-Library Loan staff. In addition, I would like to thank the staffs of the *Bundesarchiv* Koblenz; the *Institut für Zeitgeschichte*, Munich; the *Weltwirtschafts Institut*, Kiel; the Baden-Württemberg *Staatsarchiv*, Stuttgart; the *Stadtarchiv* Cologne; the *Staatsarchiv* Darmstadt; the German Historical Institute, London; the Leo Baeck Institute, London; the U.S. National Archives; and the Hoover Institution.

Finally, this book could never have been written without the help, love, and encouragement of my wife, Caroline, and our three children, Susan, Thomas, and Bradford.

Abbreviations

AHR	*American Historical Review*
Akten	Documents
BA	*Bundesarchiv*
BBZ	*Berliner Börsen-Zeitung*
BZM	*BZ am Mittag*
BT	*Berliner Tageblatt*
BVP	*Bayerische Volkspartei*—The Bavarian People's party
CEH	*Central European History*
CSV	*Christlich-Sozialer Volksdienst*—the Christian Social People's Service
C.V.	*Central-Verein deutscher Staatsbürger jüdischen Glaubens*—The Central Association of German Citizens of Jewish Faith
CVZ	*C.V. Zeitung*—the journal of the C.V.
DBB	*Deutscher Bauernbund*
DDP	*Deutsche Demokratische Partei*—the German Democratic party
DN	*Düsseldorfer Nachrichten*
DNVP	*Deutsche Nationale Volkspartei*—The German National People's party
DPK	*Demokratische Partei Korrespondenz*
DS	*Deutsche Stimmen*
DStP	*Deutsche Staatspartei*—the German State party
DVP	*Deutsche Volkspartei*—the German People's party

Abbreviations

DVF	*Deutsch-völkische Freiheitspartei*—the German Racist Freedom party
FDP	*Freie Demokratische Partei*—the Free Democratic party
FZ	*Frankfurter Zeitung*
GA	*Geschäftsführender Ausschuss*—the managing committee
HB	*Hansa-Bund für Gewerbe, Handel und Industrie*
HZ	*Historische Zeitschrift*
JConH	*Journal of Contemporary History*
JMH	*Journal of Modern History*
Jungdo	*Jungdeutscher Orden*—the Young German Order
KPD	*Kommunistische Partei Deutschlands*—the Communist party of Germany
KW	Koch-Weser
KZ	Kölnische Zeitung
MNN	*Münchner Neueste Nachrichten*
NL	*Nachlass*—Papers
NSDAP	*Nationalsozialistische Deutsche Arbeiterpartei*—the National Socialist German Workers' party—Nazis
NSDAP *Hauptarchiv*	The National Socialist German Workers' party main archive
OHL	*Oberste Heeresleitung*—the army high command
PA	*Parteiausschuss*—the national party Committee
PT	*Parteitag*—the party congress
Reichsbanner	*Reichsbanner Schwarz-Rot-Gold*—Reichsbanner Black-Red-Gold
SPD	*Sozialdemokratische Partei Deutschlands*—the Social Democratic party of Germany
S and S Laws	*Schund- und Schmutzgesetz*—trash and filth laws
USPD	*Unabhängige Sozialdemokratische Partei Deutschlands*—the Independent Socialist party of Germany
Vorstand or *Hauptvorstand*	The party executive committee
VR	*Volksnationale Reichsvereinigung*—the People's National Reichs Union

VRP	*Volksrechtspartei*—the People's Rights party
VZ	*Vossische Zeitung*
VZG	*Vierteljahreshefte für Zeitgeschichte*
WK	*Wahlkreis*—electoral district
WP	*Wirtschaftspartei*—the Economic party
Z	*Zentrum*—the Center party

Introduction

The left-liberal political tradition in Germany, although never popular, has persisted for well over a century. In the Weimar period (1919–1933), the German Democratic party (DDP) and its successor, the German State party (DStP), represented this tradition. In January 1919, the DDP received the third largest vote total in the election for the National Assembly. The election followed four years of war and a revolution, and it seemed that it might result in a socialist majority and government. This did not occur, much to the relief of the German middle classes, and instead a coalition of moderate parties—the DDP, the Social Democratic party (SPD), and the Catholic Center party—formed a government, the Weimar Coalition. The Democratic party gained several key cabinet posts and assumed the leadership in writing the Weimar Constitution. This was the beginning of a national political role for the DDP/DStP, which it maintained, although with diminished importance, until 1932.[1] The DDP/DStP had representation in sixteen of seventeen national governments during this period. Moreover, in Prussia, where the Weimar Coalition remained in power, it served from 1919 to 1932 as well. Prussia was by far the largest and most important German state (*Land*). In addition, at the municipal level of government, the DDP provided more mayors of principal German cities than any other party. Because many Democrats were trained as local government officials and the DDP could serve as a bridge between the political extremes, many city councils elected Democratic mayors soon after the revolution. They served long terms, and several were still in office when the Nazis came to power in 1933. Berlin, Hamburg, Frankfurt a/M, Dresden, Königsberg, Dessau, and many other cities and large towns had governments headed by a Democrat during the Weimar period. In addition, there were thousands of professional civil servants at all levels of government who were left liberals.

I

While the greatest significance of the Weimar Democrats was their contribution to democratic government, they are also remembered because of
their individual qualities. Many outstanding figures were active in the
DDP. Because of its following and its ideals, large numbers of teachers,
academics, and intellectuals backed the DDP. At the DDP's Party Congress (*Parteitag*) meeting in December 1919, forty percent of the delegates possessed a doctorate. Among the most prominent DDP leaders
were Max Weber, Friedrich Meinecke, Hugo Preuss, Friedrich Naumann,
Theodor Heuss, Ernst Troeltsch, and Gertrud Bäumer. Three Nobel prize
winners in chemistry were Democrats, while Thomas Mann and Heinrich
Mann were "close" to it. Many of Germany's leading journalists supported the DDP, as did the artist Max Liebermann, the portraitist of the
Weimar cultural establishment.

The left-liberal parties produced Germany's leading constitutional historians and lawyers. Preuss, who was one of the founders of the DDP in
November 1918, was perhaps Germany's leading constitutional authority.
He was asked by the socialist revolutionary government to draw up a constitutional draft before the election of the National Assembly. His committee included several prominent left liberals, including Max Weber, who
had long been associated with the desire to achieve parliamentary democracy in Germany on the English model. Later, the DDP dominated the
National Assembly's Constitution Committee, which Conrad Haussmann,
a veteran left-liberal politician, chaired. The DDP also assumed the leadership in the writing of several state constitutions and in reforming many
city governments. In later years, Democrats wrote most of the major constitutional studies and became linked in the public mind with the political
system of the Republic. Although the SPD and the Center party remained
far larger and more important than the DDP to the success of the Republic,
the DDP gained the reputation of being most in tune with the spirit and
institutions of Germany's first democracy. The DDP was the best example
of a liberal-democratic party in Germany, not unlike the Liberal party in
Britain or the Radical party in France at that time. Although political circumstances and national questions divided western European liberals, the
DDP's ideals and the values of its leaders were in the western left-liberal
mold; the DDP's brand of liberalism was not exceptional.[2]

Liberal historians close to the DDP wrote most of the standard historical
surveys of the Weimar Republic during and soon after the Nazi years
(1933–1945). They shaped the image of the DDP, painting a generally
favorable picture of the DDP and its leaders and tending to overlook the
party's "shady chapters." In foreign policy, for example, the DDP is seen
as a party which supported a conciliatory foreign policy and fulfillment of
the terms of the Treaty of Versailles. While there were pacifists and internationalists in the DDP, most Democrats were passionate nationalists who
were determined to revise the Treaty of Versailles as quickly as possible.

Their goals were only slightly less extreme than those of the extreme Right, although they were not prepared to use war to achieve those goals. Moreover, Democrats for the most part supported evasions of the military limitations placed on Germany by Versailles. The DDP has usually been portrayed as the bourgeois party which was most friendly toward Jews. After all, it generally found support in the Jewish community, and several of its leaders had Jewish ancestors. The liberal historians, however, overlooked the extent of moderate anti-Semitism in the DDP and the discrimination which Jews suffered within the party when they sought political office as Democrats. The DDP has also been portrayed as a party particularly friendly to women and young people, but in fact, it accorded them only a token role after 1920. Democrats in the Weimar period could not overcome the prejudices and values of the Protestant middle classes. Their strong nationalism and moderate anti-Semitism as well as their hatred and distrust of socialists and Catholics were deeply felt emotions and their defense of bourgeois property interests often determined their political stance. Their feelings and convictions combined to make the DDP an unreliable partner of the SPD and the Center party, the only parties besides the DDP which wholeheartedly supported the Republic. In 1919, the DDP resigned from the government rather than sign the Treaty of Versailles; national emotion overcame reason and responsibility. Although the DDP soon reentered the government, it again broke with the SPD and the Center party in 1921 and joined forces with the German People's party (DVP) to bring down the government of Centrist Joseph Wirth. National and fiscal considerations determined its actions. Increasingly, in the late 1920s, the DDP broke with the SPD and the Center party on fiscal and social policy, and, in 1930, it again combined with the DVP to destroy a government which strongly supported the Republic and a moderate course in foreign policy.

The DDP's fall from prominence and popular support was the most dramatic debacle suffered by any bourgeois party. This is usually explained as the consequence of external Weimar circumstances—the Treaty of Versailles, the inflation of 1923, the Great Depression, and various constitutional flaws. More recently, some scholars have focused on more subtle factors: social and intellectual trends which undermined and divided the middle classes and weakened the ideology of liberalism. Liberalism is seen by some of these scholars as an inadequate ideology; indeed, not an ideology at all. While both the external factors and the more subtle changes are undoubtedly basic in attempting to understand the causes of the fragmentation of the bourgeois parties and the downfall of the Republic, one must also analyze the *internal* weaknesses of parties such as the DDP and their mistakes. The DDP's internal inadequacies explain several of the causes of its decline and fall. First of all, the DDP advanced an ideological goal which proved unconvincing and unappealing. It proclaimed from the time of its founding until its demise that it was not a class party or an interest party but that it represented the entire nation, regardless of class or material interests. It attempted—although there were always many in the DDP who objected to this idealistic approach—to ignore material factors in politics and to proclaim abstract political ideals. Usually at election time, however, it climbed down from this lofty perch and appealed to people on the basis of class and interests. As a result, the German electorate soon perceived the DDP to be a party torn by contradictions and led by fuzzy-headed idealists.

Second, the DDP failed because its organization proved unequal to the task of engaging in frequent elections. It was unable to produce an effective and respected organization leader after the early death of Naumann in 1919. His successors lacked his charisma and stature. Beneath the three men who led the party from 1919 to 1933, a coterie of lesser party officials, who had remarkable staying power, were unable either to recruit new members or to energize the old ones. Above all, they failed to raise the necessary money to maintain the organization and its press. Early in the party's history, a few donors supplied a large percentage of the needed funds, but many of the wealthy contributors soon defected, and a large dues-paying membership on the SPD model never eventuated. What was lacking was not money—most members were relatively affluent—but individual commitment to the party's welfare. The party's followers became too old, tired, and dispirited by failure to work for the DDP. Only a few members believed sufficiently in the DDP's principles or mission to sacrifice time and money. As defeat piled on defeat, even the leaders wearied of the struggle, and, by 1928, some of them wished to abandon the fight. Enough persisted, however, that it maintained at least a skeletal organization in a few districts until the end of the Republic.

We know a great deal about the DDP/DStP compared to other Weimar parties; the left liberals preserved their papers and wrote memoirs. They knew the importance of private papers to historians and possessed the bureaucratic habit of saving documents. In addition, a portion of the party's archive, by chance, escaped destruction at the hands of the Nazis. As a result, the primary source material available dwarfs the sources for the other moderate bourgeois parties. The large collection of primary source materials accounts for the relatively large number of dissertations and books about the DDP. What is available not only allows the historian to reconstruct the national party's history but also occasionally to get a glimpse into the heart and mind of the German middle classes engaged in party politics. In addition, a history of the DDP/DStP also helps to explain the complicated process by which the middle classes switched from the moderate parties which backed the Republic to respectable rightist parties who opposed the Republic and finally to the radical Right which destroyed it.

By 1928, the organizational flaws in the party and its failures at the polls at all levels of government made it imperative for the DDP to join with other parties and groups to form a new party or face extinction. The DDP majority preferred to combine with the DVP, but the right wing of the DVP and the left wing of the DDP prevented this in 1930, as they had earlier. In desperation, with a national election called for September 1930, the leaders of the DDP joined with other allies: a right-wing, anti-Semitic youth organization, the Young German Order (*Jungdo*), a few young DVP members, several Christian Trade Unionists, and a small number of conservative Democrats who had not previously been active in the organization. They created a new party, the German State party, but it proved even less successful than the DDP. The DDP's left wing refused to join it, and, soon after the election, the *Jungdo* broke away. What remained was the extreme right wing of the DDP under the banner of the DStP. Without a popular base, several of the leaders repeatedly sought to find other allies, but their efforts failed. The DStP expired unmourned early in 1933, but not until it had joined with other middle class parties to sanction Hitler's dictatorship. Its members soon scattered abroad, if they were Jewish, or disappeared from the political scene. Generally, those who remained in Hitler's Germany lacked the recklessness to resist the Nazis but joined the legion of intellectual and passive resisters to nazism. Most sought simply to survive in perilous conditions. Many of them did and, following 1945, as elderly men and women, some of them again pursued an active political role and helped provide experienced political leadership in the Federal Republic and West Berlin. Chastened by their experiences and cognizant of their mistakes in the Weimar period, they helped provide a more solid base for liberal democracy in Germany after 1949.

I

German Left Liberalism before 1918
Liberalism, Nationalism, and Democracy

One of the most profound contrasts between Germany's political history and the political history of Britain, France, and most other western countries was the failure of the German middle classes to find a suitable instrument—a political party—to express their values and to forward their material interests.[1] The lack of a powerful and confident liberal political party in particular weakened the liberal impulse in Germany and contributed to the greater popularity of conservatism, socialism, political Catholicism, and, after 1930, nazism. The inability of the liberals to unite in one party not only contributed to their political impotence but to the general low regard with which most Germans viewed liberal values. The causes of this failure to unite were differences over political principles, clashes over material interests, and personality disputes and competing ambitions among the liberal leaders. Although several generations of liberal party leaders attempted to heal the divisions and unite the liberal forces, the differences were too compelling to be overcome. The weakness of the liberal parties in turn contributed to the strength of their partisan—and ideological—enemies. The failure of the liberals and the feebleness of liberalism in Germany contributed to the success of both the kaiser and the führer, and the "illiberalism of Germany" remains a compelling synthesis which has both fascinated and baffled historians.

Left-Liberal Parties, 1871–1918

During the period 1871–1918, there were several parties designated left-liberal in Germany and one right-liberal, the National Liberal party

6

(*Nationalliberale Partei*—NLP). The liberal parties combined and divided on several occasions, but all efforts to create one liberal party failed. The Progressive party (*Fortschrittspartei*), which was formed in 1861 in Prussia, and the secessionist Liberal Association (*Liberale Vereinigung*), founded in 1880, joined forces in 1893 as the Radical People's party (*Freisinnige Volkspartei*), headed by Eugen Richter. The other major left-liberal party was the Radical Association (*Freisinnige Vereinigung*), led by Theodor Barth. In 1896, another party was founded which evolved into a left liberal party. This was Friedrich Naumann's National Social Union (*Nationalsozialer Verein*), which survived as an independent party until 1903 when it suffered a crushing defeat in the national election. Most of Naumann's small but distinguished following then joined Barth's Radical Association. There was, in addition, a regional left-liberal party in the southwest, the German People's party (*Deutsche Volkspartei*), whose most prominent leaders before 1914 were Friedrich von Payer and Conrad Haussmann. Closer, ideologically, to the events of 1848–1849 and the democratic traditions of those revolutions than the other liberal parties, the German People's party was especially strong in Württemberg and Frankfurt am Main. In 1908, Barth and a few followers compounded the traditional disunity of left liberalism by forming still another party, the Democratic Association (*Demokratische Vereinigung*). The Democratic Association had a shaky independence until 1918 when most of its members joined the new German Democratic party (*Deutsche Demokratische Partei*—DDP). The other left-liberal parties, after years of negotiations, formed the Progressive party (*Fortschrittliche Volkspartei*) in 1910. It, too, went over to the DDP in 1918. From 1910 until 1918, then, there was only one important left-liberal party, the Progressive party. In a formal sense, unity among left liberals had been achieved, but there remained several distinct traditions which coexisted within the Progressive party and in the later DDP.

There were several causes for the disunity of left liberalism. The left-liberal movement seemed to attract strong personalities who put a high premium on individual freedom. There were also differences on principles, on priorities, on possible political allies and on leaders. The left liberals divided on how fast the pace of democracy should occur, and, after 1890, they were torn by the so-called "national questions"—foreign policy, imperialism, colonialism, defense budgets, and sensitive patriotic issues. Yet they were in agreement on many fundamentals. They all believed in the need for the true, responsible parliamentary government on the English model at the national level of government. After 1900, more liberals also accepted the necessity to extend the national franchise (essentially manhood suffrage) to the states and municipalities. Determined to reform the Prussian electoral system, they were nearly all monarchists

7

who also shared common attitudes toward the Socialists, Catholics, and Conservatives. In addition, they had common class and economic interests.

Left liberalism developed from a narrow sociological base. The members were largely drawn from the Protestant and Jewish urban middle classes. They represented businessmen, large and small, bankers, professional people, teachers, some farmers, certain *Mittelstand* elements (artisans and small businessmen for the most part), and a few industrial workers organized in the liberal Hirsch-Duncker unions and an even smaller Lutheran workers' movement.[2] The export industries and international bankers were especially important in the left liberal organizations in the Hanseatic cities. Most Jews voted left-liberal, and large numbers of school teachers also supported the movement. The left liberals were least popular in largely Catholic areas, heavily industrialized districts, and rural regions. Because of their small electoral base, the combined left-liberal parties received only 361,000 votes in 1871, or 4.5 percent of the votes cast.[3] In 1890, they increased their vote total to about 1.3 million, or 12 percent of the voters. Most of the gains which they registered, however, were at the expense of the National Liberal party. This was a recurring pattern in the history of the liberal parties: they primarily competed with each other. In 1912, the last election before the war, the Progressive party received about 1.5 million votes, 14 percent of the popular vote and a 25 percent increase over the 1907 election. Despite the generally upward trend, the Progressive party remained small and relatively unimportant, unable to broaden its base or to justify its claim that it represented all of the people. Nonetheless, left liberals saw the 1912 election as a portent of a brighter Progressive future.

Principles, Ideals, Values

The political principles and values of the German left liberals were rooted in the revolutions of 1848 and in the Statement of Fundamental Rights (*Grundrechte*), which was one of the few positive achievements of the Frankfurt Assembly. For the most part, the fundamental rights summarized the principles of mid-nineteenth-century "classical" liberalism. Many of the basic ideas of the American and French Revolutions were reproduced in them, although they also reflected particular German concerns and the German conception of the state. The DDP later updated the statement in the Weimar Constitution. The German left liberals wished to protect the individual from government and to create a society in which every citizen was equal before the law, regardless of religion, profession, or class. They believed in separating church and state, and they wished to eradicate aristocratic or religious privileges and to create a society in which the able individual could rise regardless of his origins. They believed in the idea of progress and the efficacy of education, and they saw Germany essentially following the liberal model of Great Britain. In their vision of the future, they saw the triumph of the middle classes, the establishment of parliamentary government, a secular society, and civilian control of the military.

In 1848, some German liberals were democrats, but revolution frightened them. They soon wanted to restrict the franchise to the well educated and prosperous. Only after 1900, spurred on by the growth of the SPD and the Catholic Center party (*Zentrum*—Z) as great mass parties, did the left liberals become democrats. A few left liberals even felt that women should have the vote. Most of them, however, opposed extending the vote. They also feared "party government," the excesses of which they saw in the French Third Republic. The march of the SPD and the spectre of socialist revolution were a nightmare to them. Although Naumann and Barth attempted to assure their followers that the German socialists were essentially moderate trade unionists and patriots, most left liberals remained wary.

The liberals of 1848 and the later Progressives were also ardent nationalists. In 1848, as has often been observed, liberalism and nationalism were complementary. Later, they conflicted and German liberals had to make some unpleasant choices, often sacrificing liberal institutions and values for national unity. Most left liberals favored a Reich which would include as many ethnic Germans as possible and regretted that millions of Germans remained outside. The Liberals soon set to work to develop the institutions of the national government and continued to try to establish the spirit and institutions of the *Rechtsstaat*, the state founded on the law and guided by the rule of law.

In the 1890s, while the left liberals grudgingly accepted the necessity for some democratic reforms and changed their position on the "national questions," they were also forced to reconsider their traditional posture on the "social question," which essentially dealt with social legislation designed to protect the urban worker against the harsh consequences of industrialism. During Bismarck's time, they were the foremost advocates of strict laissez-faire and fought his "welfare state" measures, but the Naumann left liberals and Barth's group gradually altered their stance on the social question. The Richterites, however, maintained their hostility to positive state action in the economy and society. While the Naumann and Barth liberals gradually began to see the SPD as a potential ally, Richter's followers remained fanatical anti-Socialists.

The basic political goal of the left liberals was to achieve a people's state (*Volksstaat*), a synonym for democracy which combined the idea of popular control of the government and national unity. They were also determined to achieve a people's community of social harmony and order (*Volksgemeinschaft*). This ambiguous political vocabulary was employed

9

by several German parties in varying ways and, even among left liberals, it was necessary to debate the meaning of this terminology.

The left liberals also differed on the sources of liberalism. Naumann's group emphasized the German roots of liberalism and wished to break with English and French liberal traditions and thought. Barth and Richter continued to admire English political institutions and values. The Naumann followers pointedly rejected the "natural rights" school of political philosophy and grounded their political thought on Kant, Hegel, and Fichte, and they also—not surprisingly—became "statists," accepting and even urging the need for state action in many areas of national life. They all stressed the need for a strong centralized state and represented themselves as the spokesmen for the nation, not for classes or economic interests.[4] Their sense of responsibility for the maintenance of the power and unity of the state led them to support German unification under Bismarck and Wilhelm II's *Machtpolitik*. Their statist orientation also helped them see the German parliament as a place where conflicting views could be reconciled rather than as a battleground for political power. Their deepest instinct was to achieve harmony and reconciliation in German society as well. They abhorred the Marxist idea of a class struggle.

The left liberals of Germany also desired a secular society and state. They wished to separate church and state, to build a public school system free of religious domination and uniform throughout the Reich, to end any form of religious censorship, and to guarantee academic and scientific freedom. The large following they had among teachers and journalists is largely attributable to their policies on the *Kultur* issues. On such questions, they could join with many in the NLP and the SPD against the Center party and Conservative parties.

There was no unified, coherent left-liberal philosophy in 1914, no ideology in the contemporary sense of that term. There were Manchester Liberals, who would have been more comfortable with John Bright or Richard Cobden than with Naumann or Max Weber. There were Social Liberals, such as Naumann and Barth, who saw, for varying motives, the necessity to act with the SPD. The Progressive party exhibited both statist and laissez-faire values. On occasion, an individual such as Ernst Müller-Meiningen, the Bavarian Richterite, exhibited both tendencies. For Naumann, traditional liberal values became less important than nationalist and democratic ideals. Barth, on the other hand, remained true to classic liberal values while becoming a democrat who was prepared to work with the SPD.

Domestic Concerns

A number of recent works have stressed the interrelationship in German politics between constitutional questions and social, economic, foreign, and defense policies.[5] In these studies, the political Right and Left emerge as distinct entities, with parties maintaining an ideological position consistent with the social classes and economic interests they represented. In the history of left liberalism—or in the history of the Catholic Center party—however, such simplistic economic interpretations are impossible to make. There was no neat package of beliefs, interests, and actions which can be grouped under an ideological label. It is even difficult to categorize the left liberals' thinking as left or right. On foreign policy issues, the left-liberal position generally evolved from left to right, while on constitutional, franchise, and social questions the movement was from right to left. Often, the left liberals found themselves squarely in the middle and pulled in both directions.

The most persistent domestic goal of the Progressives and their predecessors was the achievement of constitutional reform leading, specifically, to a constitutional monarchy. They wanted to reform the government by strengthening and modernizing it, to reduce the role of the Conservatives and the aristocracy, and to elevate the importance of the middle classes in the government. But they had a rather flexible timetable. The most pressing demand was the reform of the Prussian electoral system, which symbolized everything the left liberals opposed. After the *Daily Telegraph* affair of 1908, in which the kaiser and his ministers performed so lamentably, the Progressives became more impatient, insisting, for example, that the franchise used to elect Reichstag deputies be extended to the states.

The Progressive party continued the left-liberal concern with the civil liberties of the individual citizen. Sensitive to heavy-handed censorship and to any form of religious discrimination, it was the strongest political voice to safeguard academic freedom. It was also more alert to political anti-Semitism than any other German political party, although it discriminated against Jews in selecting its political candidates, preferring baptized Jews. The Progressive party was also hostile to the exaggerated militarism of the *Kaiserreich*. Most Progressives were fundamentally civilians, even though some of the younger leaders were inordinately proud of their reserve commissions. Their intense patriotism and great pride in Germany's achievements after 1890 produced contradictory currents in the party. They were uncomfortable with the combination of Wilhelm II's "personal government," the exalted status of the military officer and the aristocrat, and the combined economic-political power of the *Junker*, but above all, they hated the Conservative-*Junker* domination of Prussia. On the other hand, they were strong monarchists and did not wish to embarrass the kaiser or seem to undermine him, especially in the troubled years before the war.

Throughout the nineteenth century, most left liberals believed that one's political beliefs were independent of class or material concerns, or that at least they should be so. At the same time, however, they recognized that the SPD was a class party, as was the Conservative party, and increasingly the National Liberal party (NLP) was seen as the party of heavy industry. Moreover, despite the left liberals' curious inability to admit their own association with special interests, the Progressive party worked to win the financial support of commercial firms, shippers, liquor and tobacco businesses, the *Mittelstand*, and peasant groups, which exchanged financial backing for support of their needs in the Reichstag and state legislatures. In the decade before the war, the *Hansa-Bund* (HB) and the *Bauernbund* (DBB), both economic interest groups, were closely tied to the liberal parties. They gave financial support and in turn received favorable consideration from liberal politicians. Some left liberals became specialists in representing certain interests, and it was common to choose candidates because of the financial support they would receive from professional or economic associations. All this was clear to contemporaries, and yet the national party organization and the party's leadership preferred to believe that the Progressive party represented lofty ideals and the whole nation, not interests and classes. The Democratic party later displayed this same affectation.

Historians commonly picture the German left liberals as free traders— and, indeed, they were more prone to favor free trade than other *Bürger* parties—but by 1914, there were few doctrinaire free traders in the party. Free-trade principles had never sunk deep roots in Germany, and the developments after 1890 were not conducive to any form of internationalism. While a few traditionalists such as Georg Gothein continued to combine free trade, international understanding and peace,[6] the Naumannite wing of progressivism, which was least sympathetic to free trade, had the greatest success in winning new adherents to left liberalism. The old laissez-faire principles and the mystique of free trade as a panacea for the world's problems no longer attracted the Progressives. The only tariffs which the Progressive party opposed in a united fashion were the agricultural barriers against foreign grain.

Foreign Affairs

Until the 1890s, the German left liberals were far less interested in foreign and military problems than in domestic concerns. The budget was their principal interest and their field of expertise. While they wanted to secure civilian control of the military and to achieve annual military budgets, and they desired a greater knowledge of the decision-making process in foreign affairs, they generally felt ill-equipped to challenge the government experts and ministers. Both the lack of a foreign relations committee or a defense committee in the Reichstag and the powers of the kaiser in foreign and military affairs excluded the Reichstag from any important part in making foreign and military policy. The Reichstag was only permitted to debate the budget and to approve treaties. There was little opposition to the government's conduct of foreign affairs among left liberals, despite the embarrassing gaffes of the emperor and the construction of the Triple Entente. They seemed largely unaware of the drift toward war after 1908, and when it came, they tended to blame the professional diplomats rather than the kaiser or the military leaders.[7]

In the decade before the war—years marked by two Moroccan crises, the *Daily Telegraph* affair, Balkan wars, and the Zabern affair—the left liberals were generally reluctant to criticize the government or to suggest alternatives to its policies. Only a tiny pacifist group, mostly members of the Democratic Association, made any fundamental criticism of foreign and defense policies. The 1912 Progressive Party Congress (*Parteitag*) appeared to be remarkably unconcerned about foreign affairs,[8] although a few members were alarmed by the threatening international atmosphere. From the 1890s onwards, the most vigorous supporters of the kaiser's *Welt-* and *Machtpolitik* among left liberals were the followers of Naumann. Naumann's group, never large but numbering many intellectuals and editors, combined an older romantic nationalism with social Darwinism and the turn-of-the-century imperialist perspective. Naumann was greatly influenced by Max Weber in his world view, but he in turn had an enormous impact on journalists, professors, and young professional people. Many young people who achieved prominence during the Weimar period became his conscious followers after 1900.

Crediting intellectuals with great and immediate influence is difficult in partisan politics, but there are some exceptions. Max Weber's inaugural lecture in 1891 and Naumann's book *Democracy and Empire* (*Demokratie und Kaisertum*), which was published in 1900, were read and absorbed by large numbers of politically conscious young people. Weber and Naumann provided a more sophisticated and critical view of German affairs than Heinrich von Treitschke had done for the previous generation. Naumann combined *Machtpolitik*, imperialism, democracy, and compassion for the working class in an unusual but appealing combination. Although he was never as profound a thinker as Weber, he was an effective, popular writer and a brilliant speaker. In general, Naumann and his followers believed that Germany was irrevocably committed to industrialism but woefully unequipped by nature to compete in world trade. For its survival, Germany needed foreign raw materials and markets. Germany was seen as young and dynamic; it had to expand or die. Germany could survive as a state and a *Kultur* only through world trade, colonies, or schemes such as *Mitteleuropa*, a German-led economic union which was much discussed in left liberal circles before 1914. The Naumann circle included publicists who, while never as extreme as the Pan-Germans, advocated imperialism and German expansionism at the expense of others and shared the Pan-German view that Germany was being encircled and its future restricted by the Entente powers. During the second Moroccan crisis in 1911, Naumann took an extreme, chauvinistic position. Nonetheless, his public utterances moderated. He felt sobered by the threatening international situation, and when the war came, he sank in gloom and foreboding, which contrasted with the youthful glee of Max Weber.

Naumann's virile nationalism and strong support for imperialism greatly strengthened the statist characteristics of left liberalism, as did his advocacy of additional social legislation. His social liberalism represented a basic change in the liberal philosophy, one which paralleled developments in Britain and the United States at about the same time. He desired above all to moderate the class war in Germany and to enlist the German workingman in support of the state and the government's foreign policy. Naumann's nationalism and statist motives were self-evident, but he genuinely believed that the desired *Volksgemeinschaft* would benefit all Germans. His effort to secure a Reichstag coalition "from Bassermann to Bebel" (from the NLP to the SPD) expressed much the same objective in parliamentary terms.

From the 1890s onwards, the left liberals began to abandon their old principles and positions on defense and foreign policy. First Naumann, then Barth, and finally the Radical People's party and the German People's party began to support military and naval appropriations and a forceful, global German foreign policy. By the time the Progressive party was formed in 1910, the left liberals and the NLP held similar foreign policy positions. Barth's Radical Association voted for naval expansion before 1900, much to the disgust of Richter. It also supported efforts to increase German trade abroad and to develop German colonies. Barth attempted to combine this new course with continued support for free trade and international conciliation, remaining a warm friend of England and America, but failing to see that Germany's naval policy was alienating England. After 1906, when Richter died, the Radical People's party also changed its policies on the "national questions."

What caused this change in left-liberal attitudes? The writings of Naumann, Weber, and various publicists in the Naumann circle were undoubtedly important, and class and economic interests also influenced the change, but international events proved determinative. Millions of Germans in the decade before the war became aware that Germany could only feed and supply its people through trade expansion and colonies. Special circumstances also influenced party behavior. In the 1893 election, for example, the Radical Association suffered a serious loss. During the campaign, it opposed naval expansion, and this became a significant issue in the election. Many party members attributed the party's loss to its opposition to the growth of the navy, and they soon changed its policy and supported appropriations to expand the navy. The change in attitude toward the navy has also been explained as a result of the traditional left-liberal animus toward their historic foe, the Conservative party, which opposed both the development of the German navy and world trade and colonies. The plethora of explanations only underlines the fact that there was a change of policy and that it was not adopted without much debate and controversy. The Naumann group and the Radical Association were heatedly denounced for their changed position by both the Richterites and the South German People's party, who were not willing to support a naval buildup and colonies and risk antagonizing the British and French. Neither group had powerful international bankers in their ranks or shipping interests; their followers were largely lower middle-class people who had no stake in overseas expansion. Traditional laissez-faire values and free-trade ideas still held sway in these parties, and they were better able to resist the siren calls of intellectuals and publicists. Richter's authoritarian style of leadership was also more effective in keeping his party on the customary line. Gradually, however, a combination of economic pressures and events pushed them to support the government's foreign policy and, by 1910, there were only a few holdouts.

While the German left liberals converted to support a strong and even aggressive foreign and defense policy, they seemed to have little sense of the real danger which lay ahead. In this, they resembled their counterparts in Britain and France. The Progressives surmounted each constitutional and foreign policy crisis with no sense that the nation was headed for disaster. The *Daily Telegraph* affair of 1908, in which the kaiser had sought to clarify German foreign policy and show his friendship for Britain, embarrassed many Progressives, including Weber and Naumann, causing them to conclude that a more representative and responsible government was imperative in order to provide more capable leadership than the kaiser had demonstrated. The army's behavior in the Zabern affair outraged the left liberals. The Progressive party condemned the government's attempt to protect the army, although in view of the international circumstances of 1913–1914 it could go no farther than harsh words. Nationalist feelings silenced most *Bürger* critics and even the most contentious liberal journalists moderated their criticism of the government. It would be misleading to exaggerate the nationalism of the Progressives; they were not chauvinists and they did not passionately hate the English or the French, although they feared Russia. Paul Rohrbach, a Baltic German, was the only one who expressed the desire to carve up Russia. Most of them were hostile to Russia because they hated its reactionary government and society rather than because it represented a threat to German national interests. They did not accept the government-inspired theme of the eternal conflict between Teuton and Slav. They believed that Germany was unfairly treated abroad, and they were extremely sensitive to hostile world opinion, particularly to British attacks. They did not yearn for war, nor were they bored with peace and prosperity, but they were prepared to defend Germany's legitimate interests.

Colonialism

In the 1880s, there was no desire for overseas possessions among left liberals. Richter, Ludwig Bamberger, and Barth, among others, opposed colonies on traditional "Little Englander" grounds. The only prominent liberal who opposed colonialism on moral grounds was Lujo Brentano, an economist at the University of Munich. Naumann overlooked the most evil chapters of German imperialism, interpreting them as necessary to the growth of Germany's power overseas and to its unity and prosperity at home. Barth followed Naumann's lead in support of imperialist ventures, aggressively pushed by bankers and commercial interests in the Radical Association. At the time of the first Moroccan crisis, in 1905, all the left-liberal parties supported the government and soon afterwards backed its ruthless suppression of a native uprising in Southwest Africa. Their position on colonies and on imperialism in general was consistent with their attitude toward Germany's own minority groups.

The German liberals after 1890 never indicated any regret for the treaties which gave them millions of non-German people. They indignantly rejected these peoples' claims for self-determination or greater autonomy and supported measures to Germanize them. Only belatedly did the Progressive party back changes in the status of the provinces of Alsace and Lorraine to provide those regions with more powers of self-government, an effort ancillary to the liberal goals to reduce the power of the Prussian Conservatives and to reform the Prussian franchise. During the national election of 1907, whose major issues included the colonial scandals and the native uprising in Southwest Africa, the left liberals joined the National Liberals and the Conservatives in highly emotional nationalist attacks against the "un-German" Catholic Center party and the SPD, which had exposed the mistakes of the colonial administration and the cruelties to the natives. This electoral crusade formed the backdrop for the formation of the Bülow Bloc in 1907, a liberal-conservative coalition. Although some individual left liberals continued to be critical of German imperialist activity, the party strongly supported the foreign policy of the Bülow Bloc, of which it was a member. At the time of the Moroccan crisis of 1911, two years after the fall of the Bülow Bloc, the Progressive party backed the government's policy that had resulted in an increase in German possessions in Africa. While the National Liberals and the Conservatives regarded the African gains as a humiliating defeat because they had envisioned a larger expansion, the Progressives were satisfied. In southern Germany, where there had been a considerable growth in the export trade,

16

liberals switched over to the imperialist course. Few liberals could resist the heady consequences of nationalist flourishes. Indeed, most Progressives were exhilarated by Germany's aggressive actions. Only the tiny Democratic Association denounced the government's course.

Despite the support of the Progressive party for the government on the "national issues," the Progressives were not warmongers. Many of the most ardent imperialists at the turn of the century became more responsible after 1912. This was certainly true of Naumann, perhaps the leading "liberal imperialist" before 1914. As late as 1911, he remained an extreme nationalist but soon joined with Conrad Haussmann to work for peace. With Jean Juarès, the French socialist leader, and Ludwig Haas, a leading Baden Progressive, Naumann and Haussmann worked to improve Franco-German relations. In the Party Congress of 1912, Naumann gave the only significant speech on foreign policy, and it was directed toward promoting international understanding. He reported that he had seen in a Belgian railway station, on a recent trip to England, Bulgarian and Serbian soldiers boarding trains to return home to fight. His horror of war was manifest. He regretted that the love of one's country should lead to the hatred of others.[9] On the other hand, neither Naumann nor his party felt prepared to criticize the government's foreign and defense policies or even to express reservations about the consequences of Germany's *Weltpolitik*. The only alternative to overseas expansion which was popular among left liberals was the *Mitteleuropa* idea, simply another form of the expansion of German power and influence, which Naumann later popularized in a book published in 1915.

Military Questions—Pacifism

The change in left-liberal attitudes toward imperialism was paralleled and in some cases preceded by a change in attitudes toward military appropriations. Left liberals had for many years refused to vote for military appropriations, in part because they demanded annual military budgets rather than seven-year budgets, but also because they fundamentally opposed the values of the officer corps. The development of the German navy, however, produced a change of heart. Many left liberals saw the navy from the beginning as a national institution, not a Prussian one. Its officers, moreover, seemed more liberal and middle class. The requests to build a great navy coincided with the Boer War and the Spanish-American War when Germany appeared to be weak and vulnerable compared to Britain and the United States. In addition, as we have seen, the left liberals were closely tied to the Hanseatic seaports, shipping interests, and the export trade. The votes to increase the size of the navy tended to erode the traditional negativism toward army appropriations as well, but it was also apparent that Germany's national existence might be threatened.

The left-liberal conversion to a more positive and statist role under the pressure of international events did not mean that the left liberals had completely abandoned their old distrust of the military, and they continued to press for army reforms. In the years before international tensions became acute, the left liberals preferred a "people's army" to one led by Prussian aristocrats, but in the 1910 and 1912 party congresses, the Progressive party called for a strong military establishment at the lowest possible price. It commonly used the argument that the best defense against war was a superior army and navy. Figures such as Payer and Otto Fischbeck, a follower of Richter and the chairman of the Progressive party, led the party's defense of its votes for increased military appropriations, and they rejected international disarmament efforts as dangerous delusions. Nonetheless, the only *Bürger* pacifists of any importance were affiliated with the Progressives. Others, while not strictly pacifists, actively supported international efforts to halt the arms buildup. Some were identified with efforts to achieve arbitration of international disputes, while an even larger number attended meetings of European parliamentarians to further understanding and communication between nations. The left-liberal parties often made programmatic statements that were internationalist and even pacifistic, in contrast to their voting record in the Reichstag. The South German People's party, for example, published a program soon after 1900 which contained the following statement: "The *Volkspartei* is a party of peace. It regards war and militarism as the most serious injury to popular welfare, as well as to culture and the interests of freedom. It strives for an alliance of peace and freedom among the nations."[10] The Progressive party program of 1910 contained similar sentiments. Those in the Progressive party most commonly labeled as "pacifists" were Ludwig Quidde, Walter Schücking, Haussmann, Gothein, and Martin Rade. The German Right seldom distinguished between a pacifist in principle and a promoter of international understanding. Schücking and Quidde were truly pacifists, while the others were internationalists—antimilitary, opposed to chauvinist associations, and critical of the course of German foreign policy and its direction. Despite the small number of pacifists in the Progressive party, the Right saw the Progressives as dangerously cosmopolitan. The SPD, on the other hand, viewed the left liberals as hypocrites on national issues.

Some stout individualists, in addition to the pacifists, resisted the statist and nationalist trends in the party. Gothein, a member of Richter's Radical People's party, stands out as the most distinctive of this small group. A mining engineer by profession and a writer on economics by choice, he enjoyed close ties with Silesian industrial and business interests and was for a time an official of the Breslau Chamber of Commerce. While remaining a Manchester Liberal on social and economic questions until his death in 1940, he was also consistent on questions of foreign and military importance. Indeed, he admitted in his unpublished memoir that he found it impossible to change his views.[11] He displayed dogged courage in defense of unpopular causes and individuals, courageously defending Quidde and Schücking, in both the Progressive party and the DDP, against their detractors. He fought for international disarmament before the war, belonging to several organizations whose purpose was to achieve international understanding. Unlike most of the other Progressive party leaders, he also traveled widely before the war and had developed a rather sophisticated grasp of world affairs. He had an even more uncommon trait: the ability to detach himself from nationalist emotion and to view Germany's position objectively. In 1913, before the Reichstag Finance Committee, which occasionally debated questions related to foreign and military policy, he attempted to get the government to assure Belgium that its neutrality would never be violated by Germany. When the war broke out, he was the first Progressive deputy to repudiate the annexation of foreign lands. "Even in the days of the greatest victories, I warned repeatedly against annexing a single handful of land, and was thus attacked by *Fraktion* colleagues."[12] Before the war, he was closely associated with the liberal, internationalist newspaper, the *Frankfurter Zeitung* (FZ); during the twenties, his articles often appeared in the *Berliner Tageblatt* (BT). He also published widely on specialized economics questions in various journals. He had a proclivity for unpopular causes and served for many years as the chairman of the Defense League Against Anti-Semitism (*Verein zur Abwehr des Antisemitismus*). Colleagues in the Progressive and Democratic parties sometimes regarded his aggressive defense of Jews as being as tactless and impolitic as his support of pacifists. In the DDP, he was a prickly colleague and an uncomfortable reminder of how far the party had strayed from the historic principles of left liberalism.

Zabern

In 1913, an incident in Zabern, a small town in Alsace, showed clearly the nature of the German constitutional system and the position of the army in German society. The response of the Progressive party to the event also illustrates its moderate stance on "national questions" and its unwillingness to challenge the status quo. Zabern confirmed that the kaiser was not prepared to permit any changes in the social and political system of Germany. It also showed that when the kaiser, the conservatives, and the military assumed a common front, the opposition forces were helpless. The Progressive party showed its basic timidity, although some of its leaders employed strong language. When the news reached the Progressive politicians that the army stationed in Zabern had abused Alsatian civilians and violated the law, they were naturally excited; some were outraged. Although they had dutifully supported the government on most key issues, the principle of civilian control of the government and the military was dear to them, although it was remote from their experience. They also wished to unseat the Conservatives in order to reform the Prussian franchise. They had no desire, however, to rock the boat sufficiently to endanger the nation's security or unity. When the chancellor, Theobald von Bethmann Hollweg, failed to answer their questions satisfactorily and seemed prepared to shield the army's actions from the public, the Progressive party as well as the Social Democratic party introduced a motion of no confidence. These motions passed overwhelmingly, but in view of Germany's constitution, the motions could be and were ignored. Only the Social Democrats demanded that Bethmann Hollweg resign. The Progressive party drafted a bill to guarantee civilian control over the proclamations of martial law, but it was soon dropped when the NLP opposed it. From the beginning of the crisis, the Progressives had seemed as disturbed by its possible effects in Alsace as by the constitutional and legal implications. They feared it might stir up anti-German and pro-French sentiments there, and they sought to use the crisis to attack Prussia's dominance in Alsace-Lorraine. Naumann's Reichstag speech at the time dealt largely with the irrationalities of the German federal system.[13] He attacked federalism and supported a centralized system. It was characteristic of Naumann's oratory that he ended his speech by quoting from the German national anthem. No one, he seemed to say, should construe the motion of no confidence by the Progressive party as an unpatriotic action. A few months later, the war was on and the Zabern affair forgotten.

Was Germany on the Road to a True Parliamentary System before the War?

On the eve of the war, the German Right had a fearful vision of the future of German political developments. German conservatives were alarmed by the results of the 1912 election and feared the growth of a left-wing coalition majority which would institute additional social legislation, higher income and inheritance taxes, and lower tariffs. Landed estates would go bankrupt, profits for industry would decline, the Prussian franchise would be reformed, and German society and government would be democratized. This general view of future domestic developments supports the thesis that the ensuing war was designed by the government leadership as much to prevent a social and political revolution as to safeguard Germany's existence against hostile neighbors. The conviction of the Right that a left majority existed has recently been supported by scholars who feel that a "converging Left" promised major constitutional changes.[14] These historians envisage the Progressive party, the Catholic Center party, and even the NLP as moving closer to the SPD on a variety of issues in the decade before 1914. They see the outline of the parliamentary majority which emerged after the July crisis of 1917 and which took shape as the Weimar Coalition in January 1919. According to this thesis, only the national questions prevented parliamentary cooperation. As a result, Germany took another of the tragic turns which prevented its evolution toward parliamentary democracy. This optimism about the development of a left coalition from Bassermann to Bebel rests on two questionable assumptions. It suggests that the agreement of the several parties on a few issues could overcome their fundamental differences on others, and it assumes that the kaiser, the Conservative party, the NLP, and the right wing of the Center party would have yielded to a Reichstag majority. In reality, the disagreements between the SPD, the Progressives, the NLP, and the Center party on many questions were so fundamental that no left coalition was possible, and the kaiser and the Prussian Conservatives—strongly supported by the right wings of the NLP and the Z—demonstrated their intransigence through 1918. The profound differences between the middle-class parties and the SPD were alone sufficient to prevent any close cooperation, and this was true of 1919 or 1933—or, for that matter, today—as well as for the period 1907–1914. The Progressive party—and later the DDP—have often been represented as being closer to the SPD than any other *Bürger* party and perhaps this was true; yet there is little evidence to suggest that a partnership between left liberals and socialists was attainable, except on a limited number of issues. They had some common enemies and goals, but their differences were always greater than their commonality. They were divided not only by the "national questions" but on all issues on which management and labor took different sides. There were also class and religious emotions which were perhaps even more difficult to overcome.[15]

Some Progressives, mostly followers of Naumann, were prepared, for tactical and statist reasons—and perhaps for humanitarian reasons—to cooperate with the Socialists to improve social benefits. A larger number of Progressives was ready to push hard with the SPD for constitutional reforms and changes in the Prussian franchise. The average left-liberal member, however, was a follower of Richter, not Naumann. Richter saw the SPD as the foremost enemy of liberalism. Moreover, it should be recognized that many of the young liberals who responded to Naumann's ideas and charisma were probably stirred more by his romantic nationalism and liberal imperialism than by his concern for economic and social reforms. Most Progressives favored the National Liberal party as a political ally, not the SPD or the left wing of the Center party, even though—or perhaps because—the NLP was reactionary on the "social question" and chauvinistic in foreign policy. The impulse for liberal unity was always far stronger than a sincere alliance with the Left. At the time of the

Bülow Bloc, even Naumann was far more concerned with preserving a good relationship with the National Liberals than with anything else. Above all, he wanted a strong and viable liberal party.

In May 1914, the German government announced its opposition to any additional social legislation. The arms race and the expansion of the German army had produced serious financial problems. The trade unions, including the liberal Hirsch-Duncker unions, protested in a large demonstration in Berlin against this capitulation to heavy industry. The SPD members showed their rage in the Reichstag by refusing to rise from their seats when the kaiser was hailed, an action which many contemporaries felt isolated the Social Democrats from all the other parties and doomed whatever chance there was for social and political reconciliation. This was the kind of SPD gesture that infuriated the Progressive party and all other German *Bürgers*, but it only underscored the fact that the SPD was isolated by choice. Its republicanism, its doctrine of class warfare, and its attitudes on religion, foreign policy, and defense measures combined to set it apart, however strong the "reformist" tendencies were in the SPD. Moreover, there was a great gulf between the Catholic Center party and the liberal parties. In short, class feelings, material interests, nationalist and religious emotion combined to produce barriers which were far too strong to be overcome by a desire to reform the political system. This was conclusively demonstrated during the war and the years of the Weimar Republic.

The Progressive Party during the First World War

The effects of the First World War on individual Progressives were manifold and profound. Many served actively in the war, while others had sons, fathers, and brothers who did. They endured on the home front all of the familiar discomforts and sorrow after the first year's anticipation of an immediate victory waned. They ate poorly, worked harder, and shuddered in the cold of the last two winters of the war. However, the dozens of accounts of individual Progressives can only serve here as a backdrop for the history of the party itself.[16] And the most important topics for the Progressive party were, first, war-goals questions, and, second, the party's contribution to the development of parliamentary democracy in Germany during the war and its immediate aftermath. While these are relatively narrow topics in the history of the war, they will explain much about the nature of the DDP and its policies during the Weimar period.

The position of the Progressive party on war aims supported a course generally described as "moderate annexationism." Within the Progressive party, however, at least three groups produced variations of this middle position on war aims. They vacillated in accordance with the success of the German military forces. At the outbreak of the war, the Progressive party supported the government without question, although some of its members were dismayed at the prospect of fighting "the whole world."[17] Most members shared, however, in the initial enthusiasm for the war and the resulting social and political unity. The undeniable military successes in the first weeks produced a number of extreme annexationist war-goals plans. Matthias Erzberger's blueprint as well as Chancellor Bethmann Hollweg's were matched in the Progressive party by Adolf Neumann-Hofer's.[18] The Progressive *Fraktion*, shielded by censorship and deluded by emotion, remained ignorant of the true German military position. Not until 1916–1917 did well-informed Progressive political figures learn of the failed Schlieffen Plan and the First Battle of the Marne. In general, the party followed Bethmann Hollweg's moderate and ambiguous course, which could be interpreted as a call for widespread annexations or a "peace of understanding" or anything in between. Privately, Progressives produced memoranda which reflected the full spectrum of possibilities.

The problem of Belgium was the most persistent of the war-goals questions. The invasion of Belgium had formally precipitated the war in the west and brought Britain into the war. It was soon occupied, of course, and remained controlled by Germany until the end. The Progressive party accepted Bethmann Hollweg's candid if impolitic explanation for the necessity to invade Belgium. It generally believed that Belgium had not been a truly neutral state and that the French army had invaded it before the German forces. In its first formal statement on war aims, however, the Progressive party ignored Belgium.[19] It rejected "unclear and boundless annexation" but at the same time expressed the determination to secure Germany economically, militarily, and strategically—fence-straddling characteristic of the Progressive party's stand on war aims.

The Progressive party seemed indifferent to occupation conditions in Belgium, but in view of the number of Progressives who were in the occupation administration or who served in the armed forces there, it could not have been ignorant of them.[20] The memoirs and papers of these figures have little to say about their experiences except to represent them as a humanitarian mission. The Progressives heatedly denied the British-inspired stories of German atrocities, blaming the Belgians for the general tone of the occupation. Regardless of these questions, some Progressives realized that Belgium was a central problem in securing a negotiated peace. Haussmann and Gothein saw the necessity to renounce Belgium very early in the war, but few Progressives took this position until 1917. When the SPD attempted, in 1915, to align the Progressive party with it to renounce Belgium, the *Fraktion*, led by Payer, refused. Several Progressive publicists supported the ploy of annexing part of Belgium while keeping all of it as a pledge. A few annexationists in the party wanted to seize most of Belgium.

After the articulation of President Woodrow Wilson's war aims early in

1917 and the American declaration of war over the German resumption of unrestrictive submarine warfare, even the most befuddled Progressive politicians understood that a firm renunciation of Belgium was a necessary first step to negotiate a peace with Britain and the United States. The papal peace note of August 1917, following upon the momentous developments in the Reichstag in July which produced the Peace Resolution and the Inter-Party Committee, placed Belgium in the center of every discussion about ending the war.[21] By the time the papal note was delivered, Germany's foreign policy options were being openly debated in the Reichstag's committee rooms and in the press. Gothein and Haussmann became the most vocal Progressive critics of the government's policies after Bethmann Hollweg was replaced by the military high command of Paul von Hindenburg and Erich Ludendorff.[22] The new chancellor, Georg Michaelis, a mouthpiece of the generals, attempted to vitiate the Peace Resolution, much to the anger of Haussmann, who strongly criticized Michaelis and demanded that the government produce a forthright answer to the Pope's questions about Belgium. Haussmann felt that the opportunity to secure peace was at hand and that only Belgium stood in the way.

In 1917, when the German victories in the east drove the Russians out of the war and into revolution, the annexationists seemed to have been proven correct in their evaluation of Germany's prospects. The opportunists in the Progressive party, who had been wavering throughout the summer of 1917, once again moved close to the extreme annexationists. Payer, by this time vice chancellor, assumed a position on war aims close to that of the National Liberals, while Fischbeck also moved right on war aims. In a *Fraktion* meeting in January 1918, Gothein and Felix Waldstein supported a plea by Haussmann that the Progressive party should publicly renounce Belgium, but Fischbeck, supported by the *Fraktion* majority, refused to allow this. Bruno Ablass, Julius Kopsch—both prominent annexationists—and Friedrich Weinhausen argued against any action which would adversely affect the Germany military offensive.[23] The *Fraktion* majority insisted that only the military could achieve victory and that "pacifism could accomplish nothing." The left wing, however, refused to be silenced. Naumann, who earlier favored dominating Belgium, again urged the Main Committee, on January 24, to make a declaration on Belgium. "A positive word should be spoken about Belgium. We must not put everything on the card of (military) victory."[24] A few days later, he joined with other Progressives to warn the military masters that they must make a declaration on Belgium as a part of a general political offensive which should precede any military offensive. The government, however, continued to fudge on Belgium, while the American military buildup prepared the way for Germany's defeat. The chancellor, by then Georg von Hertling, made a statement on Belgium in February 1918, but it was so vague and confused that it allowed the most diverse interpretations.

Throughout the summer and early autumn of 1918, as the German armies continued to fall back and Germany's allies weakened, even the most obdurate annexationists in the Progressive party realized that Belgium had to be renounced, although the "pawn theory" was entertained by some until Wilson's notes during the armistice negotiations finally punctured that balloon.

The U-Boat Question

The Progressive party's attitudes toward submarine warfare revealed all of the contradictions and crosscurrents on war goals which were evident on Belgium, plus one or two additional illusions. In general, the party supported Bethmann Hollweg's policy of restraint to avoid forcing the United States into the war. It opposed initiating unrestricted submarine warfare in 1915 and was cool on the idea in 1917 as well, although it supported the government's decision. It did not accept the exaggerated claims made for the U-boat by the military. The Progressive party had few military experts who were able to contradict the army leaders, but it had several deputies who were knowledgeable about naval questions and two submarine authorities, Gothein and Wilhelm Struve, a deputy from Kiel. Both had been passionate advocates of the submarine before 1914 and had fought the policies of Alfred von Tirpitz to build a huge conventional fleet. They knew the potential and the limitations of the submarine and were well informed about the size and power of the British fleet as well. Other prominent Progressives were authorities on the United States' industrial power and realized the danger of provoking it. Bernhard Dernburg, the former colonial minister and an international banker, was in the United States in the first years of the war as a German propagandist. He witnessed the reaction to the sinking of the *Lusitania* and felt certain that a resumption of unrestrictive submarine war would produce an American declaration of war. Upon his return to Germany he and Hans Delbrück wrote a memorandum on the U-boat question, warning the government against the effects of sinking neutral shipping.[25] Max Weber, whose initial zeal for the war had soon waned, also prepared a long memorandum on the submarine question early in 1916. It warned against a policy that could bring the United States into the war on the side of the Entente. The Progressive publicist Ernst Jäckh also raised his voice against a reckless German policy. So did Walter Goetz after his return from the western front, where he served as a staff officer.

The *Fraktion* of the Progressive party found it most difficult to oppose the government. After all, it was a "state-supportive party." There was also much respect for the navy and its officers in the party. Haussmann greatly admired Tirpitz, and Bethmann Hollweg had stressed that to ensure victory *all* measures were justified.[26] With the military fronts deadlocked and

25

the peace initiatives producing no results, it seemed imperative for Germany to win the war as soon as possible. The Supreme Command—Hindenburg and Ludendorff—became convinced that the U-boat war could accomplish this and forced Bethmann Hollweg to approve. But before the U-boat offensive could begin, the Center party, strongly backed by the Progressives, undertook a curious initiative in December 1916, which revealed the opportunism of both parties and their timidity before the Supreme Command. The Center framed a resolution for the Main Committee to approve; on the one hand, the resolution supported the chancellor's cautious policy but, on the other hand, it indicated that if the military should decide to alter that policy it would support the military. The resolution stated that the ultimate responsibility should be the chancellor's, but that he should be guided by the views of the Supreme Command. Haussmann, strangely, saw the resolution as a victory of the moderates over the "blind fanatics,"[27] but in fact the majority of the Reichstag, including the Progressives, were preparing to join the fanatics. Haussmann, Erzberger, the Centrist leader, and the Socialist Philipp Scheidemann, urged the government to initiate sincere peace negotiations before it was too late, but neither the German government's effort nor Wilson's was acceptable. Many in the Progressive party seemed relieved that the emphasis was placed on a military solution. The liberal journalist Georg Bernhard, notable in the Weimar period for his leftist views in the DDP, became a clamorous supporter of the U-boat war and a protégé of Ludendorff.[28] When Haussmann sought to have the Berlin Reichstag deputy Otto Wiemer restrain Bernhard's enthusiasm, Wiemer told Haussmann that he and Müller-Meiningen shared Bernhard's feelings. While the majority of the *Fraktion* was more skeptical about the navy's claims, it nonetheless followed Bethmann Hollweg. Haussmann felt that there was no alternative but to support Bethmann Hollweg against the extreme annexationists, even when his policy forced the United States to declare war.

Few Reichstag deputies seemed to have a realistic knowledge of American industrial power, and men such as Gothein, Dernburg, and Max Weber were appalled at the lighthearted disdain with which the United States was regarded. They were also shocked by the ineptitude of the Zimmermann Dispatch,[29] although few Progressive deputies understood its significance or why the United States reacted so strongly to it. Most of them trusted the Supreme Command to deliver a military victory before the United States' full strength could be brought into the war. When the U-boat failed to deliver victory in the spring and summer of 1917 and domestic unrest grew over economic and social conditions, the demand for constitutional reform mushroomed. The result was the crisis of July 1917, the only major parliamentary crisis of the war in Germany. Erzberger, cautiously supported by Gothein, rejected the navy's submarine and shipping claims, eventually provoking a demonstration which culminated in the Peace Resolution and the formation of an Inter-Party Committee by the Reichstag majority. It became a significant institution for the remainder of the war. Most Progressives accepted the statistics and reasoning of Erzberger and Gothein on the submarine war, although a few deputies believed until the end that it was the instrument of victory. As late as April 1918, Gothein was still refuting the navy's evaluation of the "submarine success."

Eastern Questions

The Progressive party supported German territorial expansion in the east more clearly than it did in the west. Until July 1917, all elements of the party favored eastern territorial gains in one form or another. After the July crisis and the adoption of the Peace Resolution, a minority supported the principle of national self-determination in the east and qualified its earlier annexationist position. The majority of the Progressives, however, greeted the military victories in the east in the summer and fall of 1917 with wild enthusiasm and joyfully approved the harsh treaties with Russia, the Ukraine, and Romania which followed the German conquests. They were seen as golden opportunities to secure Germany's future. For that matter, many Social democrats also hailed the German victories and approved the treaties, although the SPD abstained and the Independent Socialists (USPD) voted against them. Russia had always been regarded as an ideological and national threat; the Bolshevik Revolution simply provided a new image for an old menace for both the *Bürger* parties and the Socialists. The Progressive party naturally saw the German army as a liberating force, lifting the collar of oppression from the ethnic groups of eastern Europe after generations of Russian oppression. It also approved Germany's protective posture toward the small nations of the east, nations which Naumann called *Zwischenvölker*, nations too small and too weak to exist as independent states but natural vassals of a superior state and *Kultur* such as Germany.[30] While it was generally recognized that Poland and Romania had historic claims to independence, the Germans found it difficult to imagine Lithuania, Latvia, Estonia, Finland, or the Ukraine as independent states.

It was impossible for the Germans to accept the Wilsonian version of self-determination, for his interpretation of the concept stripped Germany of valuable territory and millions of people. Nonetheless, the Progressive party could not avoid the use of the term "self-determination"—as the party understood it. It appeared with increasing frequency in the speeches and writings of Progressive figures after July 1917, although they gave the phrase wildly different interpretations. Even the most sincere advocates of self-determination for the small eastern nations combined it with German economic and military leadership in the east. The Progressive party never regarded the Peace Resolution of July 1917 as a denial of annexation through negotiation but only as a denial of the use of military force to conquer additional territory. The arguments used to justify Germany's "natural" leadership of eastern Europe varied according to the year and the circumstances, although the Progressive party tended to stress economic factors, as had Naumann in his work *Mitteleuropa*. Germany needed the raw materials and minerals, while the eastern nations required markets and technical assistance. It was a natural partnership, but Germany should clearly be the leading partner.[31] When it was apparent that Russia would have to sue for peace, Progressives advanced other arguments. Victory in the east would bring about the release of German and Austrian prisoners of war and would free troops fighting there for the final assault in the west. The victory of the Bolsheviks also produced the idea that Germany was a natural bulwark against the revolutionary doctrines emerging in Russia. Although most Progressives believed that Germany represented a superior *Kultur* and civilization, few Progressive politicians publicly employed racist arguments or discussed plans for German colonization or resettlement in the east. Some left liberal professors and publicists, however, did discuss such subjects. Meinecke, for example, in 1915, called for German expansion in the east. He wanted space for "inner colonization" and wished to join Lithuania to an "autonomous Poland." In a letter to the Progressive historian Goetz, he stressed the usefulness of such lands and peoples to Germany.[32] In the spring of 1917, three weeks before the outbreak of the March Revolution in Russia, a group of "liberal imperialists" including Meinecke, Karl Friedrich von Siemens, and the National Liberal deputy, Eugen Schiffer, all of whom were later prominent in the DDP, delivered a petition to the chancellor, signed by 20,000 people, which called for the annexation of the Baltic area and its colonization by Germans.[33] Naumann at times seemed prepared to stretch his concept of *Mitteleuropa* as far as the German armies could advance.[34]

From the autumn of 1917 until August 1918, the Progressive *Fraktion*, despite its formal support of the Peace Resolution, vacillated opportunistically on eastern war goals. On several occasions, the *Fraktion* backed resolutions, often formulated for the majority parties by Erzberger, which supported national self-determination against the imperialist designs of the Supreme Command and the rightist parties. In November 1917, the Progressives joined with the Z, the SPD, and the NLP to urge Chancellor Michaelis to make a binding declaration on Poland.[35] Later, the Progressive party repeated this demand. It is by no means certain, however, what the Progrssive party meant by Poland. How large should Poland be? How independent should it be? Probably, the Progressive party wanted a Poland of modest proportions, but what was certain was that this Poland would not include any German territory, regardless of the ethnic composition of the region. No Progressives, not even the pacifists, were prepared to cede land which was German in August 1914. Moreover, it is clear that the party wanted Poland to be economically and militarily dependent on Germany. When Wilson indicated in his Fourteen Points that Poland should have an outlet to the sea, there was no support for this in the Progressive party, not even from Gothein or Haussmann.

On the matter of war aims, the party's left wing, while generally recognizing the inevitability of the formation of new states in the east and the need for Germany to treat them with respect and understanding, could not, as a rule, think of them as equals. The "moderates"—figures such as Fischbeck, Payer, and Wiemer—were either purposely ambiguous or cynical of the eastern nations' future.[36] The party's right wing on the war-aims issue avoided the phrase "self-determination," seemingly confident that Germany would dictate a peace that would secure Germany's needs and compensate it for its sacrifices.

Only a few of the Reichstag deputies were sufficiently forthright and consistent to document their positions. Gothein's record is more clear and ample than any other.[37] He desired an independent Poland or a combined Polish-Lithuanian state. Though he believed in the principle of self-determination, he was a Silesian with coal mining interests. He certainly did not want to see Russia continue to dominate eastern Europe and naturally preferred Germany to have the leadership role. While he often pointedly rejected annexation, even Gothein had his exceptional case, a district called Bedzin, which was rich in coal; Gothein justified its annexation for "security reasons." He felt that its acquisition would improve the defensive capabilities of East Prussia, Silesia, and Posen. Naumann also favored an "independent Poland" economically bound to Germany.[38] He saw Poland as a recruiting ground for the German army and also wished to annex Bedzin.

It is more difficult to ascertain what Haussmann wanted in the east. He opposed the extreme annexationists and seemed to support the principle of self-determination. He also seemed less interested in the economic and security problems which troubled Gothein and Naumann. He preferred to support abstract ideals and general principles. Moreover, he was often ill and frequently absent from the meetings of the Inter-Party Committee, so that despite his voluminous *Nachlass* and published autobiographical materials, there are many gaps in his story. His postwar record showed him as a strong German nationalist who could never accept most of Germany's territorial losses. In view of the records of Gothein, Naumann, and Haussmann, the most idealistic of the Progressive leaders, it is no wonder that the SPD was confused about the war-goals stance of the Progressive *Fraktion*.[39] Moreover, although Haussmann claimed to speak for the *Fraktion* majority, Fischbeck continued to chair both the party and the Inter-Party Committee and favored a public repudiation of the Peace Resolution. Gothein was removed from the Inter-Party Committee as one of the Progressive spokesmen because his outspoken views were too radical for the *Fraktion* majority. There was even an attempt to unseat him in his electoral district because of his "pacifism." Despite Fischbeck's views, the Progressive party never formally repudiated the Peace Resolution, adopting a "wait and see" attitude.

After the defeat of the Russian armies and the Bolshevik Revolution, the Progressive majority joined the hurrah-chorus and voted unanimously for the Treaty of Brest-Litovsk and the subsequent eastern treaties.[40] At the same time, the left wing of the party feared the ambitions of the extreme annexationists and battled the Pan-German *Vaterlandspartei*, hoping that the civilians in the government could restrain the ardor of the Supreme Command and heavy industry. Their trust in men such as Chancellor Hertling, their colleague Payer, and the foreign minister, Richard von Kühlmann, was misplaced and naive. In the Inter-Party Committee, Erzberger, in particular, attempted to prevent a complete repudiation of the Peace Resolution and supported the principle of self-determination. The Progressive representatives generally supported him, but, like him, they voted for the eastern treaties, which made a mockery of the Peace Resolution and self-determination. After all, these were the only categorical victories of the war, as Gothein frankly admitted.[41] The Progressive *Fraktion* recognized the severity of the terms, but it also realized that there was little that the Reichstag could do to influence the treaties. Naumann spoke for the *Fraktion* in the debate on the Treaty of Brest-Litovsk in March 1918. He was by this time regarded as a strong supporter of the Peace Resolution and the principle of self-determination but defended the Progressive decision to vote for the treaty on the grounds that if Germany did not occupy the "power void" left by Russia's defeat, Britain would.[42] Other factors undoubtedly influenced Naumann's decision. Not only had he demonstrated a repugnance and fear of bolshevism, he still felt that Germany was the natural leader of east-central Europe.

As the dramatic military developments on the western front soon eclipsed the victories in the east, the incredible possibility that Germany might lose the war replaced the dream of a great German empire in the east. Meanwhile, the parties proved as impotent as ever to control events. This was demonstrated when Kühlmann, the hope of the moderates in the Reichstag, was summarily dismissed when he revealed his pessimism about the outcome of the war. The Progressive party muffled its criticism out of deference to its colleague Payer, but it always found it difficult to criticize the military leaders. By September 1918, it was apparent to most members of the Reichstag *Fraktion*, if not to the general public, that Germany faced defeat. Even Müller-Meiningen, one of the last of the illusionists in the party, had to admit that Germany would simply have to make the best of a dark prospect. It was apparent that the government, in view of the steady retreat in the west and the actions of its allies, would have to sue for an armistice.

Constitutional Reform

As we have seen, when the war broke out in 1914, nearly all Progressives favored fundamental constitutional reforms. The left liberals had demanded changes in the Prussian electoral system for generations, calling for reapportionment reflecting the increased urbanization of Germany, direct, equal suffrage, and secret voting. The basic demand was to extend the Reichstag franchise to the federal states. The old fears of democracy had largely given way to resignation—democracy was inevitable—or to the misplaced hope that the Progressive party might be able to win significant workingclass support. The arguments of Naumann and Barth and the results of the 1912 election plus the attrition of the Richter forces had muted the die-hard opponents of a democratic franchise.

During the first two years of the war, the *Burgfrieden*, the truce which prevailed in partisan politics, quieted most discussion of necessary domestic reforms. Behind the scenes, however, in small and local gatherings, left liberals continued to discuss the need for constitutional reforms, confidently expecting that they would come after the war. In addition to constitutional issues, there were other wartime concerns which touched basic liberal principles. There were complaints about the rigidities and arbitrariness of censorship, concern for the rights of national minorities within Germany, and a growing sympathy for the repeal of the Associations Act and the restrictions against Catholic orders in Germany.

The constitutional status of Alsace-Lorraine was another issue. While the Progressive party had never doubted Germany's historic and ethnic claims to Alsace-Lorraine, it had responded slowly to the grievances of the population. Soon after the outbreak of the war, however, the party leaders seemed prepared to support changes in the status of the province. But it was not until 1917 that any action occurred.[43] Many Progressives wished to see the *Reichsland* of Alsace-Lorraine become autonomous and self-governing, and they refused to support the claims of Bavaria and Württemberg to Alsace-Lorraine. On the other hand, the Progressive party never supported allowing Alsace-Lorraine to break away from Germany via a plebiscite. Most Progressives complacently assumed that the majority of the people preferred German rule and were later surprised that the restoration of Alsace-Lorraine figured so prominently in Wilson's pronouncements. The Progressive party finally supported the idea of independence for Alsace-Lorraine in order to secure peace, but the claim of France to regain the provinces had no support in the party.

The Progressive party welcomed the less dramatic improvements in the status of the Reichstag during the war, including the increase of the responsibilities of the Budget Committee and its change of name to the Main Committee. They especially applauded the increased tendency of this committee to debate foreign and military policy. During the war, the Progressives repeatedly pressed for even more powers for the Reichstag and for more participation by party leaders in the government, and there is little doubt, despite the token role which party leaders gained in the government, that the powers of the Reichstag increased. The *Bundesrat*, on the other hand, declined in power with the trend toward increasing centralization of government and greater concessions to popular control. The feeling grew among politically aware Germans that democratic reforms should occur to reward the German masses for their sacrifices and that democratic states were better able to manage the momentous problems of the war than the autocratic governments. Progressive intellectuals such as Max Weber, Naumann, and Preuss, all of whom advanced such ideas, also justified democratic reforms because they enhanced national unity and state power. Moreover, democratic reform was seen as a way of keeping the SPD responsible and supportive of the war effort. Concessions and the promises of additional reforms would help keep them in line to vote for war taxes.

There were a number of constraints on the Progressive party and the Reichstag majority which inhibited the desire for constitutional reform. The *Burgfrieden* silenced all partisan politics for a time. The need to present a united front to the world also weakened opposition. The Naumann-ites, in particular, gloried in the "community of the trenches," but all Progressives were fervently patriotic. Years later, Gertrud Bäumer and Meinecke, among others, continued to recall the spirit of unity which existed in August 1914 as one of the high points of their lives. The Progressive party was also constrained by its need to support its friend and ally Bethmann Hollweg against the extreme Right. It believed that he was moving as rapidly in introducing constitutional changes as circumstances permitted. By 1916, as the *Burgfrieden* began to break down and as working-class pressures rose against the SPD, several party leaders began to stress domestic reforms and to call publicly for changes. They realized that the German masses had to secure rewards for their sacrifices and that it was unrealistic to expect them to wait for those rewards until the end of the war. Payer made a major speech in April 1916, condemning censorship and stressing the need to achieve democracy in Germany in rights and citizenship.[44] Naumann at the same time voiced a moving plea for internal reform, while Haussmann continually pressed for a greater part for the Reichstag in making government policy.

Then, in the spring of 1917, a number of developments occurred which increased the demands for constitutional and domestic reforms. The Russian Revolution in March, the pronouncements of Wilson, the food riots, and strikes in Germany combined to dramatize the need for the Reichstag to take the lead in constitutional reform. The government also sensed the need to at least promise reforms. Bethmann Hollweg made a speech in March indicating the necessity for a new orientation, admitting that reforms were overdue while insisting that they had to await the war's end.[45] This procrastination was no longer satisfactory to some Progressives, and Hermann Pachnicke, a veteran legislator and the Progressive leader in the Prussian lower house, criticized Bethmann Hollweg's words as only words when action was needed. Shortly thereafter, another Progressive veteran, Ablass, introduced a Progressive motion in the Reichstag: "Be it resolved that the Reichstag require the Imperial Chancellor to work immediately to the end that a constitution be created in all the German Federal States with a representative body that is based upon universal, direct, equal, and secret suffrage."[46] Then came the kaiser's Easter Decree, which instead of enunciating reforms, justified their postponement. Nonetheless, he did support the removal of the three-class electoral system in Prussia and called for direct and secret elections of the Prussian lower house as well as a more representative composition of the upper house.[47] For left liberals who had been urging such changes for generations, this was progress; however, as much as they welcomed these verbal concessions to reform, they required something more substantial.

Throughout May and June 1917, while a new Reichstag committee, the Constitution Committee, held its first meetings to discuss the constitutional changes necessary to reform the government, the *Berliner Tageblatt* (BT) and the *Frankfurter Zeitung* (FZ), the Progressive party's most important press supporters, insistently called for constitutional reform. On 2 May, the Progressive *Fraktion* in the Prussian lower house backed a SPD motion which demanded the reform of the Prussian franchise and the upper house. A party proclamation (*Aufruf*) on 2 May voiced a similar request, and local Progressive and NLP organizations also showed increased reform activity.[48] Naumann, combining nationalism, democracy, and German political theory, insistently called for a *Volksstaat*, while even the cautious Payer urged speed before it was too late. Only a few Progressives advised care, lest the reform efforts weaken the war effort.[49]

When the Reichstag convened in the first week of July 1917 to vote the annual appropriations necessary to carry on the government, the SPD, the Progressive party, and the NLP together demanded constitutional reforms to achieve a responsible government. The Center party opposed parliamentarization of the Reich government while in Prussia its right wing, along with the NLP, effectively served as a brake on any constitutional reform. Despite the Prussian barrier to change and splits within parties, the impetus for reform was evident and the reformers sharpened their language. The longing for peace now combined with the pentup demand for constitutional and electoral reform. Gothein must have voiced the feelings

33

of most Reichstag deputies when he asked: "Isn't a revolution from above preferable to one from below?"[50] Ablass, a Richterite and foe of the Naumannite democratic current in the party, showed how the war had radicalized him by urging the *Fraktion* to refuse to vote for war credits until constitutional reforms were made. This, however, was too extreme an approach, and he received only scant backing in the *Fraktion*.

During the July crisis, constitutional reform took second place to the Peace Resolution in the debates, but it was the combination of these things—plus some extraneous and personal factors—which toppled Bethmann Hollweg.[51] In July 1917, the chancellor's policy of "the diagonals," his persistent effort to be all things to all men, his contradictions, and his inaction could no longer retain the trust and support of the Reichstag majority. The Progressive party was the only party which defended him. For the others, noble words and good intentions were no longer enough. The Social Democrats were not prepared to fight for him, and the Z and the NLP now joined with the Conservatives to oppose him. The crown prince, the Supreme Command (OHL), and Erzberger and Gustav Stresemann, the leaders of the Center party and the NLP, as a result of a confused and underhanded negotiation, deserted Bethmann Hollweg. In this crisis, the OHL demonstrated greater shrewdness and political talent than did the Reichstag. Of course, it had a simple charge: to replace Bethmann Hollweg with a chancellor who would accept its war goals and direction. It found its man in a colorless bureaucrat, Michaelis, named chancellor without the Reichstag's participation in the selection. The Reichstag's role was limited to confirming the OHL's choice.

The Inter-Party Committee continued to meet after the July crisis and to develop alternative policies to the OHL's. Resentment toward Michaelis soon developed as a result of his remarks about the Peace Resolution.[52] Michaelis accepted the resolution—as he understood it. His bungling of the papal peace initiative increased his difficulties with the Reichstag. It seemed imperative to the Reichstag majority—less the NLP—that an unequivocal repudiation of Belgium had to precede a negotiated peace. Some leading Progressives were so incensed by the actions of Michaelis that they demanded his replacement by a figure who would accept the Reichstag majority's leadership. Their party friend, Payer, who was now vice chancellor, defended Michaelis and urged caution, but the concerted pressure of the Inter-Party Committee forced Michaelis out in October 1917—a not insignificant step in the development of parliamentary government in Germany, although what might have happened if the OHL had wanted to retain Michaelis remains questionable.

Hertling, an aged Centrist conservative, became, after protracted negotiations, the new chancellor but soon proved to be a disappointment as well. Payer continued to serve as vice chancellor, seeing himself as a member of the government rather than as a party politician, and he not only continued apologizing for Hertling's shortcomings but delayed any progress toward constitutional reform. In addition to Payer, other Progressive politicians and National Liberals received government posts in the administration of the Reich and Prussia at this time. Robert Friedberg became Prussian vice minister president, Fischbeck the Prussian minister of commerce, while Eugen Schiffer became under secretary in the treasury. In addition, Paul von Krause, a National Liberal, and Peter Spahn, a Centrist, received positions in the justice departments of the Reich and Prussia. While these appointments of party figures had symbolic value, the reality of responsible government was as far away as ever, and the bargaining for these posts was so lengthy and often so petty that many felt the Reichstag had been discredited. The appointments were enough to satisfy many *Bürger* politicians that progress was being made, although, even in the last year of the war, figures such as Gothein, Haussmann, Naumann, and Haas continued to press for constitutional changes. Haussmann, in particular, became convinced that Germany could not win the war militarily and repeatedly urged a greater role for the Reichstag in the peace negotiations and in constitutional reform.[53] He had been the most aggressive *Bürger* critic of Michaelis, and he soon turned on Hertling as well. He wanted the chancellor to do the Reichstag's bidding but had no idea how to deal with the OHL, which dominated the government. He and other Progressives groused about military "dictatorship," but they could find no way to oppose it effectively. They made sharp attacks against censorship, stirring calls for majority rule, and helped to pry statements from the government which admitted the need for a wide variety of reforms, but parliamentary government was as unrealized in September 1918 as it had been in August 1914. The responsible moderates were convinced that the system could only be saved by timely concessions, and they continually urged the Hertling-Payer government as well as the Prussian *Landtag* to move faster; but the Conservatives refused to yield. When, in July 1918, the Reichstag reassembled to vote the necessary taxes to continue the government and the war, the SPD pressured Hertling to resign, threatening that it would not vote for the taxes. The Progressives attempted to convince the chancellor of the need to appoint Socialists to government posts, but he granted only a few minor positions. The refusal of the Center party to bring down Hertling and its coolness toward parliamentarization stopped any additional movements to achieve constitutional reforms until October 1918. Meanwhile, Haussmann was meeting with Prince Max of Baden, his candidate for the first true responsible chancellor, to prepare the way for Germany's first parliamentary government. The steps to amend the constitution to achieve parliamentary government and a constitutional monarchy had long been approved in the Inter-Party Committee. The Progressive party mounted a sharper attack on Hertling and Payer in late September, but the Conservatives continued to snarl the progress toward responsible government until the OHL and the kaiser, desperate to meet Wilson's demands in order to achieve an armistice, applied the necessary pressure and desired reforms followed. Max of Baden was named chancellor at the beginning of October and a party government was formed, including the SPD. Even the Prussian *Landtag* finally responded to the pressure for change. During October, while the Reichstag produced the amendments to the constitution to form a constitutional monarchy, the government and the nation were preoccupied with the armistice negotiations, the collapse of their allies, and the retreat of their armies. At a time when the Progressives should have been exulting in *their* revolution, they were upstaged by greater events. Even the documents from this period seem to suffer from the depressed mood and the distractions; the texts are terse and far less valuable than the earlier materials.[54] Neither the Reichstag nor Max of Baden and his cabinet performed well at this juncture.

The armistice negotiations brought the most discerning politicians to the brink of political reality, but first they had to discover that Wilson was not the detached idealist they had thought he was. Moreover, he did not control the policies of Britain, France, and Italy. Wilson's refusal to accept the German government changes, which had occurred as a genuine reflection of popular control of the government, infuriated the Progressives, but his skepticism about the nature of Max of Baden's government was well founded. Max was a prince of rather conservative hue and a close relative of the kaiser. Despite his liberal reputation in Germany, his support for parliamentary government was grudging at best.[55] His vice-chancellor, Payer, had loyally served Michaelis and Hertling and the OHL dictatorship with few qualms or complaints. In the light of this, his record as a verteran Swabian democrat who had long battled for constitutional reform was of little importance. The cabinet consisted of obscure politicians whose attachment to liberal and democratic principles was unknown not only to Wilson and his advisers but to many Germans as well. Their support for the kaiser's foreign policy and the war was better known. As the lengthy and painful negotiations continued while the war raged, it became evident that the armistice and the peace would be extremely harsh. After all the German people's sacrifices, this was a shocking outcome. Many in the Progressive party took out their anger not on the kaiser or their leaders, but on Wilson. He had betrayed his principles and had deliberately misled them.[56] He was a cheat and a charlatan. Not only the OHL but parliamentarians such as Haussmann concluded that it would be preferable to break off the armistice negotiations and continue the fight.[57] There was even irresponsible talk in Progressive circles of a *levee en masse*, led by such unlikely militants as Walther Rathenau and Alfred Weber.[58] In the first days of November, the masses and their parties, the socialist parties, had been set in motion. The revolutions in Central Europe which followed the collapse of Germany's allies were now succeeded by a mutiny in the Ger-

man navy in Kiel and the spread in less than a week of a socialist revolution throughout Germany. The brief experiment in constitutional monarchy was soon followed by demands that the kaiser should abdicate, and
the government under Max of Baden, instead of being the culmination of
the Progressive party's hopes and dreams, proved to be only a short inter-
lude before a more profound revolution.

II

The German Democrats and the
November Revolution

Two developments jolted German left liberals in the first two weeks of November 1918: the spread of disorder and mutiny, which became a revolution,[1] and the signing of the armistice agreement to end the fighting.[2] The Progressive party, now a member of the government, held several posts in the cabinet. It also had many foreign contacts through neutral countries. Yet it seemed surprised by these events and overwhelmed by the responsibility which was now thrust on the majority parties. Haussmann, who emerged as the real leader of the *Fraktion*, seemed particularly indecisive and ineffectual in the crisis. He was named by the cabinet, along with Gustav Noske, a member of the SPD, to investigate the mutiny at Kiel, which had begun on 3 November, and to secure order there. He soon abandoned his post and allowed Noske to assume the responsibility. The chairmanship of the Armistice Commission fell to the Centrist politician Erzberger, when Haussmann again refused the obligation. In this important moment, the liberal leaders seemed paralyzed at the national level of government, although at the state and municipal levels liberals assumed major responsibilities and behaved with courage and decisiveness.

The Kiel mutiny touched off revolutionary activities all over Germany in a remarkably short time. The German masses had reached the end of their endurance: misery and defeatism combined to produce an overwhelming cry for peace. Much of the accumulated resentment was then heaped on the governmental system and upon Wilhelm II personally, although his responsibility for the war and its conduct was greatly exaggerated in Germany as well as abroad. Antipathy toward the kaiser increased dramatically when it was evident that Wilson was unwilling to negotiate with those who were perceived as the kaiser's agents. As a result, demands soon arose that the kaiser abdicate, which much surprised the Progressive party.[3] In late October, the abdication question was openly discussed in the cabinet, but it was not until 4 November that it was seriously considered.[4] Meanwhile, the USPD, split off from the SPD in 1917, was demanding not only the abdication of Wilhelm II but the end of the monarchy. Under great pressure from the radicalized working class, the majority Socialists supported this demand rather than lose their supporters to the extreme socialists.

In the cabinet meeting of 4 November, the Progressive party, with Gothein as its spokesman, recognized that the kaiser had to step down in order to keep the SPD behind the government.[5] On the other hand, the party did not want to appear to be forcing the kaiser out of power; it wanted him to make the decision himself. The Progressives generally favored a regency for the crown prince's eldest son as the best solution. In the cabinet meeting on 5 November, Gothein returned to the abdication question and coupled it with the armistice negotiations, an obvious association but bitterly resented by Stresemann as well as Gothein's Progressive colleague Wiemer. Three days later, on 8 November, such niceties were made irrelevant by a SPD ultimatum demanding that the kaiser abdicate; otherwise, it would be forced to leave the government.[6] While the Progressives generally appreciated the dilemma of the SPD, they resented its pressure tactics. Gothein described the ultimatum as a "gun pointed at their breasts," while Haussmann found the SPD's action "dictatorial." In fact, the indecisiveness and timidity of the Progressives and the refusal of the NLP and the Center party to even consider abdication had forced the hand of the SPD. Gothein made a motion on 8 November, later withdrawn and never publicized, which called on the kaiser to abdicate voluntarily, but the NLP and the Z opposed the motion and Gothein withdrew it. Nevertheless, Haussmann told an informal meeting of Progressives soon afterwards that the chancellor had offered to resign and that the kaiser had been asked to abdicate but had refused. The next day, 9 November, Max of Baden resigned and named Friedrich Ebert, the SPD leader, as his successor. In addition, Wilhelm II abdicated as German emperor, remaining as King of Prussia. To the dismay of Ebert, a republic was now proclaimed by Scheidemann, but there was no alternative. The Progressives were even more shocked than Ebert by these developments, but they immediately accepted Ebert as chancellor and head of the government despite the dubious constitutionality of the transfer of power; apparently, they were still hoping against hope that the "October Revolution" and the monarchy might be preserved. They called for the Reichstag to be reconvened to retain continuity and to legitimize the Ebert government,[7] but events were moving too rapidly for that. And it was not long before the Progressive leaders were blaming Wilhelm II for the failure to preserve the monarchy. He had waited too long to act, they contended, and, as a result, the masses had been radicalized.[8]

At the national level of government, a socialist government was now formed, half SPD and half USPD, excluding the middle-class parties. At the state and local levels of government, a variety of coalition governments, usually including left liberals, continued to govern Germany and to try to maintain the flow of food and fuel to the cities. At the same time, the gigantic demobilization process was underway. This confused scene grew even more complex with the appearance of Workers' and Soldiers' Councils (*Räte*), a pale imitation of the soviets, but significant new institutions in a country with so little experience in revolution. Various socialist factions in cities, factories, and some military units controlled the *Räte*, and they were not unknown in small towns and in the countryside as well. The Progressives, with Russian examples in mind, were frightened at the appearance of the *Räte* and stirred from their lethargy. The *Räte* developed so rapidly that it seemed that there had to be a conspiracy; yet it was also evident that they were popularly based and strongly supported. In Hamburg, socialist crowds and soldiers and sailors demonstrated in the streets on 6 November, and Kiel was only a short distance away; yet no one sensed that a revolution was at hand. That evening, the city council (*Bürgerschaft*) met as usual and was amazed when a mob carrying red flags broke into the building and demanded that it help them negotiate with the local military commander.[9] In Kassel, the mayor (*Bürgermeister*), Erich Koch (after April 1925, Koch-Weser), has left an interesting account of his city during the revolutionary period.[10] He, together with the local SPD leader Albert Grzesinski, whom Koch refers to as "my pearl," managed to put the lid back on the bubbling pot of revolution. A similar development occurred in Frankfurt a/M and in other cities where left liberal city officials were respected by the SPD. The fact that Kassel was a major army headquarters for the demobilization effort also may have prevented violence. In a few days, Koch marveled that only in Germany could a people make a revolution one day and go back to work the next,[11] a generalization which would not have surprised Lenin. By the third week in November, the revolution was over in Kassel and thereafter, Kassel felt only occasional tremors from Berlin or the Ruhr. In a few cities, there were bloodier and more protracted disturbances, but Koch's experience in Kassel was probably the norm. In most places, the supply of food and coal dictated the need to support the local authorities and compelled the Progressives to cooperate with the majority Socialists.

It may be an exaggeration to say that there were no Democrats who favored the November Revolution, but there were certainly not many. The Progressives, as we have noted, wanted the political changes which were associated with Max of Baden's government and the so-called October

Revolution. They had almost no role in making the November Revolution. On the other hand, some Democrats approved of some of the changes which accompanied the November Revolution. The statement of Troeltsch, an active Democrat, that the left liberals of 1918 were more conservative than the men of 1848 must be qualified.[12] Many Democrats who deplored the character of the November Revolution had few regrets about the downfall of the empire, and they soon heaped the blame for Germany's defeat and its postwar plight on the discredited *Kaiserreich*.[13] A few Democrats enthusiastically welcomed the prospect of radical change. Max Weber's attitude toward the revolution was typical of most Democrats.[14] Initially shocked and surprised by the revolution, he soon recovered and set about energetically to educate and direct the liberal middle classes to share in the dividends which might come from change. Above all, he wanted to activate the middle classes to participate in the revolution for the sake of their own interests. He and other liberal intellectuals had often criticized the German middle classes for their refusal to accept political responsibility. Weber, like most Democrats, had long recognized the need for constitutional reforms and had become disillusioned by Wilhelm II's performance. In addition, he felt that the war had demonstrated that the parliamentary democracies were more efficient and commanded greater popular support than the great empires of central and eastern Europe. Less typically, Weber had gained a grudging admiration for the moderate socialist trade unionists during the war, and he saw them as a natural partner of the left liberals. He briefly supported the need for more sweeping economic and social changes but was frightened by the strength of the extreme left, which apparently took its cues from the Bolsheviks. He also felt that "socialist experiments" would delay Germany's economic recovery and frighten investors, particularly in the United States. His greatest concern—and this was also the DDP's most pressing goal—was to preserve the unity and strength of the Reich. He soon turned against the revolution and called it a "bloody carnival," a phrase which Democrats employed with approval.[15] In a moment of passion, which he later regretted, he declared that Liebknecht belonged in an insane asylum while Rosa Luxemburg should be placed in a zoo.[16]

The DDP, which published its founding *Aufruf* on 16 November, was compelled to define its attitude and its relationship to the revolution in the midst of revolutionary events. Not surprisingly, it soon altered its original reaction. Theodor Wolff, one of the founders of the DDP, personifies the shift in attitude. At first, Wolff, like Max Weber, welcomed the revolution and praised it excessively, but he soon recoiled from it.[17] In Wolff's opinion, the November Revolution had the correct principles, but it lacked political acumen (*Staatssinn*) and energy (*Tatkraft*). Moreover, he had no respect for the leaders of the German Revolution. He saw no Dantons, Jeffersons, or Lenins among them. They were nobodies, and he entitled it "the revolution of bunglers" ("*die Revolution des Schlemihl*"). Ernst Feder, a leading writer on Wolff's BT and a prominent member of the party's left wing and its Berlin organization, deprecated the revolution on its first anniversary.[18] In later years, the DDP continued to abuse the revolution although the rightist parties branded the DDP as a revolutionary co-conspirator, a "November criminal." It became commonplace in the DDP to interpret the revolution as simply the consequence of military collapse, not as a real revolution at all. While some members were clearly disappointed that it had failed to unite, renew, and regenerate German government and society,[19] others concluded that it all had been a terrible mistake. In later years, Democrats celebrated Constitution Day, the anniversary of the acceptance of the constitution by the National Assembly, but they never hailed the revolution. It was a misfortune (*Unglück*) and a disaster (*Unheil*).[20] On the tenth anniversary of the revolution, Koch-Weser, who was then minister of justice, was traveling in the United States. When asked by an American journalist about his thoughts on the revolution, he minimized its importance. It was, he said, no holiday for Germans.[21] It was too closely associated with Germany's defeat and the Treaty of Versailles to have favorable connotations.

The thrust of the DDP's propaganda and activities from mid-November until mid-January was counterrevolutionary, developing through several chapters and acquiring various characteristics. The DDP was involved in humanitarian relief work, the formation of Citizens' Councils (*Bürgerräte*) to counter Workers' and Soldiers' Councils, and participation in army or Free Corps forceful suppression of the Left. Its most important counterrevolutionary work, however, was to help secure SPD support for democratic elections of a National Assembly. Humanitarian relief work, primarily in the cities, was performed by thousands of anonymous officials throughout Germany, many of whom chose to become Democrats. At the national level, DDP politicians and publicists applied pressure and made propaganda directed abroad in order to speed the shipment of food to Germany. Naumann and Rathenau, to mention only two well-known personages, became heavily committed to financing and encouraging counterrevolutionary groups.[22] Goetz became a leading figure in the *Bürgerrat* movement until its reactionary activities caused him to withdraw from it in 1920, while a young demobilized officer, Eberhard Wildemuth, who was later prominent in the Young Democratic organization, fought in a Free Corps group to restore order in Stuttgart and Württemberg.[23] Less dramatic and probably more effective was the subtle counterrevolutionary work done by hundreds of local DDP organizations which worked cooperatively with majority Socialists to place a "cap on the volcano."[24] During this period, while the most urgent need was to prevent a revolution from the extreme Left, the DDP was not unmindful of the menace of its historic nemesis, the Right, and the left wing of the DDP often seemed more fearful of counterrevolution directed by *Junkers* and the army than a more radical turn to the left.

One of the most significant but least publicized counterrevolutionary activities of DDP members was performed by career officials who continued to work for, and very often simultaneously to work against, the revolutionary government.[25] Several important Democrats eased the transition from the empire to the Republic through their work at the subcabinet level while thousands of lesser officials remained at their posts. There were enormous problems to be solved, and the German socialists concluded that only experts could perform the necessary administrative work. The USPD was extremely suspicious of these bourgeois officials. Richard Müller and Ernst Däumig both warned of the dangers of allowing them to remain in the government, but they were unable to purge them. On one occasion, Däumig, who wanted to oust both Wilhelm Solf, who was acting foreign minister, and Schiffer, the acting finance minister, asked: "Don't we have any party members with sufficient organizational ability?"[26] The answer was "no." There were no Socialists with the knowledge and experience to perform these complex tasks, and the socialist government was unwilling to risk the consequences of administration by amateurs. Later, Schiffer became a prominent Democrat and Solf an active member of the party and on one occasion a DDP Reichstag candidate. Ulrich von Brockdorff-Rantzau, who was "close" to the DDP, replaced Solf. Another leading DDP figure, Preuss, acted as the minister of the interior with the special responsibility to prepare a draft constitution for the National Assembly to consider.

Democratic intellectuals at this time helped, on the one hand, to undermine the proletarian revolution, and, on the other, to justify a bourgeois revolution. They wrote long and learned articles in the popular press which certainly helped the educated middle classes accept the changes which had occurred. These articles, in turn, were absorbed by opinion molders—editors, professors, teachers, and pastors. Figures such as Alfred and Max Weber, Preuss, M. J. Bonn, Meinecke, Schücking, Troeltsch, Goetz, Heinrich Gerland, and Rade joined the *Hilfe* publicists and other left-liberal journalists to analyze the flaws of the *Kaiserreich* and the strengths of liberal democracy.[27] Most of them felt that a revolution was overdue in Germany, but that it was still possible to follow an evolutionary course built on the achievements of the October Revolution. They welcomed the advent of parliamentary democracy, the end of the Prussian electoral system, and the lowering of religious and class barriers. Most of them also supported votes for women and lower voting ages. They also approved the separation of church and state. More controversial were suggested measures to create a highly centralized state and to break up Prussia. There was even less agreement on economic and social reform measures, but one item on which all Democrats could agree was the ne-

43

cessity for the popular election of a national assembly to draft a new constitution and to secure a peace settlement.

Payer and Haussmann had demanded as early as 9 November that a national assembly be elected as soon as possible. Fortunately, the majority Socialists were as anxious as the bourgeois parties to secure such an election, and the agreement of the DDP, the Z, and the SPD on the need for an election was one of their tightest bonds. Preuss, in an article which appeared on 14 November, stressed that a true democracy could only be established through the election of a national assembly by an enlarged electorate.[28] Dozens of other Democrats and Democratic publications made the same point in the weeks which followed. It became the central theme of the proclamations of the *Bürgerräte*, and a number of military and civil officials added their weight, too. However, it was more important that the socialist trade unions and the officials of the SPD favor the election. Scheidemann, writing in *Vorwärts* as early as 18 November, emphasized that it was a necessary step to achieve peace, a stable economy, and order.[29] He stressed the need for the will of the majority to prevail. He also emphasized the necessity to cooperate with reasonable elements of the middle classes. This was sweet music to the ears of Democrats who regarded Scheidemann as an extreme radical.

In mid-December, an event occurred that was also reassuring. It was the National Congress of Representatives of Workers' and Soldiers' Councils, which met in Berlin. Moderate socialists dominated the meeting and virtually shut out the extreme Left. It was at this meeting that Max Cohen-Reuss, representing the majority Socialist position, proposed that 19 January be established as the election day for the National Assembly.[30] This motion, passed overwhelmingly, effectively proscribed the German Revolution. The DDP had a small contingent at the Councils' Congress which naturally supported the motion of Cohen-Reuss. Wilhelm Flügel, the leader of the DDP *Fraktion*, summarized the feelings of his party: "We need a National Assembly because peace is required; we need it because we must have bread; we need to have freedom (to battle) the extremes of Right and Left; we must establish laws based on the will of the people."[31]

During the weeks which followed, while the DDP campaigned for the national assembly and improved its organization, the USPD and the Spartacists took to the streets. When the SPD supported the forceful suppression of their brothers by the Army and the Free Corps, the USPD left the government in disgust. The DDP reacted sharply against the actions of the extreme Left and cheered the Army's and the Free Corps' violent suppression of them. In January, when it seemed as if the Spartacists and the USPD might succeed in fomenting a second revolution, the DDP marched and demonstrated with the majority Socialists in Berlin, Düsseldorf, and other cities.[32] It may be true that the revolution intensified class feelings among DDP members, but the DDP always made distinctions among various kinds of socialists—as it did among the variety of rightists. For the moment, it was imperative to act with the majority Socialists against the enemies of liberalism and democracy. Unfortunately for the history of party government in the Weimar period, having common enemies was never a sufficient bond to produce affection or trust, and class feelings and contrasting material interests were too strong to be overcome.

The Origins and the Founding of the DDP

During the final days of the armistice negotiations, as revolution spread through Germany, the liberal parties began discussing the need to cooperate in the first postwar election and to explore the possibility of fusing the two organizations—the NLP and the Progressive party—into one liberal party. The provincial organizations of both parties in south Germany led the movement for unity, strongly supported by the *Hansa-Bund*.[33] Jacob Riesser, the president of the HB, and Friedberg, the chairman of the NLP in Prussia, publicly called for liberal unity in the face of the socialist challenge, as did several prominent members of the Progressive party. However, factions in both parties opposed a merger. The right wing of the NLP, led by Ruhr industrialists who had been extreme annexationists during the war, feared that any movement to the left would destroy the party's traditional position.[34] The left wing of the Progressive party bitterly opposed any close cooperation, let alone a merger, with Stresemann's NLP. Stresemann himself played a double game for several weeks, assuring NLP members who favored liberal unity that it would be achieved, while telling others who fundamentally opposed a merger that he would never join with left-wing elements of the Progressive party, which he saw as an appendage of the SPD.[35] Opposition at the local organizational level also arose because of the memories of former political battles and the often bitter personal animosities which existed between local leaders of the two parties.

Despite these barriers, military defeat and the possibility of a socialist revolution compelled the NLP and the Progressive party to subordinate their feelings and discuss the possibility of a party fusion or, at the very least, electoral cooperation. On 8 November, Hartmann von Richthofen, an HB official and a left-wing NLP deputy who had broken with Stresemann on war-aims questions, persuaded the Reichstag *Fraktion* to send a motion to the NLP central committee which recommended a discussion of a fusion and of an electoral alliance with the Progressive party.[36] The following day, Stresemann and Fischbeck met to discuss how they might cooperate. Out of this conversation came a joint appeal for the election of a national assembly. Meanwhile, throughout Germany, Progressive and NLP provincial and local party organizations were joining together to create a broad middle-class party which would unite all non-Catholic elements between the SPD and the Conservatives.[37] It was an old idea but defeat and socialist revolution had produced more promising circumstances than had existed for many years. Stresemann's appointment book indicates that there was a lively discussion in his office on 13 November concerning a liberal merger.[38] The next day, the Berlin organization of the Progressive party held a *Parteitag* in which it called for a broad democratic and republican party to meet the urgent needs of the times. Stresemann surveyed the NLP leadership to ascertain its attitude toward fusion with the Progressives. The following day, 15 November, four representatives from each party met at the home of a NLP deputy to discuss what base for cooperation existed. They reached a general understanding of a common platform, program, and organization in the upcoming election but stopped well short of an agreement to fuse the two organizations. Stresemann and the right wing of the NLP preferred to wait for that until after the election.[39] Stresemann later exaggerated this meeting's consensus for fusion, claiming that liberal unity would have occurred had not a new party, the German Democratic party—the DDP—appeared the same day. According to Stresemann, the DDP shattered the hopes of all those who wanted liberal unity.[40] This is highly questionable. Individuals such as Stresemann, who was in the NLP left wing on many domestic issues, and Fischbeck, who was in the right wing of the Progressive party, could agree on most issues, but the parties still had fundamental differences. The eight leaders who met on 15 November could not speak for their parties. Indeed, given the local control of the nominating process and party organization in both parties, it was presumptuous for them even to try. It seems unlikely that they could have achieved even electoral cooperation except in south Germany, where the NLP was weak and more conciliatory and the Progressives had long worked for liberal unity.

The DDP, which was announced on 16 November, was conceived by fifteen political outsiders, most of them Berlin Jews.[41] They included Theodor Vogelstein, a young economist who later turned banker and businessman; Richard Witting, the banker brother of Maximilian Harden and close friend of Wolff; Richard Otto Frankfurter, an attorney; Hjalmar Schacht, banker and prominent member of the NLP's Young Liberal organization; Kurt von Kleefeld, an HB official. The others were businessmen, bankers, professional people, and intellectuals. Most of them had opposed annexationist war aims and favored democratic political and social reforms. They fundamentally opposed the authoritarian state (*Obrigkeitsstaat*), a term which Witting apparently coined and Preuss, who was a friend of most of them, popularized. Few of them had any political experience or even friends who were politicians, least of all Vogelstein, who was apparently the driving force behind the idea of creating a *new* party.[42] He had studied law and economics at the University of Munich where he had been a student of Brentano. Later, he was a lecturer (*Privat-*

dozent) there. He became an acquaintance of Max and Alfred Weber because of his activities in the Association for Social Policy (*Verein für Sozialpolitik*). During the war, he worked in the War Raw Materials Division, first organized by Rathenau, where he became convinced of the need for economic and social planning and for a new political order. Neither Vogelstein nor any other member of this group had any idea how to organize a political party. Several names were suggested of people who might help, but only Wolff, the chief editor of the *Berliner Tageblatt*, was home when they telephoned. He was attracted to the idea of a new party which would cut all ties to the discredited liberal parties, and he secured the permission of his publisher, the Mosse Press, to organize the launching of a new party. Wolff insisted on the name Democratic party. He brought two academic friends with him, Alfred Weber and Gerland.[43] He also invited several journalists on the BT and FZ to participate in the inner planning group, in which Wolff and Alfred Weber became the most important figures. One of the journalists was Max Wiessner, the FZ's Berlin editor, who secured the backing of the FZ editors and publisher for the proposed party. Gothein, whose internationalist views agreed with the BT and FZ, was also brought in and asked to contact certain Progressive leaders and Reichstag deputies with acceptable records. Gothein wrote to twenty deputies who, he felt, would be sympathetic, urging them to consider the DDP as an alternative to liberal fusion.[44] While he excluded the extreme annexationists in the Progressive party, he included figures such as Fischbeck and Naumann. Fischbeck was a superb party organizer and leader, and Wolff respected his ability. Gothein overlooked Fischbeck's war-aims record. Fischbeck not only possessed great organizational ability and many valuable contacts with financial circles, but he also brought the Berlin Progressive party with him. Paul Nathan and Frankfurter set to work to prepare the initial draft of an *Aufruf* to proclaim the new party, and Wolff applied the finishing polish. The following day, 16 November, the BT published the *Aufruf* with the names of sixty individuals attached who supported the principles of the new party.[45]

The *Aufruf* contained the principal motifs and slogans of the DDP in the election of the National Assembly and in subsequent years. Many of them were already part of the left-liberal political vocabulary. Nonetheless, the founders asserted that the DDP was a *new* party appropriate for a new age, a party of the middle which rejected the extremes of left and right, and a party which represented *all* of the people—not classes or material interests. The DDP would represent the *Volksgemeinschaft*. Those who were hastily recruited to sign the *Aufruf* were in some respects representative of the electorate which supported the DDP, but in other ways they were atypical. The DDP, in later years, was often called the party of education and property (*Bildung und Besitz*), and the signatures on the *Aufruf* reflected that designation. Over half of the signers had a doctor's degree, many were prosperous business and professional people, and there was a disproportionate number of journalists and professors as well. On the other hand, there were no teachers, no farmers, only one laborer, and no employees (*Angestellte*). The DDP had little luck in recruiting laborers or employees, and most farmers shunned it after 1918–1919, but it generally had strong support from teachers. Few experienced politicians signed it because many of them had left Berlin and returned to their homes, but also because the DDP founders wanted to show that it was indeed a new party. Most of the signers were Berliners. This was both a reflection of the character of the founders and also of the need to gather signatures as rapidly as possible. Partisan enemies of the DDP in later years often called the DDP the "party of the Jews" (*Judenpartei*), and the list of backers included many Jews, a detail which anti-Semites quickly noted. The large number of journalists and publishers among the signatories showed the important part which the BT and the FZ, in particular, had in its founding. Many of those who signed the *Aufruf* remained active in the party until the end, while others, such as Albert Einstein and Hugo Stinnes, either abandoned partisan political activity or turned to other parties. The important characteristic of the list of supporters on 16 November 1918 was that it illustrated the very narrow sociological base on which the DDP proposed to build a political party.

While the DDP founders gained support for their party in Berlin, Gothein and Fischbeck widened the net in the Progressive party and Richthofen and Johannes Junck recruited NLP members. Junck, like Richthofen, was a left-wing member and a foe of Stresemann. Yet many liberals, however attracted they were to the idea of a new party which would bring together most middle-class non-Catholics, did not enlist because of some of the principles expressed in the *Aufruf* and because of the reputation of some of the founders. Max Weber and Schacht, who ended up joining the DDP, were initially repelled because the DDP was avowedly a republican party. Others hesitated because of the ambiguous statement in the *Aufruf* that seemed to support limited socialization of property. Naumann was incensed because of the DDP's ties to the "cowardly" BT and its chief editor Wolff, but also because its founding had prevented a merger of the Progressive party and the NLP.[46] Nonetheless, Naumann joined the new party on 17 November, though Alfred Weber warned him that he had to maintain a "low profile" because of his association with annexationist war goals. The strong Berlin coloration of the DDP and its close ties to the BT and the FZ prevented many in the provinces from supporting it at first, but despite the misgivings of liberal leaders, the pressure of the rank and file for a united liberal party pushed them along. Virtually all of the Progressive party organizations soon went over to the DDP and so did several NLP groups. In addition, dozens of newspapers all over Germany followed the lead of the BT and the FZ.

Stresemann was persuaded to support the new party by several NLP newspapers and local organizations. He had been alarmed and angered by the news of the plans for a new party which he first learned about on 14 November.[47] He felt that it weakened the drive for a united liberal party, but he also opposed it because the DDP promised to radicalize the liberal movement. Regardless of his personal feelings, however, Stresemann acknowledged the groundswell of popular support for the DDP. On 16 November, Stresemann met with several NLP members to discuss negotiations for a fusion of the liberal parties, and the following day he met several supporters, including Bernhard, the editor of the VZ, to assess the impact of the DDP's formation. On 18 November, representatives of the three groups discussed the possibility of combining their forces. It was an unhappy occasion and an augury of future efforts to combine all liberals in one party. In the meeting, the brash young DDP representatives were offensive and arrogant. They demanded parity with the two established liberal parties in any future organization. Moreover, they announced that they could not possibly join with annexationists and reactionaries. They singled out Stresemann as an extreme annexationist. He quite naturally concluded that a fusion with the DDP would necessitate too many sacrifices for himself and the NLP.[48] The idea of working with people such as Wolff and Vogelstein and journalists of the FZ repelled him. While Wolff looked upon him as one of those who had irresponsibly prolonged the war, Stresemann believed that the BT had weakened the nation's will to fight on for victory.[49] The behavior of the DDP leaders offended Friedberg, the leader of the Prussian NLP, at this first meeting. Negotiations continued without Stresemann and Friedberg, however, and on 20 November, Progressives, left NLP members, and the DDP officially joined together as the German Democratic party.[50] Two days later, Stresemann and a group of NLP members announced the formation of the German People's party (*Deutsche Volkspartei*—DVP).[51] A few right-wing Progressives, including Wiemer and Kopsch, joined the DVP as well. Stresemann's effort to prevent the movement of the NLP members to the DDP by forming a "new" party, the DVP, had little success. The defection of NLP members continued apace. Two prominent Young Liberals (Young NLP), Bruno Marwitz and Hermann Fischer, who had spoken against the formation of the DVP, joined their colleague Schacht in the DDP on 23 November. Rumors flew that Stresemann and Friedberg had also gone over to the DDP—rumors which Stresemann repeatedly denied. He desperately wanted to preserve support for the DVP and his own leadership as well as to justify his refusal to join the DDP. He varied his explanations to fit the audience. He often stressed the ideological gulf between himself and the Wolff-Weber party, as he liked to call the DDP. Sometimes, he emphasized the rudeness and excessive demands of the DDP representatives, who wished to dominate the organization.

The DDP's delegation in the meeting on 18 November certainly was aggressive. It exaggerated the popular support which the DDP had at this early date and made too many demands. Its brusque manners offended many who were present, including several of the Progressive party leaders, but already the leadership of the DDP was shifting to Naumann and Fischbeck. Naumann was proving far more popular than he had been before the war. Stresemann, though conscious of this change in the DDP's leadership in the last two weeks of November, continued to represent the DDP as the party of Wolff and Weber. In reality, he had no intention of submitting himself to the DDP's terms from the beginning, regardless of the DDP's leadership; Gothein and Richthofen offended him as much as Wolff and Weber. Stresemann wanted to preserve the organization and principles of the NLP at all costs and could only have approved a liberal merger dictated by the NLP. He expected in the long run to rally most NLP members to the DVP, including most of those initially inclined to support the DDP.

Friedberg, on the other hand, more of a realist and perhaps more frightened by socialist revolution and the need to build defenses against it, after considerable procrastination and much confusion decided to join the DDP on its terms and to bring as many NLP members with him as possible. This turn of events so astounded Stresemann that he never seemed to understand Friedberg's motives,[52] and his apostasy remained an enigma, but sometime between 26 November and 2 December, Friedberg determined that the DVP lacked the minimal organizational and financial support to succeed. He joined the DDP secure in the knowledge that Fischbeck and other Progressives were dominant in the DDP's organization and that he would have an important voice in the organization and in the Prussian *Landtag*, the only political arena which concerned him. Haussmann and Fischbeck soon assumed control of the organization of the DDP and reshaped its Executive Committee (*Geschäftsführender Ausschuss*). Increasingly, it reflected the importance of veteran politicians of the Progressive and NLP parties who controlled the local organizations. Haussmann used his considerable influence to admit more provincial Progressives and National Liberals to the Executive Committee and to forestall some of the nominees of the Wolff-Weber group.[53] Fischbeck thought that the committee was too Jewish and included too many great capitalists.[54] On 26 November, the key members included Fischbeck; Otto Nuschke, a veteran Berlin Progressive and editor of a Mosse newspaper, the *Berliner Volkszeitung*; Richthofen; Alfred Weber; Schacht; and Fräulein Dr. Margareth Bernhard, a feminist leader from Charlottenburg who was conspicuous by her silence. Except for Bernhard, they all became prominent in the DDP organization. According to Richthofen, an HB official and a wily and supple politician with varied business interests, the real Executive Committee consisted of Fischbeck, Weber, and himself.

Weber, however, was soon a victim of bad luck and bad judgment—he contracted the flu, made an intemperate public attack on big business, and resigned the chairmanship of the party in mid-December.

While the organization of the DDP quickly changed to reflect the realities of middle-class politics, the DDP and the DVP continued to negotiate a merger. There was much confusion about these negotiations because of erratic communications between Berlin and the provinces at this time and because of Stresemann's contradictory and self-serving statements and letters. On 26 November, the Executive Committee authorized Fischbeck and Schacht to continue to negotiate with the DVP, and it assured Stresemann an "important place" in the party. Stresemann, however, no longer acted interested and stressed the differences in principle which separated the two parties. In the last days of November, the news agencies of the two parties vigorously attacked each other, although moderates in both parties continued to work for one liberal party and to stress the similarities rather than the differences,[55] and Stresemann publicly declared that his person should not stand in the way of a merger. The DDP leadership insisted that the door was open to "right standing gentlemen" in order to underline its conciliatory position, but the will to join together never exceeded such verbal declarations. It was impossible to combine at this time; the differences were simply too great to be compromised.

On 1 December, in the *Zirkus Busch* in Berlin, the DDP held a gigantic rally in which speeches were made and themes emphasized which terminated any hopes for a DDP-DVP merger.[56] The meeting was intended to demonstrate that the middle classes were prepared to adapt to the new democratic age, to defend their rights, and to fight for their political, social and economic principles. A crowd of 5,000 filled the hall and spilled over into an adjacent auditorium. Fischbeck and Alfred Weber, the chairman of the DDP, were the principal speakers in a long night of speeches. The themes were familiar ones, but they had not yet hardened into the clichés of the later years of the Republic. Many of the speakers were newcomers to left-liberal politics who stressed that the DDP was a new party fit for a new age. It was democratic and republican but also patriotic, as nationalistic and state-supportive as the other *Bürger* parties. With the exception of Fischbeck, few DVP leaders could respect the speakers or their ideas, and DVP publicists immediately distorted the speakers' remarks for their own partisan advantage. The remarks of Alfred Weber, who was on the far left of the DDP at this time, proved to be especially controversial. In the course of his speech, he accused Stinnes and Fritz Thyssen, both great industrialists, of collaborating with the French. He based his statement on newspaper reports which proved false, but his charges resulted in the arrest of Stinnes and Thyssen by Prussian officials. Weber's words and the arrests tended to discredit him as an irresponsible demagogue with a grudge against big business. The press reports angered many DDP leaders who then demanded Weber's resignation. Weber, after he had recovered from the flu, attempted to clarify his words but retracted nothing.[57] His speech became a pretext to ease him out of power and his illness gave Fischbeck the opportunity to become chairman in fact if not in name. The Progressives had had reservations about Weber from the beginning. Gothein, shortly before the rally, wrote Haussmann that Weber was neither a great nor even a lucid politician, but "clumsy."[58] Many years later, Gothein, who seldom changed his mind about anything, confirmed his earlier judgement. He remembered Weber's "unclear and dangerous words" and his vacillations about socialization.[59] Heuss, a young journalist with political ambitions in 1918, thought that Weber was too hysterical and demagogic to be a political leader.[60]

The last attempt to unify the DDP and the DVP occurred the day following the rally at the *Zirkus Busch*. The negotiators at this meeting were Schacht and Fischbeck for the DDP and Friedberg and Eugen Leidig, Stresemann's man, for the DVP.[61] Friedberg was determined to achieve a success. The DDP indicated that while it was prepared to give Stresemann a seat in the National Assembly, it was unwilling to allow him an important post in the organization. Moreover, the DDP insisted on a majority of the seats in both major committees and DVP adherence to the principles, including the republican principles set forth in its *Aufruf* of 16 November. The DVP demanded parity in the organization, seats for major DVP economic interest groups on the major committees, and satisfactory answers to questions about the DDP's attitude toward socialization and "national questions." Although the atmosphere was generally friendly, it was apparent that the two parties were far apart. Leidig was outraged at the DDP's demands, but Friedberg, in the light of the DDP's successes in building an organization and gaining financial backing, concluded that the DVP had no alternative but to accept the DDP's terms. While Stresemann had seemed supportive of the negotiations, he had clearly hedged his bets before he learned of the DDP's demands. On the night of 2 December, he gave a talk to a group of "party friends" in Dresden, advising them that a merger was probable but that they should preserve their local organization in case it failed to endure.[62] On 3 December, Friedberg, despite Leidig's opposition, agreed to the DDP's terms and on 4 December, the *NL Korrespondenz* reported the unification of the two parties.[63] Henceforth, according to this report, there would be only one liberal party, the DDP. Leidig protested to Stresemann that Friedberg had exceeded his powers. Stresemann readily agreed and repudiated his capitulation. Although many local organizations had joined the DDP following Friedberg's announcement, Stresemann indicated that the DVP would continue as a distinct organization. The future of the DVP, however, could only be determined by the NLP Central Committee chaired by Friedberg. Between 6 December and 15 December, when the Central Committee met, Stresemann worked hard to rally support for the DVP's survival. Only 61 of 229 members made the hazardous journey to Berlin for the meeting. It was bitterly cold, the trains were unheated, and the influenza epidemic still raged. In the end, the committee supported Stresemann and the continuance of the DVP, but only by a vote of thirty-three to twenty-eight. The minority protested that such a small number of delegates had no authority to make a major decision, but it was not reversed.[64]

The party leadership of both the DDP and the DVP recognized that the failure to unite was a fateful decision, and both parties soon sponsored official historical interpretations explaining why the parties were not united.[65] The DDP stressed that while it had, indeed, denied Stresemann a leading role in the party organization because of his wartime annexationist record, Stresemann's ambition and vanity destroyed the attempt to achieve liberal unity. The DVP, on the other hand, contended that Friedberg had exceeded his authority and betrayed the DVP by accepting shameful conditions. Stresemann tended to stress in his apologies that the two groups were so sharply divided by principles that a merger had never been in the cards, but he was always sensitive to the charge that his personal ambition destroyed the best opportunity to unite the liberal parties.[66] For the most part, DDP studies have accepted its interpretation, while studies of the DVP and Stresemann have generally supported the DVP's interpretation. Most Stresemann defenders have neglected the fact that, by 2 December, the DDP was not led by Weber and Wolff but by Fischbeck and Friedberg. It was not the so-called *Tageblatt* group which controlled the DDP, as Stresemann always contended, but figures such as Fischbeck, Haussmann, Schacht, Naumann, Gothein, and Richthofen. The exclusion of Stresemann was lamentable, but the gifted statesman of 1925 was not discernible in the Stresemann of 1918. The DDP viewed Stresemann as an extreme annexationist and monarchist and a man so unrepentant that he could not be trusted.[67] It saw him as Ludendorff's "young man," whose judgment was so warped and whose ability to adjust to changing times was so lacking that he was a political liability.[68] Stresemann was not asked by the DDP to abandon politics and was guaranteed a seat in the National Assembly. His future was not foreclosed. The DVP, it is true, was treated as a lesser partner, but that was in accordance with its strength and support in December 1918.

Still, the most surprising aspect of the failure to unify the liberal parties in 1918 was not Stresemann's behavior but Friedberg's. For a man of his principles and record to enlist in a political party called "democratic" was bizarre. He had opposed Prussian electoral reform until the spring of 1917, even then favoring its delay until after the war and curbing democracy through a system of plural suffrage for the rich and the well-educated. Until the end of the war, he continued to associate democracy with corruption and demagoguery. Following the meeting of 16 November, he asserted that he would never join a party which included Wolff and Weber. Nevertheless, this wealthy, conservative law professor and baptized Jew soon determined that the DDP offered the best hope for the liberal middle classes. He apparently never had second thoughts about his decision. The DVP always implied that he hungered for power, but this seems unlikely; he was an old man in poor health and died early in 1920. Instead, he was apparently motivated by conservative goals: to check the socialists and to preserve his beloved Prussia. Stresemann never understood why the DDP accepted Friedberg as an organizational leader but not himself. He was to the left of Friedberg on most domestic questions, but Friedberg was enough of a realist to compromise. Friedberg's defection was important for the success of the DDP in January 1919. He caused several local NLP organizations to join him in the DDP, some because they were confused and others because they respected his judgement, and he was an important factor in the organization in Prussia until his death.

From mid-December 1918 until mid-January 1919, the campaign for the National Assembly dominated the consciousness of the DDP. The Democrats were not indifferent to the Socialist struggle which swirled about them during this month, but they had no influence over its outcome. They had to put their trust in the SPD, the trade unions, the army, and the Free Corps to check the Spartacists and extreme Independent Socialists and to secure order so that the elections to the National Assembly could occur in peace. While the DDP's most compelling goal was to win seats in the National Assembly to block a Socialist majority, it also wished to achieve sufficient strength to participate in the government, to help write a new constitution, and to secure a just peace for Germany. The DDP successfully helped block a Socialist majority and won more seats in the National Assembly than expected.

III

The Election of the National Assembly

The founders of the DDP conceived it to be a new party divorced from the established liberal parties. They also intended it as a party not just for the middle class, but for all the people. The need to win an election, however, when combined with the unpopularity of the Wolff-Weber group, soon relegated the founders and their ideals to a secondary position, although their values and goals continued to inspire the left wing of the DDP. The left wing, which included many of the Naumann group as well as the journalists of the BT and the FZ and various intellectuals, regretted the compromises the election to the National Assembly forced on the party but continued to press for the ideas of the *Aufruf* of 16 November. During the campaign, the DDP clearly became a middle-class party of former Progressives and National Liberals. Most contemporaries saw it as the successor of the Progressive party. The composition of the DDP *Fraktion* in the National Assembly illustrates this. Although only a minority of the *Fraktion* had previously served in the Reichstag, most of the deputies had been active members of the two liberal parties and many had served them in various capacities.

Organization

The Executive Committee (*Geschäftsführender Ausschuss*—GA) directed the campaign. Fischbeck chaired it and it met twenty-eight times before the election, combining the functions of a policy-making committee, business committee, and campaign committee.[1] The Main Committee (*Hauptvorstand*), by contrast, which became the Executive Committee in stages following the election and which was chaired by Friedberg, met only once before the election.[2] In addition to these two national committees, the national headquarters of the party, the *Zentrale*, also had impor-

55

tant campaign functions. It served as a communications center, directing the flow of propaganda and campaign funds to the electoral districts (*Wahlkreise*) and to lower levels of the party organization.[3] Neither liberal party had been accustomed to a strong *Zentrale*, and most of the party leaders preferred to keep it impotent. Figures such as Naumann and Anton Erkelenz, who wanted to build a strong *Zentrale*,[4] suffered a defeat in their efforts, and most of the organizational power remained at the local level. Only very weak districts depended on the *Zentrale*'s funds and advice, although most organizations used its propaganda materials and accepted its monetary allotments. The "local notables" who traditionally dominated the liberal party organizations remained in control of candidate selection and the campaign in most districts, although some political newcomers did emerge in the party organization and new voters among women and young people provided valuable help to the party during the campaign, particularly in the execution of the "little tasks" of organizational work. Some of the notables were sensitive to the democratic changes which had occurred and welcomed broadening the organization, but, for the most part, the DDP organization consisted of middle-aged males.

The direction of the *Zentrale* was in the hands of a professor, Hermann Schreiber, assisted by two highly experienced professional organizers. Reinold Issberner, who had been a functionary in various left-liberal headquarters since the days of Richter, and Hermann Kalkoff, who had a similar career in the NLP. They relayed instructions and materials to more than one hundred paid party secretaries and thousands of hardworking volunteers throughout the country. Many of the party secretaries were likewise former employees of the liberal parties. The *Zentrale* also directed the production of dozens of brochures and hundreds of different flyers and leaflets, many of which were written by political candidates and representatives of various interest groups. The *Zentrale* also supervised for the GA the party newsletter, the *Demokratische Partei-Korrespondenz* (DPK), and the first party journal, *Das demokratische Deutschland*, which was first edited by Ludwig Bergsträsser. Many district organizations and city groups also published newsletters, newspapers, and periodicals. The DDP always had many willing writers and editors.

Finance

The demands of the campaign necessitated an unprecedented effort to secure funds. In 1911, the year before a national election, the Progressive party's national organization raised only 26,000 M, half of which went to pay professional party secretaries and the other half for the expenses of the *Zentrale*.[5] The 1912 election saw some improvement in the organization thanks to the greater success which party leaders had in raising funds for the party. The Progressive party had a Finance Committee, which raised money and distributed it where it would do the most good. Most of the party's funds, however, were raised at the local level through large contributions from a few individuals. Ten percent of all funds raised for the party were to be sent to the *Zentrale*, a requirement not always observed. This kind of indiscipline was characteristic of liberal organizations. In 1912, the party received only 1054 individual contributions.[6] While some of the local organizations were well financed, most of them were desperately poor. The Berlin local organization brought in six times as much money as all the other local organizations combined. The only interest group which made significant financial contributions to the Progressive party organization was the HB, which also supported the NLP. Contributions to the Progressive party were also made by tobacco and spirits manufacturers, the textile industry, department stores, banks, and stock market interests. A substantial portion of the help came from Jews. This was especially true in Berlin and in Saxony,[7] although Jewish financial "angels" were present in virtually every district.

In 1919, because the socialist threat was so ominous, the financial fortunes of the left-liberal party improved dramatically. The DDP seemed to be the only popular non-Catholic middle class party and the only *Bürger* force in politics capable of halting the achievement of a socialist majority in the National Assembly. The fund raisers of 1919 generally had important connections to commercial, banking, or industrial circles. Once again, the HB was a major contributor, and in this election, it gave most of its funds to the DDP. Schacht was an important fund raiser, and certain candidates—especially Dernburg and Naumann in Berlin—attracted generous support.[8] Friedberg also tapped significant "money bags." Bankers such as Carl Fürstenberg, Solly Segall, and the Arnhold brothers made generous contributions, as did a number of prominent industrialists. Rathenau, Siemens, Robert Bosch, Max Bahr, and a factory director, Isidor Stern, contributed to the party, and so did Stinnes. Locally, many DDP leaders, including Hermann Luppe of Frankfurt a/M., raised much money from frightened local industrialists. Some of the largest businessmen and industrialists formed the Council for the Reconstruction of German Economic Life (the *Kuratorium für den Weideraufbau des Deutschen Wirtschaftslebens*—the *Kuratorium*). It included Rathenau and Siemens and raised 1,000,000 M for the DDP during the campaign.[9] The Tietz family, founders of the Hertie department store chain, was also an active backer of the DDP, as were other department store interests. The amount of money which rolled in exceeded the ability of several local organizations to spend it. As a result, they were able to build up a war chest for future campaigns. Peter Bruckmann, the treasurer of the Württemberg party and an important industrialist, reported that on 23 December, the DDP in Württemberg had 1,700,000 M in the bank.[10] While a few thousand individuals and companies made large contributions, the effort to build a dues-paying membership modeled on the SPD's organization failed. There were well over a million party members in January 1919, but there is no indication how many paid dues or made contributions. Many members did, however, contribute volunteer labor to local organizations or the *Zentrale*. Local party headquarters were filled particularly with young people willing to help. Many who had never been active in political work before were fired by the ideals of the DDP and its leadership—or frightened of socialism—and their labor was vital to the success of the organization.[11] Some early converts, however, soon became disillusioned.[12] The DDP also received contributions from several professional and economic interest groups. Officials' (*Beamten*) organizations backed the DDP, as did the farm association, the German Farmers' League (*Deutscher Bauernbund*—DBB), which had previously been affiliated with the NLP. The Hirsch-Duncker trade unions seem to have made their contributions directly to labor candidates of the DDP, although the amounts which were given, if we can judge from the experience of Erkelenz, must have been modest. Erkelenz had little financial help in 1919 and conducted a barebones campaign. Some supporters, such as the Mosse Press, helped the propaganda effort by turning out vast amounts of political propaganda without charge, but other newspapers were only interested in the money they could make from DDP orders and political advertising. There were great contrasts in the amount of money which candidates had available in various districts. In Berlin, for example, Dernburg and Naumann received generous support, while Elly Heuss-Knapp had nothing.[13]

Despite the relatively large amounts of money which poured in—relative to 1912 and later elections—the *Zentrale* complained that there was still not enough to do the job properly. Though hard-pressed to take care of the demands of local district organizations which lacked financial support or candidates able to attract funds, the *Zentrale* did have enough beyond its own needs to grant each district 20,000 M, but that was a small amount even by German election spending standards. Although rich local organizations were expected to contribute a percentage to the *Zentrale*, they seldom made more than token payments.

Stresemann and the DVP looked on enviously as the DDP seemed to swim in money. Many wealthy NLP members bet on the DDP to win and backed their bets with money.[14] Stresemann moaned that the DDP had "enormous financial resources" at its disposal and contended that the entire Jewish banking community stood behind it.[15] Obviously, the big businessmen, industrialists, bankers, and interest groups who backed the DDP were interested not only in seeing the DDP win and the SPD and USPD lose, but they also wanted to control the economic and social policies of the DDP. The party toned down its earlier radicalism, but it remains uncertain whether this was the result of pressure by economic and financial interest groups or the consequence of the assumption of control by veteran

Progressive and National Liberal politicians. There is some evidence that contributors could and did put pressure on the party or candidates to steer the party in certain directions. The *Kuratorium*, for example, insisted that one of its members, Eduard Arnhold, should be placed on the party's Finance Committee in exchange for a contribution. Contributions were made to individuals who were prepared to support certain interests and withheld from others who were too far to the left or too independent. It is probable that pressure from big industry and business helped force Alfred Weber's resignation and influenced the selection of candidates who would be relatively conservative on economic and social issues, although the control of the party organization by traditional liberals seemed more important. However, the DDP's direction would have been to the right even without the pressure of wealthy interest groups. The verbal flirtation with socialization was the passing fancy of a small number of relatively unimportant Democrats; most abhorred threats to private property.

Ideology

In both the founding *Aufruf* of the DDP and the principal election statement of 14 December, the party made sweeping and specious generalizations intended to win supporters and to avoid serious division within the party's electorate already committed to left liberalism.[16] From the beginning, the several left-liberal traditions and new ingredients stirred in by the revolution produced divisions which could only be bridged with innocuous slogans or by nationalist appeals. There was, nonetheless, a left-liberal ideology.[17] The slogans reflected fundamental values. The ideology may not have been as dogmatic or "scientific" as the ideologies of the left, but it served the major parties of western democracies for generations. Moreover, the ideology had evolved. By 1919, traditional German liberalism had been overtaken by Naumann's social liberalism without extinguishing the earlier political liberalism as Wilsonian internationalism was overlaid on the traditional view of the state and nation. Already in Germany a vigorous democratic spirit had arisen in the southwest and in many cities of the north, and many saw the need to take a more active role in leading and administering the state. Proclaiming itself to be a liberal, democratic, and republican party, the DDP believed that the power to govern emanated from the people and should be exercised by its elected representatives. It still espoused the traditional individual rights and civil liberties, but it made a major change in its social and economic program which proved to be highly controversial and divisive. It favored a social program to secure the poor laborer, programs for women and children, widows, orphans, and disabled soldiers, rural health programs, rights for trade unions, the eight-hour day, factory legislation, and much else—a far cry from classical liberalism. The DDP in 1919 seemed to distrust great wealth and wished to impose controls on it. It even wished to confiscate war profits and welcomed the breakup of the great landed estates which had nourished its avowed political enemy, the *Junkers*. It renewed the traditional demand that men of ability and education should have a "free road" to rise in the social order and that hereditary wealth, class, and religion should count for less than they had in the past. While much of this was traditional left-liberal fare, it was updated with current terminology and analysis and given new life and meaning by the revolution. In foreign affairs, the DDP seemed to support a break with power politics and militarism. Outwardly at least, the party embraced the idea of a league of nations and the principle of peaceful adjudication of international disputes by international organizations.

The difficulty with programmatic statements, which were intended to both establish the ideology of the party and its program as well as to attract voters, is to determine how sincere the authors of the program were and, even more difficult, to evaluate how representative the ideas were of the values of the rank and file Democrats. Probably those who wrote the statements really believed in them, for the authors mostly came from the left wing of the party, but it is highly questionable whether the rank and file member accepted all of the provisions of the statements. The economic and social program, strongly influenced by the Naumann followers, was certainly unacceptable to the many Richter followers and to most former National Liberals, while the idealistic statements on foreign affairs were probably even less representative and were soon revised by the words and actions of the DDP following the election. In addition, the party was seriously divided on several issues because of conflicting regional interests.

Centralism versus Federalism

Although the election *Aufruf* and the party's electoral propaganda carefully skirted the emotional issue of the relationship between the national government and state and local governments, the DDP found itself caught between contradictory forces. The DDP sought to identify itself with the national unification movement of the nineteenth century and the achievement of a highly centralized and uniform Reich. While Preuss and likeminded Democrats such as Max Weber prepared a constitution for a centralized Reich which would have reduced the power of Prussia and broken it into several states, other Democrats, because of regional interests, favored a strong federal system and feared a centralized regime. Moreover, there were Democrats such as Fischbeck and Friedberg who wished to retain Prussia's size and strength as it had been. The Germans in the south prized their states and distrusted "Berlin," and the DDP could not ignore these sentiments. The Hanseatic cities and the Hanoverians also had much reason to fear a powerful Prussia. The DDP's task was to find a compromise between centralism and federalism that could satisfy most of its members.

Church and State

There was much greater consensus in the DDP on church and state questions and on educational issues. These will be examined below in greater detail when the DDP's contribution to the Weimar Constitution is analyzed, but they also intruded in the campaign. Historically, the left liberals were anticlerical and wished to separate church and state. They also desired a uniform, national, and secular school system, feeling that religious instruction, if given at all, should be taught after school by laymen. Although some of the emotion had dissipated on these issues over the years, some Democrats were still passionately anticlerical. This was especially true of those living in dominantly Catholic areas or rural regions where the Lutheran Church was an important institution. Jews also strongly supported the anticlerical position. Although there was a group of deeply religious members—mostly followers of Naumann—most Democrats were agnostics who believed that religion was a personal question which should not affect politics.

The DDP's determination to separate church and state and to secularize the schools—goals which it shared with the SPD and the DVP—alarmed both Catholics and the Lutheran establishment, and they fought back vigorously. In the face of the fury of this counterattack, the DDP pulled back. It continued during the campaign to support the separation of church and state and used the phrase "A Free Church in a Free State," but it was at pains to accomplish the financial independence of the churches only when their congregations could support them. Naumann, ably seconded by Bäumer, was largely responsible for softening the DDP's stand.[18] They feared that the DDP might alienate large numbers of potential voters if it continued to pursue a dogmatic line. The DDP's retreat failed to appease the clergy, however, and they heavily attacked it during the campaign and urged the faithful to vote for either the DVP or the DNVP rather than for the *Judenpartei*.[19]

There were many regional variations on clerical issues. Although *Wahlkreis* organizations generally supported the national guidelines of the party, local circumstances produced varied emphases. In Bavaria, for example, where the German National People's party (DNVP) was not organized and the DVP merged with the DDP, anticlericalism emerged as a major theme. The Bavarian DDP attacked the Catholic Bavarian People's party (BVP) in vehement tones.[20] On the other hand, in Pomerania, where the Lutheran Church was allied with large landowners, the DNVP was the enemy. The DDP's electoral propaganda in Pomerania featured the need to break the power of the old order—conservatives, local aristocracy, and the Lutheran Church.[21]

Naumann and Social Liberalism

The greatest change in left liberalism between 1912 and 1919 was the increased influence of Naumann. The fact that Berlin, one of the centers of Richter's influence, should put Naumann at the head of its list was symbolic of the change. The influence of Carl Petersen in Hamburg, elected the city's *Bürgermeister* in 1924, was another sign of the change. Petersen, a member of the Hamburg "establishment," was, nevertheless, a fervent follower of Naumann. Although he continued to stress traditional liberal values, he also emphasized what he called "social capitalism," social security, and job security.[22] The programmatic phrase-makers and many of the propagandists in the Berlin *Zentrale*—men such as Frankfurter, Nuschke, and Bergsträsser—were also profoundly influenced by Naumann, and the labor wing of the DDP was also partially under his spell. Erkelenz joined Naumann's philosophy to the older traditions and ideas of the Hirsch-Duncker unions. There was an increased statist tone to the left-liberal goals which was undoubtedly strengthened by wartime and postwar circumstances. One can err, however, by representing the DDP as a Naumann party and by overlooking the strong core of traditional laissez-faire values which were still popular in some regions—Silesia and Württemberg come to mind—and which were still advanced by some *Mittelstand* associations and by the HB.

Interest Groups

The unclear ideology of the DDP was further muddied by the need to appeal to the material interests of a great variety of vocational and professional groups and economic interests. To win support of these groups, the DDP had to promise to seek state support for their interests. The *Aufruf* of 15 December called for state protection for workers, support for artisans, small businessmen, farmers, civil servants, the clergy, and for dependents of "fallen" or crippled German servicemen. These promises were detailed during the campaign in dozens of specialized appeals to a great variety of interests in which the DDP promised help for votes.[23] The DDP's claim to represent all of the people seems to have been supported by its promises to various interest groups. It wooed virtually every group in the nation with the exception of large landowners and heavy industry. Campaign literature and party publications held out promises to trade unions, *Angestellte*, fishermen, farmers, members of the *Mittelstände*, civil servants, teachers, and businessmen. Representatives of groups most likely to support the DDP also appeared on DDP candidates' lists and in the party organization as guardians of special interests. Veteran spokesmen for *Mittelstand* groups, which were often unpopular with the intellectuals and the Naumann followers because of their anachronistic social views and blatant materialistic concerns, gained high list positions and often wrote the electoral literature. Karl Böhme, a former National Liberal who had sat in the Reichstag for a time as a representative of an anti-Semitic party, became a DDP leader because he headed the DBB, although his political and economic outlook was at variance with most of the DDP's program.[24] Erkelenz became a major figure in the DDP initially because of the hope that large numbers of workingmen might be persuaded to support the DDP, while Karl Hermann of Reutlingen in Württemberg became a deputy in the National Assembly because he was a leader of an artisans' group. Discredited extreme annexationists also gained places because of their ability to win voters from interest groups which they had long represented, although some of them, such as Kopsch, had to await the 1920 Reichstag election to return to the German parliament.[25] The scramble for votes and money tarnished the DDP's idealism but assured its electoral success.

Candidates and Candidate Selection

Candidates were even more important in the campaign for the National Assembly than party programs or promises to interest groups. The best known figures in the DDP received several constituencies from which to choose, but candidates were chosen to represent local concerns as well as the national program of the DDP. The national organization of the DDP only rarely influenced nominations or the composition of a list, although, occasionally, the GA helped to facilitate the shift of candidates from one district to another to strengthen the DDP's effort. This was particularly true when electoral committees offered a candidate, such as Naumann or Gothein, the choice of several districts.[26] The election method established by the provisional socialist government for the election to the National Assembly, the d'Hondt system, which provided for proportional representation and party lists, also made it possible for parties to cooperate for their mutual benefit. The DDP constructed its lists to appeal to a variety of interest groups, but the local committees generally chose a figure to head the list who was regarded as the best man available in the *Wahlkreis* to represent the district's interests and to attract support to the party. In the early years of the Republic, the DDP could nearly always elect its top person on the list, but in the election to the National Assembly, it often elected two individuals and sometimes three. The party found it essential to have a person who knew the district intimately—its needs and its prejudices. Although a nationally prominent figure compatible with the district's needs occasionally was acceptable, it was seldom advantageous to have an outsider. There were often great differences in the party from district to district. An individual who may have been acceptable in Berlin, Frankfurt, or Hamburg might have been unwelcome in Silesia or Bavaria. Böhme observed that outside of Berlin, few districts admired the values and outlook of the *Berliner Tageblatt*.[27]

Securing alliances with other parties became the responsibility of the GA, but its attempt to ban list connections with anti-Semitic and reactionary parties—the DNVP in particular—as well as with the SPD were not totally successful. There was no list connection with the SPD but there was one with the DNVP. The GA also tried to support DVP figures who were ideologically compatible. Overall, however, the attempts to gain list connections in 1919 were not important in the DDP's success since it gained only three seats in this way.[28]

The lowering of the voting age and the extension of the franchise to women, plus the normal phenomenon of first-time voters, produced millions of new voters in 1919. The DDP made token accommodations to these developments by including a few women and "youths" in high enough list positions to secure election, but for the most part it favored mature men. While the national party sincerely wanted to respond to the new democratic currents, the local organizations controlled the nominating process. The only major reform effected barred double candidates—candidates who sought election both in the state legislatures or constitutional assemblies and in the National Assembly. Double candidacy was such an established practice in the liberal parties that the DDP did not entirely succeed in preventing it, but the party did manage to reduce the number of double candidates, and the practice ceased after 1919.

The most notable failure of the national organization to control the nominating process, however, was its inability to elect to the National Assembly a number of individuals who had strongly contributed to the founding of the DDP and to its electoral success. Those victimized by local control of the nominating process included Preuss, Max Weber, Gerland, Schacht, Heuss, and Rathenau; lesser figures who were unsuccessful included Bergsträsser, Heuss-Knapp, Vogelstein, Kleefeld, Martin Carbe, an important figure in the Mosse Press, and Bernhard, who had soon abandoned the DVP and Stresemann and sought a DDP mandate. Neither Wolff nor Alfred Weber apparently aspired to sit in the National Assembly. Most of the prominent "victims" were intellectuals, journalists, Berliners, and Jews, candidates without a constituency and targets of prejudice, although their friends and supporters often blamed the DDP's "bureaucracy" for their defeat.

The case of Max Weber illustrates the problem of trying to win election to the National Assembly when one lacked a constituency or a well-established political record. Weber had gained much publicity because of the series of articles he wrote in the *Frankfurter Zeitung*. The Frankfurt a/M organization of the DDP designated him as the city's choice for the top list position in the *Wahlkreis*. The GA supported this decision. The district assembly, however, had the power to construct the list, and it moved him so far down that he could not be elected to the National Assembly. Last-minute efforts were made to find him a high list position in another district, but they failed. Three men placed above Weber in Hesse-Nassau were elected: Schücking, Luppe, and Koch.[29] Koch, a former National Liberal who had sat in the upper house of the Prussian assembly, was an able and aggressive administrator who had done a superb job as mayor of Kassel during the war. Luppe was deputy mayor of Frankfurt a/M. and a recognized expert on municipal problems and the "social question." Schücking, one of Germany's best-known pacifists and a professor of international law at Marburg, had had a controversial academic and political career, but, unlike Weber, he had previously paid his partisan dues and had been a Reichstag deputy for the Progressive party. Weber and his friends apparently assumed that he would be given a high list position in the district, but he failed to work to assure it, although he made a number of speeches for the party during the campaign and wrote several important newspaper articles. He also aided the Preuss committee in its constitutional deliberations at this time. Curiously, he seemed to have little appreciation of the role of party notables in the organization. He also overlooked the district prejudices toward the *Frankfurter Zeitung*. He was regarded as its candidate. Moreover, his home was in Baden. When the hurried efforts of the GA to find him another mandate failed, Weber soon accepted the decision, but his wife and friends never recovered from the blow. They claimed that the DDP "bureaucracy" had deprived the Republic of the counsel and guidance of a great German. He seemed disappointed only because he had been unable to speak personally in favor of certain constitutional provisions which he strongly supported. There is no way, of course, to determine how effective Weber might have been in the National Assembly, but the three men who were elected all had outstanding government careers throughout the Weimar period.

That Preuss did not gain a seat was even more shocking. Preuss had been an active Progressive and was deeply involved in Berlin politics for years. He, like Weber, had written a number of articles during the war and the revolutionary period which gained much attention. An eminent constitutional authority, he had been selected by Ebert to prepare a draft constitution for the National Assembly to consider. The fact that he had never gained professorial standing in a university because he was a Jew and a democrat also had elicited much attention and compassion. Wolff and Gothein worked hard to secure him a seat, but no local party organization wanted him.[30] He had made many personal enemies in the Berlin organization and was the epitome of the radical Berlin democrat, which doomed his chances in most provincial districts. His personality and dogmatism offended many. In addition, his strong unitary views and plans to weaken Prussia were highly controversial. His Jewishness was also held against him.

Rathenau was likewise a victim of anti-Semitism, but his economic views, too, were regarded with suspicion. He was associated with wartime government regulations and controls, the support of a planned economy, and big industry. The prevailing spirit in the DDP was to dismantle the wartime controls and to free the economy from government interference, and the party was generally strongly opposed to socialism and "socialist experiments." Furthermore, Rathenau's rather exotic appearance and life-style made it difficult for many Democrats to accept him.

Schacht's failure to gain a seat was even more surprising.[31] He had not only helped in founding the DDP and in attracting many National Liberals, but he had also been an important fund raiser during the campaign. A member of the GA and a vigorous and effective campaigner, Schacht was, however, a political novice without a support base or constituency. He was also too proud to solicit support. Less well-known in 1918–1919 was the young Württemberg journalist Heuss, who was living in Berlin, remote from his home and political base. Although he had influential backers, there were too many worthy candidates with significant constituencies ahead of him.[32] Haussmann told him bluntly that there were too many lawyers and journalists who sought office in the DDP.[33] With the exception of Heuss and Gerland, later elected to the Reichstag, the unsuccessful candidates soon faded from the scene. Preuss obtained a high list position in Hesse-Naussau in the 1920 election but was denied a mandate by the DDP debacle of that year. Schacht, Rathenau, and Heuss, of course, achieved prominence later despite their political setbacks in 1919.

The delegates elected to the nominating assemblies of the various *Wahlkreise* were chosen to select candidates to represent the party's principles and the district's interests. In general, they chose candidates they knew and trusted. They preferred experienced people to amateurs and local candidates to outsiders. They usually ignored women and youth: only six of the seventy-five deputies elected by the DDP were under forty years of age, and only five were women.[34] The most attractive candidates were well-known liberal leaders of proven record who were effective speakers. The officials of middle-class professional associations were also prized because, presumably, they could influence the voting behavior of their associations. All *Bürger* parties, as a result, competed to win white-collar trade union leaders and officials of *Mittelstand* organizations, employer groups, and civil servant and farmer associations. In districts where these interest groups had a large membership, their leaders often gained a high list position, but even when their groups were relatively unimportant in a district they were given a high enough list position to tell their members that the DDP cared about their organization. Women, young people, academics, and occasionally Jews were granted the same kind of token recognition. The leaders of interest groups often disappointed the DDP, and many DDP leaders, in time, questioned the practice of rewarding them.[35] For one thing, it was difficult to prove whether they actually delivered the votes of their members. Moreover, they often turned into one-issue candidates who embarrassed many in the DDP because of their narrowness and crass material interests. Their commitment to the entire program of the DDP was usually minimal. Moreover, they were often poor speakers and clumsy colleagues.

The GA's efforts to coordinate the candidate selection process for maximum effectiveness generally failed because the local organizations were determined to control the nominating process. Several veteran DDP politicians, however, served as brokers to push some candidates, barter others, and to help with juggling lists and giving inexperienced local leaders advice. Haussmann was active in Württemberg and Bavaria in this type of work, and Richthofen operated in Schleswig-Holstein and Lower Saxony.[36] Some veterans disdained this kind of interference and concentrated on winning in their own districts, with only an occasional outside speech to aid the party's cause. Naumann, whose health had deteriorated, seemed to be above this kind of activity, while Gothein, who was frequently asked for help, seemed often preoccupied with personal problems and the task of winning a seat for himself. He did, however, continue to speak and to write for the party, and he did much during the course of the campaign to reassure conservative Progressives who had serious doubts about the DDP.

The Campaign

The campaign for the National Assembly occurred during the most trying circumstances. The army was demobilizing, while revolutionary disturbances and strikes continued to occur. The coal and food shortages produced appalling social conditions in the cities.[37] Millions were weakened by malnutrition or were victims of the flu epidemic. Meeting halls, trains, and street cars were unheated. Occasionally, candidates used automobiles to reach their speaking engagements, traveling on primitive roads in terrible weather conditions.[38] Munich had a unique atmosphere because of the revolution there. In Berlin and a few other large cities, the Spartacist uprisings produced special kinds of dangers. DDP candidates in Berlin encountered street battles on·their way to speaking engagements and were sometimes forced to take shelter in nearby buildings before their trolleys could safely proceed.[39] Extreme leftists seized the DDP party headquarters in Berlin and sacked them in several cities. In Berlin, newspapers which supported the DDP, such as the BT, were silenced for several days by the Spartacist occupation of the Mosse Press building.[40] All during the campaign, there was the possibility of renewed leftist violence or a counterrevolution from the right. However, the genteel people who carried the DDP banner had the courage to continue under these conditions and even to revel in the danger. This was true not only of the frontline veterans but also of women party workers, candidates, and older men who had little experience with violence. Most of them seemed excited by the opportunities and challenges which confronted Germany and eager to build the new democracy.[41] They not only wished to prevent a socialist majority, but they were eager to renew and refurbish German institutions and to promote economic recovery. Occasionally, they confided their fears and depression in their diaries or in letters,[42] but, publicly, they demonstrated great courage and confidence. The malaise which infected them after 1928 was not seen in 1919. The candidates often spoke to six large meetings a day and many smaller ones, and in addition to their speaking chores—and the need to write their speeches—most candidates also wrote for newspapers and produced campaign literature. Since few of them had campaign managers or a staff, they often had to do the routine chores as well. In some districts and in the large cities, the local organization made the necessary arrangements for facilities, but often the candidate had to shift for himself. On occasion, mistakes were made and candidates of two parties with two different audiences would appear in the same hall simultaneously. At other times, debates occurred between two or more parties. The meetings were well attended and the audiences seemed more involved in politics than ever before. It seemed a propitious beginning for the Republic, although many in the DDP saw the need during the campaign for the establishment of citizenship schools to educate the German people in political issues and the democratic process.

The Press

The greatest asset the DDP had in 1919, aside from the generally excellent quality of its candidates, was the support it received from the press throughout the Reich. Despite serious newsprint shortages and strikes, hundreds of newspapers were published at this time and many of them supported the DDP. The Center party and the SPD, of course, also had large numbers of newspapers behind them, while the DVP, the DNVP, and the extreme Left had less impressive backing. The Right, from the beginning, sought to tie the DDP to the BT and the FZ, and these newspapers did support the Democrats aggressively in 1919. They printed the party's major pronouncements and acted as bulletin boards for the Berlin and Frankfurt DDP organizations. They had a national distribution and helped tie the DDP together, but the provincial newspapers were still probably more important to the success of the party. They adjusted the DDP's program to local conditions and traditions, gave powerful support to local party organizations, and often helped produce pamphlets and leaflets.

The *Zentrale* and the *Wahlkreis* organizations produced most of the DDP's publications.[43] Some of the large city party organizations also edited and wrote campaign literature. The publications varied enormously. Some of them publicized the principles and the program of the DDP, while others appealed to class, vocational, and professional groups. Several sought to explain the differences between the DDP and the SPD or the DVP. Others clarified the DDP's positions on controversial issues. Many were defensive, answering the allegations of the DVP and the DNVP in particular; the DDP proved sensitive to the charge that it was betraying middle-class interests and values. The GA selected leaders to write pamphlets to appeal to certain constituencies. Pachnicke, a veteran left liberal close to *Mittelstand* groups, wrote a pamphlet which appealed to artisans, Alice Salomon wrote a pamphlet for women, and Dernburg produced one against bolshevism. Other pamphlets and leaflets appealed to farmers, fishermen, or government officials. Millions of copies of DDP publications poured from the presses and were distributed by party workers. In addition to the conventional media and methods long employed in German politics, the DDP sought to use "American methods."[44] Nuschke produced a film, and the party employed soundtrucks, although it was too early for radio. The conventional methods of communicating the party's message, however, remained the speaker and the newspaper story or the leaflet.[45]

Much of the DDP's time and effort was taken up in answering the charges of the *Bürger* opponents to its right. The DVP castigated the DDP for its opportunism and its alleged betrayal of middle-class interests.[46] The DVP and the DNVP condemned the DDP's republicanism and its association with the BT and the FZ, which were alleged to have a cosmopolitan "Jewish spirit."[47] The most persistent effort of the *Bürger* parties to the right of the DDP associated the DDP with the revolution and the SPD. Although the shattered organizations of the DVP and the DNVP, as well as their association with the war and the empire, made their propaganda relatively ineffectual in 1919, their persistent, slashing attacks, in time, did much to weaken the DDP.

Election Results

After several weeks of exposure to the conflicting claims of the parties during the campaign, the German people went to the polls on 19 January. They elected a majority of candidates who supported a parliamentary democracy and a republic. The DDP became the third largest party in the National Assembly;[48] only the SPD and the Z exceeded its seventy-five–person *Fraktion*. Even more rewarding to the DDP partisans was the fact that the USPD and the SPD had been denied a majority of the seats and were thus unable to form a socialist government. In addition, the DDP had decisively defeated its main rival, the DVP. Although the total liberal vote was not very different than its proportion of the vote in 1912, the left liberals had greatly exceeded their previous vote. The National Assembly *Fraktion*, as it turned out, contained the core of the DDP's leaders until the DStP expired in 1933. Most *Fraktion* members were backbenchers who said little and who left no trace on the history of the period. Some soon drifted away from the DDP while others resigned in anger. Many met defeat in June 1920, when the DDP's popular vote was halved and the *Fraktion* reduced from seventy-three to thirty-nine. Some proved poor choices. In general, however, the major committees, the *Fraktion*, and deputies of the state legislatures elected in 1919 provided nearly all the Democrats of any importance for the next thirteen years. Little new blood came into the leadership after the first elections, and most of the major figures of 1919 remained loyal.

IV

The Configuration of DDP Politics

The National Assembly and the Weimar Coalition

Between 20 January and 5 February 1919, negotiations to form a coalition government occurred among the SPD, the Z, and the DDP.[1] The SPD, the largest party in the National Assembly with 165 mandates, took the lead in forming a government, and when the USPD refused to cooperate, the SPD turned to the DDP, with Fischbeck representing the Democrats. Only later, when the DDP insisted, was the Center party invited to join the coalition, but it proved most reluctant to coalesce with historically rival parties. Socialist actions during November and December undermined the close cooperation which had been achieved earlier in the Inter-Party Committee and the government under Max of Baden. In the end, however, the three parties overcame their mutual repugnance and joined forces in what came to be called the Weimar Coalition. The National Assembly elected the SPD leaders Ebert as president and Scheidemann as chancellor. The SPD received seven cabinet-level posts, the DDP three, and the Center party three. Of the three DDP Ministers, two, Preuss and Schiffer, owed their positions to the services they had performed for the *Rat der Volksbeauftragten*, the interim socialist government, while Gothein was acceptable because of his wartime record on war goals. Preuss became minister of the interior, Schiffer finance minister. Gothein was a minister without portfolio, as was Erzberger, who continued to be the armistice negotiator for Germany. Erzberger and Noske, the SPD defense minister, achieved recognition as the most powerful men in the government.

Many in the DDP were shocked by these selections and by the manner in which the government was formed.[2] The Center party proved even more alarmed, reluctant either to approve this government or to share responsibility.[3] Both the DDP and the Z had concentrated during the campaign on preventing a socialist majority; neither had given much thought to how Germany should be governed after the election. The socialists had embittered the Center party because of their antireligious activities in November and December, particularly in Prussia, and the Center party remained emotionally monarchist. Nonetheless, after a considerable debate, the Z accepted the yoke of responsibility which it bore throughout the years of the Republic. When the DDP resigned from the government in June along with Scheidemann and others because of its opposition to the Treaty of Versailles, the SPD and the Z reformed the government with Gustav Bauer of the SPD as chancellor and Erzberger as finance minister and vice-chancellor. The DDP reentered the government in October 1919, and the Weimar Coalition remained in office until June 1920, with only one cabinet shakeup in March 1920 following the Kapp *Putsch*. Democrats found this coalition particularly difficult to accept because of the major part which Erzberger had in it. Most Democrats believed him an incompetent coward, if not a traitor. They saw Erzberger's realism as defeatism and his ebullience as indifference to Germany's suffering, but what was most unforgivable about Erzberger was that he was an amateur, without the necessary education or experience to conduct important negotiations with foreign states or to sit as a minister.

There were also questions about the DDP's ministers within Democratic ranks. The DDP's ministers were not "main stream" left liberals and not representative of the *Fraktion*. Preuss, a radical democrat of a type best known in Berlin, owed his position to the sponsorship of the SPD. Schiffer was a former National Liberal. Gothein was of a singular mold, the last of the "classical liberals" and regarded as a pacifist. In addition, anti-Semites noted that all three had Jewish ancestors. Preuss was an especially unpopular choice in the DDP, although it was understood that his responsibilities were largely tied to the constitution draft which his committee had prepared. Preuss was barely confirmed by the *Fraktion*.[4] He had an awkward status because the DDP had not secured him a seat in the National Assembly. Schiffer, the minister of finance, enjoyed great popularity among conservative Democrats in 1919. He had an excellent record as an administrator and had shown flexibility and toughness while serving in both the wartime Prussian government and in the interim socialist government. The left wing of the DDP, however, viewed Schiffer as a reactionary and an opportunist. He proved to be a poor team player and made some glaring mistakes.[5] When he resigned at the end of April, he was replaced by Dernburg, another conservative.

The DDP's *Fraktion* in the National Assembly, seventy-five strong, consisted for the most part of men in their forties and fifties. Only seven were younger than forty and only eight older than sixty. The group included only five women. Forty of the seventy-five had previous parliamentary experience and most of them had been active in the liberal parties before 1918, which contradicted the image of "newness" which politicians such as Erkelenz and Bäumer tried to convey about the DDP.[6] Most of them were solid and rather affluent business and professional men. A small number of intellectuals, academics, journalists, farmers, and workers balanced a few plutocrats. Nearly all members who expressed a religious preference designated themselves Protestants. Only two listed themselves as professed Jews, although at least ten had Jewish ancestors. Only one, Erkelenz, designated himself as a Catholic, although six were professed Catholics. But the most impressive feature of the *Fraktion* was the high educational level of the members. Only eighteen of the seventy-five had not attended a college or university and all but a handful of these, mostly farmer or labor representatives, had gone to specialized schools beyond the *Volksschule*.

In the prewar Reichstag, most liberal party leaders were budgetary specialists, but the Republic offered more diverse legislative opportunities. During the war, many deputies had acquired specialized knowledge in foreign and military affairs and later spoke in the Reichstag on these topics. In the *Fraktion*, men such as Johannes Heinrich von Bernstorff, the former German ambassador to the United States, and Dernburg made the major DDP speeches on foreign affairs. Haas, who had served as an army officer during the war, became the party's specialist on military questions, although several members contributed to these debates during the course of the Republic. Other *Fraktion* figures became spokesmen for certain economic or professional interest groups. A few members interested themselves in *Kultur* questions, particularly educational ones. Gothein, much to the dismay of the Naumann group, insisted on speaking on economic and fiscal questions. Several also specialized in legal and judicial questions. Erkelenz became one of the experts on social questions. He was also one of the generalists prepared to speak on a variety of topics. Naumann and Schiffer, during the National Assembly, also considered themselves generalists, but they were not always as well prepared as they should have been. In general, though, the *Fraktion* was well briefed and the speakers made able presentations. The DDP *Fraktion* felt that the level of its contribution to the debate was far higher than that of most parties,[7] but then the DDP always had a very high opinion of itself.

The *Fraktion* had a chairman, an Executive Committee, and a business manager, but only the *Fraktion* chairman was of much importance. Payer served as chairman until the vote on the Treaty of Versailles; yet most recognized Naumann as the leader of the party even before he received that honor in July at the first *Parteitag*. Payer, at seventy-two the oldest member of the *Fraktion*, was soon called *der Alte*. His support of annexationist war goals in the governments of Michaelis and von Hertling compromised him, and the Naumann group in particular deprecated his leadership qualities. He became chairman, however, because many deputies felt that he would best defend *Land* and communal interests. Nearly everyone agreed that Naumann was a disappointment as a politician and parliamentarian in the National Assembly.[8] Never having been an assiduous parliamentarian, he was often bored by committees and *Fraktion* meetings, and his illness during this period—he suffered from severe asthma—seemed to have debilitated him. But Naumann had a nobility of character, a charisma, which elevated him above other leaders of the DDP, and it was a tragedy that he died so soon after he was elected the party's first chairman. His followers were the most impressive group of newcomers in the *Fraktion*—intelligent, aggressive, and determined to achieve the goals of "social liberalism." They were better prepared, by temperament and ideology, to accept a democratic Republic, and they were more sympathetic toward the DDP's partners in the Weimar Coalition than was any other faction in the party.

In February 1919, what lay ahead for Germany was uncertain. How would party government work? How could parties so historically divided cooperate in the terrible circumstances of postwar Germany to achieve a new government and to conclude the peace? Although most of the circumstances which bedeviled the National Assembly are beyond the scope of this study, they should never be forgotten. The burden which the stresses and uncertainty of the times placed on these middle-aged politicians proved almost unbearable, and they came on top of four horrible war years in which many had been front-line soldiers and others had suffered devastating family tragedies. Was it any wonder that so many died so young and others were often ill and incapacitated?[9] Or that politicians such as Koch or Erkelenz, relatively young and energetic, should have risen to prominence so quickly? Despite all of the difficulties and uncertainty, the parties of the Weimar Coalition had the courage to face the future, to battle for their ideals and for Germany's existence. Their work was little appreciated at the time, but historians should grant them their due.

The DDP and the Treaty of Versailles

The deliberations of the Entente and associated powers in Paris on the peace treaties were never far from the thoughts of the DDP's deputies throughout the spring of 1919. They sensed, despite their later protestations of shock and surprise, that it was going to be a harsh, punishing treaty. In the last days of April, the German peace delegation, including several prominent Democrats,[10] went to Paris to receive the terms. The delegation was in a combative mood and determined to refute the treaty clause by clause. This spirit also prevailed in the DDP *Fraktion* in the National Assembly. On 7 May, when the text was delivered to the Germans, most of the terms were known in a general way, but the document confirmed the most pessimistic predictions. Brockdorff-Rantzau, a friend of Wolff and close to many in the DDP, struck the defiant note of outrage which most Democrats felt. For several days afterwards, the DDP continued to hope that if the government held fast it might be able to split the Entente and secure better terms. Later, led by Erzberger, they chased another illusion that the so-called honor clauses, articles 227–231, dealing with the questions of war guilt, reparations, and war criminals, might be eliminated.

On 12 May, when the National Assembly convened in Berlin, the DDP united with the SPD and the Center party as well as with the political Right to reject the treaty.[11] The DDP's speakers were Haussmann, Andreas Blunck, and Quidde. Haussmann had been, as we have seen, one of the first Progressives to work for a negotiated peace during the war and had been attracted to Wilsonian ideals before they gained popularity in left-liberal circles. He had placed much hope in Wilson's ability to implement his ideals in the treaty. Now he showed his profound disillusionment with Wilson in his speech, illustrating repeatedly the discrepancies between the treaty itself and Wilson's earlier statements on the basis of which Germany had agreed to the armistice and the treaty.[12] Haussmann pronounced the treaty not only intolerable and unfulfillable but unacceptable. He established the position that the DDP could never sign such a treaty. He contended that the treaty undermined democratic hopes in Germany, dooming the prospects for an enduring peace. Blunck, who represented Schleswig-Holstein in the National Assembly, attacked the application of Wilson's principles of self-determination to Schleswig and branded the plans to give German territory to Denmark as unfair.[13] He stressed the hypocrisy of the Entente powers, who denied "German Alsace" a plebiscite and refused permission to "German Austria" to join the Reich. Quidde, a leading pacifist and an old enemy of intolerant nationalism, spoke last in the debate. He testified to the unity of the National Assembly against the treaty and pleaded for continued opposition to it regardless of the consequences. "No one has more cause than we pacifists to come forward with great sharpness against these peace terms," he declared.[14] He described the treaty as the antithesis of the kind of peace which pacifists wanted. The terms destroyed the hopes for peace and for the league-of-nations idea. The implementation of self-determination was unfair and not uniform. Quidde judged the planned plebiscites a fraud, "a mere show," and a "mockery of free elections," and demanded an international, neutral, fact-finding committee to judge the question. Quidde, who had been hounded for years by rightist parties because of his convictions, brought down the house with his conclusion: "We were promised a peace which was to lead to a new world of international order and justice, and we are offered these terms! What a tragedy it would be for humankind if these terms were to become a reality! And therefore it is: No! again No!

75

and for a third time, No!" (Stormy cheers and applause.) Scheidemann, the Socialist chancellor, and Konstantin Fehrenbach, the Centrist president of the National Assembly, made similar, highly emotional speeches urging defiance.

In the cabinet meeting on 12 May, the DDP sought unsuccessfully to get the other government parties to reject the treaty out of hand,[15] arguing that the best hope for a favorable revision was to remain defiant. It assumed that the Allies could be divided by a tough and united opposition. Several Democrats speculated about the alternatives which Germany had and what the future scenario might be. Naumann thought that if the DDP held fast, the government would fall. It would be impossible to form a new government, and the British and French would then find out how difficult it was to occupy, govern, and feed Germany.[16] Germany, according to Naumann, had become a "prisoner state," and he bitterly attacked Wilson for his unchristian attitude. Erkelenz at first saw three possibilities for Germany: Germany might be occupied totally and ruled by its enemies; the League of Nations might be asked to govern Germany; or, the government might accept the treaty and then resign.[17] Erkelenz, however, soon reached the conclusion that the *Fraktion*'s position was unrealistic and that it had to remain with the SPD and the Center party. He not only had a better sense of what the mass of people were thinking, but as a veteran he also knew the full horror of a resumption of war or total occupation.

The *Hauptvorstand* debated the position of the party on 18 May and unanimously supported the *Fraktion*.[18] Nothing, Fischbeck declared, could be worse than the treaty. A single member demurred, one Heinrich Beck, a *Stadtrat* from Dresden. He argued—over the verbal protests of the members—that the treaty was not as final as Fischbeck and the others had described it. He felt that it was still possible to negotiate the removal of the most objectionable provisions. He angered many when he compared the DDP's tone of opposition to the rigidity of the German Nationalists (DNVP), but in reality, they were behaving similarly. The DDP's leaders were determined to demonstrate the party's patriotism, which Naumann later admitted and defended.[19] Although the DDP refused to demonstrate in the streets against the treaty with its *Bürger* rivals, it wanted to proclaim that no party loved Germany more than the DDP. Behind the scenes, some party leaders also began to hold talks with DVP figures in the eventuality that the government would fall and an alternative coalition of *Bürger* parties would be formed.

Several *Fraktion* members broke away from the majority at this time and favored signing the treaty. On 12 May, apparently only Pachnicke, a veteran Progressive of no clear orientation, favored signing, but soon several deputies joined him, led by Payer and Richthofen. Payer counted fifteen who opposed the DDP majority position, even though only seven voted against the majority in the formal vote. The rest opposed the treaty.[20] There was no commonality among the dissidents. Three came from the southwest, which feared not only the effects of occupation but a French-inspired separatist movement. Württemberg, at least, remembered the Napoleonic occupation, and Payer's position had much support. Two of the dissenters were from Saxony, one from Thuringia, and Richthofen represented a district in what is now Lower Saxony. They included the oldest member of the *Fraktion* and some of the youngest, and there was no particular ideological kinship. In general, they concluded that acceptance would be less harmful to Germany than rejection. They also wished to preserve a common front with the other parties of the Weimar Coalition for future considerations. The Naumann group, which often was quoted about the need to bridge the classes and to forge a working relationship with the SPD, proved to be more "national" than "social" when the chips were down. The women in the *Fraktion*, most of them Naumannites, united in opposition to the treaty.[21]

The DDP press split on the treaty.[22] Although the great majority of DDP newspapers supported the *Fraktion* majority's position of defiance, there were some notable defectors. Both the VZ, which had swung over belatedly to the DDP after initially favoring the DVP, and the FZ favored signing the treaty. The BT, however, strongly opposed it on 7 May and never wavered in its opposition. It often printed articles by DDP leaders, such as Haas, who vehemently denounced the treaty. The FZ groped its way to its final position, working through several intermediate stages before finally concluding, on 16 June, that Germany had to sign the treaty.

Between 12 May and 23 June, there were dozens of *Fraktion* and cabinet meetings which debated the alternatives before the government. Erzberger became the driving force behind the idea of a conditional acceptance, arguing that the treaty was acceptable if articles 227–231 were dropped. He became convinced that the Allies would exclude them and persuaded the Center party to accept this idea. Public opinion in the electorate of the SPD and the Z raced ahead of parliamentary parties and pulled them along. The DDP refused, however, to change its position and seemed to have been supported by its voters. Initially, three or four members of the cabinet supported Erzberger and ten were opposed, including the chancellor, Scheidemann.[23] On 16 June, the Allies delivered an ultimatum: either sign within seven days or face invasion. By this time, the German peace delegation had returned to Weimar, determined to discredit Erzberger's position and to back up the opponents of the treaty. Nonetheless, when the cabinet again voted whether to accept or reject the treaty, the tally was evenly divided, seven for and seven against. In the face of the DDP's stubborn opposition, it seemed apparent to Erzberger that the government would have to be reformed, and he began to lead the negotiations. He had no desire to be chancellor himself, but he felt that someone had to take the initiative. He attempted to persuade several Democrats to serve in a reformed government, asking Dernburg to remain as finance minister and trying to persuade Bernstorff to enter the government. The DDP forestalled these moves, however, by announcing that no Democrat who wished to remain in the party could serve in a cabinet in which the party was not officially represented. On 20 June, in an apparent effort to show that it was not completely negative and inflexible, the DDP presented its own plan for conditional acceptance. The conditions were four in number: first, Danzig, West Prussia, and that area's railway grid should be placed under the administration of the League of Nations; second, the Treaty of Versailles was to be revised within two years; third, the total indemnity bill should be determined by neutral experts; fourth, Germany should be admitted to the League of Nations on 1 February 1920. It remains unclear what the DDP hoped to accomplish by this proposal, which the cabinet promptly rejected. Wolff later described it as "frightfully dilettantish," and it certainly ignored some basic realities. The same day that the DDP presented its plan, Scheidemann resigned as chancellor and the DDP abandoned the government, forcing its ministers to relinquish their posts. A new cabinet, headed by Socialist Gustav Bauer, was formed, consisting of only SPD and Z representatives. Erzberger, the DDP's *bête noire*, was the most powerful man in the government as finance minister and vice-chancellor.

On 22 June, the government received the formal permission from the National Assembly to sign the treaty conditionally—less articles 227–231. The Center party insisted on this step.[24] The Allies, however, brushed aside this request and demanded unconditional acceptance within twenty-four hours. Several hours later, the National Assembly voted to accept the treaty unconditionally by a majority of 237 to 138, with five abstentions. The DDP voted against it, an action explained in a formal statement.[25] It was convinced that Germany could have secured a better peace had the government parties remained united in their opposition to the treaty. As had been agreed with the SPD and the Z, the DDP issued a statement saying that it knew that the SPD and the Z also realized that the treaty was "unbearable and unfulfillable" and that they voted for the treaty only because they feared that the consequences of rejection would be more harmful than those of acceptance. The DDP also took the occasion to defend the work of the Weimar Coalition and to indicate that it would continue to cooperate with the government. An article in the party's official journal, *Das demokratische Deutschland*, emphasized the desire and need to remain close to the SPD, which it characterized, for those who still may have been confused, as a democratic party with no ties to Lenin or Trotsky![26]

Because Payer had broken with the *Fraktion* majority and voted for acceptance of the treaty, he resigned as *Fraktion* chairman. Schiffer replaced him, making the major speech for the party in the treaty debate of 22 June.[27] Many Democrats opposed his selection because he was a former National Liberal and had broken with the SPD on fiscal policy and were bitterly unhappy with his speech. Some thought that the pacifist, Schücking, would have been a better selection, although this would have been inappropriate given the belligerent mood of the *Fraktion* majority. Schiffer's speech was poorly organized, far too long, and characterized by the emotional "hurrah patriotism" which the DDP condemned in others. The DDP, he said, preferred to look annihilation in the face and to go down with honor, a statement which produced strong approbation in the DDP and derisive catcalls in the SPD. The most controversial portion of his speech, for the DDP, included some gratuitous remarks about the Weimar Coalition and the future course of coalition government. He implied that the DDP might join with rightist parties in the future because of its profound differences with the SPD on economic and fiscal policy.

Schiffer's remarks reflected the growing disenchantment with the obligations of coalition membership and, in particular, the tax and socialization legislation which the SPD and the left wing of the Center party forced on the DDP. Indeed, the divergence between the DDP and its partners on economic, fiscal, and social legislation was so great that the DDP might have been forced to leave the government even if the Treaty of Versailles had not been an issue.[28] Despite these growing differences with the coalition partners, it was unwise and maladroit for Schiffer to include references to them in a debate on the treaty, and left-wing Democrats who still hoped there might be a way to remain in the government immediately attacked him. The *Fraktion* majority, however, was relieved to be out of the government. It despised Erzberger and blamed him for the retreat which had forced unconditional acceptance of the treaty. Naumann allegedly told Erzberger on the afternoon of 23 June: "Today we still need you, but in a few months, when the overall situation will have changed, we will get rid of you."[29] Soon, Naumann and others in the DDP were calling the Versailles treaty the "Erzberger peace."

The debate and the vote on the Treaty of Versailles were the outstanding events of the National Assembly for the DDP. Their importance even overshadowed the writing and acceptance of the constitution. Only a few deputies—most notably Koch-Weser and Luppe—ever regretted the party's decision to leave the government and to desert its political allies. Most contended they would have preferred occupation to "slavery." In later years, the DDP always saw the Treaty of Versailles in its most extreme and theoretical form, and it could never accept the losses: Posen was Polish, Alsace-Lorraine French, a part of Schleswig Danish, Danzig and the Saar controlled by the "French puppet," the League of Nations, the colonies "stolen," the army and navy reduced to pathetic reminders of Germany's former power. Little wonder that treaty revision proved to be the

DDP's dominant foreign policy theme. The DDP's vote on the treaty resulted in serious short-term and long-term consequences. It broke up the Weimar Coalition at a critical moment. In the long run, it helped to weaken cooperation and sow distrust among the parties dedicated to maintaining the Republic. It guaranteed the primacy of foreign policy in the DDP and strengthened its statist and nationalist values.

But also it produced disputes and splits within the DDP as well. When the DDP left the government, it compelled its cabinet officers to resign. Preuss was especially upset, in part because he sympathized with the SPD's views on the treaty, but also because he wanted to supervise the writing of the constitution.[30] The breakup of the Weimar Coalition disturbed the left wing, but many more Democrats were relieved that the alliance with the SPD had ended and the party could now oppose the tax and socialization measures being prepared. When the first Party Congress convened in July 1919, these internal differences were still evident, and they produced a passionately angry debate between Naumann and Richthofen.[31] A recent study of the DDP's foreign policy concludes that the vote on the treaty caused the DDP to abandon reason, responsibility, and pragmatism.[32] The vote certainly foreshadowed the DDP's tendency to move to the right toward the non-Catholic middle-class parties in moments of crisis, and also showed the DDP's penchant to make nationalist flourishes when the real issues might be taxes or economic and social policy. In the DDP, nationalism became a smokescreen to hide the divisive interests and conflicting ideals within the party.

The DDP and the Weimar Constitution

The general consensus among historians is that the DDP bore the greatest responsibility for the Weimar Constitution and that, among Weimar political parties, its political values were most in accord with it.[33] Indeed, most studies feel that its contribution to the constitution was its most outstanding accomplishment. This was also the perception of most active Democrats. When the work on the draft constitution began in mid-November 1918, the Preuss committee included several Democrats who kept the party leaders well informed about its deliberations. The constitution committee, chaired by Haussmann, was formed soon after the election. It met sporadically for several months, but the constitution did not move from the committee chambers to the floor of the National Assembly for debate until after the decision on the Treaty of Versailles. The constitution was approved in early August, signed by President Ebert on 11 August, and went into effect shortly thereafter. During the long period while the writing of the constitution occurred, the general public, as well as several parties, remained uninterested. But not the DDP! Most active Democrats watched with great interest the progress of the document through the legislative pipeline. While some parties were particularly interested in certain sections of it, only the DDP, and to a lesser extent the DVP, proved interested in the entire constitution. It was the DDP which gave it its name, the "Weimar Constitution," and Preuss is often called the "father of the constitution," although some Democrats felt that Haussmann deserved the title. Haussmann's years of legislative experience enabled him to guide its passage skillfully, while several other individual Democrats made important contributions to it. DDP stylists polished most of its sections, and DDP committee members achieved several vital compromises included in the final draft. Naumann is generally credited for the statement on basic rights, while Max Weber greatly influenced the section on the office of the president. Koch and Ablass resolved several sticky problems which slowed the constitution's passage. Koch wrote the section on the initiative and the referendum and was also responsible for the compromise words of article 1: "The German Reich is a republic." Apparently, Koch also coined the term *"Land"* for the federal states. Ablass made several editorial suggestions, including the compromise wording of the basic school formula. Koch made his reputation in the DDP in the Constitution Committee, and Ablass capped off a long political career with his work there. Preuss's contribution, on the other hand, was so controversial—and so misrepresented—that it helped destroy his hopes for a political career.

Though, historically, German left liberals had looked to Great Britain for their constitutional model, when circumstances determined that Germany should be a federal republic rather than a centralized constitutional monarchy, constitution makers principally studied the constitutions and traditions of France and the United States while borrowing democratic constitutional devices and practices from a number of sources. The Weimar Republic was conceived as a parliamentary democracy with a strong president. It was wrong to label the Republic as a foreign import, as the right-wing parties did, for it owed much of its inspiration to German history and theorists. On the other hand, the Republic conformed to the general spirit of the liberal democracies of the West, and it accomplished what the DDP wanted: a representative and responsible government.

The most devisive issue within the DDP was the conflict between the unitarists and the federalists. The constitution necessarily touched the most fundamental relations between the Reich, the *Länder*, and communities. Preuss and his committee were determined to give the constitution a decided unitary, if not centralist, character, but even they wished to preserve German traditions and practices at the local and communal level, which came under the rubric self-government or autonomy (*Selbstverwaltung*).[34] The DDP unitarists, however, wished to reduce the power of the *Länder* and to destroy the spirit of particularism. Naumann, most of his followers, and Koch were strong backers of the unitary state.

The problem of Prussia constituted another major issue. Preuss and his draft recommended cutting up Prussia into three or four medium-sized *Länder*. The SPD and some of the DVP also favored a unitary state and a reduction in the power of Prussia, but the Center party strongly defended federalism. It soon alerted the states and municipalities against the Preuss draft constitution and led the fight for "states' rights" in the National Assembly. On 25 November, a conference of most of the states met in Berlin to assert the rights of the states and their determination to hold on to their traditional governmental powers. During January and February, the DDP held a series of meetings to discuss this question.[35] The plan to break up Prussia aroused strong feelings that caused people to retaliate against Preuss in a personal way. Southwestern federalists such as Payer and Haussmann and the Bavarian contingent joined forces with the "preserve Prussia" group, the Hanseatic cities, and representatives of the smaller states to attack the Preuss draft. Even Hanoverian particularism revived. Although Preuss, Naumann, Koch, and Luppe denied that they were centralists who wished to impose a French system on Germany, many Democrats feared this break with tradition at a time when Germany was threatened from without and by French-inspired separatist movements. Many feared that any strongly divisive reorganization would stimulate the French and Poles to interfere in German affairs. There were also strong emotional ties to some of the states and their dynasties. The Prussian Progressives fought changes which might have disturbed their power base in the Prussian cities. Preuss found himself on the defensive against other parties and was caught in a vicious crossfire in the DDP.[36] Never one to turn his cheek, Preuss fought back. In Berlin, there was an effort to read Preuss out of the DDP, and several Prussian local organizations passed resolutions to deny him a seat in the National Assembly. They were angered to learn that he had obtained a seat in the Prussian Constitutional Assembly before the full implications of the constitution were known. His enemies now constructed a stereotype. They saw him as doctrinaire, dogmatic, pedantic, sarcastic, and arrogant, a characterization which recent scholars find false and malicious.[37] He remained an outsider in the DDP until his death in 1925. At that time, he received many fulsome accolades, some of which were insincere.

The final provisions of the constitution on *Reich-Länder-Kommunal* powers and relations were the result of difficult and unsatisfactory compromises. Germany moved a step closer to a unitary state, but the powers of the central government fell far short of what the SPD and many in the DDP wanted. The federalists, on the other hand, felt that the *Länder* had lost too much. In subsequent years, the DDP continued to prepare constitutional reforms, most of which aimed to reduce the power of the *Länder* and end the costly duplication of functions and the plethora of representative bodies in Germany. Many Rhinelanders, including Konrad Adenauer, had hoped for the formation of a new *Land* in the Rhineland, but that was rejected, as were most of the efforts to reduce Prussia's size and power. But at least, as Erkelenz reminded his constituents, Prussia was now democratic and looked to the West.[38] The rallying cry of the DDP constitutional reformers by the mid-twenties, led by Koch-Weser, was the "decentralized unitary state." It became a major campaign theme in 1927–1928. It involved the consolidation of the smaller *Länder* and the reduction of duplicate government functions.[39] The DDP was almost alone, however, in its desire for constitutional reform. After the mid-twenties, the DDP also sought to reform the electoral law of 1920 to which Koch-Weser had made a great contribution. It wished to reform proportional representation to reduce the size of the districts and the number of mandates in each district. These reforms had little support from the other parties and little appeal; the general public seemed indifferent to them. The financial crisis after 1929 showed that the DDP's reforms were probably sound ideas to improve government efficiency and to reduce government costs, but without mass support there was no way to effect the reforms.

The DDP largely shaped the nature of the office of the president in the constitution, including the array of emergency powers—notably article 48—granted the chief executive. The DDP wanted to make the president a powerful figure in the German government, and it realized this intention. Only a few Democrats such as Wolff, Erkelenz, and Bernhard seemed to fear the office. Wolff preferred the French system where the parliament elected a president with few responsibilities or powers. He always feared a monarchical revival and did not trust the German people to make responsible choices in electing a "strong man." Many intellectuals in the party had criticized the process by which leaders were chosen in the empire, and the war seemed to demonstrate that the leadership in the parliamentary democracies surpassed the German semi-authoritarian system. Some of the intellectuals apparently wanted the president to be an *Ersatz* kaiser or even a führer,[40] but most Democrats wanted an American-style president, a democratically elected leader with considerable powers. Although the model did not yet exist, most of them seemed to have in mind a figure comparable to the president of the French Fifth Republic. In a democratic age, there did not seem an alternative to a popular election, and in the end, they created a presidental office neither American nor French. The emergency powers granted the president, which in retrospect are so significant, were seen by the SPD as well as the DDP as a protection for popular rule, not as a means to subvert it. The president was not intended to dominate the government nor to become a quasi-dictator; his office was supposed to complement the work of the Reichstag and the cabinet. Because of the DDP's central part in creating the president's office and because of some isolated remarks of intellectuals close to the DDP, the party has been accused of having an affinity with fascism, of longing for a führer.[41] This is absurd. What the DDP wanted was a strong but democratic leader able to overcome the divisions and weaknesses of the Reichstag and still responsible to the people. This desire existed after July 1930 as well, when the DStP succeeded the DDP and the crisis of German democracy deepened.

The DDP backed the SPD's desire for various devices to make the government more accountable to the people and to widen the franchise. It supported the initiative and referendum, proportional representation, and votes for women and young people, although not unanimously and not without reservations. There was a general sense that the pace of change was outstripping the German people's preparedness to exercise the great powers granted to them. Preuss, for example, had doubts about the wisdom of the initiative and referendum, while Naumann strongly attacked proportional representation. Old *Freisinnige* such as Müller-Meiningen opposed votes for women and for young people. The *Fraktion* and the party activists, however, approved these democratic reforms overwhelmingly. The first Party Congress, in July 1919, upheld the *Fraktion*'s judgment and no significant opposition developed. One delegate opposed the five-year term for the Reichstag in favor of a three-year term, but this was the only specific opposition registered by a PT delegate. Most of the complaints at that time and at the December PT in 1919 were against taxes and economic and social measures approved by the *Fraktion*.

Educational issues were also controversial in 1919. Debated at length in DDP party meetings, education seemed to have affected the rank and file members more personally than other constitutional questions. As we have seen, left liberals had a long-established educational philosophy and a program based on liberal fundamentals. The DDP continued the tradition. It preferred a uniform, national, and secular school system, and the crux of the educational debate was over religious instruction in the schools and religious influence on the intellectual and moral development of German youth. Although most DDP members stood ready to approve moderate compromises with the wishes of the Z and conservative Lutherans, a fervent minority of fanatical anticlericals and Catholic-haters hindered the leadership. In general, the DDP's position resembled the SPD's but clashed on fundamental grounds with the Center party. The Centrists wished to make the parochial school the rule and insisted that clerics give religious instruction during regular school hours. They also wanted state support for parochial schools. Most Democrats believed that religion was a private concern and opposed state support for parochial schools and religious instruction in public schools. The DDP extremists still demanded the *Einheitsschule*, a uniform, secular, national school system.[42] Most Democrats, however, by 1919 favored a school model called the *Simultanschule*—later usually called the *Gemeinschaftsschule*—the prewar system in Baden. The DDP and the SPD found it acceptable, but the Center party deplored it. In the *Simultanschule*, instruction was given in the Lutheran,

Catholic, and Jewish faiths, and it was provided that any student, with parental permission, could skip religion classes. Religious instruction was voluntary, then, and after regular school hours. The system, though sufficiently flexible to take into account local needs and parental wishes, was still awkward for Jews, small Protestant sects, and "free thinkers."

There were two school compromises during the course of the debate and passage of the Weimar Constitution. The SPD and the Z concluded the first school compromise following the DDP's resignation from the government in June. The DDP assumed from the earlier deliberations that the *Simultanschule* would become the regular (*Regel*) primary school and expressed shock when it learned that the SPD had yielded to Centrist pressure and adopted the parochial school (*Bekenntnisschule*) as the norm. The DDP was furious with the SPD, which felt that it had to make concessions to the Center party on this, and used whatever power it had to reverse the decision. This became possible when both the Center party and the SPD urged the DDP to return to the government. Three Democrats, led by Luppe, negotiated a second school compromise at the last minute.[43] According to this agreement, the *Simultanschule* became the norm and the parochial school the exception. The law still permitted three kinds of elementary schools: the *Simultanschule*, the parochial school, and a completely secular school with no permitted religious instruction. The second school compromise angered and embittered the Center party, and the church hierarchy soon began a movement to overturn it by attempting to secure passage of a national school law.[44] By the mid-twenties, this campaign gained ground as the Center party slipped to the right, and it was combined with a Centrist fight to secure concordats between the Vatican and the national and *Länder* governments. The DDP seemed unable to understand the concern of the Catholic church, which regarded the *Simultanschule* as a surrender to worldliness and secularism. This was also the attitude of conservative Lutherans, who were to be found in the right wing of the DVP and in the DNVP.

The final constitutional issue that was important to the DDP was "the flag question." The debate over whether to support the new flag proposed by the Constitution Committee or the old flag of the empire and the Hohenzollerns divided the DDP. Though not important in the history of the party, it was symbolic of the DDP's sensitivity to the "national questions." On such issues, the DDP generally felt compelled to vote with the other Protestant middle-class parties for fear of being derided as unpatriotic and too closely tied to the SPD. Like the school question, the flag issue reappeared in the mid-twenties to divide the party. In 1919, most Democrats had originally assumed that the flag of the empire would continue to be the flag even though the Reich had become a Republic. Preuss, who favored the retention of the term *Reich*, also favored the old flag—the black, red, and white colors—as a symbol of continuity. There were other

Democrats, however, who wanted a sharp break with the past and, more-over, wanted to link the new German democracy with the revolutions of 1848, which had adopted the black-red-gold standard of the youth organizations. Most Democrats in the southwest favored the change.[45] The Naumann group also favored the standard of 1848 at first because it was a symbol of *Grossdeutsch* aspirations, the movement to unite all the lands which had belonged to the German Confederation, the course rejected by Bismarck. The new Austrian Republic adopted the black-red-gold colors to facilitate *Anschluss*, and apparently the Austrian ambassador persuaded Preuss to change his mind on the flag.[46] The SPD readily accepted the new colors while the Center party, much more reluctantly, also adopted the black-red-gold. When the first vote on the flag was taken in the Constitution Committee, the DDP contingent voted four to one for the black-red-gold. Only Koch, a strong Prussian, a reserve officer, and a former National Liberal, voted for the black-red-white colors. At this time probably a large majority of the *Fraktion* would have approved a new flag. The forced signing of the Treaty of Versailles, however, made the old flag a symbol of nationalist defiance. On 3 July, the DDP *Fraktion* rejected the new colors, forty-three to fourteen, although in the plenary session the margin was reduced to thirty-six to nineteen with many abstentions. Most of those who strongly opposed the new flag were north Germans, former National Liberals or Naumannites, whose nationalist rage against the treaty produced a change of heart. The Württembergers and the left wing of the DDP, which wanted a clean break with the past, approved of the change. The leadership divided: Naumann, Petersen, Koch, Gothein, Fischbeck, Schiffer, and Dernburg opposed the new flag, while Hauss-mann, Payer, Erkelenz, Nuschke, and Quidde favored it. All of the prominent followers of Naumann, save Erkelenz, voted against the change.[47] Ablass suggested the compromise in the Constitution Committee; the black-red-gold flag became the official emblem of the Republic, but the merchant ships would continue to fly the old colors. For the DDP, this was agreeable because it appeased the maritime interests in the Hanseatic cities, which strongly supported the DDP. Foreign observers, however, felt that the compromise reflected the German determination to stay linked with the past and the monarchy. This was an accurate assessment of many in the DDP's right ring who remained emotionally identified with the past. Nevertheless, the DNVP soon attacked the new flag as the symbol of Catholic clericalism (black), Marxist internationalism (red), and Jewish cosmopolitanism (gold). Although the *Reichsbanner-Schwarz-Rot-Gold* was established in 1924 to honor the Republic's flag and to protect its institutions, Preuss, before his death in 1925, noted with sadness that the German people had still not warmed to the Republic or its symbols. In the DDP, the *Reichsbanner* never elicited much support; it was too closely tied to the SPD for DDP tastes.[48]

V

Left, Right, and Center in the DDP

Economic and Social Issues and the Role of Interest Groups

Left liberalism, as we have seen, lacked a firm ideological foundation, and DDP members sometimes changed their orientation during the course of the years of the Republic, but there were, nonetheless, fairly well-defined groups within the party which had clear preferences in economic and social policy and which attempted to shape the DDP's policies to advance their own and their constituents' interests. There was a left wing, the Social Liberal or Social Republican group, a right wing, generally called the business wing in the secondary literature, and a group of centrists which drifted right after 1924.

The Left Wing

From 1919 to 1924, the relatively strong left wing of the DDP consisted of individuals and groups who were stout supporters of the Republic and who hoped this newly achieved democracy would result in a new economic and social order as well. The changes they had in mind were not radical but sufficient to distinguish their advocates from those who essentially wished to preserve the pre-1914 economic and social system. In general, the left wing saw the Weimar Coalition as the best means to advance progress along a wide front, and it rejected various suggestions for alliances of middle-class parties (*Bürgerblocks*) which excluded the SPD. Although they often became angry and impatient with the SPD and the left wing of the Center party, they felt that the preservation of democracy in Germany depended on continued close cooperation with them.

Unlike the DDP's right wing, they were prepared to make substantive concessions to the working class.

There were several subgroups within the left wing: the followers of Naumann; the labor group (Hirsch-Duncker unions,[1] the *Gewerkschaftsbund der Angestellten* [GDA],[2] and the *Gewerkschaftsring*);[3] the Young Democrats;[4] the Women's Committee;[5] the publishers, editors, and journalists of the large urban newspapers which supported the DDP;[6] teachers and certain *Land* and municipal officials; university professors and intellectuals.

The Naumann Group

Naumann had far more followers during the Weimar period than he had in the Progressive party, but their commitment to his philosophy and vision varied considerably. The Naumann group provided the ideological leadership of the DDP, as we have seen, and many of the party's leaders were self-conscious Naumannites. They included Naumann's successor as the party leader, Petersen; Erkelenz, the leader of the left wing of the party and chairman of the *Vorstand* from 1921 until 1929; Bäumer, the most prominent woman in the party and one of the vice-chairmen. The second rank of leaders included such prominent Naumann followers as Heuss, Wilhelm Heile, Dora and Martin Rade, Goetz, and Gustav Stolper. Koch-Weser, who succeeded Petersen as the party leader in 1924 and who remained the most important leader of the party until 1930, is often identified as a Naumann follower, but Koch-Weser's debt to Naumann was minimal, and he deprecated Naumann's leadership qualities.

Before Naumann's death, his words and writings were the indispensable source of the meaning of his political and social philosophy, but, after his death, *Die Hilfe*, the small highbrow journal which he founded and edited, became the best source for the amorphous Naumann tradition. His close followers continued to edit the journal and to supply many of the articles for it. Heile, Heuss, Bäumer, Erkelenz, and Goetz served as editors or leading contributors throughout the Weimar period, with Bäumer and Erkelenz sharing the greatest responsibility for it and serving as co-editors for several years. Dozens of Social Liberals or Social Republicans wrote for it and shaped its peculiar character.

Bäumer, one of Naumann's most prominent admirers, devoted much of her life to perpetuating Naumann's memory. She was a brilliant and highly energetic person, one of the first women to graduate from a German university.[7] After achieving an outstanding academic record, she turned to teaching, social work, and feminist politics. She became the leader of the major feminist organization in Germany before the war, the Federation of German Women's Associations (the *Bund der Frauenvereine*). She had played a token role in the Progressive party, as we have seen, but earned

88

an important leadership position in the DDP, where she led a major constituency that promised to have great importance in the DDP, which
boasted that it was the "women's party." This claim was attributable to the
prominence in it of several leading bourgeois feminists. Bäumer served in
the National Assembly and the Reichstag from 1919 to 1932, specializing
in *Kultur* questions—education and church-state matters. In addition, she
secured an important official post in the Ministry of the Interior. This was
largely the result of the pressure of the DDP and, in particular, of Koch-
Weser's assistance while he was minister of the interior. She wrote and
spoke on many topics, producing a veritable torrent of words. Despite this
impressive record, however, Bäumer lacked warmth and a common touch
and practical political gifts. Bäumer adored Naumann and worked to keep
his ideas alive, but she was completely uncritical in her evaluation of his
importance. Usually numbered in the left wing of the DDP in the early
years of the Republic because of her economic and social views, she
turned to the right after the mid-twenties. Like Naumann's, her nationalism was passionate and romantic. She became the greatest enthusiast for
the DStP in 1930 and later apologized for Nazi aggression. Indeed,
Bäumer embodied the darkest currents in the DDP—extreme nationalism,
statism, romanticism, racism. Regardless, she was always listed among
the top half-dozen leaders of the party. She had numerous party responsibilities, serving on many committees and attending frequent party meetings.

Bäumer's family included many Lutheran pastors and theologians,
while Erkelenz, by contrast, stemmed from skilled Catholic workingmen
and advanced into politics through the Hirsch-Duncker trade union movement, the liberal unions which preached self-help and antistatism.[8] Naumann's social liberalism attracted him because it shared with his union the
desire to diminish class tensions and to achieve social harmony. He became a union officer before the war and a follower of Barth, but when
Barth broke away from the Progressive party, Erkelenz remained and became the party's token labor figure, just as Bäumer was its token feminist.
Naumann, recognizing Erkelenz's potential, introduced him to the proper
books and journals and helped him improve his writing. Erkelenz also
became friends with the philosopher Leonard Nelson and the rural re-
former Adolf Damaschke. When the war came, Erkelenz served although
he was thirty-six and married. He suffered a bad wound on the western
front but spent two more years in the army in the east before his separation
from the service. He never advanced beyond lance corporal, probably because he besieged the army with requests to be permitted to return home
because of the hardship his absence created for his family. He worked in
a manufacturing plant in the last year of the war. When the revolution
occurred, he served in a Workers' and Soldiers' Council and in the Neuss

Bürgerrat, which advised the mayor during this tense period. He also worked to revive the Progressive party in the Düsseldorf area but immediately joined the Democratic party when he learned of its formation. Like Bäumer, he wanted a *new* party which would make a clean break with the prewar liberal parties. He obtained a high list position because of his labor ties and campaigned as a self-conscious workers' representative, but he soon broadened his outlook and sought to represent a more diversified constituency—the DDP's left wing. In the National Assembly, he became an aggressive and effective *Fraktion* member, although his leftist views and blunt manners antagonized many in the DDP's right wing. By 1920, he was the acknowledged leader of the left wing. Erkelenz became one of the *Fraktion*'s generalists who volunteered to speak on a variety of subjects, although many in the right wing questioned his ability to speak for the *Fraktion* on foreign policy or economic questions. Like Bäumer, he worked extremely hard, but, unlike her, he lacked the education and the sponsorship to secure a high civil-service position. He earned his living as a journalist and, at first, as a union official. He wrote for a number of union newspapers, *Die Hilfe*, the DDP press, and edited a union publication. In 1921, at the DDP's Bremen Party Congress,[9] Erkelenz won a significant victory and became the chairman of the *Vorstand*, second in importance to Petersen in the party leadership. The election of Fischer, a leader of the business wing, as his deputy, diminished the triumph of the left wing and added greatly to Erkelenz's difficulties. Fischer and Erkelenz fought each other until Erkelenz's retirement in 1929.

Although Erkelenz initially saw himself as a Naumannite, he came under other intellectual influences. Rathenau and Bernhard were soon more important to him that Naumann. The "councils ideas," which stemmed from the factory councils movement and Arthur Feiler, an FZ editor, also influenced his economic and social thinking. Later, by the mid-twenties, he turned away from the idea of a planned economy and the welfare state back to Hirsch-Duncker traditions of self-help and union self-administration of welfare programs and social security. After 1927, when he made a trip to the United States, he became increasingly concerned with profit-sharing ideas and with the role of technology in modern life. His ideas were imprecise, but apparently he was most concerned to moderate the class struggle and to give the worker a greater share in decision making in the productive process. He remained a trade unionist with a compassion for the underdog and the unlucky, uncommon sentiments in the DDP. Like all of the Naumann group, he emphasized the role of the DDP as the bridge between the working classes and the middle classes, and the failure of the DDP to achieve this was perhaps his most crushing disappointment. His efforts to improve the DDP organization also failed. In his last years in the DDP, he became locked in an unpleasant and bitter rivalry with Koch-Weser, Werner Stephan, and Fischer. His professional relationship with Bäumer in editing *Die Hilfe* also became disagreeable. His disappointments and frustrations combined after 1928 to produce the physical and mental breakdown which forced his retirement in 1929.

When Naumann died in 1919 he was succeeded as party leader by Petersen.[10] Petersen won a narrow victory as a compromise candidate determined to continue the Naumann tradition in the DDP. An early Naumann convert and enthusiastic follower, he was a member of the Hamburg business and social "establishment" where his family had long been prominent. His family saw his support of Naumann and left liberalism as a radical aberration which he should outgrow in time. Petersen, in fact, soon turned to the right and became an early advocate of a DDP-DVP fusion and of *Bürgerblocks*, but he was so affable and so fine a figurehead that he made few enemies in the party, and in Hamburg, he was not only a popular but an effective leader. He became mayor in 1924, which precipitated his resignation as the DDP's chairman, and he remained Hamburg's and the Hamburg DDP's leader until 1933. At the national level, however, he was a failure. He helped squander the DDP's early advantage and allowed the organization to fall apart.[11] He became best known as a popular orator, speaking at great length in sweeping generalizations but seldom saying anything memorable. Although too good-natured and too fuzzy in his thinking to be an effective leader, he continued to pronounce his support for the ideals of social liberalism and for the democratic Republic in such ringing language that he remained popular until his death in 1934.

Heile, another prominent Naumannite, descended from a long line of farmers in Lower Saxony; his family had farmed the same area for over four hundred years. He broke with tradition, attending a university where he was educated as a marine engineer but then discovered student politics and Naumann. He seemed destined to become a professional youth leader before the war. He served on the western front and was badly wounded several times. Finally, he was invalided home and went to work for Naumann on *Die Hilfe*. He became Naumann's editorial assistant and man Friday. When Naumann died, Heile seemed to lose whatever intellectual anchor he had ever had. He won election to the National Assembly but soon alienated his Hanoverian constituency by his unitary views and his confused effort to square them with Hanoverian particularism. He soon drifted away from both the DDP—after failing to be renominated in 1920—and from *Die Hilfe* to become a professional internationalist enthusiast and organizer. His efforts to return to DDP and DStP politics in 1930 failed, although his enthusiasm for his internationalist causes never slackened.

Heuss was attracted by Naumann while the former was a young man in Heilbronn, which Naumann represented for a time in the Reichstag.[12]

Later, he studied under Goetz in Munich, one of the intimates of the Naumann circle and an active National Social party member. Like Goetz before him, Heuss also came under the spell of Brentano, a Social Liberal before Naumann. From the university, he entered journalism, first in Heilbronn and then in Berlin. He gained admirers in Württemberg along the way who believed him a promising politician, but he failed to secure a favorable list position until May 1924 when he won a seat in the Reichstag. After serving from 1924 until 1928, he suffered a defeat, but he was reelected as a member of the DStP in 1930 and remained in the Reichstag until the end of the Republic. During these years, Heuss worked as a journalist and editor. In addition, he had an appointment as a professor at the *Hochschule für Politik*, a Berlin institution partially supported by the Carnegie Foundation and based on Naumann's desire to educate the German public in politics and public affairs. Heuss combined a sincere support for liberal democracy and for the Republic with relatively conservative views on economic and social questions and on the "national questions."

These brief biographies of the leading Naumannites illustrate the variety of views which existed among Naumann's followers. Essentially, they were bourgeois democrats, strong supporters of parliamentary democracy. They were also passionate patriots, although Erkelenz and Heile became internationalists. None, save perhaps Rohrbach, could be called a militarist or warmonger. They became more conservative on economic and social questions during the Weimar period, and Petersen, Heuss, and Stolper, to cite only three examples, became identified with the business wing. They all continued to stress the role of the DDP as a bridge to connect the working class and the middle classes, but most of them identified themselves with the interests and values of the businessman. Above all, the Naumannites longed for social harmony and national unity, wishing to recapture somehow the spirit of the "community of August 1914."[13] They also generally esteemed the virtues of moderation and rejected the values and methods of extremist parties. They differed on whether the DDP should be left of center—and closer to the SPD and the Z—or right of center—closer to the DVP—but these were important distinctions in the Democratic party. As ambiguous and contradictory as the Naumann heritage seems from our perspective, it offered many young Germans—and some who remained young at heart—a vision of Germany which they found exalted. Naumann touched the lives of thousands and helped to politicize them. They tended to overlook the contradictions and above all remembered his voice and his bearing and his vision of overcoming class divisions. He opened their eyes to political and social realities and yet fired them with idealism and hope. There were not many political figures who were his equal in the early years of the twentieth century.

The Labor Group

The nonsocialist unions which moved close to the DDP during and shortly after the revolution were an essential part of the kind of party which the Naumannites desired, a party which spanned the social classes. The hope was that unions would attract large numbers of workers to the DDP, allowing the middle classes, workers, and employees to learn to work together within the party, providing an example for all of German society. The hope soon faded, and only a small number of nonsocialist workers and employees ever joined the DDP. The DDP found it difficult to support even moderate measures such as the eight-hour day and social insurance without producing divisions in the party, and the social gulf between the classes remained within the party. Workers and employees were never comfortable in the DDP; it was too bourgeois, respectable, well-educated, and snobbish. The decline of the nonsocialist unions also soon affected the importance of the labor group in the party. Although few in number, the labor members were influential enough to elect several of their leaders to the National Assembly and the Reichstag as well as to *Land* parliaments. The major committees of the party also always included labor representatives, and the *Reichslist* usually provided for at least two labor representatives in the top fifteen positions. Erkelenz remained the leading labor figure in the DDP, although ironically he soon tired of union work except for union journalism, which earned him a living, preferring to turn over most of his union responsibilities to Ernst Lemmer, Bruno Rauecker, and Gustav Scheider. Union affairs bored him, as he frankly admitted to old friends.[14] Scheider, the head of the GDA, served in the Reichstag most of the years from 1919 to 1932, but without distinguishing himself in the eyes of DDP leaders. Goetz, who was succeeded by Schneider as Leipzig's DDP representative in 1928, indicates that Schneider was not regarded as a worthy representative of the university and commercial city of Leipzig, even though he was a hardworking advocate of the white-collar group.[15]

In the Reichstag, the union representatives of the DDP joined with the SPD and the Center party to sponsor social legislation. The DDP especially wanted to achieve remuneration and benefits for white-collar workers which were equal to those of blue-collar workers. Since the DDP failed in this and too often supported the interests of employers, it soon failed to convince the employees (*Angestellte*) that it really cared about them. As a result, the white-collar workers drifted away from the DDP, first to the DNVP and then to the Nazis. Occasionally, a railway clerk, an office worker, or a metal worker appeared on a DDP committee or on a candidate's list, but more often, a union officer achieved this recognition. The DDP had a Labor Committee (*Arbeitnehmer-Ausschuss*), which Erkelenz and then Rauecker chaired, but it was small and insignificant and ignored after 1928. After 1930, the Social Republican Circle (*Sozial-republikanischer Kreis*), tiny and scorned by the business wing, kept alive the concept of economic democracy in the DStP, but this basic trade union goal was most forcefully represented by the socialist General Confederation of Unions (*Allgemeiner Deutscher Gewerkschaftsbund*).

The Young Democrats

Another one of the subgroups of the DDP which was generally on the left of the party was the Young Democratic Organization (*Reichsbund demokratischer Jugend*). It began with much promise in 1919 when 20,000 attended its first national convention in Berlin, but the initial enthusiasm died away, and the membership dropped even more drastically than the membership of the DDP so that, by the mid-twenties, only a few thousand members were active in the organization. In 1929, for example, 2,000 attended the national convention, and only three chapters seemed to have much vitality: Hamburg, Berlin, and Nürnberg. The DDP's increasing conservatism and hostility to pacifism combined with the nation's growing economic woes, hitting the young disproportionately hard, radicalized the Young Democrats and pushed many of them toward the SPD. In the early twenties, many Young Democrats had followed their parents and joined the DVP or the DNVP, although few well-known Young Democrats became Nazis. Wiessner, the first president of the Young Democrats and a prominent journalist, did become increasingly conservative and later served the Nazis, and one of the Young Democrats' leaders, Hans-Werner Gyssling, became a Nazi party member, although he soon regretted his opportunism. These, however, seemed to have been exceptional cases. Many of the Young Democrats were Jews, such as Hans Kallmann, a major leader for several years; a sizable minority were pacifists, and pacifism alone would have deterred them from turning right. In general, the Young Democrats remained truer than their elders to the founding principles of the party and to the Republic. They also fought what they saw as the remilitarization of the Reich under the duplicitous leadership of Gessler and were especially angered by the construction of the new battle cruisers which the DDP first opposed and then supported in the late twenties.[16] In their economic and social views, they were on the far left of the party. The Young Democrats' leader in the late twenties was Lemmer, regarded as a socialist and an irresponsible demagogue by many conservative Democrats.[17] Another prominent Young Democrat in the late twenties, Erich Lüth, became so controversial for his pacifist and economic views that he was compelled to resign from the DDP. Lemmer, on the other hand, soon conformed and remained in the Reichstag until 1933. The Young Democrats virtually disappeared after 1930. They had never been a large group and left little mark on the period. Ignored even in the works devoted to Weimar political youth organizations, they fought largely unreported and forgotten struggles for their ideals and often displayed considerable courage, but most senior Democrats had little regard for them. An exception was the *Regierungspräsident*, Ferdinand Friedensburg, whose papers demonstrate his support for them and frequent contacts with the organization. Perhaps the Nürnberg chapter of the Young Democrats was the most noteworthy. Against great odds, its leaders, Otto Stündt, a young businessman, and Julie Meyer, an instructor in the Nürnberg *Volkshochschule*, fought for democracy against Julius Streicher and the Nürnberg Nazi organization, alongside the embattled mayor, Luppe. In general, however, the Young Democrats embarrassed their elders in the DDP.[18] Even moderate figures such as Koch-Weser, Bäumer, and Heuss, who strongly supported the Republic, never seemed to understand or appreciate them. It is little wonder, therefore, that most Young Democrats turned to the SPD.

The Women's Group

The Women's Committee (*Frauenausschuss*) of the DDP was generally on the left of the party on economic and social questions, especially on issues which affected women and children. Most of the women prominent in the DDP had been inspired by Naumann; many had also had practical experience as social workers and teachers of children in the appalling social conditions of German factory towns or Black Forest handicraft sweat shops. They were as determined as socialist feminists to improve the social conditions of the poor, but they could not accept socialism because of their bourgeois backgrounds and religious convictions. They wished to heal the social rifts in German society, not widen them, and they blamed the SPD for enflaming the class war. In Britain, women of this type might have joined the Labour party, but the SPD demanded a more dogmatic commitment, and German social barriers and prejudices were even more formidable than those in Britain. At any rate, Naumann gave them what they were looking for—a movement combining democracy, patriotism, respect for the rights of women, the social gospel, together with practical attention to the major social problems of the nation.

It was assumed in 1918–1919 that, because the DDP had attracted most of the non-Catholic, bourgeois feminist leaders, it would win a large following from nonsocialist women. This proved as illusory as the hope that the Democratic party would attract large numbers of workers and employees. Initially, the fear of socialism and idealistic expectations produced a rather large number of female activists, but the feminist leaders seemed unable to attract many newcomers and the DDP leaders soon overlooked the female component in the party. The women's groups received less and less respect and fewer positions of prominence in the party, which quite naturally angered and embittered the leading women in the party. This anger is particularly evident in the papers of Marie-Elisabeth Lüders, the most aggressive woman in the DDP attempting to advance women's rights.[19] Perhaps, to some extent, the Women's Committee deserved the treatment it received. Most of the women active in it had rather narrow interests; they were seldom prepared to discuss anything other than the problems of women and children. On the other hand, the scope of their activity was limited by the sexist attitudes of the party leaders and of German society. Despite the discouraging course of the DDP and the slight role in it accorded to women, they dutifully met, framed their motions and resolutions, and filed their records. A few of them also appeared as members in the major committees and in the Reichstag and state and local government. Only Lüders and Bäumer were in the Reichstag after 1920, and although she was probably a more valuable party member than Bäumer, Lüders had to fight for a high list position in every election. Other prominent women members were Martha Dönhoff, an effective Prussian *Landtag* deputy, Else Ulich-Beil, a Saxon political figure and official, Maria Baum, Marianne Weber, Dora Rade, and Elly Heuss-Knapp. As a group, perhaps their most glaring shortcoming was their inability to attract young women to politics. Indeed, they often repelled them.[20] It was particularly unfortunate that Bäumer garnered so many offices and honors and came to symbolize the Democratic party woman.

The Large Urban Newspapers—BT, FZ, VZ

The three great urban newspapers which supported the DDP most of the time from 1918 until 1933 were another important leftist element in the party. While the BT, FZ, and VZ always insisted they were independent newspapers and often clashed with the Reichstag *Fraktion* and the *Vorstand* between elections, they generally supported the DDP during the major elections and served as a sounding board for DDP politicians and as a party forum. Several important journalists, as we have seen, helped to found the party, and a number of them gained political posts as a result of their party membership. Perhaps the most notable was Rudolf Oeser, an FZ editor who became a cabinet officer in the early twenties and later administered the nationalized railway system. Nuschke enjoyed a prominent career in the Prussian *Landtag* while Bernhard served a term in the Reichstag. In addition, many journalists were active in the organization. The most vocal was Wilhelm Cohnstaedt, an FZ editor and a leader in the Hessen-Nassau DDP organization. He was a significant member of the *Vorstand*. In the course of the twenties, as the DDP drifted to the right in search of middle-class voters, the gap between it and the three newspapers opened wider and wider. In the mid-twenties, they split from many in the DDP *Fraktion* on the *Schund- und Schmutzgesetz* and the issue of the indemnification of the princes. Another basic difference between the DDP and "its" press revolved around Otto Gessler and the administration of the

Reichswehr, which shall be examined shortly. The great newspapers were also firm friends of the Weimar Coalition and opposed to *Bürgerblocks*, while the *Fraktion* and the DDP organization vacillated in their feelings and policies toward the SPD and the Center party. Provincial Democrats and the great urban newspapers also had contrasting—often subtle—social and national values. Even urbane leaders such as Heuss and Bäumer, who lived and worked in Berlin, came to see the "Berlin press" as an enemy and felt that its influence was harmful to the party.[21] Though some contemporaries tended to see these newspapers as the DDP's greatest asset in politics, this was not the conclusion of most right-wing Democrats and many moderates. The internationalist flavor of the papers' positions on foreign policy and their strong support of the SPD were highly controversial in the DDP; their opposition to a merger with the DVP and *Bürgerblocks* was also resented.

As they sometimes did on foreign policy questions, the three newspapers took different lines on economic and social policy. The VZ reflected Bernhard's corporatist philosophy and his strong support of a planned economy. The BT, on the other hand, took a rather conventional liberal position, strongly antisocialist and pro–laissez-faire. The FZ's economic and social philosophy was less clearly defined. Feiler, responsible for the economic section in the DDP's program of 1919, in general set the economic policy of the FZ and wrote many of its stories on economic policy and politics.[22] Cohnstaedt, perhaps the leading political writer, relied heavily on Feiler for information and advice about economic questions. Once a student of Brentano and also greatly influenced by Kant, Feiler attempted to blend social liberalism with Kantian ethics. He employed many of the ambiguous phrases, such as economic democracy, which Erkelenz and Bäumer also favored in the early years of the Republic, and his ideas were really moderate and only mildly critical of capitalism, but the business wing denounced him as a socialist, often demanding that the economic provisions of the program be rewritten. Like others on the DDP's left, Feiler sought a system between socialism and unregulated capitalism. He helped draft article 165 of the Weimar Constitution, which established the hierarchies of councils which rested on the factory councils of the large factories and other enterprises, and for a time he had a seat on the Reich Economic Council (*Reichswirtschaftsrat*) at the pinnacle of the pyramid of councils. He also served on several important DDP committees. Feiler's economic program remained the DDP's program to the end despite the attempt of some in the business wing to substitute the Stolper program in 1929.

Teachers and Public Sector Officials

The DDP won the initial support of relatively large numbers of teachers and officials soon after the revolution. They welcomed the changes in society and government which the revolution made possible, but most of them could not support the SPD. The DDP fitted their temperament and expectations: it was democratic, liberal, and mildly reformist, but not really revolutionary. They flocked to the party, and many gained positions of prominence. Teachers and public sector officials also left their bureaucratic mark on the party's records. One can see this in the extensive and orderly collections of private papers as well as in the portion of the party's archive which has survived. They kept diaries, wrote memoranda, letters, articles, books, and memoirs. They preserved much of the DDP's history either consciously or out of bureaucratic habit. In the beginning, officials of all ranks joined the DDP, but the senior officials soon defected to the right, and by 1928, most of the lower officials and employees had gravitated to the SPD or the Center party. Until 1928, most of the civil servant and teacher contingent was on the party's left wing on most issues. They even formally supported the democratization of the civil service, although within limits which maintained the educational standards and traditional training of officials and teachers.

In the early years, the presence of so many officials in the DDP's leadership—Petersen and Koch to cite only two examples—and its highly educated, bourgeois character, only slightly diminished by the presence of a few trade unionists and *Mittelstand* representatives, made the DDP an attractive party to officials. The DDP understood them and their desires: to adapt to a new order of things while maintaining the best of the traditions associated with government service. It also understood their hunger for security and status. Only a small number of Democratic leaders, led by Gothein, was hostile to government officialdom in principle and constantly sought to trim the officials' numbers and privileges. The DDP was aware of the harsh blows which inflation dealt them and, at first, was sympathetic, but in the end, as the DDP's economic and social policies became more conservative, economic orthodoxy outweighed compassion in the DDP's *Fraktion*. In 1926, Peter Reinhold, the DDP finance minister, won the plaudits of businessmen by reducing taxes, but the following year, when the Centrist finance minister Heinrich Köhler raised the wages and salaries of government employees and officials, the DDP opposed him. As a consequence, thousands of officials who favored the Republic turned to the SPD or the Z. The DDP also showed little interest in compensating the victims of inflation, including many teachers, academics, ics, and officials. The alternatives were complex and divisive, but in the end the DDP favored only a token compensation.[23]

In the later years of the Republic, government officials still active in the left wing of the DDP tended to be *Land* and municipal officials. The best examples were Friedensburg, an ardent republican and a sincere democrat,[24] and Luppe.[25] Both held out against the pressures which drove most of their party friends and colleagues to the right. Luppe unfortunately never achieved the same prominence in national politics that he did at the municipal level, but Bavaria did not provide a promising stage for a left-liberal career, and he was always exceedingly conscientious about his responsibilities to the city of Nürnberg. He was, at any rate, too radical on the "national questions" to win the trust of the DDP's *Vorstand* and its *Fraktion*. He helped to expose Gessler as a strong monarchist and showed sympathy for the party's pacifists, although he himself was not a pacifist. There were several prominent left-wing members in the Prussian *Landtag* and other state parliaments. Hermann Grossmann, a Prussian official, was the most strident voice in the party calling for the democratization of the civil service. He also frequently criticized Gessler and the military.

Historically, as we have noted earlier, the teaching profession had been attracted to the ideals of left liberalism, and teachers flocked in large numbers to the DDP in 1919. A number of leading officers of national teachers' organizations were in the DDP, including Konrad Weiss, a school inspector from Nürnberg who was perhaps the DDP's most militant spokesman for the interests of teachers. In addition, there were several prominent ministers of culture in the *Länder*. They included Troeltsch and Carl Heinrich Becker in Prussia, Willy Hellpach in Baden, and Johannes Hieber in Württemberg. There were always teachers or educational administrators in the Reichstag in the early years of the Republic—twelve in the National Assembly. The educators aspired to become a major force in the party, but they were never able to organize their numbers effectively to control party policies or to win support for their material goals. The DDP's teachers were, for the most part, public employees vitally concerned about salaries, working conditions, and "rights." They were cruelly punished—as all people on relatively fixed incomes were—by the economic blows of the twenties, but when they turned to the DDP for support, they were usually disappointed. Weiss and Bäumer devoted much time and energy to battle for their educational ideal, the *Einheitsschule*, and they were strong opponents of clericalism, but they came up short in the struggle for decent salaries for teachers. The DDP always proved more effective in fighting for noble ideals and lower taxes than for higher salaries and better retirement programs. As a result, it lost its credibility and support among teachers. The prominence of leaders such as Fischer and Gothein in the party and the dominance of the *Fraktion* by men of wealth drove the teachers out and into the SPD. There were also some examples of former Democratic teachers who turned to the right and documented instances of a few who became Nazis.[26]

Academics and Intellectuals

Another group usually found on the left of the DDP consisted of a glittering array of prominent professors and intellectuals, many of whom left papers, wrote their autobiographies, or have been the subject of specialized studies. Because the DDP's academics and intellectuals tended to be highly individualistic, it is difficult to generalize about them without constantly making exceptions, but it can be said that they were never very important in the DDP, which is contrary to the observations of a number of secondary studies of the DDP by individuals whose forte is intellectual history. These intellectuals probably, at first, helped to attract a portion of the educated middle class to the DDP, but in the long run they were a dubious asset. Intellectuals and academics, with only a few exceptions, were always on the fringe of the party, helping with the advertising, but they were seldom at the center, holding down the key committee posts or taking an active part in parliamentary life. The academics who were elected to the National Assembly and the Reichstag—figures such as Goetz, Bergsträsser, Hellpach, Erich Obst, Gerland, Wilhelm Vershofen, and Schücking—generally found parliamentary affairs frustrating, boring, and time-consuming. They preferred to spend their time and energy in professional pursuits; politics was a secondary interest.

The intellectuals in the DDP were even less influential than the professors. They wrote articles for the left-liberal journals and, if gifted with a more popular touch, in the DDP press. Occasionally, one of them made a major speech at a DDP gathering, as Heinrich Mann did at the Hamburg PT in 1927.[27] Sometimes, a group of academics and intellectuals circulated and signed petitions in behalf of the DDP. Although there is little evidence that these efforts won any votes for the party, this activity may have increased their sense of well-being. Bonn, a professor, publicist, and intellectual, was a useful gadfly in the party. He was able to bridge the university, the popular press, and politics. He often spoke at the Democratic Club in Berlin and before major committees of the party on economic questions. Like most of the economists in the party—or figures such as Gothein and Hermann Dietrich, who thought of themselves as economists—he was highly opinionated, but unlike the rest he had a sense of humor. Harry Kessler was another DDP intellectual who occasionally appeared at party gatherings.[28] From his diary, it would appear that he was utterly bored with party politics and politicians, even though he was a candidate for the Reichstag in 1924. Apparently, he hoped for a diplomatic career and felt that activity in a political party might help his chances. Heuss aspired to win a Reichstag seat but was forced to earn his living in journalism. He also had a valid claim as a professor and intellectual. His writings on politics and the arts, not to speak of his later biographies, were distinguished not only by their contents but by their style. His letter writing and oratory attained high levels of literary achievement. These achievements, however, did not count for much in politics, and he had several frustrating years trying to break into Württemberg politics before he achieved his ambition in 1924. Heuss was a greater success in the Reichstag than most academics and intellectuals. His conservative position on economic and social questions and his strong nationalism helped his effectiveness, but he also had a common touch and considerable charm—rare qualities in the DDP. Most of the DDP's academics and intellectuals were handicapped by their arrogance and aloofness; they would not suffer fools or climb down from their pedestals.[29]

The DDP was not successful in attracting many medical doctors, lawyers, pastors, or engineers. To remedy this and to give some kind of focus to the needs and concerns for those in the "free professions," it formed a committee in April 1929, the conventional DDP way to recognize an oversight. But the Committee for the Free Professions, formed too late to be of importance, was never popular and soon disbanded.

The Right Wing

The right wing or business wing had a more settled and homogenous character than the left wing. It consisted primarily of businessmen, industrialists, bankers, farmers, and certain *Mittelstand* elements. On occasion, officials, professors, and intellectuals also supported the economic and social positions of the right wing. However, the policies and values of businessmen and their allies generally shaped the program and character of the right wing. It was led by two party committees, the Committee on Trade, Industry, and Commerce (*Reichsausschuss für Handel, Industrie, und Gewerbe*), whose permanent secretary was Ernst Mosich, and the Employers' Committee (*Unternehmerausschuss*). In the early years of the party, the nonpartisan Curatorium for the Reconstruction of German Economic Life (*Kuratorium für den Wiederaufbau des deutschen Wirtschaftsleben*) also had much influence on the business wing. The most important interest groups outside the party affecting the right wing were the HB and the Congress of German Industry and Commerce (the *Deutscher Industrie und Handelstag*—DIHT), the German Chamber of Commerce, whose leader after 1925 was the prominent Democrat Eduard Hamm and whose titular head was Franz von Mendelssohn, who also had many ties to the DDP. Mendelssohn occasionally provided money for the DDP at election time. The business wing opposed socialism, trade unions, and high taxes, but favored programs and taxes to aid business. Despite the general agreement among the members, rifts and contradictions persisted within the right wing. The interests of farmers clashed with those of businessmen, and commercial interests sometimes clashed with industrial interests. Even within an industry there were divisions. The needs of *Mittelstand* groups were at variance with the large department store interests in the party and the major banks; the values of the *Mittelstand* sometimes clashed with the traditional, laissez-faire liberals. Even the farmers within the DDP divided on tariff policy. The grain and wine producers favored tariffs while the cattle feeders and breeders opposed them.

By 1924, it had become apparent to many in the DDP that a party with such diverse interests could not endure. How could one party represent the interests of electronics moguls such as Rathenau, Siemens, and Phillip Wieland, Schleswig cattle breeders, East Prussian grain growers, international bankers such as Dernburg and Mendelssohn, Black Forest clockmakers, small wine producers in Hesse, and retail clerks in Berlin? In fact, under the conditions of the Weimar Republic and in the light of German traditions, one party could not represent them, although the NSDAP tried. The binding ties—fear of socialism and a general desire for parliamentary democracy—were not strong enough to sustain a democratic integrationist party. In the competition to control policy making in the DDP, the business wing tended to be better led and financed than the left wing and by 1924 effectively controlled the party. In general, the various interest organizations close to the DDP's business wing traded financial support to the DDP in exchange for influence in determining the fiscal, social, and economic policies of the party. Financial support became a club which kept the party in line in the areas which really counted for businessmen, who were less concerned about foreign policy, civil liberties questions, or *Kultur* issues.

The HB was the principal business pressure group close to the DDP. Most of its members owned small or medium-sized businesses and industries dependent on the import of raw materials and the export of finished products.[30] In politics, they generally supported the DDP or the DVP. Several of its DDP members were prominent in the tobacco industry while others were important in the garment industry in Berlin. Before the war, Stresemann represented a group of HB members in Saxony who were chocolate manufacturers. The HB's greatest strength lay in the Hanseatic cities of the north and in Berlin, where many members were Jews. Its president was Fischer, the treasurer of the Democratic party and one of its vice-chairmen.[31] His chief concern within the party was to checkmate Erkelenz's "radical influence." After most of the great industrialists and businessmen abandoned the party, Fischer remained behind to help keep the DDP responsible and attentive to the interests of HB members. The programmatic statements which the HB published in the Weimar period indicate that the organization was primarily interested in lowering the costs of government and in cutting taxes, and at times its program sounded like warmed-over Manchester liberalism. The HB did what it could to block the Erzberger tax laws and then to undo them. It also sought to roll back social security measures, including the eight-hour day. It fostered "self-help" social insurance programs to replace government ones. Richter would have been delighted with its fulminations against socialism. Only the "very weak"—a term never defined—should receive government assistance. The HB also strongly advocated the merger of the DVP and the DDP, the Liberal Association,[32] and *Bürgerblock* governments.

The most active business representatives other than Fischer were Dietrich, Dernburg, Wieland, August Weber, Hamm, and Carl Melchior. Dietrich had been a NLP member and, from the formation of the DDP, he was on the extreme right of the *Fraktion*. Although Dietrich's business card described him as a peasant from a small village in Baden, and he did own land and forests there, he was a rich businessman with varied interests who entertained in a palatial house in Berlin.[33] Although he posed—not insincerely—as the spokesman for the small peasant and *Mittelstand*, his greatest concern was to create a favorable climate for business in Germany. He became the party's most important representative on the Reichstag budget committee from 1920 to 1930 when he became minister of agriculture in the Hermann Müller government. As minister of economics, minister of finance, and vice-chancellor under Heinrich Brüning, he was partially responsible for the disastrous deflationary policies of the Brüning government and became tied in the public mind—and in that of the DDP and the DStP—with unpopular taxes and the *Osthilfe* program to bail out *Junker* landlords at public expense. Dietrich had favored agricultural protection in 1925, unlike the DDP, and after 1930, he abandoned other traditional left-liberal positions on taxes and tariffs.

Dernburg's diverse economic interests are difficult to catalog, but he is generally identified as an international banker. His social circle included some of the wealthiest men in Germany. Wieland, a Württemberg industrialist who barred Heuss's political ambitions for several years, also had varied economic holdings but was known primarily as the owner of an electronics firm in Ulm. Prominent in the Committee on Trade, Industry, and Commerce and an arch conservative in the *Fraktion*, Wieland, although he had one of the worst attendance records of any Reichstag deputy, was often chosen to voice the party's positions on fiscal and economic questions. Like Dietrich and Dernburg, he seldom attended party meetings; the power of the leaders of the business wing was demonstrated not in DDP committees but in the *Fraktion*. Fischer, Wieland, Dernburg, and Dietrich usually spoke for the party in the Reichstag on economic and fiscal questions.[34] This was even true in the early twenties when the left wing supposedly was still important in the DDP and parties held the power in government which bureaucrats eventually usurped. The same conservatives who rigged the committee agendas and the speakers' lists to exclude the Social Republicans saw to it that the right wing dominated the discussion of taxes and even *Sozialpolitik*. For the most part, the left wing spoke only on questions which did not threaten property. But the right wing was not exclusively interested in taxes and property rights. Fischer, for example, had a rather enlightened record on civil liberties questions, and Dernburg forcefully and effectively advocated the policy of fulfillment and international reconciliation. Dietrich seemed genuinely interested in peasant problems and in aiding the victims of inflation. Moreover, they were undoubtedly sincere in feeling that Germany's economic recovery necessitated measures to improve business conditions, while social programs, education, and "big government" only hampered the economy and delayed prosperity. In time, most of the right wing of the DDP concluded that the political system prevented economic prosperity and had to be replaced by something more effective with greater authority. According to one source, Hamm, minister of economics in Marx's first two governments and an important adviser of Cuno, seemed in particular to have given up on the Weimar Republic.[35]

Within the business wing a small group of intractable and mostly elderly men clung to Richter's ideals with stubborn determination. Although they modified their policy of free trade considerably, they continued to believe in many of the tenets of classical liberalism in the teeth of Weimar conditions and German traditions. They attempted to have all wartime controls and regulations removed as soon as possible, insisting that the road to economic recovery must be paved with lower taxes and smaller government. Although most of the recent studies of the Democratic party have ignored this group, the leadership could not. They turned up in the Reichstag and *Land* parliaments and on major committees of the party and at the party congresses because they still had strong rank and file support in several electoral districts.[36] The HB also made concessions to their principles and prejudices. Gothein, as we have seen, was still battling for traditional liberalism as if its principles were self-evident truths. He had simple solutions for all of Germany's economic problems: cut taxes and reduce the size of government. He seemed utterly unconcerned about the material welfare of the worker or the small farmer; the business of Germany was business. The left wing of the DDP quite naturally saw him as a tool of big business, but in fact he had no master except perhaps Adam Smith. The other prominent Richterites, Fischbeck and Kopsch, who initially were spokesmen for *Mittelstand* and local chamber of commerce concerns, continued to voice the feelings of small businessmen. Laissez-faire principles may have been regarded as anachronistic by the followers of Naumann and the journalists of the major DDP newspapers, but they remained vital in the business wing. Indeed, the prevalence of such views in the right wing of the DDP and in the DStP helped to blind the party to the need for state intervention when the Great Depression struck and dulled its capacity for finding innovative solutions to the depression.

Mittelstand

The concept of the *Mittelstand* has been analyzed thoroughly by several scholars as has the role of the *Mittelstand* in politics during the Weimar period.[37] The term generally includes groups from the older, pre-industrial middle class as well as the so-called new middle class. In the DDP, the most clearly identifiable *Mittelstand* members were self-employed artisans, small businessmen, office workers, retail clerks, and lower-level government employees. Small farmers are usually included in the *Mittelstand* as well but will be treated separately here. The significance of the *Mittelstand*'s contribution to the political instability of Weimar Germany and to the dissolution of the bourgeois parties is generally recognized.[38] In response to a variety of economic and social problems and in its attempt to find political representation for its material interests, the *Mittelstand* deserted or was driven out of the established bourgeois parties. Millions of *Mittelstand* voters abandoned the two liberal parties and the DNVP between 1920 and 1928. The failure of the DDP to respond to their needs doomed whatever hope it had to remain a large and important party.

The Progressive party had recognized before 1914 that the *Mittelstand* groups were potential left-liberal voters and it sought—rather half-heartedly—to understand their concerns and to develop programs to meet them. Several Reichstag deputies in the Progressive *Fraktion* specialized in *Mittelstand* problems. In Württemberg, for example, where there were relatively large numbers of self-employed artisans and peasants, Haussmann worked effectively to win their support and brought them with him to the DDP. In Baden, Silesia, East Prussia, Hamburg, and Berlin, the DDP initially had deputies with close ties to master bakers and green grocers, although it proved less successful in establishing associations with retail clerks, white-collar workers, and factory technicians. For the most part, the *Mittelstand* specialists were followers of Richter, but others in the DDP, especially the former National Liberals and the Naumannites, showed little compassion for their plight and little desire to understand their problems. They seemed embarrassed to have such clumsy, ungrammatical figures representing the DDP in parliament. A few carpenters, tailors, and house painters were elected on the DDP ticket, but it was more common to advance the business managers or secretaries of *Mittelstand* organizations. In the National Assembly, for example, Franz Bartschat, a tinsmith, gained a seat, but his significance was attributable to the fact that he was the head of a guild which numbered several thousand in East Prussia. In Württemberg, much to the displeasure of young Heuss, Hermann, active in retail trade associations, won election. The DDP hoped that artisans and small businessmen in other districts would be alerted by their professional organizations to the DDP's action in selecting a *Mittelstand* deputy. It seems, however, that the *Mittelstand* organizations were not deceived by such gestures. The DDP generally underestimated the intelligence and opportunism of the *Mittelstand*. *Mittelstand* representatives were not motivated by partisan principles or loyalties. One figure, Andreas Kerschbaum, a farmer who had a DDP mandate in the Reichstag from 1919 to 1924, representing Unterfranken, belonged to four parties during his career—the NLP, the DDP, and two peasant splinter parties. His loyalty was not to a party but to the interests of small farmers in northern Bavaria. Bartschat became the most well-known *Mittelstand* figure within the DDP organization and won election several times to the Reichstag. In 1920, Wilhelm Kniest, a carpenter, gained a seat from Hesse-Nassau, thanks to his high position on the *Reichslist*, while, at the same time, a house painter succeeded in winning a place in the Prussian *Landtag*. In February 1924, following the resignation of Petersen from the Reichstag, Johannes Büll, the chairman of a small businessmen's association in Hamburg, replaced Petersen and remained in the Reichstag until 1930. During these years, Büll became the principal spokesman in the Reichstag *Fraktion* for *Mittelstand* needs, but in 1930, Stolper, regarded by Büll as a spokesman for high finance, bumped him from the top list position in Hamburg.[39]

Throughout the Weimar period, the DDP/DStP substituted token candidates for a *Mittelstand* policy. The DDP had a *Mittelstand* Committee by 1920 and occasionally held a *Mittelstand* Day, but the party lacked any real commitment to the interests of these groups. This became clear soon after the appearance of the *Wirtschaftspartei* (WP) in 1920,[40] organized by a former Democrat and master baker, Hermann Drewitz. The BT, reporting the WP's first meeting, predicted that the WP would make heavy cuts into the vote of the middle-class parties, and it did.[41] The regional leaders of the DDP, within a few months, reported that large numbers of Democrats were leaving to join the WP. The WP also placed the DDP on the defensive by labeling it a party of big business and big banks as well as a friend of the SPD and Jews.[42] The WP, unlike the DDP, was an avowedly Christian party. The DDP and the DVP, also weakened by the WP, reacted to the WP's formation by ridiculing its crass materialism and narrow interests, but the DDP responded somewhat and began occasionally to advance "pocketbook issues" which previously it had been too haughty to emphasize. Lüders, in particular, became active in the fight to compensate the *Kleinrentner* class ruined by the inflation. The revaluation question, which spawned new parties and worried the government for several years, was only one of several economic and social issues which tormented the *Mittelstand* and weakened the DDP. The new *Volksrechtspartei* sheltered several disgruntled groups, while a House Owners' party, formed to fight a Prussian house tax designed to penalize property owners who had profited from inflation, won the backing of hundreds of thousands of lower middle-class voters. New parties were organized to aid landlords, tenants, the *Rentner*, as well as various peasant groups. By 1930, there were over thirty national parties. Every new party took voters from the DDP, but the most damaging competitor, the WP, did much to destroy it as a political force. In the 1928 election, the WP received about the same number of votes as the DDP, but in 1930, its total exceeded that of the *Staatspartei*. In July 1932, however, the WP virtually disappeared along with the two liberal parties and most of the peasant parties. Here and there the DDP/DStP retained some strength at the *Land* and local levels, in part because local organizations responded more effectively to *Mittelstand* concerns than the national party. In Prussia, for example, the DDP voted against the house owners' tax, although the national party favored the tax because it felt that those who had profited from the inflation—such as the house owners—should pay compensation to those who had suffered losses from the inflation. Regardless of these occasional desertions of "fiscal responsibility" and efforts to achieve equity, the interest parties always outbid the DDP for the *Mittelstand* vote.

In the face of the proliferation of special interest parties, most of which focused on problems of the urban *Mittelstand*, and because of the drastic decline of the DDP's organization, several Democrats advocated that the DDP become a *Mittelstand* interest party and abandon its integrationist goals. Frankfurter, an urbane Berlin lawyer who represented the Ullstein press and many clients in the film industry, urged this course in the *Vorstand* and in correspondence.[43] In effect, he argued that if the DDP could not beat the interest parties it should join them. Although it is questionable how sincere Frankfurter was in making this proposal—as chairman of the Organization Committee he may have been playing the devil's advocate— it was promptly negated by Koch-Weser and the *Vorstand*, who remained true to the Naumann integrationist mission of the DDP. Koch-Weser argued that the DDP had to represent *all* the people and political ideals, not just the material interests of a few. Such local organizations as the DDP in Cologne, led by Hans Goldschmidt, a professor of political science, also pressed the national party to meet the needs of the *Mittelstand* and the *Angestellten* and urged a party policy to make them the mass base of the party. After the 1928 election, when it became apparent to nearly all leading Democrats that economic factors had been the most important determinant in the DDP's loss, Stephan emphasized the central part which the loss of support of *Mittelstand* organizations had played.[44] According to him, only in Württemberg, Baden, and Bremen could the DDP expect to receive important *Mittelstand* support in the future. Elsewhere, the base of the DDP's electorate, the *Mittelstand*, had turned to other parties.

Agriculture

The DDP's rural supporters were generally found in the right wing of the party.[45] They shared the businessman's antipathy for socialism and trade unions and preferred to ally politically with the DVP and the DNVP. They were also generally conservative on the "national questions." The farmers had specialized problems and needs, however, which made it difficult for them to be comfortable with *any* urban political party representing diverse interests. While in 1919 a sizable number of farmers throughout the Reich voted for the DDP, they soon turned elsewhere. In 1920, many deserted the Democrats and by 1924, few farmers remained. The

DBB, which had supported the DDP in 1919 and whose leaders became prominent in the organization, grew disenchanted with the nature of the DDP and its voting record. It began to lose its members to other farm organizations which were politically close to the DNVP. Its leader, Böhme, resigned from the DDP in 1924, but his deputy, Fritz Wachhorst de Wente, a former NLP deputy, remained behind. In 1925, the DDP ended whatever chance it had to win farm votes by opposing agricultural protective tariffs while favoring tariffs for industry and commerce. Only the small group of cattle breeders and feeders in northwest Germany opposed agricultural protection. While most Democrats favored bilateral trade treaties which favored industry and commerce at the expense of agriculture, most farmers were convinced that high protective tariffs were imperative for their survival. Although the DDP had little support from farmers after 1925, it continued to attempt to retain its rural supporters with electoral slogans and by placing well-known farm figures on electoral lists and major committees. Active Democrats such as Hugo Wendorff, the former Prussian minister of agriculture, Ernst Siehr, the East Prussian *Oberpräsident*, Theodor Tantzen, the former minister president of Oldenburg, Heinrich Rönneburg, and Wachhorst de Wente reminded farmers that the DDP still had agricultural spokesmen in its leadership, but the DDP's votes were generally cast against the farmer. Even in the period 1930–1933, when Dietrich became prominently identified with the *Osthilfe* program to aid grain producers in the northeast, the DStP opposed his protectionist measures, and many traders in farm commodities resigned from the party in protest against Dietrich, the DStP's leader.

In 1927, a year in which farm foreclosures increased dramatically, the DDP finally reconciled some of its internal differences on agricultural policy and produced an agricultural program and an Agricultural Committee, but once again, to use a rural metaphor, the DDP had closed the barn door too late. Neither a farm program nor a committee could overcome the DDP's voting record in the Reichstag. In addition, the DDP was too closely associated with urban groups and interests most farmers found offensive. The DDP was too wealthy, too well-educated, too closely tied to Berlin, Jews, banking, and commercial interests to appeal to agricultural groups.[46]

The Pragmatic Center

The so-called pragmatic center consisted of a group of men and women with weaker economic interests and a less dogmatic ideological stance. They provided a kind of cushion in the struggle between the two wings of the party and the various interest groups to determine party policy on economic and social issues, often framing the compromise resolutions which became party policy and resolving internal contradictions. The middle ground constantly shifted and many of the individuals who occupied it were in transition from left to right. Bäumer, for example, in 1919–1924, occupied a position on the far left of the party on economic and social questions. She often joined with figures such as Cohnstaedt or Erkelenz. In the middle and late twenties, however, Bäumer moved to the right, largely because of foreign policy and *Kultur* questions, and, in time, this affected her position on economic and social questions as well. Koch-Weser also moved from left of center to right center if for different reasons. Increasingly, he believed that the preservation of the Republic and the DDP necessitated a *Bürger Sammlung*; in particular, he was convinced that the DDP and the DVP had to develop the closest of ties if not a merger, although he still had reservations about joining with the DVP's right wing. He also became convinced, along with Bäumer and Stephan, that many in the DDP's left wing were harming the party, an evaluation strengthened by the fact that these people were also his personal party enemies. His diary and correspondence provide many examples of his growing estrangement from the left and his increasing attraction to politicians on the right such as Oscar Meyer. The improvement in his personal fortune through profitable connections with banks and business interests probably also contributed to his growing conservatism. Outwardly, as the party leader, he sought consensus, avoiding an ideological label and often hiding his true feelings. As a result, it is difficult to determine how much of his shift of ground was based on principle and how much was the result of personal opportunism. Moreover, his sensitivity to criticism and his pride sometimes affected his actions. One may also interpret his words and actions as the consequence of his concern for the welfare of the party and for German democracy.[47]

Haas, by temperament and by lack of major economic interests, was another influential moderate. Generally, on economic and fiscal questions, he voted with the business wing, but he clearly placed the welfare of the party and the Republic above any personal considerations. His election as *Fraktion* chairman in 1928, after Koch-Weser became the minister of justice and resigned the post, was a recognition of his disinterestedness and his general accord with the *Fraktion* majority. His highest priorities were to restore the vitality of the Weimar Coalition and to produce a consensus in the party. He often assumed a mediatory position, trying to dispel misunderstandings of various sorts and to explain the decisions of the *Fraktion*. He also served as a liaison to the SPD, the left wing of the Center party, the *Reichsbanner*, and the Jewish community. When he died of heart failure in 1930, the party's major conciliatory voice was silenced, and no one replaced him.

Stolper, another example of a DDP centrist on most questions, was an Austrian who had been converted to Naumann's *Mitteleuropa* vision and became the editor of *Der deutsche Volkswirt*. In 1925, aided by financial help from Schacht and Albert Vögler, a conspicuous figure in heavy industry, he moved his journal to Berlin. He had many friends in the DDP and was coopted into the *Vorstand*. He enjoyed considerable success with his journal and in the party. For several years before Stolper moved to Berlin, there had been opposition in the business wing to the economic portion of the DDP's 1919–1920 program. Many businessmen felt that it did not distinguish the DDP clearly enough from the SPD and thought it supported socialization too strongly. At the time of the 1927 PT, many at the congress, including Petersen, expressed the need for a new economic program. Many thought that a new program could more clearly define the DDP's principles. A year later, in June 1928, and over the reservations of several of the party's leaders, the *Vorstand* named a committee representing all wings of the party, with Stolper designated as its chairman. Stolper, taking his responsibility seriously, attempted to organize the committee to write a draft program, but he ran into opposition from several sources. Koch-Weser feared that an economic program would open up the old divisions in the party. The left wing of the party, led by Bernhard and Lemmer, set out to obstruct the committee's work, aided and abetted by Erkelenz.[48] Several in the business wing encouraged Stolper to persist even if he had to write the program himself, although Mosich and Fischer, who were given advance information about the principal provisions of Stolper's draft, had serious reservations about it.[49] Nevertheless, most members of the major committees expressed general approval and, as a result, Stolper received an invitation to present his program to the *Parteitag* at Mannheim in October 1929. As it turned out, Stolper's long speech presenting his ideas was the highlight of a meeting depressed by the news of Stresemann's death.[50] It took Stolper over two hours to read the document, and its content impressed many. Others, however, clearly had made up their minds before the reading for or against it on the basis of Stolper's well-known reputation. Those in the far left wing, such as Bernhard, saw it as a capitalist apology.[51] The most conservative businessmen believed it was too radical. In the debate at Mannheim, Schneider and Goldschmidt for the left and Andreas Colsmann, a businessman from Württemberg for the right, sharply criticized it. Schneider attacked it because it had little to say about unemployment and wage policy. He also thought the statement on monopolies too weak. The business wing, represented by Colsmann, denounced Stolper's tax proposals, his plan for a tobacco monopoly, and his support for the public sector. Stolper, who saw himself as a centrist, defended it as an attempt to find the median position of the party.[52] In fact, it was less a party economic program than a statement expressing Stolper's personal economic philosophy and an attempt to analyze the effects of the war on Europe's economy and society. While it praised capitalism, it also addressed the needs of the worker.

The reaction to the draft program substantiated Koch-Weser's fears that it would exacerbate the DDP's internal divisions. As a result, it soon received a quiet burial and never became the DDP's economic program. It did not revive the party's fortunes or achieve party unity on economic and social issues, but for Stolper it was a personal triumph; he soon had more speaking engagements than he could fill. It also sparked renewed interest in the DDP in a few districts, but it did not stimulate any significant efforts to regenerate the party.

The DDP's Legislative Record on Economic and Social Legislation in the National Assembly

It would serve no purpose to analyze here the legislative record of the DDP for the entire period of the Republic since *Zehn Jahre Deutsche Republik*, edited by Erkelenz, devotes several chapters written by legislators to this subject, and the *ABC Bücher* also have authoritative brief essays on various issues.[53] The party journals and press also devoted much space to the legislative work of the Reichstag *Fraktion* and the most important *Land* parties. In the end, however, it is extremely difficult to attribute legislative achievements to the DDP. The DDP was always a member of a coalition government, and laws were a joint product of the government parties. Only when the DDP was in the opposition—which was rare—did it have a distinctive posture, and in the opposition, it often seemed more interested in embarrassing the government than in advancing positive alternatives to government policy. After 1924, the DDP was too small to have much influence even when it was a member of the government. By the late twenties, parties were less important in the law-making process than bureaucrats. The president assumed greater importance and the emergency provisions in the constitution were employed ever more frequently.

The DDP made its clearest contribution to major legislation during the National Assembly. At that time, the DDP was relatively large and important and it held significant cabinet posts. Party and personal records are also much more extensive for the early years of the Republic so that it is easier to chart the murky passage of bills on the way to becoming laws. Deputies, for example, took notes in *Fraktion* meetings and preserved them. The press coverage was more extensive and there were many more DDP journals and newspapers. The first major decision of the National Assembly in the economic and social field was to approve the socialization of monopolistic industries.[54] Later, this law became article 165 in the constitution. The DDP vaguely supported the socialization of monopolies in its electoral propaganda and in its 1919–1920 program, but many in the party opposed it. The business wing believed that it represented an undesirable and unnecessary capitulation to the SPD. The *Fraktion* majority, however, concluded that it was tactically necessary to prevent the radicalization of the workingman and the weakening of the majority Socialists. Only a few Democrats favored the socialization of monopolies because of its merits. While Naumann and Erkelenz defended the need to stay aligned with the SPD and the left wing of the Center party in order to build a "dam against the red flood," the business wing saw the government as part of the "red flood." They shared Stresemann's opinion that the DDP had "capitulated to the streets." While the DDP generally opposed socialism at the national level, it accepted municipal socialism and the continuance of state socialism in Prussia without a murmur. Later, it also supported the nationalization of the railway system, and a Democrat, Oeser, was the first administrator in charge of the railway system. At the December 1919 PT, Friedrich Raschig, an industrialist and National Assembly deputy, defended the efficiency of Prussian socialism.[55] The opposition to the nationalization of the electrical grid came largely from DDP mayors who wished to preserve municipal socialism. The DDP opposed "socialist experiments," nationalization in new and untried areas for doctrinaire reasons. It feared any development which might harm productivity and impede economic recovery. The DDP wanted to restore the German export trade and to win foreign loans, especially from the United States, and it knew that the United States government strongly opposed socialism.

The first measure to implement the law to socialize monopolies was a bill to nationalize the coal industry. When the SPD announced that this was one of its goals, the business wing of the DDP contended the DDP had been betrayed and professed to be surprised.[56] While the SPD had never disguised its objective to socialize coal, the DDP still found socialization difficult to defend. The *Fraktion* chose veteran and rather conservative deputies, Pachnicke and Dernburg, to explain its support. They argued that it was imperative for labor peace and for Germany's economic recovery to support the law.[57] In the *Hauptvorstand*, the *Fraktion*'s decision came under heavy fire from two former National Liberals, Marwitz and Otto Keinath.[58] A major debate occurred in the committee, in which Bernhard and the labor wing defended socialization and the necessity to bolster the stock of the majority Socialists among German workingmen. A similar bill to nationalize the potash industry passed soon after the coal bill.

No one in 1919 could anticipate that these nationalization measures would never be fully implemented. The *Bürger* parties in 1919 did hope that by procrastination and foot-dragging they could weaken the laws, and in the end they were successful as several Democrats later boasted.[59] Even though the DDP helped slow down the implementation of socialization, it felt compelled to vote for several tax measures in the summer and autumn of 1919 which to the business wing seemed as threatening to private property as nationalization.[60] These so-called Erzberger tax laws placed the DDP in a terrible position. The DDP was in the opposition when they were introduced and it might have won popularity by opposing them, but the DDP realized the perilous condition of German finances and elected to act responsibly. The DDP knew that the pre-1918 government and, in particular, the former finance minister Karl Helfferich, were culpable. It realized that the government had to impose high taxes and institute severe governmental economies to avoid runaway inflation and to gain international credibility. Even Gothein, whose continual wail against high taxes never ceased, appreciated that Germany had to pay at least as much taxes as its enemies.[61] As a result, the DDP, with great misgivings and some mild criticism of the tax bills, approved the first tax proposals.[62] Schiffer shouldered part of the responsibility for the new taxes as a previous finance minister, but Erzberger had to endure the storm of abuse from the rightist parties and their press. He was the object of an unmerciful campaign of vilification in which the business wing of the DDP and nearly all of the DDP newspapers shared. It led to Erzberger's political fall in 1920 and his assassination in 1921.

The DDP endorsed some aspects of the Erzberger tax reform program, approving the centralization of the tax system and the weight placed on income and property taxes. It quibbled about the tax rates and some of the new taxes, but it immediately came under fire from the HB and various middle-class interest groups for its failure to combine with the DVP and the DNVP against the tax program. When the DDP rejoined the government in October 1919, it approved the whole package of tax laws, including great increases in income, property, and inheritance taxes, a war profits tax, a continuation of the wartime business turnover tax (*Umsatzsteuer*), and, finally, a capital levy (*Reichsnotopfer*), which middle-class groups thought would destroy capital and ruin the middle classes. The government introduced the tax program in stages and voted on it sequentially over many months. As each segment was debated and approved, the opposition swelled and became more violent. By October and November 1919, hundreds of thousands of people who had voted for the DDP in January deserted it for the DVP or the DNVP. The DVP, in particular, fattened on the DDP's decision to be "responsible." The DDP offered a statist defense: it had a duty to support the legitimate government of Germany and to safeguard the future of the Reich. The right wing of the DDP *Fraktion*, led by Gothein who had opposed the party's return to the government, attempted to win the *Fraktion*'s support to oppose the tax program, but it failed. Gothein contended years later in his memoirs that the decision to reenter the government and to support the tax program destroyed the DDP. But what was the alternative? If the DDP wished parliamentary democracy to succeed, it was imperative to support the majority Socialists and the left wing of the Center party. To undermine the government at this stage might well have precipitated a civil war or the intervention of the Entente in German affairs. As a result, the *Fraktion* majority concluded that it had to swallow its repugnance and vote for the taxes, although nearly half of the *Fraktion* absented itself on the vote for the *Reichsnotopfer* and others either voted against it or abstained.

The Second Party Congress of the DDP (First Special PT) occurred soon after the Reichstag recess for Christmas and while the indignation against the government was at its peak. Fischer, who was not a deputy in the National Assembly, received considerable support when he attacked the *Fraktion*, but it was Gothein, who had opposed most of the government's policies, who received the greatest applause.[63] The Fischers and the Gotheins, however, did not control the DDP at this stage of its history; the business wing lacked a majority and there were only a small number of Richterites in influential positions in the party. Most of the delegates realizèd the dilemma of the *Fraktion*, and it received a vote of confidence. But in the months which followed, the party made few efforts to justify the program, and only a few deputies had the courage to defend it.[64] The party attempted to moderate the administration of the tax program as much as possible, condoning the failure to implement the Erzberger tax program. No one could have predicted that the capital levy would never be collected or that most of the harsh direct taxes would be scaled down to a much lower level. Despite the decrease in actual tax collections, the business wing of the DDP continued to advocate cutting government costs and raising indirect taxes. Members of the business wing argued that such steps would make it easier to borrow money and to build capital, the German economy would revive, business would prosper, and the benefits, in time, would trickle down to everyone. In the age of Thatcher and Reagan, this has a familiar ring. Later, when the inflation hit, the DDP did not blame its own unwillingness to accept higher taxes; it blamed the French.

One is always struck in studying domestic political history how much time is consumed in legislative bodies on taxes. Certainly, taxes haunted the history of the DDP and contributed to the unpopularity of several of its leaders and of the party. Time and again the DDP felt compelled to support unpopular taxes which weakened its support among the middle classes, but, on other occasions, it succumbed to pressure from its middle-class followers and opposed the SPD and the Center party to retain middle-class support. In October 1921, the DDP deserted the Joseph Wirth government because it could not accept the tax program of the SPD. In March 1930, it helped scuttle the Müller government rather than maintain unemployment compensation at levels demanded by the SPD. In each instance, the principal cause of the fall of the government was the inability of the DVP and the SPD to agree on fiscal and *Sozialpolitik*, but the DDP chose to support the DVP rather than the parties of the Weimar Coalition. While it is true that the Center party, in 1930, had moved to the right and preferred to work with the DVP rather than the SPD, a viable compromise might still have been achieved if the Müller government could have been preserved somewhat longer. The DDP's decisions to bring down the Wirth and Müller governments—ostensibly because of Upper Silesia and fiscal responsibility—were significant acts which weakened German democracy by destroying the unity and strength of the only parties which unreservedly supported the Republic. Unpopular taxes, on several occasions, rubbed off on the DDP leaders and, in particular, those who performed as finance ministers. Of the four Democrats who served as finance ministers in the national government, only Reinhold, who was in the cabinet in 1926–1927, gained popularity in the DDP and among middle-class voters because of his policies, and largely because he reduced taxes. Dietrich's record was more typical. He became identified with new and unpopular taxes and subsidies to *Junker* landlords which hurt the DDP/DStP as well as his personal reputation. Hermann Höpker-Aschoff, the Prussian finance minister from 1925–1932, sometimes described by right-wing Democrats as the greatest Prussian finance minister since Johannes Miquel, gained a reputation among leftist parties as a heartless figure, indifferent to the suffering of the poor and supporting harsh taxes. The DDP—which in 1919 seemed anxious to become a party of all the people—clearly emerges in its fiscal policies as an essentially middle-class party.

The last measure of the National Assembly which illustrates the DDP's economic and social philosophy and policies was the Factory Council Act (*Betriebsrätegesetz*).[65] Debate on it raged from March 1919 through February 1920 with many interruptions when issues with higher priority intervened. The idea of factory councils had little relationship to Workers' and Soldiers' Councils. They had a long history in Germany; Naumann and the Hirsch-Duncker unions approved the idea before the war as a way of alleviating the class struggle.[66] In 1919, the SPD, the Center party, and the left wing of the DDP led by Bernhard and Erkelenz, backed the factory councils with varying motives, although all of the trade unions reacted cooly to the idea. The unions had made significant advances during and immediately after the war and feared giving up their power to an unknown entity. Although Erkelenz's influence in his union was at its height at this time, he had a difficult time persuading it to approve the factory councils idea. The business wing divided on it. A few employers saw that the factory councils could be useful to improve worker-management relations, but most of them fought the idea, particularly after the SPD decided that workers should be put on corporate boards, company books should be open to the councils, and councils should share in hiring and firing labor. As with the tax laws earlier, these new powers for the councils split the DDP apart.[67]

The Factory Councils Law which eventually passed could not be separated by rank-and-file Democrats from the socialization measures and taxes because they all threatened middle-class property and privileges. As a result, the DDP worked hard to slow the progress of the Factory Councils Act and to reduce the powers of the councils in areas which were normally the province of the employer. The procedural haggling, which was a part of the delaying strategy of the DDP, went on for months. When the DDP returned to the government in October, Koch-Weser argued that the best hope to modify the law would result from the DDP's presence in the government. The DDP ingeniously delayed the bill by amendments and protracted committee hearings, but the SPD and the Center party, which had the votes to approve it without the DDP, allowed only minor changes. It reached the floor of the National Assembly in mid-January 1920 after thirty days of committee hearings, a record length for hearings in Germany. The debate on the bill lasted three days, including a Sunday, which was also highly unusual. When the bill became law on 4 February 1920, the parties reached predictable conclusions about it.[68] The Independent Socialists described it as a travesty of the new industrial and social order which they had in mind. Employers, on the other hand, viewed it as a fundamental reduction of their traditional rights. Only a few naive optimists, such as Erkelenz, thought the law promised a new day in industrial relations. Although Feiler and Bernhard also greeted it with joy and saw it as a fundamental reform in economic and class relations, the Factory Councils never achieved the importance which the law and the constitutional provisions promised. The councils became advisory groups in some large factories and business establishments for a few years, but the regional councils never functioned, and the *Reichswirtschaftsrat*, at the peak of the hierarchy of councils, had only a brief and vain existence. Several Democrats, including Rathenau, Vogelstein, and Feiler, participated in its deliberation, while Max Weber refused to serve as a DDP representative. Despite the failure to translate the factory councils idea into practice in any meaningful way during the Weimar period, the movement lived on in modified form during the Nazi years and gained a new life after 1949 in the Federal Republic. For the DDP majority, the 1920 Factory Councils Law was a tactical concession forced by the need to maintain the Weimar Coalition and to apply the brakes against too rapid economic and social change. The business wing saw it as an outrageous assault on property rights, while to the left wing, it seemed to promise a new day in labor-management relations.

No party or nation had the answers for the economic and social problems between the wars. They were extremely complex, and the discipline of economics was even less developed than it is now. One is still struck, however, by the inadequacy of left-liberal solutions for these problems in the Weimar period. The DDP, after all, boasted that it was a party of brains and education. It included in its ranks several economists who were in touch with the most advanced thinking about economic and social questions as well as practical businessmen, industrialists, and bankers, many of whom were deeply involved in international trade. After the deaths of such major DDP intellectuals as Naumann, Max Weber, and Rathenau, the most innovative economic thinkers were Bernhard, Feiler, Erkelenz, and Bonn. They all believed in the need for state planning and interference in economic life. Erkelenz soon reverted to a more traditional liberal approach, although he continued to be a strong defender of unions and of a compassionate social security system. In general, they seemed to be aiming toward a corporatist system similar to those which have become common since 1945, but they were utterly incapable of influencing public policy. Only Reinhold, among the DDP political leaders, toyed with deficit financing and seemed prepared to depart from traditional liberal policies. For the most part, the Democrats supported the economic policies of the government—regardless. Their statism was more evident than their economic policies, and the possibility of another runaway inflation paralyzed thought and action.[69] This was particularly true between 1929 and 1932 when the DDP and the DStP proved unable to suggest alternatives to a deflationary fiscal policy and a protectionist trade course. Only Erkelenz argued, among DDP/DStP leaders, that it would be best to stimulate the economy through spending and by increasing purchasing power, but his suggestions were tentative and largely confined to obscure trade union publications and private correspondence. Apparently Bäumer only began to think of alternatives to the Brüning-Dietrich policies after Hitler came to power,[70] while Lüders, who had a solid grounding in economics and often popularized complex economic theories and developments in women's magazines, seemed to have no ideas of how to deal with unemployment or to stimulate the economy. Most left liberals—Dietrich, Stolper, Meyer come to mind—were traditional liberals in the mold of Herbert Hoover. The Democrats were not unmindful of the social and political consequences of unemployment, farm foreclosures, and business failures, but they seemed stultified by the scope and depth of the depression. They were, of course, not alone in their ignorance and helplessness. The SPD and democratic socialism had no viable solutions for the problem either.[71] It seems apparent that, by 1929, the wellsprings of left liberalism had dried up; liberalism was indeed obsolete. It had no answers to the principal problems of the era.

VI

The DDP and the "National Questions"
Foreign and Military Policy

The DDP, as we have seen, inherited the national traditions of 1848 as well as the liberal imperialism and moderate annexationism of the Progressive party. It demonstrated its strong nationalism early, resigning from the government rather than approving the Treaty of Versailles. The DDP's opposition to the treaty was its major concern throughout the Weimar period. Indeed, it was obsessed with the need to revise the treaty. Disproving the "war-guilt lie" was a related preoccupation. It is true that the DDP, by 1921, supported the "fulfillment" of the treaty's terms, but that was a revisionist ploy. The DDP refused to be content with a negative rejection of the hateful treaty. Instead, it sought principles which would reconcile its revisionism with self-determination and democratic values and found them in the *Grossdeutsch* tradition of 1848, the Naumann *Mitteleuropa* "solution," and a selective application of Wilsonian ideas. In its development of a military policy, the DDP showed both traditional attitudes and an adaption to realities framed by the Treaty of Versailles.

The gray-clad warriors returned to Germany as defeated heroes, and their officers were lionized in the DDP as long as they made deferential gestures toward the institutions of the Republic. Hindenburg, in particular, represented virtues and sentimental associations for which most Democrats had profound respect. Only the tiny pacifist group and those who agreed with the values of the major newspapers supporting the DDP did not share these feelings. Gessler served for over seven years as minister of defense and during this period was perhaps the most popular DDP leader, largely because of his close association with the military. Because of these nationalist sympathies, the DDP became a part of the general conspiracy to cloak the *Reichswehr*'s circumvention of the arms limitations. The DDP's support for disarmament through the League of Nations was largely a tactic to achieve military equality for Germany while most Democrats ridiculed the Kellogg-Briand Pact.

In the light of these generalizations, which shall be discussed more fully and documented below, it is difficult to understand why the *Bürger* parties and many contemporaries saw the DDP as leftist, internationalist, pacifist, or as a strong supporter of treaty fulfillment. To some extent, its *Bürger* rivals misrepresented the Democratic party in order to damage it politically. There was also a tendency to focus on the extreme left wing of the DDP even though its influence waned sharply after 1920. The problem, as in so many other areas, was the heterogeneous character of the party: it spoke with many voices on foreign and military policy. There was a vast difference between the foreign and military ideas of a Rohrbach or a Gessler and a Quidde or a Bernhard. But they were all Democrats. While there was always some diversity in the major committees and in the *Fraktion* of the Reichstag, the strong nationalist position generally prevailed. By 1930, the internationlists and pacifists had been driven from the *Staatspartei*, and the foreign policy of the party became indistinguishable from that of the DVP and the other right-of-center parties.

To illustrate the actual policies and values of the DDP in the area of foreign and military policy we will focus on selected issues and events.

Upper Silesia and the Fall of the First Wirth Government

In May 1921, the Allies announced the decision on reparations, the details of how much Germany owed, and the schedule of the payments and interest charges. This decision had been anxiously awaited for two years. The sum to be paid was $31,500,000,000, and it was on this figure that most Germans concentrated their fury. The technical arrangements for payment were largely ignored. The announcement aroused the same kind of incredulous, outraged response as had Versailles, although, in both instances, many in the DDP were forewarned. The London Agreement became the London Ultimatum in German parlance and the Fehrenbach government, which included the DDP, fell because of it. It was replaced by another government headed by a Centrist chancellor, Wirth, who invited the DDP to participate. The DDP *Fraktion* at first voted sixteen to fifteen against acceptance, but finally, agreed to join the Wirth government, for statist reasons. Gessler, Schiffer, and Rathenau accepted ministries.[1]

To undertake the burden of fulfilling the London Agreement, the government needed to find additional tax revenues.[2] The SPD and the left wing of the Center party favored severe taxes of the wealthy and especially of heavy industry, while the right-wing parties preferred taxes on consumer products and food. The DDP, charactistically, divided. A year earlier, in June 1920, the Democrats had suffered a terrible defeat, and the DVP and the DNVP had gained most of its lost supporters. The exodus of right-wing members did not, as one might expect, radicalize the party but increased the dominance of the business wing. Then, in 1921, the pressing need for additional tax revenues and the necessity to fulfill the Allies' demands confronted the DDP. While the choice between literal acceptance and outright rejection seemed simple, the Wirth government chose an alternative. In effect, the government pledged to fulfill the Allied terms as much as possible while working to reduce the demands and seeking assistance from America and Britain. At the same time, the government had to convince the German voter that fulfillment was the best road to treaty revision. The "fulfillers" contended that by seemingly fulfilling the treaty terms, including reparations payments, Germany would win support in the West and the terms would be lightened.[3] Most Democrats found this difficult to believe, even after their "party friend," Rathenau, became the most persuasive voice in favor of the policy and the tactic.[4]

The necessity to increase taxes in order to fulfill Allied demands merged with another problem in the summer and autumn of 1921: the need to accept the League of Nations' decision to divide Upper Silesia. Like reparations, this was a problem too complicated for the peacemakers to resolve at Paris. Upper Silesia was an area of mixed German and Polish populations, with each nation having legitimate historical claims. The fact that the area included a major industrial region and rich coal mines naturally increased its significance to Germany, which had already lost significant mineral deposits. In general, the industrial and urban areas were German and the rural areas largely Polish. Workers and farmers tended to be Polish, while the middle classes were German or Jewish and preferred to be governed by Germany. In view of these circumstances, the League commission had little choice but to divide the area, but most Germans were convinced that France dictated the settlement. Although an adverse judgment was expected, the result seemed far worse than most Germans had anticipated.[5] The DDP again showed its rage, but this time, rage was accompanied by a deep psychological depression; many wondered whether Germany could remain a viable state after such enormous losses.

Before the League announced the decision on Upper Silesia, the DDP had threatened to resign from the government if the decision damaged Germany severely; now, it followed through on its threat. It remains doubtful, however, whether the party resigned because of Upper Silesia or because remaining in the government meant approving a tax program which would have alienated its middle-class supporters. Perhaps both factors coalesced, but it was politic for the DDP to concentrate its fire on Upper Silesia. Even more important, the DDP leadership felt it imperative to act jointly with the DVP, fearing that acting independently might speed up the ongoing exodus to the DVP and the DNVP.

Wirth formed his second government without the DDP, but, surprisingly, Gessler remained behind in the cabinet of "trusted men." Rathenau, who held the rather unimportant Ministry of Reconstruction, was forced to step down along with Schiffer. The DDP's left wing, valuing Rathenau's ability highly, wanted Gessler, the darling of the business wing, to step down too.[6] Shortly after the formation of his second government, Wirth named Rathenau his foreign minister, but this was clearly his personal choice, not the DDP's decision. The People's party strongly opposed placing Rathenau in such a trusted position, and it used the occasion to break off negotiations for a great coalition, which the DDP consistently preferred.

The DDP's performance in this crisis of October 1921 was reminiscent of its behavior in the vote on the Treaty of Versailles. It used an issue which aroused national emotions to shield the real issue, fiscal responsibility, and deserted the only other parties closely identified with supporting the democratic Republic—the SPD and the Center party. Instead, it preferred to join with the DVP, still monarchist and controlled by its heavy industry wing. The DDP feared that if it did not join with the DVP on taxes at this juncture, it might lose more supporters. Though based on a real foreboding, the DDP's decision was a disquieting one. At a crucial stage in the Republic's history it chose to appease its business wing rather than to accept responsibility for a necessary if unpopular level of taxation.

The DDP's Eastern Policy

The DDP's policy toward eastern Europe was shaped by several factors: its attitude toward the Soviet Union and communism; its feelings about the "successor states" of East-Central Europe; its reaction to the plight of German ethnic minorities which lived scattered throughout Eastern Europe; Germany's need for trade, for raw materials and markets in the East; the *Reichswehr*'s requirements for hiding places for illegal arms and training facilities; Naumann's *Mitteleuropa* ideas; and a desire to escape from the grasp of the Allies. As a party of liberal democrats, small traders, and exporters of finished products and consumer goods, the DDP looked more to the West than to the East for friends and customers, but as the heir of Naumann's *Mitteleuropa* views, it also had an obsessive concern for the welfare of German ethnic minorities in the East. And, given Germany's economic circumstances, it could not ignore various trade possibilities with the East. The DDP found it difficult to include the Soviet Union in its conception of the European state system, and it never really accepted the importance of the "successor states." Only gradually did it grasp that the USSR might become a partner against the Versailles system. Moreover, there seemed to be a need to checkmate what was perceived as an aggressive and expansionist Poland, requiring closer cooperation with the

Soviets. The DDP also became aware of how it might use the principle of self-determination to advance German interests in Eastern Europe by exploiting the grievances of the German minorities.

In spite of the several reasons for closer ties to Eastern Europe, there were not many ardent "Easterners" in the DDP. Bernhard, who was elected to the Reichstag in 1928, was the most notable.[7] He remained true to his prewar "continentalist" foreign policy position, which emphasized close ties to France and Russia but hatred for Britain, but he had more detractors than followers in the DDP. Hellpach, whose political views were even more eccentric than Bernhard's, was also an "Easterner." He promoted the "Eastern connection" in his writings and speeches.[8] There were others who based the need for closer relations with the Soviet Union on history and economics and who believed that Germany might exploit the USSR's isolation advantageously. Bergsträsser, a historian with a penchant for current affairs who represented the DDP in the Reichstag from 1924 to 1928, wrote in 1919 that the Soviet Union could provide an "Eastern counterbalance" and strongly supported a German foreign policy which could play off East against West for Germany's advantage.[9] Haussmann urged the Foreign Office to use the Russian-Polish War in 1920 in every way that it could to advance Germany's interests in the East.[10] Rathenau also appreciated the mutual benefits of German-Soviet economic and military cooperation, while Haas, who had been stationed in Poland during the war, stressed the economic prospects in the East and made two trips to the Soviet Union to substantiate his views. Other prominent Democrats also traveled there, perhaps partially from curiosity but also to learn what advantages Germany might gain.

Much has been written about the Genoa Conference and its famous byproduct, the Treaty of Rapallo, in which Rathenau figured so prominently as foreign minister.[11] As has often been noted, it was ironic that such confirmed "Westerners" as Wirth and Rathenau should have concluded this treaty, which generally regularized relations between the Soviet Union and Germany, while stimulating additional contacts; yet they were both strong nationalists who were prepared to play the Eastern card for Germany's gain. Several months of negotiations preceded the dramatic signing of the Treaty of Rapallo, but it apparently came as a surprise to the British and French and to many well-placed Germans in the Genoa delegation as well, including Bonn and Goetz. Bonn, in particular, soon shared Rathenau's alleged second thoughts about the treaty. His misgivings included the fear that the government had overreacted to the rebuffs received at the hands of Lloyd George. Soon, however, the dominant impression in the DDP and throughout the country was that Rapallo had been a major foreign policy *coup*, the first independent action of a German statesman since the armistice. Koch reassured Rathenau in early May 1922, between the signing and the debate on the treaty in the Reichstag, that the impression made by the treaty in Berlin was entirely favorable. He anticipated that it would aid him in his district.[12] Most Democrats demonstrated delight that Germany had boxed the ears of the Entente and had ended a passive, docile role in foreign affairs.

But in the first *Parteiausschuss* meeting following the signing, two days before the debate in the Reichstag and two weeks before Rathenau was assassinated, it still seemed necessary to justify and defend the treaty. Several members expressed doubts about its wisdom.[13] Bonn felt that it might jeopardize Germany's economic recovery, a stance contradicted by Dernburg, when, speaking for the *Fraktion* in the Reichstag, he stressed its economic importance.[14] He indicated that it was a response to the hostility of the French and the Poles; Germany wanted to live in peace with its neighbors, he argued, but they would not allow it. He also deplored Lloyd George's frequent references to Germany's responsibility for the war as a deterrent to the establishment of normal relations. In a meeting of the *Vorstand* two weeks later, the Treaty of Rapallo was accepted as an accomplished fact and scarcely mentioned, but treaty revision remained a major theme.[15] One of the leading revisionist spokesmen, Gerland, who had once been on the far left of the party in the Wolff-Weber group, had moved to the right because of the national questions. Although he rejected a *Machtpolitik*, he bemoaned the German position in Europe despite the gains of Rapallo. The Poles, he pointed out, were still in Upper Silesia, the French in Alsace, the Belgians in Eupen and Malmédy, and the Italians in Bozen (the Trentino). Gerland received support when the DDP, at about the same time, showed its fiery nationalism by participating in a "protest day" against the Treaty of Versailles which stressed the terrible treatment the Rhinelanders were receiving at the hands of the occupiers.

In the years between Rapallo and the second major treaty with the Soviets, the Treaty of Berlin (1926), the DDP fully accepted the Eastern connection. The Treaty of Berlin was not even controversial, appearing as a natural complement to Germany's other treaty arrangements.[16] The anger and fear stirred by the treaty in Warsaw and Prague went unnoticed in the DDP, but then the small states of eastern Europe were seldom noticed or respected in the DDP. By 1926, German foreign policy rested in the confident hands of Stresemann, whose abilities the DDP recognized. Although routinely attributing the origins of his policies to Rathenau and Wirth and viewing him as their successor, the DDP strongly supported him and his policies. Under Stresemann, "fulfillment" with its unfortunate connotations of spinelessness and cowardice, had given way to "national *Realpolitik*," a phrase apparently coined by Stresemann and quickly adopted by the DDP.[17] Even in the left wing of the DDP, the terminology changed from "fulfillment" to "policy of understanding." Europe was still in the quietly hopeful atmosphere following Locarno, and the DDP's large urban newspapers, once highly critical of Stresemann, now praised him.

Wolff and Stresemann ended their bitter personal and political enmity. The left wing of the DDP, however, including the big newspapers, still expressed reservations about Stresemann's party and opposed any talk of a DDP-DVP merger. In general, despite recent efforts to revise the "Locarno era" image,[18] this *was* a happier time, especially if one ignored the high level of unemployment, the fragmentation of parties, and the lack of public support for democratic values and institutions. Many Democrats simply disregarded the erosion of support for the Weimar Republic reflected in the continued deterioration of the party organization.

The DDP's Western Policy

The Ruhr Invasion

When Wirth fell from office the second time, in November 1922, in a tangle of reparations and tax problems, he was succeeded as chancellor by Cuno, a Hamburg shipping executive. Cuno was not a DDP member, but he maintained close business and personal ties with the DDP.[19] Indeed, it was probably Petersen who suggested his name to President Ebert, and Petersen became a major defender of Cuno and his government. The DDP strongly supported Cuno until Stresemann replaced him as Chancellor in August 1923. The fall of the Wirth government has been studied in great detail, and the policies of the DDP and the DVP are often blamed. Although it was unlikely that the Great Coalition could have ever existed for a long period of time because of the major differences between the DVP and the SPD, the willingness of the DDP to side with the DVP on fiscal questions torpedoed the government. The DDP compounded its responsibility by attempting to blame the crisis on the French and the SPD, characteristically obfuscating the real causes of a problem to maintain party unity. According to the Democrats, the French were blindly determined to cripple Germany permanently, while the SPD was motivated by class hatred and a stubborn refusal to make any accommodations to the legitimate needs of others.

During this time, the reparations question naturally dominated every political discussion, and various solutions were suggested to resolve the problem. Germany, according to the DDP, could not pay the required sums; it needed loans to restore its economy. With restoration achieved, Germany could begin to pay the reparations bill. The Western powers, however, were not prepared to accept this solution and repeatedly warned the German government that it had to either pay reparations on time or face the consequences—invasion and occupation of areas such as the Ruhr. Throughout the autumn of 1922, the crisis brewed; yet the invasion of the Ruhr in January 1923 caught most Germans by surprise, including the DDP.[20] In the first serious discussion of the Ruhr invasion, Bernstorff, the former diplomat, took the position that Germany was fortunate that

only the French and Belgians had invaded, while Oeser, the DDP's trans-
port minister in the Cuno government, offered the vague hope that the
crisis might split the British and French. He cited the friendly support
which Viscount Edgar D'Abernon, the British ambassador, offered the
German government. The dominant note of the debate, however, was
struck by Petersen. He seemed to revel in Germany's isolation and the
return of the spirit of national unity which had prevailed in August 1914.
While Gessler and Oeser tried to quiet the DDP's fear of a possible Polish
invasion, many in the party seemed to prefer fantasy and hyperbole—
strange behavior for reasonable and moderate men and women. Articles
denouncing the French and Belgians in the most extravagant terms filled
the party's principal journals.[21] In Kehl, a left-liberal stronghold across
the Rhine from Strasbourg, the opera *William Tell* was performed while
the sense of German outrage was at its peak. When the opera ended, the
audience joined in a lusty chorus of the German national anthem "to show
their unity and hatred of the conqueror" and then took to the streets to
condemn the French as the Belgians had condemned the Dutch in the
Revolution of 1830.[22] While today scholars stress that the Ruhr invasion
isolated France, in Germany, at the time, German misery and isolation
were emphasized. Germany's tie with the Soviet Union went largely unmentioned, although we now know that it helped restrain the Poles.

Berlin's response to the Ruhr invasion—passive resistance—received
the enthusiastic support of the DDP. The long-range implications of passive resistance, including the inflationary effects of printing large quanti-
ties of paper money to aid the unemployed, were ignored. By February,
some leading Democrats unobtrusively began to question the government's policies in private correspondence. In the March 1923 meeting
of the *Parteiausschuss*, however, the general tone remained highly excited
despite Oeser's effort to provide a cool and factual analysis of the situation.[23] The meeting ended with an emotional call for freedom and
self-determination. In July, the DDP's journal, *Das demokratische
Deutschland*, changed its name to *Deutsche Einheit* (German Unity) to
memoralize the national mood, but the atmosphere had changed even before the first issue appeared under the new title. In July, some Democrats
openly criticized the failure of passive resistance and its harmful economic
and fiscal effects. Richthofen, always the realist, expressed doubts about
the government's policy, and so did Erkelenz.[24] Erkelenz argued that
French policy had failed and it was, as a result, the right moment for
Germany to launch diplomatic initatives to resolve outstanding questions
left by the Treaty of Versailles. He concluded that passive resistance, in
addition to being harmful to the German economy, had been too negative.
A more positive policy was needed.

By July, the problem of inflation, dramatically worsened by the Ruhr
invasion, rivaled the Ruhr occupation as a major issue. Democrats as in-

dividuals, as well as the party organization and its press, were devastated by the inflation.[25] As a result of the increasing worry about inflation, the president of the *Reichsbank*, Rudolf Havenstein, received sharp criticism, but he remained in office several months longer than Cuno, who was replaced by Stresemann in mid-August. Stresemann's cabinet, which included Oeser and Gessler, soon concluded that passive resistance had to end. The DDP strongly supported this conclusion. It subsequently claimed that Schacht, who replaced Havenstein, restored the value of German currency; Schacht was the "savior of the mark." When Stresemann fell at the end of November, the DDP blamed the SPD, but it applauded the decision of Wilhelm Marx, Stresemann's successor, to retain Stresemann as foreign minister.

We know now that 1924 became the year of Germany's fiscal and economic stabilization as well as the beginning of its restoration as a respected major force in Europe. For the DDP, 1924 also meant two national elections. In May, it suffered a decisive loss and came under heavy attack from the extreme right, particularly from a racist party, the German Racist Freedom party (*Deutsch-Völkische Freiheitspartei*—DVF). In November, it recovered somewhat. In both elections, foreign policy issues were highlighted, and the DDP found it difficult to defend its support of "fulfillment." It was also forced on the defensive by attacks that it was a handmaiden of socialism and of Jews. Between the elections, a number of conservative Democrats, several of them prominent leaders, defected to the DVP, muttering about "cowardly fulfillment" and excessively close ties to "Marxist betrayers of the people."[26]

The Dawes Plan

The Dawes Plan is generally viewed today as a German victory—as a way out of inflation, the Ruhr occupation, and social misery and toward bearable reparations payments, American loans, and the Treaty of Locarno.[27] The process, of course, was hardly that lineal or simple. The Dawes Plan was bitterly fought as an unprecedented interference in Germany's economic affairs, and many of the Democrats who defected in 1924 concentrated on these charges to justify their action. Those who remained in the party had to make the best of the plan, and soon the DDP's left wing and most DDP centrists hailed the Dawes Plan as the beginning of Germany's recovery. Erkelenz, for example, defended the plan as a scheme which provided Germany with opportunity to gain the economic security and investment capital it needed. He looked forward to a new period in German history when the government could concentrate on domestic problems and reforms.[28] Of the three speakers representing the DDP in the debate on the Dawes Plan, only Schiffer, who soon left the party, appeared guarded and pessimistic about it.[29] Most active Democrats, alarmed by the abusive attacks of the extreme right in the May election, wanted to minimize internal differences preceding the November election. This cautionary spirit probably also contributed to the defectors' failure to lure many Democrats to accompany them. In a special meeting of the Party Congress in November in Berlin, Koch, with his knack for expressing the mood of the majority, represented the Dawes Plan as the beginning of a fundamental change in Germany's position.[30] As he saw it, Germany had surmounted a great divide and could look forward to better prospects. The need to defend the party against its partisan enemies engendered some of this optimism, but there seemed to be a sincere recognition that Germany had indeed turned a corner and better things lay ahead—for Germany as well as for the DDP.

Locarno

The diplomacy behind the agreements which come under the rubric "Locarno" is beyond the scope of this book.[31] I am primarily interested in the DDP's position and in the part it played in gaining support for the treaties. In addition, I want to demonstrate how the Locarno agreements spurred additional demands for treaty revision.

The Rhineland Pact, a key provision which asked Germany to accept freely the western territorial sacrifices made in the Treaty of Versailles, shocked few Democrats still active in 1925. Most had already mentally relinquished Alsace-Lorraine and Eupen-Malmédy, although the DDP voiced the usual regrets for the record. In 1919, most Democrats would have found it outrageous to accept the Rhineland Pact; in 1925, it appeared inevitable. With the departure of Gerland and Alexander Dominicus, both of whom had strong emotional and personal ties to Alsace, there was only slight resistance. Rohrbach and Müller-Meiningen denounced the agreement, but the leadership ignored their opposition. The fact that the DVP as well as some members of the DNVP favored Locarno eased the situation for the Democrats, as did the central importance of Stresemann in the negotiations. Thus, the party did not have to look constantly over its shoulder to ward off blows from its *Bürger* party rivals; moreover, the DDP press did an outstanding job of "selling" Locarno to the public, which Stresemann greatly appreciated. Most Democrats perceived from the beginning that the Rhineland Pact secured Germany against future French incursions. There also seemed little doubt that Locarno might further a more aggressive revisionist stance in the East. The Democrats approved Stresemann's refusal to even discuss an "Eastern Locarno" and immediately noted the British position, which apparently approved revision by negotiation. Koch-Weser, in his Reichstag speech supporting Locarno, indicated that for Locarno to have any political value it must lead to a revision of the Treaty of Versailles.[32] Shortly afterwards, at the Party Congress in Breslau, the eastern revisionist theme dominated the meeting.[33] Although these meetings always included spokesmen from German communities in Eastern Europe, the Breslau PT featured them. Delegates representing Memel, the South Tyrol, Austria, Danzig, the Saar, and the Sudetenland attended. Elisabeth Brönner-Höpfner, a DDP deputy in the National Assembly, self-consciously representing the "lost province of Memel," reassured the delegates that, while Memel had been betrayed, it was and would remain German.[34] German parents, she contended, still raised their children as Germans and would continue to do so. Probably the most repeated phrase at this meeting with respect to former German territories was: "It is German and will remain German." The "tragic fate" of the South Tyrol was also a prominent subject at this PT.

Although nothing came of this wishful thinking about treaty revision in the East during the immediate post-Locarno period, the years 1925–1929 proved to be relatively prosperous and stable. The DDP's leaders now had more time and money to travel and to take long holidays in the exclusive spas of Europe. Even Erkelenz, who had little money, found sponsors to enable him to travel to America and Poland and other nations. The party's rank and file, now largely urban middle-class men and women, were also more affluent. The greater prosperity and the post-Locarno atmosphere in international relations produced more optimism than Germany had known in a decade. Many in the DDP became excited about the famous meeting of Stresemann and Briand at Thoiry in 1926, and Germany's admission to the League of Nations seemed a favorable sign. The hopes that Thoiry presaged a general settlement of outstanding issues between Germany and France or that League membership might lead to treaty revision were, in time, disappointed, but the optimists could always find something to cheer about. For example, a series of bilateral trade treaties at this time, including one with France, appeared most promising. There were also numerous meetings between European parliamentarians, which produced a comforting if misleading feeling of understanding and comradeship among the "democratic forces." The German Right frowned on such gatherings, especially when Germany's delegates went to Paris for a meeting and spoke French! Bäumer was attacked by a female German Nationalist because of her participation in this meeting. The DDP's internationalists, including recent converts such as Bäumer, bravely faced this rightist criticism and defended their work for international understanding and peace. They never tired of repeating that treaty revision would come after trust and understanding had been achieved between Germany, France, and Britain. Erkelenz was especially active in promoting close relations with British Liberals, including several pacifists. He also used *Die Hilfe* to develop better relations with France and Poland. The British, in particular, were prepared to forgive and forget, although the French remained determined to enforce the treaty and the British government proved unprepared to abandon France. Gradually, it also became apparent that the DDP gained little from Streseman's successes, in large part because the German public refused to recognize the benefits of his diplomacy for Germany, and, by 1927, a more insistent revisionist campaign began to demand a reduction in reparations payments and the end of the Rhineland occupation.

Other Foreign Policy Questions

Anschluss

There were few issues on which there was more agreement in the DDP than on the need to join "German Austria" to the Reich. Most DDP policy statements and electoral pronouncements called for *Anschluss*, and Democrats agreed that it was necessary for the survival of both countries. From the formation of the party until Hitler's coming to power, the DDP never stopped working for this objective; no party identified itself more closely with *Grossdeutsche* foreign policy goals than the DDP.[35] As early as November 1918, the DDP cultivated close relations with Austria's Left-Liberal party in order to forward *Anschluss*. Many of the most ardent supporters of *Anschluss* were supporters of Naumann's *Mitteleuropa* vision during the war. Although the German and Austrian governments necessarily adopted a discreet position on *Anschluss*, the Democrats, as individuals, acted as leading propagandists for it. Nearly all the DDP's leaders participated prominently in associations which advocated union with Austria. Many also had business or personal connections to Austria. In general, the Democrats saw the *Anschluss* movement as an attempt to complete the work of the men of '48, and they justified it on the grounds of self-determination and economic necessity. *Anschluss*, however, was never seen as an end in itself, but only as part of a larger plan for Germany's expansion.

The most active Democrats in the *Anschluss* crusade included former Naumannites such as Heile, Bäumer, Heuss, and Jäckh. Stolper, who had been active in the Austrian Left-Liberal party, bridged the two parties and the two countries and forcefully advocated *Anschluss*. Heuss, a close friend of Stolper's, was also a major figure in the pro-*Anschluss* agitation. Although *Anschluss* languished for a number of years, it gained new life under Brüning when he and his foreign minister, Julius Curtius, a member of the DVP, attempted to secure an Austro-German customs union.[36] The *Staatspartei*, as we shall see below, strongly backed this initiative.

Auslandsdeutsche

At the first party congress, Naumann had emphasized that *Grossdeutsche* ideas had to be kept alive and ties maintained with "our brothers."[37] His followers eagerly accepted this charge, often using the same emotional language which Naumann employed. "The isolation of East Prussia and the cutting off of Upper Silesia have left bloody wounds on the body of a maimed Germany," wrote Koch-Weser.[38] He described the loss of Eupen-Malmédy and the German colonies as "unmitigated robbery." The DDP claimed that no German party was more concerned about the *Auslandsdeutsche* than it was, an assertion validated by much evidence.[39] Most party leaders belonged to associations whose chief purpose was to promote German feelings and ties among German ethnic communities abroad; some of these organizations employed extreme nationalist and racist propaganda not too far removed from Nazi agitation. Other groups, such as the American-based Carl Schurz organization, in which Erkelenz was deeply involved, were moderate, confining their work largely to German cultural activities and exchange programs. One can see diverse motives in the work of DDP members on behalf of ethnic Germans living abroad. Some were concerned to protect them from hostile ethnic majorities; others had economic motives such as promoting German exports or business ties with German communities. Many were simply curious about the life of Germans outside the Reich. Sometimes this fascination acquired racist characteristics. The literature about the *Auslandsdeutsche* frequently expresses a sense of regret that these good Germans, through no fault of their own, had been forced to leave Germany and to live outside it and would never be fulfilled until they became truly German, living under a German flag.

In the twenties, the DDP stressed the rights of self-determination of nations. This was ironic, given the indifference of left liberals to such questions before 1919. Self-determination was used to justify retaining "lost territories" and even, as in the case of the Sudetenland and the Trentino, to support the annexation of territories which had never been in the German Empire (1871–1918). While the DDP handled these questions with greater delicacy and circumspection that did the extreme Right, the polite language could not camouflage the DDP's ultimate intentions. Wherever possible, the Democrats wanted German minorities living abroad to be reunited with the Reich. Koch-Weser declared in 1924 that "there is and will be an *Irredenta* until there is a union of true Germans with the Motherland," while Heuss, an officer in the *Bund der Auslandsdeutschen*, declared, with reference to the ethnic Germans of the South Tyrol, that they had God-given and human rights which could only be expressed by political institutions that represented their political cultural individuality.[40] After Germany joined the League of Nations in 1926, the DDP worked within the League to improve the conditions of German minorities. Koch-Weser was particularly active in this work. Indeed, the DDP saw the League chiefly as an organization in which Germany could work to improve the conditions of German minorities; it showed indifference to other minority grievances.

Other Eastern Goals

While *Anschluss* and the condition of German minorities in the East
were the DDP's most important concerns, other foreign policy subjects
vied for attention. Danzig, the Polish boundaries with Germany, and Upper Silesia continued to be vital interests to most Democrats. The Sudetenland was of less importance, and there seemed to be little interest in the
Baltic states or Romania and Yugoslavia except for the travel supplements
to illustrated papers close to the DDP. One suspects that the DDP's concern for the German minority in Italy combined a desire to embarrass the
NSDAP, which pointedly omitted this German minority from consideration in order to appease Mussolini, with a show of sympathy with all
ethnic Germans living under foreign rule. More significantly, the DDP
never accepted the finality of Germany's eastern boundaries and waged
steady propaganda against the Polish Corridor and the status of Danzig.
Erkelenz seems to have been the only DDP leader who showed any objectivity toward Poland. The decision on Upper Silesia continued to rankle
Democrats, although, in fact, the cooperation achieved between Poland
and Germany after 1921 was a pleasant surprise to those, such as Schiffer,
familiar with the work of the Polish-German Commission. German industrialists continued to exploit the coal resources, and large numbers of Germans lived on in Upper Silesia; yet the DDP seemed to be unwilling to
accept this accommodation. A similar situation existed in Danzig, where
Polish economic and port development made the old port of Danzig irrelevant while emigration and better understanding between Germans and
Poles eased the friction between them. Most Democrats, however, ignored
the progress made to secure the Germans in Danzig and continued to agi-
tate for the return of former German territory. The DDP made exceptions
only for districts where the predominance of the Polish populations was
overwhelming.

After the September election of 1930, the *Bürger* parties and the
NSDAP confronted the Brüning government with strident demands for
treaty revision in the East. Curtius and Bernhard W. von Bülow, once an
active Young Democrat and now a prominent official in the Foreign Office,
adopted a more aggressive tone toward Poland and Czechoslovakia and
attempted to develop new tactics to force a faster revisionist pace.[41] The
desire for an Austro-German customs union was only a part of their plan.
The *Staattspartei* applauded these moves and responded with fury when
France blocked the customs union. The DStP was represented in the cabinet by Dietrich, the unchallenged leader of the party after Koch-Weser
was forced to resign his Reichstag seat and to give up his party positions.
Dietrich's nationalist credentials were impeccable, and his speeches in
these years often stressed foreign policy goals. He favored such terms as
living necessity (*Lebensnotwendigkeit*), a term sounding rather like the

Nazi cry for *Lebensraum*, which Bäumer, among others in the DStP, embraced as a particularly apt term after the Nazis came to power.[42]

The Young Plan and the Freeing of the Rhineland

The reduction of reparations payments and the achievement of greater security against France, attained in the Dawes Plan and the Locarno agreements, actually stimulated German demands for more concessions. Stresemann's pressuring of Belgium for territorial concessions was a part of this development.[43] In addition, Germany wanted a reduction in reparations payments and a termination of the military occupation of the Rhineland. Stresemann worked quietly but forcefully along these lines after 1925, never relaxing the pressure on the British, French, and Belgians. He always asked for more than he could reasonably expect to get. Then, on 17 September 1928, Stresemann finally achieved a breakthrough in the form of an adjustment in the reparations payments and a subsequent Allied pledge to remove the occupation forces. After months of difficult negotiations, this agreement became the Young Plan. Once again, as in the case of the Treaty of Locarno, to non-Germans it seemed a German triumph, but the right-wing parties bitterly opposed it, and the DNVP and the NSDAP forced a national referendum. It met defeat, but the alliance of right-wing forces at this time was an ominous sign, and so were the indications of a deepening depression throughout the country. The liberation of the Rhineland—the termination of military occupation—represented the only happy moment of the period. It was a deliriously joyous occasion for the German Democrats, a time of thanksgiving and celebration.[44]

The DDP viewed the Young Plan with considerble coolness, and prominent figures in the party, including Dietrich, at first opposed it. The frenzied rightist assault on it, however, forced most Democrats to come around. In order to defend the Republic against its enemies, they were compelled to favor the Young Plan. Dernburg, speaking for the DDP in the Reichstag, caught the mood of most Democrats: "We have no enthusiasm for this treaty. We march to muffled drum beats on the way because we must."[45] While a few efforts were made to depict it as the culmination of a succession of republican foreign policy successes, the only thing the DDP could cheer about was the "freeing of the Rhineland." Several Democratic party orators addressed patriotic rallies at the time, but Adolf Korell, a Lutheran pastor from Rhine-Hesse who specialized in patriotic bombast, received the most publicity. He had been an early follower of Naumann, known for his long benedictions at party gatherings and for his defense of the local wine industry in the Reichstag.[46] He was a stormy, temperamental figure who had gained a measure of fame in the party in 1923 when he defied the French occupation and was briefly jailed. His most publicized moment in the Reichstag came when he physically defended a colleague, Alfred Brodauf, a pugnacious and conservative jurist, from an assault by an angry Communist deputy who attacked Brodauf with a newspaper holder. Korell, a decorated war hero, became the *Fraktion*'s champion for the moment, and, years later, *Fraktion* members recalled his action with great pride. He later broke with the party on its support for a trade treaty with Spain and lost his mandate, but the DDP applauded his patriotic harangues in the summer of 1930 and joined the thousands listening to his speeches.

The evacuation of the Rhineland by the Allied forces stimulated a surge of new demands for the repudiation of the Treaty of Versailles altogether, and the DStP competed with other *Bürger* parties, now under pressure from the Nazi successes, to demand the dismantling of the peace settlement.

Colonial Questions

The DDP/DStP included a number of men with extensive colonial experience. Dernburg and Solf were former colonial ministers, while Wilhelm Külz served as a colonial official in Southwest Africa. Several Democrats belonged to various colonial associations. Külz, in particular, played an active part in them and often addressed them,[47] while Rohrbach, Hamm, Dietrich, and Schacht supported organizations which desired a return of the colonies. In the late twenties, Schacht became the most publicized advocate of this cause. The Bavarian branch of the DDP, always more belligerently nationalistic than the national party, became closely identified with the colonial cause. Perhaps it was the DDP in Bavaria which was responsible for inducing the *Löwenbräu* brewery to turn out millions of beer coasters with slogans supporting German colonial aspirations or which placed the funeral wraths at the *Feldherrnhalle* which carried the words, "the colonies."[48] The DDP always responded angrily to the charge of the Entente states that Germany had been a bad colonial master, and while it conceded that there had been some dark chapters in the colonial administration, it insisted that the abuses had been remedied before the war and hardly justified the "theft" of the German colonies. In fact, it contended, the German record was as good if not better than that of the Entente. In its desire to regain the colonies, the DDP remained, of course, completely blind to the extension of the principle of self-determination to Africans and Asians. Moreover, the DDP proved unable to establish any rational or cogent arguments to justify regaining territories which had previously been of little economic or strategic importance.

The DDP and the League of Nations and Pan-Europe Plans

The idea of a league of nations had had supporters in Germany even before the end of the war. Erzberger, the Centrist leader, wrote a book in support of the league-of-nations idea, while Bernstorff, Schücking, and other members of the DDP pacifist group strongly backed the league idea. After the formation of the League of Nations by the peacemakers at Paris,

133

however, enthusiasm for the League waned in the DDP. The part played by the League in the Upper Silesian decision, the Saar, and Danzig, as well as in the various plebiscite votes, discredited it, making the League seem a French puppet. Only the pacifists and the internationalists in the DDP continued to believe that it represented the best hope for disarmament and a lasting peace. In 1925–1926, when Stresemann coupled German entrance into the League with the Locarno agreements, interest in it increased, but the DDP continued to have a limited view of the League's potential. It was seen primarily as an instrument to secure treaty revision and better protection for German minorities in eastern Europe.[49] Most Democrats found it difficult to rise above traditional nationalist values and to embrace internationalist ideals, and even strong republicans such as Haas and Heuss remained cool to the League of Nations. Erkelenz, Lüders, and Schücking, on the other hand, strongly supported its work. Perhaps the most surprising convert to internationalism was Heile, a fiery nationalist during and immediately after the war, who turned his back on Naumann's narrow nationalism and embraced a variety of internationalist causes. He contended that his internationalism had evolved out of Naumann's *Mitteleuropa* work, but Naumann would not have recognized Heile's orientation by the mid-twenties. Bäumer and Koch-Weser also became identified with League work. Bäumer resumed her pre-war activity in international women's organizations and social programs which the League sponsored, while Koch-Weser labored in the League of Nations' Minorities Commission. Most Democrats, however, seemed wary of the League or any kind of international organization. This distrust was especially marked toward the Pan-Europe movement of Count Richard Coudenhove-Kalergi, which, for a time, Briand allegedly supported. Koch-Weser attended Pan-Europe meetings, but his commitment to the organization was not great. Heile's Society for European Understanding (the Verband für Europäische Verständigung) was another version of Pan-Europe, which included Britain and Russia. It was not much more popular than Coudenhove's scheme in the DDP, although Heile worked assiduously among Democrats to propagate his views and to raise money for the organization. He also repeatedly denigrated Coudenhove's ideas. The Inter-Parliamentary Union, a harmless and largely social gathering of European parliamentarians which met in various European capitals, gained more support in the DDP than Pan-Europe ideas. Lüders and Schücking attended its meetings regularly. Several Democrats also worked in the international Liberal Society, which involved joint meetings with the British Liberal party and the French Radical Socialists, as well as other European liberal parties. There was also a Young Liberal international. It seems clear, however, that the DDP felt only a minor commitment to internationalism; it remained a party of conventional nationalists.

The Military Question

Hawks, Pacifists, and Doves

It is difficult to identify any DDP "hawks" or militarists, with the possible exception of Külz, during the years of the Republic. The military had no enthusiastic supporters in the DDP; the *Reichswehr* was even less congenial than the prewar army. The "pacifist faction," by contrast, was easy to identify because of its professional associations and because its values were openly espoused. However, the term "pacifist" was used in an ambiguous manner. Some right-wing Democrats labeled anyone who supported international understanding or cooperation a "pacifist." Gothein, for example, who had once been branded a pacifist himself, identifies Haas as a pacifist.[50] Haas was occasionally critical of the *Reichswehr* and favored conciliating France, but he was not a pacifist as that term was generally employed in the interwar period. Prominent boosters of the League of Nations, such as Bernstorff, were also called pacifists, and so was Rathenau, whose efforts to achieve agreements with France were undertaken to promote Germany's economic recovery. To reduce the confusion over the use of "pacifist," the DDP differentiated them into two groups: the "radical pacifists" and the "healthy pacifists." The radicals were led by Fredrich Wilhelm Foerster and submitted their ideas to the journal *Die Menschheit*. Foerster himself was not a Democrat, lived in Paris, and had few friends or followers in the DDP. Quidde, a "healthy pacifist" in the opinion of most Democrats, refused to turn his back on Foerster, corresponding with him and occasionally publishing in his journal. Heile, though corresponding with Foerster, did not share his views. Only two Democrats in the late twenties were usually singled out as "radical pacifists": the retired General Paul Freiherr von Schoenaich and Lüth.[51] Additionally, there was the former Democrat Hellmuth von Gerlach, who still had many friends in the left wing of the party.[52] The principal distinction between the two groups of pacifists was how each viewed certain "national questions." Both groups rejected war and violence and deprecated armed forces and the military, but the "radical pacifists" rejected patriotism as well. The "healthy pacifists" were not only patriotic but more moderate in temperament. They wanted peace and international understanding and deplored war as a solution, but they loved their country. Quidde, for example, made one of the great speeches which denounced the Versailles treaty in 1919 and refused to accept it. There were several other prominent examples of "healthy pacifists" in the DDP: General Berthold von Deimling,[53] Kessler, and Illa Uth, whose pacifism apparently resulted from her profound distrust of the *Reichswehr* and its leadership.

The "doves" and internationalists were often close to the "healthy pacifists" and sometimes cooperated with them. Many individuals in the DDP could be placed in this group. While they did not abjure war as an instrument of national policy and would have fought in defense of their country, they were horrified at the thought of another war and deeply suspicious of the military services in all countries. They saw armies as a cause of war rather than as a means to prevent war. The internationalists supported international organizations whose purpose was to prevent war and worked for peace through a variety of professional and political associations. They included prominent journalists such as Wolff, Bernhard, Nuschke, and Cohnstaedt and party leaders Erkelenz, Luppe, Ulich-Beil[54] and Heile. Dernburg might also be included in this group, and many contemporaries would have counted Bäumer, Heuss, and Koch-Weser as well, although they appear, in retrospect, to have been strong nationalists. The political right often derided the *Hochschule für Politik* as a den of internationalists, partially because it received support from the Carnegie Foundation, but its leading members remained ardent nationalists. Heuss, at least, was not only a strong nationalist but an apologist for the military and for his friend Gessler.[55]

In the debates on foreign policy and military questions in the major committees of the DDP and at the Democratic Club in Berlin, the hawks, pacifists, and doves made characteristic contributions. Sometimes the lines between them blurred. Generally, the party leaders attempted to avoid those votes which would be so divisive that their results would be difficult to repair, but it could not prevent the airing of differences. In 1924, when the party came under heavy attack from the right because of its alleged pacifism, the leaders responded by demonstrating their patriotism and support of a strong revisionist foreign policy. At the same time, the party's pacifists were relegated to low list positions and suffered heavy attacks in party meetings. Deimling, for example, a moderate and level-headed person, was relegated to a low list position despite the strong backing of Wolff and Erkelenz. Echoes of party strife in the 1924 elections continued to be heard early in 1925, and in February, a passionate debate took place in the Democratic Club on the "pacifist issue." Rohrbach precipitated it by attacking Quidde and lumping him with the radical pacifists who opposed *Anschluss* and favored exposing Germany's evasions of the military provisions of the treaty. Rohrbach wanted the DDP to stress national goals and to purge all party members who might sully that image. To achieve this, he attempted to remove Quidde from the party committees of which he was a member. His campaign against the pacifists failed, however, although he renewed the attempt in January 1926 when he once more attempted to have Quidde expelled from the party. After his second failure, Rohrbach resigned from the DDP. In 1927, Erkelenz reopened the "pacifist issue" by reprinting an article from *Die Menschheit* in *Die Hilfe* which documented the aspirations of some *Reichswehr* leaders to circumvent the treaty restrictions.[56] Erkelenz was immediately attacked by the

DDP's right wing. He was called an honorary member of Foerster's circle and his patriotism was questioned. Despite the absurdity of the charge, Koch-Weser, at odds with Erkelenz on several other issues, attacked him sharply. At the same time, Koch-Weser accepted Gessler's assurances that the document was false and the officers loyal. Meanwhile, the Nobel Committee announced that it had awarded the Peace Prize to Quidde. The DDP's leaders at first seemed reluctant to admit that he was a Democrat and it was only belatedly, with leftists like Cohnstaedt applying the pressure, that Quidde was commended by the party for his fight against the Treaty of Versailles and the radical pacifists![57] When, somewhat later, Schoenaich attacked Gessler and revealed additional details about the *Reichswehr*'s transgressions, he was met by such a storm of abuse in the party that he soon resigned. In his statement explaining the reasons for his resignation Schoenaich indicated that the DDP's leadership was hostile to peace work. Surprisingly, the individuals he named as most opposed to his work were not extreme rightists but Bäumer, Koch-Weser, and Bernstorff. In 1930, Quidde and Lüth again were attacked, and Lüth was forced out of the DDP, the victim of a concerted drive led by Stephan, who sometimes served as Koch-Weser's hatchet man.[58] The DStP made all pacifists and internationalists unwelcome, and Quidde founded an alternative democratic party. The internationalists either joined with him or the SPD. Although the DDP majority had never been comfortable with pacifism or internationalism, the DStP was intolerant toward both. In the DStP, national loyalties triumphed over individual opinion. So much for freedom of the individual and intellectual freedom, the heart of liberalism.

The DDP and the Military Services

The DDP proved ambivalent from the beginning toward the *Reichswehr* and the navy.[59] For statist and patriotic reasons, it wanted to support the armed forces, but it retained the old left-liberal prejudice against the professional military man. It also disliked the type of professional army and navy which the treaty had compelled Germany to adopt, preferring a conscript military force and a small corps of professional officers and noncommissioned officers. A few members initially favored a Swiss-style militia. When it became apparent that the professional army decreed by the peacemakers could not be altered, the DDP sought to democratize and republicanize the military, while at the same time placing the military forces outside politics. Many of the Democrats' fears were erased when their party friend Gessler became the defense minister following the Kapp *Putsch*. A small faction on the left wing, however, remained suspicious of the military and of Gessler. The pacifist group, the big city newspapers, and several individuals—Tantzen, Erkelenz, Luppe, and Bruno Hauff, a *Reichsbanner* activist—had the courage and the convictions to continue to expose the mistakes and shortcomings of the military. The party majority, however, was content to pass innocuous resolutions which, in essence, called on the military to reform itself. When the press or Erkelenz or the SPD revealed the transgressions of the *Reichswehr*, most active Democrats responded with anger and resentment.[60] The party leadership, with the exception of Erkelenz, tended to wink at the lies and deception of the military and allowed Gessler to deceive the party, although, on occasion, Koch-Weser became angry when Gessler's lies became too blatant.[61]

Before the war, few active left liberals had any military experience beyond the required year or two of active service and occasional short periods as reserve officers. There were no professional military men in the liberal parties, and the government prevented Reichstag deputies from gaining any sensitive information or significant experience in military affairs. By the twenties, however, there were many front-line veterans in the party's leadership who approached military questions from a different perspective. Although they did not lionize the officer corps, they realized how impractical and naive it was to think of German army development proceeding along the lines of the Swiss militia. They also had a less stereotyped picture of the professional military man. The veterans did not constitute a subgroup in the party or a lobby for a particular military policy, and they seldom publicized their military records or specialized knowledge. The two most prominent former officers, Deimling and Schoenaich, were pacifists. Only a few Democrats attempted to use their military service to forward their political careers, and the DDP did not conspicuously support veterans benefits or increases in the *Reichswehr*'s budget. There were a few leaders, however, whose military records became known to the general public. Lemmer, the leader of the Hirsch-Duncker unions and the *Gewerkschaftsring*, continually reminded his audiences of his youth and his front-line fighting record. He had volunteered at sixteen and served with distinction and became active in the paramilitary *Reichsbanner* after its founding in 1924. Külz, an infantry company and then battalion commander for four years on the western front, had his war record publicized when the French accused him of being a war criminal. A French court convicted him in 1924 but, needless to say, the German government did not deliver him to the French, and he never admitted or denied the charges. Haas's accomplishments in the army became known largely because Jewish organizations used them to demonstrate the falsity of the rightist charges that the Jews were shirkers during the war. Personally, Haas was modest about his war record, but the Jewish community made him into a war hero.[62] Goetz, Erkelenz, Stephan, Korell, and dozens of other DDP leaders also served in combat during the war, but, in most instances, the experience had little effect on their political careers.

Haas personified the DDP's contradictory feelings toward the military. He had performed his required military service around 1890 but became disillusioned by the anti-Semitism which he encountered in the army. He could not win a reserve officer's commission and was even denied the insignia of a noncommissioned officer's rank, because he was a Jew. Though a middle-aged Reichstag deputy when the war broke out, he felt the need to demonstrate his patriotism—and the patriotism of German Jews. He volunteered and served with distinction in combat on the western front in 1914–1915, winning several military decorations and a commission before being transferred to Poland as a "Jewish expert" in the effort to convince Polish Jews to support Germany's plans for Poland. He returned to the Reichstag before the war ended and went on, as we have seen, to become a popular and moderate Democrat and an ardent republican. A leader of both the *Reichsbanner* and the *Republikanische Union*, he wrote frequently in its weekly publication, the *Deutsche Republik*, and in the BT. In foreign affairs, he had been one of the strongest opponents of the Treaty of Versailles, but he favored the policy of fulfillment and worked toward reconciliation with France. Although Haas generally supported the *Reichswehr* against irresponsible attacks, he wanted it to become a loyal republican institution. When Gessler resigned as defense minister early in 1928, Haas spoke for the DDP in a characteristic manner,[63] commending Gessler for his good intentions but stressing how far short he had fallen from the goals he had set to democratize and republicanize the *Reichswehr*. It should not be surprising that the SPD saw Haas as an apologist for the military while the Right denigrated him as a pacifist and a Jew and often interrupted his speeches in the Reichstag with anti-Semitic interjections. He also had enemies in the right wing of the DDP and, in 1924, in the face of the surge of radical anti-Semitism of that year, he was lowered on the *Reichslist* and an effort was made to remove him from the Reichstag.[64] Koch-Weser, rather belatedly and lamely, came to his defense, maintaining that Haas was reliable on the national questions; but these incidents must have sickened Haas.

Otto Gessler and the DDP

Gessler was the Democrat most prominently identified with military questions in the twenties.[65] A Bavarian and a nominal Catholic who was elected to the National Assembly while he was serving as the mayor of Nürnberg, he claimed to be a follower of Naumann. Deeply conservative, he never disguised his monarchical sympathies; he always preferred to use the term "Fatherland" to "Republic" when speaking of the government. This was no particular handicap among most Democrats, and it won him respect in the *Reichswehr* and among rightist parties. Indeed, in time, he enjoyed more support from the Center party than the DDP and also had many friends in the DVP. He was a member of every government from October 1919 until early in 1928, first as minister of reconstruction and then as defense minister. There were those, including General Hans von Seeckt, who supported Haas for defense minister in 1920, but Haas had few illusions about how a Jew would be able to function as defense minister.[66] In 1920, Gessler seemed an admirable choice, but little was really known about his political values and temperament. In the years which followed, he abandoned the effort to reform the *Reichswehr*—despite much reform talk—and became a willing tool of the army. He made only cosmetic alterations. In fact, he spent much of his time as defense minister serving as a shield for the army and navy, fending off hostile questions with skill and humor. He was masterful in handling his "party friends," who were only too willing to accept his assurances about the loyalty of the *Reichswehr*.[67] The party regarded him as one of its greatest assets, and he was in great demand during election campaigns as a speaker. During the period 1925–1927, however, he became less and less believable to more and more Democrats, and many finally realized that he had deceived them all along. He resigned from the *Fraktion* in January 1927, a year before he stepped down as defense minister. Gessler was not a dupe but a willing partner of the *Reichswehr* leaders. He shared their nationalist and statist values and their determination to evade the treaty, as did his close friends in the DDP.[68] The DDP's left wing saw Gessler as a conservative nationalist early in his career and grumbled for years about his failure to democratize and to republicanize the army. Wolff, Preuss, Tantzen, Grossmann, and the FZ regularly attacked him in the press and in party meetings, much to the dismay of most of the party leaders and the rank-and-file Democrats, who were grateful that he retained his formal tie to the party as long as he did. After he resigned under fire, the party overlooked his mistakes and eulogized him.

There were a few instances in which the DDP's actions conformed to its rhetoric on reforming and democratizing the *Reichswehr*. The support which some army units gave the Kapp *Putsch* produced a widespread hostile reaction to the army in the DDP, but fears of communism and hostility to the general strike called by the trade unions checked their determination to bring the army to heel. In 1923, at a time when the *Reichswehr* had to deal with attempts, from both sides of the political spectrum, to overthrow the government, the DDP believed that the army was completely even-handed in dealing with the extremes, a judgment few historians would share. It seems clear now that the *Reichswehr* dealt much more firmly with the Communists. Between 1923 and 1925, fewer military questions seemed to be of concern to the Reichstag or the general public, but late in 1925, the first of a number of disturbing reports about the *Reichswehr* and its leadership surfaced, raising doubts about Gessler's loyalty to the Republic. Emil Ludwig, the author, disclosed a conversation he had had with Luppe, in which Luppe revealed details of Gessler's monarchical sympathies and his close ties to the Bavarian royal family.[69] About the same time English and French newspapers reported a number of instances of German evasions of the size limitations on the *Reichswehr*, and French leader

Edouard Herriot attacked these evasions, particularly the existence of the so-called "black *Reichswehr*," in several speeches.[70] There had been reports of secret formations drilling in remote locations in Germany since 1923, and several prominent Democrats, including Koch-Weser, had received reports from friends and relatives about these evasions of the treaty. There were also published reports at this time of growing links between the *Reichswehr* and various extreme rightist groups. The DDP's press tied these various strands together to produce a picture of a conspiracy of alarming proportions. Then, in the fall of 1926, the son of the German crown prince reviewed some army units and Seeckt admitted that he had permitted this.[71] Seeckt, who had become a *Bürger* hero for his part in building the *Reichswehr*, was forced to resign and, for a time, Gessler enjoyed a reprieve from leftist criticism. It seemed that the civilian minister of defense was in charge after all. Then, in December 1926, while Stresemann labored in Geneva trying to reduce the treaty constraints on Germany, the *Manchester Guardian* published details about the *Reichswehr*'s activities in the Soviet Union from information apparently supplied by dissident Communists. *Vorwärts*, the principal SPD newspaper, republished this material, and Scheidemann made a sensational speech in the Reichstag in which he called upon the government to resign. The motion failed, but it had a surprising outcome: Scheidemann's action embarrassed the SPD and the DDP was furious. Koch-Weser, who believed that it was morally responsible to evade the Treaty of Versailles,[72] regarded Scheidemann as a traitor for revealing *Reichswehr* secrets. Nevertheless, he concluded that the *Reichswehr* needed a firmer hand, that Gessler's attempts to deny the existence of the "black *Reichswehr*" were unconvincing and mistaken, and that because of these shortcomings he should resign. Soon afterwards a scandal in the navy, the so-called *Phöbus* affair, not only implicated Gessler, but Koch-Weser and Reinhold, the DDP finance minister, as well. Gessler finally resigned, but Koch-Weser and Reinhold escaped any serious repercussions from the affair.[73]

The *Phöbus* affair overlapped with an internal DDP crisis which resulted from Erkelenz's publication in *Die Hilfe* of some documents previously published in *Die Menschheit*.[74] The documents were the texts of two lectures allegedly given by *Reichswehr* officers who described plans to reorganize the army, increase German army reserve strength, improve its offensive capabilities, and even test the will of the Allies to halt overt violations of the treaty. Gessler at first branded the documents false and joined the DDP's right wing in denouncing Erkelenz. Erkelenz defended his action by contending that the documents had already been published abroad as well as in *Die Menschheit* but had been misrepresented in the German press. He felt obliged to set the record right by publishing the documents, which, despite Gessler's disclaimer, he believed to be authentic. Erkelenz was correct, as it turned out, and Gessler had to admit that the documents were obtained by espionage, but Koch-Weser continued to censure Erkelenz. Erkelenz, however, refused to back down. How, he asked Koch-Weser, does Gessler have the nerve to denounce us for "lying" when he has been lying to us for years? And, he asked, is Gessler a liar, a dupe, or just a simpleton? Erkelenz also resented the imputations made at the time in the DDP's right wing that he was unpatriotic. As a front-line soldier for three years, he did not think his patriotism should be questioned. In the face of Erkelenz's firmness and righteous anger, Koch-Weser retreated somewhat but advised him to be more tactful in the future in his criticism of the *Reichswehr*.

When Gessler resigned in January 1928, he was replaced by the retired General Wilhelm Groener, Ludendorff's successor as quartermaster general, who was socially friendly with several right-wing Democrats such as Schiffer and Meinecke. Groener enjoyed a good reputation in the DDP as an officer who had behaved wisely and responsibly in 1918–1919 and who had made his peace with the Republic. He managed to avoid any major difficulties or adverse publicity, although there were signs that the *Reichswehr* was drifting closer to rightist political forces, including the NSDAP, and Groener was doing little to prevent it. Groener's reaction to DDP press criticism soon disillusioned several DDP journalists. Although his democratic credentials were tarnished, there were few major problems in the *Reichswehr* under his leadership. The only important military issue between 1928 and 1930 was the furor over the construction of two modern supercruisers, the ships later called "pocket battleships."[75] Although construction of the ships was legal under the treaty and had been discussed since 1920, it flew in the face of impending disarmament negotiations as well as the financial crisis which accompanied the onset of the Great Depression. To rob domestic programs for an expensive and seemingly meaningless naval construction program seemed outrageous to the Left and to many Democrats. Despite strong lobbying by Groener and naval leaders among Democratic leaders, the DDP at first voted against the construction of *Panzerschiff A*. The DDP explained that it opposed the construction both for financial and military reasons. Moreover, it had not been demonstrated how the ship could strengthen Germany. In the May election of 1928, the DDP repeatedly defended its vote against rightist attacks but soon afterwards reversed itself to support the construction in order to prevent the Müller government from falling. This was a turnabout which puzzled its friends and angered many in the left wing of the party. It outraged the Young Democrats.

The Müller government formed after the 1928 election included two Democrats, Koch-Weser and Dietrich, but the SPD, the great winner in the election, dominated the government. Soon after the formation of the government, Groener and Hindenburg put pressure on the government to reverse its position on the *Panzerschiff*, arguing that if it did not, Groener would have to resign and the government would be endangered.[76] In the face of this ultimatum, the SPD changed its position and the DDP yielded as well. The DDP, as was its custom, engaged in a long and divisive debate over the *Fraktion*'s flipflop. The arguments used to defend its change of position were weak and unconvincing because it was necessary to protect Groener and Hindenburg. Many active members were understandably confused. While the urban press along with the tiny pacifist group attacked the decision to support the ship construction, the right wing and the party regulars approved the change. The most clamorous debate occurred in the *Parteiausschuss*.[77] Koch-Weser indicated that he, personally, still opposed the construction. He added to the internal dissension, however, by attacking the young pacifist Lüth for discrediting the party and by censuring the Hamburg organization because of its failure to control him. In the intraparty debate, Heuss was the principal proponent of the ship construction, while Ulich-Beil was perhaps the most effective voice against it. In the end, the PA gave the *Fraktion* a vote of approval but insisted that each member be allowed to vote according to his or her conscience on the issue. When the debate occurred in the plenary session of the Reichstag, Lemmer, the leader of the Young Democrats, who had previously spoken forcefully against the construction, now spoke—badly and illogically—in its favor.[78] As a result of the *Fraktion*'s decision, many Young Democrats who had remained loyal during the election now turned away from the DDP to the SPD, although the SPD's behavior had not been any more consistent or commendable than the DDP's. The SPD jeered Lemmer's remarks because of his reversal, but it was largely responsible for the change of position of the government.

For the DDP, the *Panzerschiff* construction proved to be another issue which split the party down the middle. The coeditors of *Die Hilfe* personified the division. Bäumer approved the change of position and wrote an editorial supporting it, while Erkelenz, ill at the time and unable to participate in the Reichstag debate or the party meetings, opposed. How, Erkelenz asked Bäumer, could loyal party members, who only a short time earlier had been told that the *Panzerschiff* was unneeded and unwise, now accept the party's assurances that it was vital and proper?[79] Bäumer responded that the switch was justified since rank-and-file party members supported it. She had made a speaking tour through the provinces and discovered that most members supported the naval construction.

In order to develop a more coherent and united position on defense questions, Haas soon called for a DDP position paper on defense policy. The *Vorstand*, under fire right and left because of the DDP's recent vacillation, approved Haas's suggestion and appointed a committee—which included Külz and Bäumer—to write the paper. Külz did most of the work, and it became known as the Külz Defense Program. The left wing immediately opposed the need for such a program, attacking the draft program when it appeared.[80] Erkelenz, Cohnstaedt, and Uth led the opposition. Bernstorff also opposed the defense program because it ignored the League of Nations and the disarmament negotiations which had started. The right wing, on the other hand, supported Külz. Fischer, a reserve officer, defended the program because it helped to achieve a more positive relationship with the *Reichswehr*. Stephan, who was on the right of the party on national questions, defended the Külz program as well. He felt that the DDP had to be seen waving the flag in order to retain its middle-class supporters. Bäumer agreed; she wanted to fix in the voters' minds the image of the DDP as a strong nationalist party. Many voters had seen the DDP at the time of the election as a party of rich Jews, intellectuals, and international bankers and traders, and Bäumer and others wished to alter this perception of the party. Koch-Weser opposed the program because of the devisive consequences of all such party documents, and he was surprised at the support for it in the *Vorstand*. Only four members voted against it. The opposition in the PA and among the rank-and-file Democrats, however, was much more widespread. Erkelenz and Bäumer again disagreed on a basic party policy. Bäumer wanted to publish the Külz program in *Die Hilfe*, while Erkelenz opposed publication. Finally, it was published in *Der Demokrat* and became the DDP's official statement on defense policy. Its effects were negligible. It belabored the obvious, divided the party, and won no new recruits. Instead, the controversy surrounding the Külz program widened the split between left and right, between generations, as well as between the Berlin and Hamburg organizations and the provinces. It was about this time that figures such as Bäumer, Koch-Weser, and Heuss came to feel that the big city press, the Young Democrats, and the Social Republican circle were destroying the party. It was also at this time that the idea of a new party in league with loyal and nationalistic young people as well as other *Bürger* forces was conceived.

In the year following the furor over the Külz program, the right wing of the DDP attempted to purge the DDP of its leftists. Despite the constant attrition of the DDP members and the party's weakened organization, the right wing believed that it could attract new recruits from the middle classes if it ousted its controversial radicals. Stephan and other rightists created the "Lüth affair" and drove Lüth from the party. Lemmer, who earlier had shown his compliance in supporting the construction of naval vessels, received heavy attacks because he and the labor group continued to use the phrase "economic democracy," and because he had permitted the Young Democratic organization to become a pacifist forum. Once again, Lemmer retreated. Wolff's and Alfred Weber's old dream of a small but pure party was finally being achieved but in a perverse manner which Wolff, at any rate, deplored.

The *Staatspartei*, which I shall examine shortly, culminated the trend to the right in the DDP. In its short lifespan the only defense issue of any importance was the construction of *Panzerschiff B*, which was not a controversial issue and provoked little debate in the party. The only notable opponent of ship construction was Ulich-Beil, who coupled an attack on the cozy relationship which had developed between the *Reichswehr* and the NSDAP with opposition to *Panzerschiff B*. She charged that Dietrich and other members of the government had ignored the *Reichswehr*'s ties to rightist parties.[81] The other left-wing Democrats who remained in the DStP, figures such as Cohnstaedt, Lemmer, and Nuschke, proved to be either opportunists, cynics, or terribly confused. Most *Staatspartei* members believed the enemy was on the left, not in the *Reichswehr*. They feared and loathed the Nazis but, in 1930, did not perceive them as the greatest threat to the Republic. The DDP's allies were thought to be the "responsible right," the "state-supportive right," a force whose importance diminished as its supporters flocked to the NSDAP.

After the Nazis gained power as Germany's largest political party, the former DDP/DStP members watched the revival of German military strength and Hitler's bold steps in foreign policy with a mixture of pride and alarm. As Hitler dismantled the peace settlement step by step, many must have cheered.[82] After all, most Democrats were as insistent as Hitler on the need to abolish the Treaty of Versailles. Of course, they did not want war, and they abhorred the Nazi domestic policy, but they were loyal Germans. Most of them remained in Hitler's Germany, silent from fear and cautious by nature. Several were arrested and briefly detained in jail to frighten them into compliance. A few resisted. Many Jews and those with Jewish spouses fled, although not all of them escaped. Regardless of whether they remained or fled, Jews and non-Jews and right and left Democrats blamed Versailles for Hitler and Hitler for the war and absolved the German military of responsibility for either.[83]

VII

Divisive Domestic Issues during the Years of Party Crisis, 1925–1929

The Presidential Election of 1925

The death of Friedrich Ebert in February 1925 began a series of domestic developments which, while of little importance individually, together showed a pattern which starkly exposed the DDP's divisions and contradictions as well as the divisions in the Weimar "democratic camp." Each event had constitutional implications, each should have been resolved by early compromises, but, for one reason or another, it was impossible to solve them. While Ebert's death necessitated two elections to elect a new president and dragged on for several months,[1] the Weimar Coalition parties opened the door to the rightist parties by their failure to agree on a candidate in the first election. The SPD nominated and backed Otto Braun, the Center party Wilhelm Marx, but the DDP had *two* candidates, Otto Gessler and Willy Hellpach. Stresemann's opposition destroyed Gessler's candidacy, which had some support in the DVP as well as in the Center party and the DDP.[2] Hellpach, the former minister of culture and minister president of Baden, better known as a professor of psychology at Heidelberg, found little backing outside of the DDP. In the second election, the Weimar Coalition parties agreed to back Marx, a rather colorless former chancellor and veteran Reichstag deputy, who also led the Catholic educational association.[3] The DDP found it difficult to support him because of his faith and his ardent support for confessional education. Hindenburg, on the other hand, the candidate of the right, including the DVP, had much support in the DDP.[4] Following the election, which Hindenburg won narrowly—if the KPD voters had supported Marx rather than their own candidate, Marx would have won—there were bitter recriminations between the parties and within the DDP over the outcome.[5] Stresemann came under attack because he had opposed Gessler; the choice of a Catholic as the Weimar Coalition candidate was seen as a horrible mistake; the Center party saw itself the victim of religious bigotry. Within the DDP, placating Hellpach's wounded ego proved impossible since he never forgot the DDP's inadequate work on his behalf.[6] The basic mistake, however, was that the Weimar Coalition parties failed to agree on a candidate in the *first* election; that was what opened the door for Hindenburg. The election results seemed to prove to contemporaries how little Germany had changed and that it still longed for a kaiser. More certainly, it demonstrated that the middle classes had indeed shifted to the right since 1920. It seems apparent that Democrats voted for Hindenburg because he was a Protestant and a national hero, not because he was a monarchist. Within the DDP, the drawn out campaign and the bickering and recriminations seemed to have widened the gap between the left and right wings of the party, separating the emotional anti-Catholics and strong nationalists from those who still believed in the Republic and the spirit of the Weimar Coalition.

The Flag Question

The flag question, apparently resolved by compromise in the National Assembly, unexpectedly revived as a controversial political issue in 1926, when Chancellor Hans Luther and President Hindenburg, seeking the approbation of national groups and monarchists, extended the privilege of exhibiting the imperial flag from merchant ships to overseas consulates and legations.[7] This was accomplished by an executive order without consulting the Reichstag. The DDP cabinet ministers, Gessler, Külz, and Reinhold, who represented the right wing of the party, approved Luther's action, but many in the left wing strongly protested this "monarchist" action. The leadership of the organization, which was never able to control its cabinet officers, sought to minimize the internal upheaval over this issue by restricting discussion of it to the *Vorstand* and a few guarded public statements. This failed to silence the opponents in the Democratic party, however, and soon, much against its will, the DDP found itself in a central position on the flag question. The SPD, which was in the opposition, introduced a motion of no confidence in the Luther government. The DDP, while regretting the decision of Luther and Hindenburg, feared the consequences of supporting the SPD motion of no confidence and framed another motion of no confidence. This motion expressed a lack of confidence in Luther, personally, but not in his government. Koch-Weser justified the motion by pointing out that Luther was a non-party expert.[8] When the DNVP abstained, much to the surprise and annoyance of the DDP, the Democratic motion passed, compelling Luther to resign. The DDP, as a result, gained credit—or discredit—for overthrowing the government. The *Fraktion*'s parliamentary ploy to avoid supporting the SPD's motion had backfired, greatly embarrassing the party. Moderate and conservative Democrats heavily attacked the DDP *Fraktion* for destroying an admired government on a relatively unimportant issue. On the other hand, the strong republicans in the left wing of the DDP and even some moderates in the party rejoiced in Luther's fall; for them, Luther's decision had seemed highhanded, and the republican symbol was a major issue of principle. They saw Luther and Hindenburg bidding for monarchical support and circulated rumors of an effort to restore the monarchy.[9]

After Luther resigned, a new government under third-time Chancellor Marx was formed in May 1926. The DDP retained the same ministries it had had under Luther.[10] The executive order on the flag remained in force; it was never countermanded. In the end, however, the DDP lost much more than it gained from its republican flourish urged by the left wing. Koch-Weser's deficiencies as a leader were attacked. Some of his enemies even contended that he had engineered the crisis in order to win a cabinet position for himself.

The Princely Indemnification Issue (*Fürstenabfindung*)

The question of the disposition of princely properties produced a deeper division in the DDP and the nation than either the presidential election or the flag question.[11] The national referendum supported by the SPD and the KPD to expropriate the property of the dynastic houses touched a fundamental liberal concern, the sanctity of private property. On the other hand, many in the DDP's left wing felt that the princes should suffer along with the rest of the population for the military defeat for which the *Kaiserreich* had been responsible. Article 153 of the Weimar Constitution provided that private property could not be expropriated without fair compensation, but it included a loophole which indicated that, if the general welfare demanded it and if due process were exercised, expropriation was legal. The *Länder*, acting independently, began soon after the revolution to address this question, but the many legal tangles became even more complicated during the inflation era of 1922–1924. Ultimately, many of the cases concerning the expropriation of princely property ended up in the courts, where sympathetic judges made generous settlements in favor of the dynastic families. These judgments outraged many leftists, and a movement developed to block such judicial actions. In the face of a KPD demand for total expropriation without compensation, the DDP, in December 1925, introduced legislation in the Reichstag to give the *Länder* full powers to solve the problem. This would enable Bavaria, still emotionally monarchist, to provide a generous settlement for the former ruling family, the Wittelsbachs, while allowing the Prussian *Landtag* to gain control of the vast Hohenzollern properties "for the people." The KPD and the SPD responded to the DDP plan by banding together to support a national referendum to expropriate all dynastic properties without compensation. The motto of the referendum became *"Keinen Pfennig den Fürsten"*—not a penny for the princes. Securing sufficient signatures to hold a referendum proved easy, but when, after weeks of passionate oratory and violent demonstrations, the election occurred, the referendum lost.

The referendum divided the DDP down the middle. The big city press, together with the Hamburg and Berlin organizations, the Young Democrats, and individuals such as Erkelenz, Wolff, Nuschke, and Rönneburg—business manager of the Reichstag *Fraktion*—favored the referendum. Most of the provincial organizations and moderate and conservative members opposed it. The HB fought it with almost religious fervor as an attack on the principle of private property. Conservative Democrats led by Hans Delbrück, Rohrbach, and Richard Bahr, organized a committee to oppose the referendum.[12] It was not difficult to find Democrats to fight it; it was enough that the KPD and the SPD—and Wolff and Bernhard—favored it for a clear majority of Democrats to oppose the referendum. On the other hand, many in the DDP resented the active role which Hindenburg took in the struggle against it. Initially, the *Vorstand* and the *Fraktion* issued statements denouncing the referendum and asking members to oppose it as an assault on private property. The left wing fought back, however, and the DDP retreated to a neutral position. After a good deal of confusion it was decided that this issue should be treated as a question of individual conscience; the party would not take a position.[13] This decision angered many right-wing Democrats who felt that a strong defense of private property was imperative in the face of the socialist challenge, and several, including Schacht, resigned from the DDP in protest.[14] Although Schacht had not been active in the party since 1924, his leaving was a blow since the DDP traded heavily on his reputation as the man responsible for restoring the value of the German currency. Throughout the controversy, the DVP heavily attacked the irresolute DDP position which the *Bürger* parties interpreted as a failure to defend middle-class interests.[15] But when the Reichstag, following the defeat of the referendum, resolved the question of dynastic properties, it essentially adopted the original suggestion of the DDP and allowed the *Länder* to determine the disposition of dynastic properties. The DDP never received any credit for this outcome. All that was remembered in later years was that the DDP had pursued a divided and confused course of action and that Schacht had resigned from the party because it had not sufficiently defended private property against the socialist parties.

The Trash and Filth Law (*Schund- und Schmutzgesetz*)

The image of the DDP as a party deeply divided and badly led gained reinforcement in the next crisis for the DDP, which was the effort to regulate the sale and distribution of pornographic literature to children, the *Schund- und Schmutzgesetz* (S and S Law). Once again, the party divided on a question of principle: censorship versus freedom of the press. Once again, the right and left wings disagreed, although their split was not identical on every issue. The DDP minister of the interior, Külz, introduced and defended the measure for the government in November 1926, although Bäumer apparently drafted the law in the ministry. The Center party and its ally on clerical issues, the DNVP, had sponsored similar legislation for several years without success, and the DDP had anticipated, as early as 1919, that such a law would be necessary. Troeltsch had defended the need for it at the DDP's PT in December 1919. Then, in 1926, the DDP joined with its usual clerical foes to sponsor the legislation to censor "filthy literature." Bäumer, Külz, and Heuss provided the DDP leadership in support of the law.[16]

The opposition to the S and S Law came from the leftist parties, the DDP's large city press, and passionate civil libertarians. Moderates such as Koch-Weser, who opposed it in principle, soon were caught in a cross fire from both extremes. This was at a time when the DDP continued to lose members to economic interest groups and to a number of avowedly Christian parties. The DDP did not wish to offend the sensibilities of its "Protestant wing" and its educators, many of whom favored the S and S Law. On the other hand, the DDP found censorship repugnant in any form; it ran counter to the traditions of historic left liberalism.

In the end, after a heated debate within the major committees of the DDP and weeks of acrimonious press controversy, the vote in the Reichstag occurred.[17] Koch-Weser and a majority of the *Fraktion* opposed it, but in the opinion of the DDP's left wing and its major press supporters, the DDP did not oppose it strenuously enough.[18] As a result, some of the major publishers withdrew their financial support from the DDP for a time, and Wolff resigned from the party. Wolff had few admirers in the party, and there was no general exodus on this issue, but his departure showed how badly divided the party remained and how difficult it was to agree on fundamentals. The leadership, which desperately strove to hold the party together, received a pummeling from both extremities of the party. Clearly, the contradictions within the DDP were tearing it apart.

The S and S Law proved less harmful to the freedom of the press and the wealth of the DDP publishers than had originally been feared, but it nonetheless grievously damaged the DDP.[19] The BT, in particular, sharply attacked Bäumer and Heuss, who had been occasional allies of the Left and strong supporters of the Republic. The party leaders, particularly Külz and Koch-Weser, lost prestige because of their flabby performance, and the enmity between provincial organizations and the "Berlin press" increased. Even anti-Semitism, never far beneath the surface, reappeared. The staffs of the major DDP newspapers, who had supported the DDP as the Republic's best hope, became disaffected and increasingly backed the SPD, although the publishers generally continued their formal support of the DDP during election campaigns.

Kultur Questions

The *Kultur* issues which gained prominence between 1925 and 1929 stemmed principally from the Center party's and the BVP's achievement of a Bavarian concordat in 1925, their campaign for a national school law and a Reich Concordat in 1926–1927, and the Center party's attainment of a Prussian concordat in 1929.[20] The DDP and the SPD, often supported by the DVP and the WP, opposed this clerical resurgence but not in any cooperative, concerted manner. Each party had a somewhat different interpretation of these questions and sought to use them for whatever partisan advantage it could derive from them. The DDP resolutely opposed these measures, with the exception of the Prussian concordat, which most members accepted after all references to education were deleted. Indeed, the Center party saw the DDP as its staunchest enemy on these questions.

The Bavarian concordat became law in 1925. It passed by a comfortable margin in a predominantly Catholic *Land* over the strenuous objections of the small Bavarian DDP party. As an extreme measure granting generous benefits to the Catholic church and to confessional schools, it frightened Democratic school administrators outside Bavaria and alerted them to fight the proposed Reich school law favored by the Center party and a Reich concordat in the years which followed.[21] The DDP felt that the Bavarian concordat was clearly unconstitutional, and it denounced the Luther government for not challenging it in the courts. The Bavarian concordat revived the *Kultur* issues in the DDP and breathed life into the Culture Committee (*Kulturausschuss*), in which Bäumer and Heuss had important roles. They were in great demand as speakers and writers on *Kultur* subjects in these years and often aroused great emotions and "stormy applause" at party gatherings.

The DDP proved most adamant and united in its opposition to the national school law and the Reich concordat sponsored by the Center party, the BVP, and the DNVP in 1926–1927, a period when right-wing governments prevailed at the national level and the DDP was in the opposition. Contemporaries generally connected the two measures, and the DDP fought them together. As we have seen, the Center party never really accepted the school compromise of 1919, but then neither did the DDP. Both parties sought to pass education laws to secure their educational goals, but neither succeeded. By 1925, the Center party was turning right for a variety of reasons, but its clerical goals seemed to have been the greatest impetus for this development. Marx, for example, became convinced that educational issues were the best way to get Catholics to support the Center party.[22] Unfortunately, while clerical issues helped to unite the Center party and built bridges to the DNVP, they weakened the Weimar Coalition in Prussia and alienated several of the Center party's left wing, especially Wirth, the former chancellor, and Heinrich Imbusch, a leader of the Catholic coal miners' union. As strong supporters of the Weimar Coalition and the Republic, they were angry and alarmed at the Center party's turn to the DVP and the DNVP. The DDP echoed their emotions, if for somewhat different reasons. Friedrich Mück found the Center party's clerical pursuits "sheer idiocy."[23] Along with most Democrats, he felt that the schools offered no threat to religion. The courts had decreed that all *Länder* must permit religious instruction, and nearly all schools taught religion in one way or another. Although the DDP would have preferred a more uniform and secular school system, it generally admitted that the schools reflected community and parental desires. The Center party's demand for a Reich concordat was even more puzzling to Democrats.[24] Characteristically, the Democrats took up the pen to battle these two measures and debated them in major committee meetings and in the DDP press.[25] Some members of the party became so worked up over these old issues that they had to be warned by cooler heads to avoid a *Kulturkampf* mentality which might irreparably alienate the Center party.[26] In fact, however, frictions between Protestants and Catholics still existed in many districts, and educational questions were at the center of the difficulties. While Heuss and Bäumer and several Democratic educators stirred up Democrats to resist the Center party's clerical goals, Koch-Weser and Erkelenz worked to calm the party. While a few members believed that these *Kultur* issues could win new voters and others encouraged a new *Kulturkampf* in order to move closer to the DVP and perhaps secure liberal fusion, more often than not the *Kultur* questions produced division rather than unity.

At the 1925 PT in Breslau, Hellpach, who loved to play the devil's advocate, initiated a spirited debate with Heuss on the historic attitudes of the Catholic church and the Lutheran church toward democracy.[27] Hellpach, speaking in a predominantly Lutheran and Jewish assembly, contended that the Catholic church had been far more supportive of democracy than the Lutheran church. Heuss, a prominent member of the DDP's "Protestant wing," heatedly challenged Hellpach's facts and his interpretation. Although they seemed to settle the matter amicably enough at Breslau and brushed their differences off as a misunderstanding, it wounded relations between them, affected Hellpach's self-esteem, and led to additional publications and speeches by them, accentuating differences within the DDP. At the same time, the small DDP Catholic group came to feel out of place in a party which increasingly emphasized its Protestantism.

In retrospect, one can only wonder about the excitement which these issues aroused. The Reich school bill never had a chance to become law, and the Reich concordat had even less support. The tactics of the Center party in aggressively pushing these clerical measures remains even more of a riddle. Was this the only way it could retain the Catholic vote? After May 1928, when the SPD won a smashing victory, the clerical proposals were sidetracked, but the Center party remained determined to implement them under more favorable circumstances.

The Prussian concordat presented a greater challenge to the DDP than the above-mentioned clerical issues and had to be handled with greater care. Although the DDP's strength in the Prussian *Landtag* had declined proportionately to its losses nationally, it continued to be a member of the Prussian *Land* government. Höpker-Aschoff, who had been named minister of finance in 1925, remained in that important post until 1932. The DDP wished to preserve its position in the Prussian government at all costs, but in order to achieve this, it had to appease the Center party. This necessitated a compromise on the Prussian concordat. Led by Braun, the Socialist minister president, the government drafted a concordat which omitted any references to education and which permitted only a few administrative reforms desired by the Catholic church.[28] This proved satisfactory to the DDP and the DVP as well. The Center party and the papal nuncio Pacelli were not happy about this outcome but were forced to accept it. Some members of the DDP, most notably Bäumer, were also distressed by this compromise. She regarded the Prussian concordat as a threat both to historic liberal principles and—even more important to her—to Protestantism. When Erkelenz, a nominal Catholic who saw the Prussian concordat as a necessary and wise compromise, permitted Höpker-Aschoff to write an article in *Die Hilfe* urging support for the concordat, she angrily attacked Erkelenz.[29] She had been under the impression, she wrote, that she controlled *Kultur* contributions to *Die Hilfe*, not Erkelenz, and she strongly opposed his presumption in making *Kultur* policy for the journal they jointly edited. She also opposed the Prussian concordat in the major committees of the party and at the 1927 and 1929 party congresses, where it received equivocal approval. On this issue, however, she was in a small minority. Most members of the party were reassured when educational questions were eliminated from the Prussian concordat.

The *Kultur* issues were not a major cause of division within the DDP, and the fact that the DVP generally saw eye-to-eye with the DDP on these questions appeased the right-wing group which was most likely to defect. The only division of any importance was on the Prussian concordat. Although Koch-Weser and some others attempted to turn these *Kultur* issues into electoral dividends, they neither attracted nor repelled voters. Only the school issue stirred much popular excitement. The greatest harm done was to the unity and spirit of the Weimar Coalition and, ultimately, to the Republic. Old suspicions were again aroused among parties which generally supported the Republic; anti-Catholicism revived in the DDP, while the Center party tended to blame the DDP for its defeats.[30] Coalition governments, always difficult to operate under the best of conditions, became increasingly hard to maintain—especially after the Great Depression hit in 1929 and 1930. The constant pressure of the DVP to be admitted to the Prussian *Land* government, sometimes favored by the Center party and some Democrats, also produced coalition problems. Furthermore, the continued inability of the DVP and the SPD to agree on fundamentals and the tendency of the DDP to back the DVP and move away from the SPD in times of crisis also contributed to coalition instability. At the same time, the growth of special interest parties and, after 1930, extremist enemies of the Republic produced great pessimism about the future of democracy in Germany.[31] The Center party's frustration at not achieving its clerical goals caused it to embark on a course which indirectly led to its support for Hitler's dictatorship to preserve Catholic institutions.

The DDP's history in the last years of the Republic moved against a backdrop of quarreling parties, government instability, and economic crisis. The DDP suffered repeated defeats at the polls, partly because of these factors but also because of the divisive issues treated in this chapter which helped to destroy the party's organization and its will to survive.

VIII

The Formation and Breakup of the *Deutsche Staatspartei*

Following the national election of May 1928 and the communal and *Länder* elections in the autumn of 1929, the DDP was no longer a viable political organization.[1] Since at least 1926, the DDP had been crippled by the growth of special interest parties, especially the *Wirtschaftspartei*. By the fall of 1929, the DDP also became aware of the growing importance of the NSDAP. The special interest parties and the NSDAP threatened not only the DDP but also the other traditional Protestant middle-class parties, the DVP and the DNVP. Another marked trend after 1928 was the general drift to the right among these parties; *Bürgerblocks* at the municipal and *Land* level became increasingly common. At the same time, the DDP became more and more critical of the SPD and less inclined to cooperate with it, despite the frequent professions that its coalition preference was the Great Coalition, which included the SPD. Two events epitomized the DDP's rightist shift: in January 1930, the Württemberg DDP entered a rightist government, which produced a tremendous furor; in late March, the government of Hermann Müller fell when the DVP and the DDP refused to support the SPD's policies to fund unemployment compensation and other social services. Given this rightist move and the defection of many left-wing Democrats, plus the decay of its organizations, the DDP needed to seek political allies with which it might join in forming a new political party. In the period 1920–1930, there were several possibilities: the DVP; the WP; the Christian Social People's Service (*Christlich-Sozialer Volksdienst*—CSV), a nascent Protestant party; one or more of the several peasant parties; the political arm of the Young German Order (*Jungdo*), the People's National Reichs Union (*Volksnationale Reichsvereinigung*—VR).

Most active Democrats favored some kind of a merger with the DVP, preferably on the DDP's terms, although many were prepared to make far-reaching concessions. Some were willing to sacrifice the DDP's left wing, if necessary, to effect the union with the DVP;[2] many hoped that a party could be constructed of a DVP shorn of its right wing and a DDP divested of its leftists. This, of course, had been the goal of the DDP's business wing since 1918, and there had been many efforts to combine the two parties, but the left wing of the DDP and the right wing of the DVP had blocked a merger. In the DDP, Petersen and Fischbeck led the liberal unity campaign, and in the DVP, a few left-wing figures also favored this course. After 1928, conditions to produce a merger seemed brighter than they had in years. After all, the two parties had worked closely together in many areas in the mid-twenties and some of the intense animosity between them had died down. And, although the DVP's decline was not as precipitous as the DDP's, it was being undercut by the same forces which were killing the DDP. Stresemann saw the trend and concluded that the DVP had a bleak future. In the two years before his death in October 1929, Stresemann met with several political leaders to discuss, in general terms, the possibilities of closer cooperation. He talked and corresponded with both Koch-Weser and Artur Mahraun, the leader of the *Jungdo*, and discussed the possibility of a *Bürger-Sammlung* with Koch-Weser a short time before his death.[3] By 1929, the Liberal Association was moribund but an organization with similar goals, Front 1929, had taken its place. There was little enthusiasm for these nonpartisan groups in the established parties, however, and most of them soon perished. Nevertheless, the idea that the middle-class parties should join to form a large new party between the SPD and the NSDAP remained alive.

While several leading Democrats devoted themselves to saving the DDP through a political merger of some kind, a profound disillusionment set in about the shortcomings of the German parliamentary system and the "party system." The system's imperfection was well established before the onset of the Great Depression, but the depression exposed its flaws for all to see. The government seemed incapable of dealing effectively with the economic and social problems which the depression aggravated. The failure of the government increased the number of political parties and political instability. In the confusion and weakness, many Democrats, like the general population, began to hunger for leadership and authority.[4] The DDP continued to promote its suggestions for a constitutional and electoral law reform, but they were inadequate to deal with the problems facing Germany after 1928 and were ignored by other parties. The DDP, which can be seen as a microcosm of the national system, repeatedly sought palliatives for its organizational problems instead of facing up to the basic causes of its decline. Many members, disgusted with the bickering and quarreling over relatively minor issues, called for more effective leadership. They often blamed Koch-Weser for the party's woes.[5] He, in turn, became even more sensitive to criticism and more dictatorial, so that Erkelenz compared him to Richter and denounced his "dictatorship."[6] Although Koch-Weser seemed to be responding to the requests for stronger leadership, he was also increasingly at odds with the party's left wing. He had moved closer to the business wing after 1924 and had joined the Liberal Association, becoming its honorary chairman, which greatly angered the left. The inability of the *Fraktion* to agree on basic issues was also blamed on his leadership. Nonetheless, he repeatedly won votes of confidence and was authorized to conduct negotiations for the party to achieve a new party from the ruins of several. In order to safeguard these negotiations, he rarely confided in the major committees. It seems clear, however, that he hoped to fuse with the DVP.[7] But the DVP, now led by Ernst Scholz, was not interested; it preferred to look to its right for allies. The WP also rejected Koch-Weser's overtures. When Koch-Weser was censured for the failure to find suitable allies, he blamed Scholz's stubbornness and unwillingness to make reasonable compromises.[8] In fact, neither leader wanted to see his party fold its tent and disappear, but that was probably the only solution to maintain a liberal party. Long after Koch-Weser and Scholz had lost their leadership posts, attempts were made to bring the DStP and the DVP together, but liberal unity was never achieved. The best chance for a partnership with another party was with the WP, but the DDP, which had always treated the WP with condescension and contempt, shrank from this political marriage. And what did the left liberals have to offer? They were still tarred in *Bürger* ranks as leftists and tied to revolution, fulfillment, the SPD, and controversial Jews. At the local level, the barriers between the parties were even greater than at the national level. How, for example, could the DDP organizations in Bremen or Breslau overcome generations of fighting the DVP or its predecessor, the NLP? Many political wounds simply would not heal. How could the DDP organization in Saxony forget that the WP won many of its members through the lowest kind of demagogic politics?

The leaders of the *Bürger* parties conducting these political negotiations in the spring and summer of 1930 knew the seriousness of the situation. Support for the Brüning government was shaky and the economic situation continued to worsen. While the NSDAP gained ground in state and local elections, the KPD won SPD followers. It was evident from the time Brüning formed his minority government that new national elections would be required soon, but most Democrats hoped that somehow the decision might be delayed. The prospect of new elections made it even more critical for the DDP to find political allies. When the efforts to secure deals with the DVP and the WP failed, the DDP's leadership became desperate. This explains the curious alliance which became the German State party—the DDP, the VR, a few young DVP members, some Christian Trade Unionists, and a few individuals with liberal connections. The DStP was always seen, however, as only the first stage of a comprehensive party which would occupy the middle ground between the Center party and the DNVP. But with the Reichstag dissolved in July and new elections ordered, circumstances compelled Koch-Weser to join with the only elements prepared to accept the DDP. While the DStP always had the appearance of a hasty improvisation, in actuality the DDP's leaders had been in communication with the varied elements which joined the DStP for many months. DDP leaders such as Koch-Weser, Lemmer, Bäumer, and Stephan found the VR especially attractive.[9] It was reputed to have 900,000 dues-paying members. Even the name, German State party, was often considered a preferable term to German Democratic party.

The VR was the political wing of the *Jungdo*, a right-wing, paramilitary *bündische* organization with medieval trappings. It seemed to have little in common with the DDP, but the Democrats as well as Stresemann had watched it carefully for several years. Its youthful character and its alleged large membership were attractive to smaller parties with few youthful members. These assets overcame whatever doubts many in the DDP had about the nature of the VR, some of whose characteristics seemed bizarre to the urban sophisticates of the DDP. The *Jungdo* dressed its members in distinctive uniforms, sported a Teutonic cross as its emblem, and called its leader, Mahraun, führer or *Meister*. It had a strong Prussian and Christian character and its bylaws included an "Aryan paragraph" which excluded Jews from membership. Many of its members were war veterans who had had Free Corps experience, and, until 1924, it was indistinguishable from several other such groups. During 1920–1921, it marched in patriotic rallies with the *Stahlhelm* and the NSDAP, and Koch-Weser viewed it with much distrust when he was minister of the interior. At that time, he thought it a subversive group seeking to undermine the Republic. Jewish organizations grouped it with other prominent anti-Semitic radicals as a hostile force.[10] After 1924, however, the *Jungdo* began to change. It made its peace with the Republic, supported Stresemann's foreign policy, and even became known for its Francophile tendencies. Mahraun also toned down his personal anti-Semitism, although the *Jungdo* still barred Jews. It placed its greatest stress on hatred of the Soviet Union and communism, but it also featured propaganda against plutocracy and often deplored the unstable German party system. In the late twenties, it became increasingly alarmed about the growth of "interest politics" and hoped to elevate the state above vested material interests. The *Jungdo* favored constitutional changes to reform the electoral system, and it wanted to strengthen the executive branch. Although previously it had scorned "politics," the *Jungdo*, because of its growing political concerns—and possibly because its membership was declining—decided to participate in partisan politics. The VR first ran candidates in the *Landtag* elections in

Saxony in the spring of 1930 and won two seats. Several prominent Democrats noted this development with great interest and exaggerated the importance of the VR's "victory."

In addition to the VR, two other groups and several individuals were also drawn toward the DDP in the spring of 1930, partly as a result of Koch-Weser's actions and partly because of the general *Sammlung* and crisis fever. One group consisted of the February Clubs, dissident young members of the DVP who were either associated with or inspired by the *Kölnische Zeitung*, a major right-wing liberal newspaper. This group included people such as Josef Winschuh, who edited a newsletter, *Deutsche Führer Briefe*, and often wrote for the KZ and other liberal newspapers. Another constituency consisted of several Christian Trade Union leaders and others close to the *Gewerkschaftsring*. Several individuals who were Democrats but who had been relatively inactive in the organization were motivated by the emergency to become more active partisans. They included figures such as August Weber, Wolfgang Jaenicke, the *Regierungspräsident* in Breslau, Friedensburg, the *Regierungspräsident* in Hesse-Nassau, and Stolper.[11] Höpker-Aschoff, the Prussian finance minister, also became more deeply involved in national politics at this time. With the exception of Friedensburg, they were right-wing Democrats favoring closer ties with the DVP and constitutional and electoral law reforms. Weber, for example, formerly chaired the Liberal Association and was an HB official. They criticized the DDP leadership and saw the need to restructure the party and to shake up the Reichstag *Fraktion*.

As it became evident that the DDP had little chance to join with one or more of the existing parties, it became imperative to reach an understanding with the VR, which supposedly had a large membership. This necessitated weeks of negotiations. Koch-Weser took the lead, aided by Lemmer, in particular, although several others assisted. Dietrich suffered a heart attack in May at the critical stage of the negotiations and was out of action for six weeks, convalescing at Marienbad. Lemmer, the left-wing leader, who was a determined foe of a merger with the DVP, strongly advocated fusion with the VR. This greatly puzzled many in the Young Democratic organization, not to speak of his Jewish friends.[12] Could one explain it on the basis of Lemmer's and the VR's common hatred of plutocracy? August Weber, relatively old, rich, and conservative, also seemed to be an unlikely negotiator in this context, but he was wily and flexible and had many contacts. Stephan was also an important figure in the background to the DStP. He had been the DDP's general secretary for over six years when, in 1929, he resigned to accept a government civil service position at the invitation of Stresemann. He remained active in the DDP and became chairman of the Organization Committee, replacing Frankfurter in the general organizational change following the resignation of Erkelenz as chairman of the *Vorstand*. Stephan had long been at odds with Frankfurter, the last holdover of the founders of the DDP, whom he regarded as an ineffectual dilettante. Stephan, the most sophisticated student of political behavior and elections in the party,[13] also wanted to replace many of the fossils of the *Fraktion* with younger and abler people. By 1930, Meyer had, in effect, replaced Fischer as the business wing's leading spokesman, although Fischer remained treasurer of the party. In addition, following Haas's heart attack, Meyer, the deputy *Fraktion* leader, became the real *Fraktion* leader.[14]

There were several other Democrats who felt the need to do "something" in the spring of 1930, although they were generally baffled as to what should be done. Hellpach, the party's choice for the presidency in 1925 and one of its deputy chairmen, had long called for a right-wing *Sammlung*. He resigned his Reichstag seat in March, allegedly because Koch-Weser had moved too slowly to merge with the non-Catholic *Bürger* parties. In fact, Hellpach's distaste for democratic politics and his hatred for Koch-Weser had become pathological. Thoroughly disillusioned with the practice of parliamentary government in Germany as early as 1926, his Reichstag experience after 1928 had confirmed his feelings.[15] He was convinced that the system was so corrupt and inefficient that only an authoritarian government could succeed in restoring order and respect. Although after 1933 he became, for a time, a Nazi apologist, he was, in 1930—at a time when it was still common in the DDP to lump the Nazis with the left as a socialist party[16]—one of the few Democrats who saw that the NSDAP was a fascist party and that fascism, not the Left, was the greatest threat to German democracy. Hellpach's disenchantment with German parliamentary government was an example of a general trend among left liberals which the DStP articulated. Another perennial malcontent, Tantzen, also resigned from the Reichstag in the spring of 1930, largely in protest against Dietrich's agricultural and tariff policies.[17] The *Fraktion* had disassociated itself from Dietrich's policies and many members had attacked them, but the party had not been as hostile as Tantzen wanted it to be. Moreover, it refused to endorse his special demand for aid to a small number of farmers in northwestern Germany. Tantzen's and Hellpach's actions were isolated and extreme and found little sympathetic response among the rank and file. Their actions did indicate, however, the depth of feeling against the party's leadership, and they were symptoms of a general frustration directed toward parliamentary government.

With the DDP's left wing impotent and confused and its moderates and rightists eager to form a new group or party of some kind to the right of center, the reception of the announcement of the DStP was overwhelmingly favorable. It only became apparent gradually how high the price had been to secure allies. Initially, however, the DStP received overwhelming support from the left wing to the right. It is still common to represent it as a lurch to the right, but this ignores the enthusiasm which many in the left wing displayed. Bäumer, Lemmer, the Social Republican Circle led by Hans Muhle, the Hirsch-Duncker Unions, and even Erkelenz's old friend and party secretary Adolf Lange,[18]—but not Erkelenz—joined the DStP. The Berlin *Mittel* organization, led by Feder, seems to have been the only exception, although several Young Democrats' organizations, including the Berlin and Nürnberg ones, refused to join it. The DStP also received instant and significant backing from the newspapers and party journals which had previously supported the DDP. Aside from Erkelenz, who had been disaffected and ill for two years and thus relatively inactive, all of the major leaders of the DDP joined the DStP. Though both Heuss and Stolper were uneasy about some of the partners, they joined it, served it, and were numbered among its leaders. Bäumer proved to be the most uncritical enthusiast for the DStP. Although she has recently been depicted as a proto-fascist,[19] at the time, she was still numbered as a member of the left wing of the DDP. Lemmer, like Bäumer, had wished to avoid a *Sammlung* with rightist parties and fought a merger with the DVP; yet he eagerly joined with the VR! Bäumer, as we have seen, was a romantic nationalist and statist in the Naumann tradition. She had also become bitterly opposed to certain left-wing elements in the DDP, mostly Jewish journalists in Frankfurt a/M and Berlin, who were too cosmopolitan and rational for her tastes. Lemmer, on the other hand, had many friends in this circle. He was particularly close to Feder. Bäumer, and probably Lemmer as well, had become increasingly disappointed by the nature of the Young Democrats, who had become increasingly pacifistic. Bäumer was certainly enamored of the VR in part because its members were youthful, Christian, and nationalistic, and while Lemmer's support seemed more opportunist, he too could be carried away by nationalist emotion and fond memories of front-line *Kameradschaft*.[20] Both Bäumer and Lemmer longed to recapture the "community of August 1914." Both also had a distaste for plutocrats. Once they committed themselves to the DStP and the alliance with the VR, neither seems to have looked back or regretted his action. Heuss and Stolper, on the other hand, whose economic and social views were rightist, were sincere democrats and liberals and strong republicans, and they soon regretted the compromises which had to be made to form the DStP.[21] They were especially disturbed by the anti-Semitism of the VR—Stolper because he was a Jew and Heuss because he had many Jewish friends. The memoirs of the DDP/DStP members are more equivocal for this period than for any other, and it was the "Jewish question" which seemed to produce the later reluctance to deal with this period openly and honestly. Meyer, a baptized Jew, has a disingenuous account of his relationship to the formation of the DStP, while Lemmer's memoirs are evasive and deceitful. Heuss's recollections are not much more edifying, while Toni Stolper tends to obscure her husband's importance in the DStP. The distinguished secondary accounts of the Weimar period by Democrats—Eyck, Hajo Holborn, Friedensburg, Berg-strässer—tend to further the masquerade. Bäumer, Meyer, and Koch-Weser, who also had Jewish ancestors, tried to argue that the VR was not anti-Semitic, although the *Jungdo* had been. They contended that the "Aryan paragraph" was no different from the restriction a Jewish lodge might impose for membership.[22] When this question was later aired in committee meetings, Bäumer, at least, said that she would have never agreed to a merger with the VR if she had known that the VR was *still* anti-Semitic, although one must doubt her sincerity in the light of her words and actions after 1933. On the other hand, the repugnance with which Lüders, Friedensburg, and others viewed the VR's anti-Semitism indicates that "everybody knew," just as "everybody knew" the plight of the Jews after 1933 and what was happening to them after 1942.[23]

At the outset of the merger talks with the VR, Koch-Weser warned that, while he and Mahraun shared the same goals, they spoke a different political language, but he never allowed this to slow the merger.[24] The other DDP leaders were also well aware of the differences between the principles of the DDP and VR; yet they pushed on regardless. At the same time, they continued to negotiate with the DVP, the DSV, the WP, and the anti-Semitic wing of the DNVP, although nothing came out of these talks. The key DDP meetings which aired the possibility of a new party in a general way were on 5 May and 25 May.[25] These meetings of the *Vorstand* and the *Parteiausschuss* displayed the characteristic left-right divisions of the DDP, but they ended by giving Koch-Weser the power to negotiate for the party and an overwhelming vote of confidence. The *Fraktion*, on the other hand, was less popular, but its most vociferous critics, Hellpach and Tantzen, had little support. The 25 May meeting was expected to be a battleground, and it was a turbulent meeting. A small group heavily attacked Koch-Weser and questioned his veracity. When he sought to identify his views with the left wing, which opposed the Brüning government on several scores, Heinrich Landahl, a young Hamburg member, strongly criticized him and pointed out the discrepancies between his words and the actions of the *Fraktion*. Landahl and others were appalled at the idea of a fusion with the DVP, the only negotiation known at this time. On the other hand, right-wing representatives such as Hellpach, Gothein, and Stolper larded their remarks with sharp attacks on the SPD, blaming it for the crisis of the parliamentary system. Hellpach and Koch-Weser both commented favorably on the qualities of the VR during the course of this debate, although nothing as yet was said about a merger with it. Meyer, the acting *Fraktion* leader, angrily assaulted Landahl for misrepresenting the *Fraktion*'s actions. He declared the DDP's goals and principles remained the same: a democratic republic; a social republic; a liberal *Kultur* policy.

In the weeks which followed the May meetings, the negotiations between the DDP leaders and others continued at a rather unhurried pace despite the mounting political crisis. The DDP leaders went on their usual long June vacations. There were several stories in the press about the possibilities of a cooperative working arrangement in the Reichstag between the middle parties, but nothing came of this talk. Koch-Weser continued his negotiations, much to the annoyance of Erkelenz, who denounced their secret character and ridiculed his efforts.[26] In the second week of June, when the national income fell below expectations, the Brüning government asked for an emergency tax levy to raise the needed revenue, which the DDP, the DVP, and the SPD opposed.[27] The DDP disapproved Brüning's attempt to raise the needed taxes under the authority of article 48, in part because the DDP was fearful of the overuse of article 48. Meanwhile, the unemployment numbers mounted, and street fighting between the Communists and Nazis became common. Then, on 16 June, the Brüning government fell, and Hindenburg ordered new elections.[28] Many Democrats denounced the decision to hold national elections in the summer of 1930 as blind and irresponsible, but, at the same time, they had helped to bring down Brüning and were unable to suggest any constructive alternatives to his policies. They knew about the growth of the extremist movements—local organizations had been sending in reports about the NSDAP's growing political effectiveness—but it was still more common in the DDP to ridicule the Nazis than to respect their power. The great success which the NSDAP had in the Saxon *Land* elections, which proved to be a portent, was alarming but soon overlooked in the avalanche of bad news.[29] Koch-Weser finally informed the *Vorstand* of his negotiations with the VR and told it that a merger with the VR was pending, although many prominent Democrats later contended that they had never heard about these negotiations. Meanwhile, Bäumer, Külz, and others were speaking and writing in support of a merger with the VR. Külz, the leading Saxon Democrat, had previously received generous support from Jewish industrialists and bankers in Saxony, but he now dismissed the anti-Semitism of the *Jungdo* as an inconsequential matter. A strong nationalist with fond memories of his military experience, Külz felt the VR would be a valuable partner of the DDP.[30]

As the DDP began to organize its allies into a new party, the party organization prepared to fight another election. Early in the campaign, prescient politicians in several parties warned that the election in September 1930 would be the most decisive in the Republic's history. On 19 July, the DDP issued the election *Aufruf* with the now conventional warnings against the extremes of right and left, but the committee which wrote the *Aufruf* had little sense of the real peril which lay just around the corner. The day before the release of the *Aufruf*, 18 July, a small trusted group met in secrecy to discuss the alternatives which the DDP had remaining.[31] Present, in addition to Koch-Weser, were Bäumer, Lemmer, Külz, Dietrich, August Weber, Höpker-Aschoff, and—apparently—Stephan. Absent were four of the party's vice chairmen—Erkelenz, Hellpach, Fischer, and recently named Meyer. The group concluded what had so long been apparent: the DDP by itself had no future. It was told that the negotiations with the DVP had failed, although there was still some hope that some left-wing DVP members might be split off from it. The only sizable pool of voters which might join with the DDP was the VR. On 23 July, a larger group met and this time the leader of the VR, the *Jungdo*'s *Meister* and führer, Mahraun, and his deputy, Otto Bornemann, were present. Koch-Weser and Mahraun had met several times during the past two months, but this was the first opportunity some of the DDP leaders had had to meet him face to face. He seemed as eager as Koch-Weser to coalesce. Although no representatives of the February Clubs or the Front 1929 were present, they were mentioned as promising allies. No reference was made to the Christian Trade Union (CTU) personalities who soon joined the DStP.

The following day, 24 July, Koch-Weser addressed a large DDP meeting at the Kroll Opera House in Berlin to inaugurate the Berlin organization's campaign.[32] He said nothing about the negotiations with the VR or the possibility of a new party, although he stressed many of the statist motifs which became familiar DStP propaganda themes. The following day the *Vorstand* met, and Koch-Weser still remained silent about the new party.[33] Only Bäumer mentioned the VR, stressing its admirable social goals and youthful character. Stephan later marveled at the *Vorstand*'s lack of curiosity and the willingness to allow Koch-Weser full powers to negotiate for the party. In the end, the *Vorstand* gave him its blessing to proceed as he saw fit. The next day, 26 July, another meeting occurred, this time with representatives from each of the groups who joined the DStP. They discussed the *Aufruf* to proclaim the new party and the *Aufruf* signatories. In addition to the familiar DDP and VR names, this meeting included the DVP members Winschuh, Theodor Eschenburg, a young historian; Fritz Baltrusch, a CTU leader with considerable trade union and government experience, who was Lemmer's friend; and Erich Obst, an academic who had been active in the DDP in the early years of the party until he became alienated by the *Fraktion*'s conservative economic policies. They apparently joined together to produce the *Aufruf* published on 28 July supported by the signatures of fifty individuals, mostly Democrats but many of them rather obscure members of the party.[34] The DDP's pacifists and best-known Jews were not invited to sign, but several of the later leaders of the DStP, including Heuss and Stolper, were also missing. There seemed to have been a deliberate attempt to find new names as a symbol of the fresh directions and ideas which the DStP was supposed to represent. Actually, the *Aufruf* contained little that was new or fresh, although it stressed a nationalist and revisionist foreign policy and reflected a disillusionment with the political system and parties which the DDP had never publicly emphasized. It seemed calculated to drive out the DDP's left wing and to attract people from the rightist parties.

Two days after the appearance of the *Aufruf*, the *Parteiausschuss* of the DDP met, confused and angry by the appearance of a new party led by the DDP's leaders, professing ideas and goals which only its extreme rightists had previously articulated.[35] They were all aware of Koch-Weser's effort to achieve a *Bürger-Sammlung*. The newspapers contained much news about this, and the party publications and politicians had been dropping clues for months, including favorable comments about the VR. The nature of the *Sammlung* and the tone of the *Aufruf*, however, still shocked many members. Once again, they attacked Koch-Weser, but Stephan exaggerates when he contends that the PA might have rejected the new party had it not been for a great speech of Koch-Weser which turned the meeting around.[36] His opponents in the meeting—mostly pacifists, Jews, and idealistic internationalists, with the possible exception of Mosich—proved unable to transform their personal indignation into an organized opposition, in part because many of the most forceful people in the left wing deserted them. Koch-Weser stressed that the DStP was only a beginning of a *Sammlung* and that the VR was compatible with the DDP. He also sought to reassure them on the Jewish question. Mahraun had told him, he said, that the VR was not anti-Semitic—not any longer. The new party had vocal support from Muhle, the chairman of the Social Republican circle, from Stolper, Höpker-Aschoff, Külz, and others. Heuss gave his qualified support. Hellpach, on the other hand, who had often called for something similar, spoke sharply against the proposed new party and called for Koch-Weser's resignation. He saw Koch-Weser as a barrier to successful negotiations with the DVP, which remained the primary objective for many right-wing Democrats. A few opposed the DStP on the basis of liberal principles. Quidde and Bruno Weil, a functionary of the moderate Jewish organization, *Der Centralverein deutscher Staatsbürger jüdischen Glaubens* (CV), asserted that the DStP *Aufruf* was a clear declaration against pacifists and Jews. Stündt, who soon formed an alternative left-liberal party with Quidde, predicted the DStP would fail and denounced the proposed alliance as a disgrace. When the vote was cast, however, only five members voted against the new party. Many later said they had reservations about it, but like Weil and Heuss they voted for it. Those who could not swallow this curious alliance and the thrust of the *Aufruf* turned to the SPD or the Association of Independent Democrats (*Vereinigung unabhängiger Demokraten*), which was renamed the Radical Democrats (*Radikaldemokratische Partei*), shortly after the election. They soon concluded they would be unable to present candidates in the election. Good intentions and noble ideas were insufficient in themselves to build a political party, as Wolff had discovered when he had founded a short-lived

Republican party. Although the Radical Democrats won few supporters, they at least had a clear conscience.

Meyer shaped the party organization in several motions which were quickly approved. Speed was imperative. An Action Committee of sixteen, later enlarged to twenty-two, then undertook the difficult task of selecting the candidates from the various groups, proportionate to their membership. The DDP, the only constituency with any political experience or organization, received about half of the top list positions. Four men—Koch-Weser, Mahraun, Winschuh, and Erich Glimm, a VR who formerly belonged to the DNVP—constituted the party executive. They determined that Mahraun should lead the party outside the Reichstag, while Koch-Weser was to be the party leader inside the Reichstag; however, Mahraun's role was soon being contested by many DDP local organizations. The Action Committee functioned badly from the beginning and soon *Wahlkreis* and other local groups as well as the DDP *Vorstand*, which still functioned, began to interfere in the selection of candidates. In districts with conflicts between the DDP and the VR candidates, Koch-Weser and Mahraun often resolved the dispute in an authoritarian manner. These actions produced more displeasure in the DDP toward Koch-Weser and because of this, as well as because of his inept handling of news about the negotiations with the DVP, Höpker-Aschoff replaced him on 2 August. Koch-Weser announced that he was taking a short leave of absence, but it turned out to be the end of his political career. Höpker-Aschoff and Mahraun seldom could agree on anything, and whatever direction there had been at the top of the organization quickly deteriorated. The only remaining structure was the old DDP organization as the VR showed little interest or skill in electioneering. Stephan led the campaign and Bäumer and Bornemann handled much of the propaganda chores of the national organization, but most of the work and the fund-raising had to be done at the local level, where the new party received tepid support. When local candidates were well known and respected, such as Jaenicke in Silesia or Heuss in Württemberg, there was some effective organization work, but most of the people who voted for the DStP did so from habit rather than conviction.[37]

In the course of the campaign, the DStP defined its positions somewhat more clearly and sharpened its image, but this sometimes had adverse effects. Not only could many DDP members not support it, but many *Jungdo* members who had opposed this political venture in the first place were repulsed by the compromises Mahraun had made and by the DDP as a political ally. The DDP defectors generally turned to the SPD, while the VR dissidents seem to have either voted for the NSDAP or not voted at all. In addition to Erkelenz, Bergsträsser and two DDP *Wahlkreis* chairmen joined the SPD, while many DDP government officials quietly switched to the SPD or the Z. Many Democrats, however, could not bring themselves to join parties they had denounced for years and tried to find justifications for supporting the DStP. Most convinced themselves they were voting for the old Democratic party, and many local organizations continued to call themselves the DDP. Either because of lack of funds or doubts about the future of the DStP, they used their old letterhead or stamped over it. Many local organizations were still calling themselves "Democratic" in March 1933 in the last regular election of the Weimar Republic. Given the character of many of the VR leaders and the *Jungdo's* program, the most surprising development was the willingness of veteran and respected Democrats to vouch for the DStP and its goals. Martin Rade, Alfred and Marianne Weber, Max Weber's widow, and Maria Baum, a close friend of Erkelenz, were numbered among the many prominent Democrats who publicly endorsed the State party.[38] Even Hellpach finally came around after Koch-Weser was replaced by Höpker-Aschoff, calling the DStP an "interesting experiment." The major urban DDP newspapers, which had been drifting to the right along with many Democrats, also supported the DStP but with varying degrees of acceptance.[39] The BT adopted a rather passive, detached position toward the DStP, and Wolff, who, privately, had called the DStP the "Koch-Weser and Parcifal *Vereinigung*," went on vacation in the midst of the campaign. The FZ, quite understandably, seemed more concerned about the rise of the NSDAP than the fate of the DStP. The VZ, now managed and controlled by the younger and more conservative members of the Ullstein family, showed little of the spunk which it had when edited by Bernhard.[40]

The hastily formed party organization soon broke down, as did personal relations among Democrats and others. The DDP discovered that the VR had no interest in the election fight, and Democrats ended up doing most of the campaign work and fund-raising. Yet the VR claimed a large share of the top list positions. The selection of candidates was greatly complicated by the need to satisfy several constituencies in addition to the usual DDP ones. Soon, the Action Committee was heavily attacked because of its choices, and many prominent Democrats were "sacrificed" or had their feelings bruised in the struggle. The lack of firm written guidelines to regulate the distribution of top positions led to much confusion. When the VR attempted to acquire the top slots in DDP strongholds such as Erkelenz's former district Düsseldorf-West, the local DDP organization and the DDP's *Vorstand* became involved and tried to influence Koch-Weser and Mahraun to select Democrats. In this particular example, the VR prevailed, infuriating Democrats. The VR, on the other hand, often objected to Democratic candidates, particularly if they were veteran politicians, women, "plutocrats," or Jews. There were unpleasant quarrels in organizations throughout the country. Most of the prominent women in the DDP soon tasted the DStP's hostility to them; the Nazis were not the only anti-feminist party in the election of September 1930.[41]

Stephan, a veteran in the art of building lists, played an important part in this process in 1930 and relates the difficulties which the party leadership encountered.[42] Many distasteful bargains had to be struck, although Stephan was not unhappy to see many DDP veterans lose their seats; he had attempted for years to purge the *Fraktion* of elderly and lazy deputies. In many districts, the local organizations were strong enough to determine their own choices. The papers of Stolper, Heuss, Friedensburg, and Jaenicke provide much detail about the selection process in Hamburg, Württemberg, East Prussia, and Central Silesia (Breslau).[43] Stolper was hawked from district to district before he found a congenial constituency, but he gained a seat at the expense of Büll, the leading *Mittelstand* figure in the DDP *Fraktion*.[44] Heavily assailed by anti-Semites, including some in the VR, Stolper occasionally regretted his decision to run for office.[45] But he at least won a seat, while several experienced and able Democrats were pushed aside in favor of inexperienced and sometimes raffish newcomers.[46] The DDP had been content too long with running established figures who could raise their own campaign funds, but the DStP leaders determined to purge many of them. Unfortunately, the replacements were often no more able or popular, and some of the VR selections seemed bizarre to Democrats.

The need to stress different campaign themes and symbols in order to demonstrate the "newness" of the DStP compounded the usual strains in selecting candidates and building lists. Although the DDP leaders as well as the VR determined to display a vigorous and fresh image, they often differed on emphasis and priorities. The VR wanted to represent the DStP as a nationalist movement attempting to reconcile the imperial past with the Republic. It always insisted on displaying the old flag and sometimes refused to show the black, red, and gold, while many Democrats still revered the republican colors and scorned the old banner. The VR was more inclined to stress the Christian character of the DStP as well. Although many conservative Democrats were not averse to driving out radical Berlin Jews, they were usually not openly anti-Semitic. They neither counted on the VR to link Jews, the stock market, and plutocracy, nor did they anticipate attacks on such respectable figures as Stolper and Meyer. While they had differences on the Jewish question, the DDP leaders and the VR essentially agreed on employment of the political vocabulary of the Naumannites, stressing such terms as "national," "social," and "*Volksgemeinschaft*." Still, it is an exaggeration to represent the DStP as essentially a triumph of the Naumann ideology.[47] Many Democrats were shocked to discover that "democracy" as well as "liberalism" were largely omitted from the DStP's statements and to learn that the VR's scorn for the Weimar system rivaled the Nazis'. The VR and the DDP agreed most on foreign policy goals featuring a more blunt and far-reaching demand for treaty revision than in previous campaigns, but the DStP showed a greater distrust of international institutions and ideals than the DDP, forthrightly attacking pacifism.

The DStP's enemies ridiculed its contradictions and its pretensions. The illustrated Nazi *Boebachter*, for example, published a cartoon which showed Mahraun dancing a jig to the order of Jewish Democrats designated as Melchior, Mosse, and Ullstein.[48] For many Democrats, the "interesting experiment" soon became a nightmare. While some DDP and VR candidates running on the same list were in general agreement and respected each other, others soon clashed and their differences became known to the public. Local Democratic organizations, angered and frustrated by the need to work with their "new friends," took out their resentment on Koch-Weser, forcing him to resign from the Action Committee.[49] Höpker-Aschoff replaced him and proved to be a more resolute defender of the DDP's interests and of Jewish candidates like Stolper. He was as committed to the principles of the *Manifesto* as Koch-Weser and as desirous of purging the *Fraktion* of unpopular veterans, but he was offended by the illiberal and boorish behavior of the VR.

Because of local conditions or personal values, many candidates soon deviated from the general thrust of the *Manifesto* and the *Aufruf*, which seemed pessimistic about the survival of the Republic and democratic values. Stolper, for example, stressed the need to work closely with the SPD, a stand which reflected both Hamburg realities and his personal conviction that the Republic could only survive if the SPD shared in the government. Heuss remained consistent with his past record and the atmosphere of Württemberg. He was conservative on the national questions and on economic and social issues, but "liberal" and republican on constitutional subjects. The speeches and writings of Bäumer and Koch-Weser, on the other hand, reflect their disillusionment with the "party system" of Weimar and their conviction that the DStP's principles were in harmony with traditional DDP values. Lemmer and Mahraun, sharing a penchant for nationalist emotion and front-line bathos, demonstrated this by appearing on the same platform and publishing their speeches together.[50] Dietrich, on the other hand, stressed rather dry economic and fiscal subjects and punctuated his speeches with calls for thrift, moderation, and responsibility, while Höpker-Aschoff echoed Dietrich's emphasis but often tied fiscal reform to constitutional and electoral law reform.[51] Both Dietrich and Höpker-Aschoff were strong nationalists, but their demands never exceeded the Brüning government's policy. Few of the DStP speakers dwelled on the social misery of the depression, although they did evince a greater awareness of its political effects than they had in 1923. Nearly all of the DStP speakers attacked "interest politics" and the fragmentation of parties because of the tendency for most parties to associate with interests. Most of the campaign themes would have been employed by conservative Democrats even if the DStP had never been formed. It was only in what Külz and Bäumer called the "little matters" that differences appeared between the mainstream DDP tradition and the DStP. Because the "little matters" were rooted in classic liberal principles, they were of crucial importance to many Democrats. The "Jewish question," in particular, came to symbolize the basic differences between the DStP and the DDP.[52] Dietrich, who, like so many Democrats, had often received generous contributions from Jewish supporters in the past, had little luck in 1930 in raising campaign contributions from businessmen and industrialists. He was reduced to begging money on the grounds that at least the DStP had driven the Berlin radicals out of the party.

The importance of the rising Nazi party during the campaign also concerned the DStP. It was, of course, in the election of September 1930 that the NSDAP became a mass party, polling over 6.4 million votes and 18.4 percent of the votes cast, results rather similar to the DDP's best effort in January 1919. Although most DStP leaders still seemed more frightened of the left than of the NSDAP, the violence which the Nazis caused during the campaign produced much concern. Lemmer later reported that the Nazis broke up every one of his electoral meetings in Pomerania, and, while this may have been an extreme example, every DStP candidate encountered Nazi thuggery in one form or another. In past campaigns, Jewish candidates—Bernhard, for example—had tasted Nazi violence, but in 1930 all candidates suffered harrassment and efforts at intimidation. The Nazis, riding a crest of electoral successes, including the most recent in Saxony, were well financed and prepared, but what struck many Democrats was the energy and commitment of individual party members. The DStP, by contrast, seemed weak and its propaganda inept. Before Koch-Weser stepped down from the Executive Committee on 2 August, a publicity photograph was taken of the group.[53] As propaganda, the photograph must have been disastrous. Nothing in it suggests that these leaders represented something fine and new. Koch-Weser appears angry, exhausted, and resigned to something distasteful; Mahraun glares at the camera, hostile and forbidding; Eschenburg, representing the February Clubs, alone has the appearance of youth and intelligence but is dressed like an effete British aristocrat of the period; Glimm, by contrast, resembles an American gangster—open coat, vestless, dull, brutal face.

The DStP had no illusions during the campaign that it would achieve a victory. The only question was how great its loss would be. As it turned out, it lost about 200,000 votes and its Reichstag delegation was reduced from twenty-five to twenty, too few to form an official *Fraktion*. Once again, the question arose whether the DStP should continue. As usual, the active members concluded that it had to continue. But there were other questions as well. What would be the relations between the principal partners who had formed the DStP, the DDP, and the VR? Who should lead the party now that Koch-Weser was discredited and Mahraun's image tarnished? Should Koch-Weser, Lemmer, and Bäumer, the strongest boosters of the DStP, be permitted to retain their mandates in the aftermath of the defeat?

While the leadership pondered these questions, it also began to analyze the election results with a kind of fascinated horror.[54] The DStP's loss appeared insignificant beside the depletion of the *"Bürger* middle" in the Reichstag. The growth of the NSDAP, moreover, had been paralleled by a great increase in the size of the KPD at the expense of the SPD. Throughout the Reich, the DStP losses ranged from 25 to 33 percent, but the DVP and the DNVP had suffered even greater defeats. Indeed, the only *Bürger* competitor of the DStP to register a slight gain was the WP, but its leaders soon concluded that it had peaked. The SPD, which had drawn large numbers of DDP defectors in 1928 and 1930, lost nearly a half million votes and ten seats in the Reichstag. National events were so overwhelming that it may be helpful to concentrate on one city as a model. Frankfurt a/M was, in 1919 and in later elections, one of the DDP's strongholds, although it showed a decline throughout the period. In 1930, the DStP received about 19,000 votes compared to 23,600 in 1928. The DVP had about the same percentage loss, while the WP registered a slight gain. The NSDAP, however, climbed from 13,700 votes in 1928 to 68,400 in 1930! There were similar results in the largely Protestant areas throughout Germany. In the heavily Catholic areas, the major industrial areas, and large cities, Nazi gains were not as impressive, but everywhere the Nazis won great victories and apparently obtained support from all classes. In Frankfurt a/M, the SPD also lost support to the KPD in keeping with the national pattern. From the beginning, the DStP election analysts realized that the significance of the election overshadowed the future of the DStP. Nevertheless, the leadership necessarily focused on the party's problems.

As they tried to explain the dimensions of the defeat, the immediate reaction of many disgruntled DDP members was to blame the controversial alliance with the VR, even though the decrease in support conformed with a ten-year trend.[55] Mahraun blamed former Democrats for the defeat, particularly controversial Jews, pacifists, and plutocrats.[56] He charged that these Democrats had alienated his followers. The Democrats who were most responsible for the merger—Koch-Weser, Lemmer, and Bäumer—tended to be more even-handed in assessing responsibility; Bäumer and Koch-Weser continued to assert that there had been no basic differences in principle between the DDP and the VR, an astounding assertion in the light of the charges and countercharges of both the DDP members and the VR during and after the campaign. Koch-Weser, Jaenicke, and Lemmer stressed that it had been the pressure of time which had adversely affected the campaign, diminishing the effectiveness of the partnership in many ways. Misinterpretations of remarks and statements which might have been corrected in the span of a normal campaign caused much damage.

Bäumer seemed to be the least repentant of those who had engineered the DStP, but Koch-Weser, Lemmer, and Stephan also aggressively defended the necessity to join with the VR and the other allies.[57] Lemmer attributed much of the responsibility for the failure to the rigidities and negative attitude of the DDP *Fraktion* members. Stephan also largely blamed the failure of the campaign on the DDP. He and Bäumer tended to remember the good qualities of the VR leaders and to stress the strengths of the VR which the DDP lacked. None of the prominent defenders of the VR and its leaders seemed to be troubled by the anti-Semitism, belligerent nationalism, or nostalgia for the imperial past which were repeatedly displayed during the campaign.

There were some Democrats, however, who were contrite. Höpker-Aschoff felt humiliated by the failure and angry because the VR had violated its promises. Meyer was also chagrined at being led astray by Mahraun's assurances and claims. He charged that the VR had lied about the Jewish question and he apologized for the "indecencies" which DDP members had suffered at the hands of the VR. As it turned out, Jews had been routinely purged from published lists of DStP supporters and discouraged from seeking office on the DStP ticket. Meyer as well as Koch-Weser emphasized the significance of the failure of the DVP to join the DStP, and Meyer blamed the VR for the DVP's decision, a charge which Mahraun indignantly denied. Koch-Weser more accurately placed the responsibility on Scholz's shoulders. Stolper, sickened by the anti-Semitic attacks on himself, angrily denounced the VR leaders in private correspondence following the election. Mahraun, he charged, was an alcoholic whose eyes were glazed by midday; Baltrusch he dismissed as "grotesque," while August Abel and Arthur Hesse were described as "political illiterates."[58] In the three weeks following the election, the VR continued to attack Stolper, Meyer, Reinhold, and Höpker-Aschoff, building the case for its decision to leave the DStP. The DStP Democrats overlooked their gullibility in accepting the VR's claims as well as their moral failings in joining with partners who violated basic liberal tenets. They had either never attended a *Jungdo* rally or read a VR publication or—even more contemptible—they were prepared to ignore their principles. There was no excuse for any Democrat to be ignorant of the VR, its leaders, and its ideas. Koch-Weser, Bäumer, and Stephan certainly knew the *Jungdo*'s record in detail. The whole party should be condemned, however, for trusting Koch-Weser and the others. Heuss had serious doubts about the wisdom of the merger and Koch-Weser's leadership, but he remained silent.

Some members looked beyond the wrangling within the DStP and attempted to find more basic explanations for the outcome. Many blamed the results on economic factors.[59] The economic burdens of the middle classes had mounted steadily, they said, and the government had done little to help. The farmers and the *Mittelstand* especially had been hurt by forces beyond their control. It was only natural for them to take out their anger on "the system." Why they voted for the NSDAP, however, was puzzling. Why would people who allegedly wanted order, peace, and work vote for a radical party which seemed to promise upheaval and social unrest?[60] Several DStP commentators noted this irrational trend. Later on, Stephan concluded that nationalism had played a large part in the outcome, but he also noted that most of the NSDAP's supporters were young people, many of whom were white-collar workers who feared the effects of the depression on their income and their social status. Several Democrats commented on the part which new voters and traditional nonvoters had probably had in the outcome. Stolper, who labeled the habitual nonvoters as the "dumbest of the dumb," seemed bitter that such people, reacting against the traditional parties and voting for the extremes, had the power to determine the outcome of the election.[61]

Once the election was over, the most pressing problems concerning the future of the DStP had to be solved first by the Reichstag delegation. Immediately following the election, some former Democrats and VR deputies decided to take separate paths. Others, however, wanted to persevere together in fighting for a place in politics for the "state-supporting middle classes."[62] Meetings were held and letters written to try to iron out the differences which the campaign had exacerbated, but some members seemed more interested in obstructing the peacemakers and began making wild charges. The VR made some impossible demands to increase its power in the party organization, while some Democrats wanted to reverse some concessions already made. Between 27 September, when it was determined that the DStP should continue, and 7 October, when the VR announced it was going its separate way, there were dozens of meetings and much confusion. Clearly, each of the two principal components of the DStP felt abused and betrayed by the other. Jaenicke, a conservative Democrat from Breslau and one of the new deputies, kept a diary for the period from 17 September to 9 October, in which he recorded his participation in meetings as well as conversations with individuals and an occasional rumor.[63] During the campaign, largely isolated from much reliable news from outside his district, he had assumed that the partnership of the Democrats and the VR was working as well nationally as it was in his district in Silesia. There, he had established a good relationship with the Number 2 man on the list, Naumann, a VR man and, like Jaenicke, a former army major. Jaenicke wanted to preserve the DStP as the basis for a larger *Sammlung* of *Bürger* parties and felt that VR membership in the DStP was imperative for this.[64] He was shocked to learn soon after the election how much August Weber and Höpker-Aschoff hated Koch-Weser and how many members wished to deprive Lemmer, Bäumer, and Koch-Weser of their Reichstag mandates in retaliation for their responsibility in creating the DStP. To prevent the breakup of the DStP, Jaenicke met with Mahraun and Bornemann on 24 September. They assured him that the VR would remain in the DStP, but a few days later, the always loose ties began to fall away. Several Democrats attacked Abel, one of the VR leaders, when he publicly advocated that Germany should leave the League of Nations. Soon afterwards, Stolper and Reinhold, both DStP Reichstag deputies, were assailed by the VR because of their association with Jewish and foreign business interests. At about the same time, Bornemann denounced Meyer because of his Jewish ancestry. During the same period, several Democrats revealed other examples of VR bigotry during the campaign as well as the ineffectiveness of the VR organization in the election. On 4 October, Mahraun abandoned all pretenses of maintaining good relations with the Democrats and blamed them for the election failure. He especially censured Jews and pacifists among the Democrats, while holding up Koch-Weser, Bäumer, and Lemmer as outstanding examples of cooperative Democrats. Two days later, a stormy meeting occurred in which the partners attacked each other with few restraints. Meyer and Stolper announced that they could not remain in a party which included the VR, and Stolper read to the gathering Bornemann's attack on Meyer. Bäumer had the gall to defend Bornemann and her own relations with the VR on the grounds that they were both attempting to win over the anti-Semites of the VR by, in effect, meeting them halfway. She was also Koch-Weser's only defender among the Democrats. Lemmer remained true to the VR by defending Mahraun against Democratic assailants and commended him for a "brave" speech he had made, attacking anti-Semitism. Höpker-Aschoff, in the face of Koch-Weser's and Lemmer's defiant determination to retain their Reichstag mandates, summarized the majority sentiment: Koch-Weser must lose his seat, while Lemmer and Bäumer, who had important constituencies—labor, youth, and women—would retain their positions. Koch-Weser fought back. "I'll fight if you want to fight," Jaenicke quotes him as saying. Jaenicke also recounts a blow-by-blow account of the conflicting recollections of Koch-Weser and Höpker-Aschoff over Koch-Weser's "retirement" from the Action Committee. While Höpker-Aschoff reported that Koch-Weser had been derelict in his duty and had fled the battle, Koch-Weser contended that he had been asked to leave the Action Committee temporarily and had complied with Höpker-Aschoff's wishes. He continued to defend the necessity for the DDP to gain allies and the contribution which the VR had made to the campaign. He clearly preferred some VR members to some Democrats. "If you think you can build a party with people like Merten (Otto Merten, the DDP organization leader in Berlin) and Frankfurter (the former Organization Committee chairman) and by sacrificing me, you will be surprised," Jaenicke has Koch-Weser say. Koch-Weser was obviously still bitter at the "Berlin *Richtung*" which had rejected him. Stolper then belabored what most of them knew: they had made a terrible mistake joining with a reactionary group. "We are divided from the VR by a 'whole world,'" he opined. Rather than continue with the VR, he preferred to join with Gottfried Treviranus's Conservative People's party (*Konservative Volkspartei*). This statement produced an interjection from Lemmer: "I'll remember those words a quarter of a year hence!" Meyer told Jaenicke after the meeting that he thought the best solution was to join with the Center party, the only viable middle-class party. He also expressed the opinion in this conversation that any party which included Jews and defended them had no chance to become a mass party and would fail. On the other hand, on philosophical grounds the Jews could not be excluded. This distasteful brawling among former friends and colleagues finally came to an end two days later when the VR leaders announced their departure from the DStP in a formal press conference. They could not resist making several demeaning references to the "old DDP."

The obituaries for the "interesting experiment," to use Hellpach's phrase, were written 8 October. The FZ's account, measured and sympathetic, reflected both the growing conservatism of the paper under great financial pressure, as well as the personal evolution of Cohnstaedt, the paper's leading political writer.[65] It was unfortunate, the FZ contended, that the tactics in forming the DStP had obscured its ideals and goals. But, of course, those same ideals and goals, expressed in the *Aufruf* and the *Manifesto*, had begun the breakup of the party. The DStP press as well as the DStP's business manager, Wilhelm Rexrodt, also evaluated the brief-lived merger.[66] Rexrodt stressed that the experiment had failed because the DVP had not been induced to join the *Sammlung*, and the blame for that he placed on the VR. On a more positive note, Rexrodt continued that the DStP had succeeded in decisively separating itself from the SPD, an old goal of the business wing. He admitted that the *Aufruf* had alarmed many Democrats and produced such initial controversy and misunderstanding that many left the party before the campaign began. Instead of the *Aufruf* binding the divergent groups together, which was the intention of its authors, it had hastened their separation. In addition, the Action Committee, a weak institution from the beginning, multiplied the organizational problems instead of resolving them. Then, according to Rexrodt, the VR had attempted to use the DStP for its own selfish ends. Its anti-Jewish statements had produced unsavory actions which disgusted many Democrats, and its false membership totals were also deplorable. The VR had claimed 400,000 members, but only a small fraction of that number were active or had even voted. Although the DDP claimed only 130,000 members, they were organized in 1250 working local groups. The VR was organized, as it turned out, in only twelve of thirty-five districts. Rexrodt, who wrote under the supervision of the new leaders, Dietrich and Höpker-Aschoff, asserted that, in reality, the VR had never wanted to merge with the DDP and the others. It had only wanted to dominate them for its own ends. The wonder, as Feder noted after the VR press conference on 8 October, was that the DDP had been able to work with the VR for two months.[67]

Soon after the VR departed, the leadership made several personnel changes to keep the organization functioning until a party congress could meet. Höpker-Aschoff became chairman, and August Weber and Rochus von Rheinbaben, a former DVP member active in the Front 1929, were named vice-chairmen. Dietrich was the acknowledged leader of the party, but his cabinet duties left him little time for the DStP. Koch-Weser, without party offices or a Reichstag place, attempted to rally his friends to support him so that he might remain in the Reichstag but failed.[68] He later attempted to rationalize his loss by indicating that constructive work in the Reichstag was impossible and that the party posts meant nothing to him, but he missed the limelight and the responsibility which he had enjoyed so long. It was unfortunate that his career ended on such an unpleasant note. When one compares the leadership of Koch-Weser with Petersen or Naumann, he must be seen as superior to either of them as a party leader. Energetic, intelligent, he eagerly—perhaps too eagerly—assumed responsibility. But he lacked the charisma, warmth, and human qualities to bind men and women to him in friendship and affection. He was also inclined to be too impulsive and, in his last years, too authoritarian. In the course of his career, he made many enemies but few friends.[69] Koch-Weser's enemies derided him as a "little man," both physically and in personal qualities, but he still towered above most of them. He wanted to save a political role for the liberal middle classes as well as himself but became desperate after he was unable to secure an agreement with the DVP. Had he been willing early to sacrifice his own political career and to subject the DDP to the DVP, perhaps a merger might have been achieved, but he was not prepared for such a bargain and neither was the DDP. He never quite overcame his bitterness at being pushed aside when the DStP failed, but after 1933, in Brazil at his cattle ranch, he continued to write and to plan for Germany's future. In many ways, Koch-Weser was the typical German Democrat of the Weimer period, and his *Nachlass*, which reveals the man—warts and all—is his monument.

The DDP terminated itself and officially founded the DStP on 8 November 1930 at the Party Congress in Hannover.[70] Those who wanted the old title rather than *Deutsche Staatspartei* were overwhelmed, but the mechanics of the meeting were reminiscent of the old party, and nearly all of the participants were Democrats. Fischer, who chaired the meeting, was still the party's treasurer. Petersen, old and ill, delivered the elegy for the DDP but not many wept. Petersen embodied the continuity to the early days of the DDP as well as to the Progressive party before it, and his words and style remained unchanged. He could still excite people with his rhetoric and he was still loved. At the same time, he was the most respected figure in the Hamburg organization, which, along with the Württemberg DStP, remained the strongest local organization in the party. If only he had had Koch-Weser's ambition and energy, he might have become the leader many in the DDP so desperately wanted. Following Petersen's predictable oration, Höpker-Aschoff addressed himself to the present and the future of the DStP. Brutally turning his back on the DDP, he defended the necessity for the DStP. A new party was imperative; the DDP had failed. He bravely asserted his confidence in the future, apologized to no one, and showed few regrets. He again demonstrated his strong nationalism and conservative values and ran roughshod over a pacifist, Willy Braubach, who had the temerity to appear at the meeting and to challenge the new direction of the DStP. Figures such as Höpker-Aschoff, Dietrich and Reinhold Maier were obviously in charge, and conservatism was in the saddle. They presided over the last years of the party, years in which the DStP became a smaller splinter group than before but nevertheless refused to quit.

IX

Left Liberals after 1930

The history of the DStP from its formation in November 1930 until its termination in July 1933 was characterized by a progressive deterioration and loss of support until its formal dissolution under Nazi pressure. After that, the DStP leaders sought cover within Germany, engaged in various compromises with the regime, or scattered for safety in other countries. The great hopes the founders of the DStP had in July 1930—to breathe life into the *Bürger* middle of German politics—failed utterly. The VR, as we have seen, soon broke away, and most new recruits had little interest in it after the electoral debacle. What remained in the DStP was the DDP's right wing, a few former left-wing members who apparently could not bear to give up politics, and individuals, such as Winschuh, who could not easily or quickly desert it. The business wing of the DDP provided most of the leaders and the program for the DDP's successor, although it was gravely weakened by defections and deaths and by the general aging of the party. To distinguish the DStP organization from the DDP, the names of the major committees were changed—the *Vorstand* became the *Geschäftsführender Vorstand* while the PA became the *Gesamtvorstand*. In the last six months of the party's history, a three-man executive committee, the *Arbeitsausschuss*, was formed because of Dietrich's ineffectual leadership. The formal structure of the DStP counted for even less than it had in the DDP. The committees seldom met, leaders provided little leadership, and hardly anyone contributed money to the DStP. As a result, the party could not afford much propaganda and there was little news about its activities. The party's former press support disappeared as publishers increasingly sought to separate their investments from partisan politics. In addition, there was little desire to associate with a "loser." Individuals who had previously made sizable contributions to the DDP either husbanded their shrinking resources or turned to other parties.

The organization mirrored the DStP's decline. In the early years when money was plentiful, the DDP printed and widely distributed the protocols of the major party meetings, and dozens of party publications regularly appeared even between elections. In time, these practices were curtailed, and it became common to summarize the discussion in meetings rather than to reproduce the verbatim record. However, the editing, typing, and reproducing of the materials for wide distribution was thoroughly professional, presided over by Issberner, a key figure in the *Zentrale* and the party archivist.[1] As the party declined, its publications steadily decreased in number, but the party headquarters continued to turn out a large volume of information about the party's activities and positions on issues, and its newspaper service distributed stories to hundreds of newspapers about the party. In the DStP, by contrast, it proved impossible to maintain professional party secretaries or even competent officials in the *Zentrale*. The staff soon consisted of a part-time general secretary and business manager—first Rexrodt and then Nuschke—Issberner, and a part-time typist. With the exception of a new journal, the *Deutscher Aufstieg*, a weekly, the publications were cheaply printed and produced. The protocols seem to have been assembled and typed by volunteers. Few of the committees could afford to distribute notes of their meetings or sponsor publications even at election times.

Although no reliable membership statistics are available for the DStP, it would seem that the paid membership number declined precipitously. The most committed members of the DDP who had aided in the "little tasks" of party organization had been women, young people, and the left wing. Most of them turned away from the DStP, apparently to the SPD, between 1928 and 1930. Those who remained soon reacted against the blatant male domination and the scorn for the youthful members and the left wing apparent in the DStP's leadership. Through 1928, Jews were active in party organizations throughout the Reich, but most of them, especially young Jews, rejected the DStP. The party missed their help. Soon after the election of 1930 several DStP leaders visited local organizations throughout the country and discovered that they had either disappeared or had been transformed into social clubs for senior citizens. Only in Württemberg and Hamburg did the DStP organizations display any vitality. The most important committees of the party—the Women's Committee, the Young Democrats (now the *Reichsbund der Staatsbürgerlichen Jugend*), and the *Beamten* Committee—soon expired.

The leadership of the DStP changed considerably after July 1930. Koch-Weser remained on the sidelines, bitter and inconsolable but unable to separate himself from the party. Erkelenz became a member of the SPD. Fischer alone retained his old position of importance into 1932, although he was far less involved than he had been. The former vice chairmen and honorary chairmen, except for Petersen, were no longer active. The most prominent women in the DDP in 1929—Bäumer, Lüders, Ulich-Beil, and Dönhoff—still worked for the DStP, but they were accorded little respect. Several of the youth leaders, such as Lemmer and Jaeger, were active as well, but the organization was pathetically small. The most important leaders in the national party were Dietrich and Höpker-Aschoff, but neither seemed particularly interested in leading a splinter party. A few of the strong local organizations still functioned. Petersen in Hamburg, Merten in Berlin, and Albert Hopf and Heuss in Württtemberg kept those organizations alive, although they were feeble compared to their earlier years. In Saxony, Külz and Goetz still fought on, although it was a losing battle, while in Oldenburg Gustav Ehlermann had even less chance to succeed. Otto Baumgarten in Schleswig-Holstein presided over a dismal political scene. Hundreds of former Democrats, who were accustomed to defeat and disappointment, continued, from habit, to attend party meetings and to assume small responsibilities. Most were deeply pessimistic about the DStP from its founding, but what were the alternatives if one were bitten by the political bug? Besides, it was still interesting and exciting to argue politics and discuss public issues. They remained intensely political men although they often laughed among themselves about the small size and unimportance of the party. The last Reichstag delegations sometimes referred to themselves as the "last of the Mohicans." The national organization was an empty shell; Nuschke and Dietrich alone kept it going. Dietrich remained the outstanding figure in the DStP although, until Papen replaced Brüning in May 1932 and he lost his cabinet position, he seldom had time for the party. Then, either Dietrich or hs wife was ill so that he was frequently at health spas and unable to be politically energetic.[2] There was much grumbling about his failure to be a more diligent leader, especially by Heuss and Lüders, but no one had the ambition to unseat him or replace him.[3] In the last six months of the DStP's history, the Hamburg and Württemberg organizations finally shouldered him aside and replaced him with a triumvirate of an old and ailing Petersen, a youthful and energetic Maier, the Württemberg minister of economics, and Dietrich. Maier became the rising young man in the DStP in its last years.[4] He was not bound by dogmatic adherence to traditional liberal principles nor bowed down by the sense of helplessness and defeatism common among the DStP veterans. But there was little either he or the new *Arbeitsausschuss* could do under the circumstances. The conditions in these years dispirited the bravest men and women, often leaving them unable to deal with anything but routine and trivial party activities. The level of debate in the party meetings, if we can judge from the summaries, was pedestrian and uninspired.

A good example of the DStP's devotion to the trivial was the attempt, led by Nuschke, to write a statement of guiding principles—*Richtlinien*—to give the DStP a program and a set of goals which would distinguish it from the DVP and the DDP.[5] It was easy enough to rename the committees, but the statement of principles proved too difficult. The leadership polled the local organizations for suggestions and asked them to make recommendations. Perhaps the most thoughtful list was compiled by Paul Helbich and the Ruhr DStP organization,[6] although virtually all of the points mentioned were familiar DDP demands. It did stress the need to strengthen the executive and to weaken the power of the parties and parliament, but this was a familiar emphasis also stated by Dietrich and Höpker-Aschoff in the election of 1930. It also emphasized the need to decentralize Prussia's administration to diminish the SPD's importance in Prussia. Dozens of organizations submitted lists, although they were slow to turn them in and most of them proved to be uninspired catalogs of familiar DDP goals. They even lacked the right-wing and statist thrust of the 1930 statements which had so offended the DDP's left wing. After nine months, the statements were finally collated and a statement written in which no one seemed interested. It was perhaps a harmless form of wheel spinning, but a more resolute effort to improve the financial condition of the party or to find a more aggressive leader than Dietrich or Höpker-Aschoff might have been more useful.

This pathetically weak, ill-financed, and indifferently led party fought three national elections between October 1930 and March 1933, several important *Land* elections and numerous city and local elections. As the same general pattern of defeat became evident in all of them and it was apparent that the DStP was incapable of contesting elections alone, the DStP had no choice: it had to either find electoral allies or join with other parties in a new party. As a result, it made frequent efforts, some apparently sincere and others half-hearted, to gain allies. The most notable new effort to achieve a *Bürger-Sammlung* was the formation of the *National-Verein* by Wildemuth,[7] but there were dozens of regional and local attempts by conservatives, liberals, and peasant leaders to combine before it was too late. At the *Land* and communal level, many of the temporary alliances were successful, and they probably helped to retard the decline of the *Bürger* parties. At the national level, however, the DStP proved unable or unwilling to achieve such alliances, largely because there was no consensus on which parties were desirable allies. Some members, particularly in Prussia, preferred the SPD or the Center party, both of which would probably have been cooperative in the critical election of July 1932. Others, however, continued to favor the DVP, which had turned to the right to the DNVP and the NSDAP. Still others wanted to join with small peasant or Protestant parties. The key meetings to discuss a list connection for the July election of 1932 were the meetings of the *Geschäftsführender Vorstand* and the *Gesamtvorstand* on 7 July.[8] The members who attended both meetings were, for the most part, familiar DDP leaders, including Bäumer, Dietrich, Nuschke, Barteld, Rönneburg, Fischer, Höpker-

Aschoff, Heuss, and Leon Zeitlin, one of the few Jews still active in the DStP. Winschuh, who had been given Koch-Weser's Reichstag seat, was also present. Before the meetings, there had been a concerted if quiet effort to depose Dietrich, but this failed for want of a candidate and was not mentioned during the meetings. The dominant topic was list connections. Dietrich explained that several list connections had already been explored, including one with the Z, another with the SPD, and even one with the BVP, but for one reason or another they had all rejected the DStP's offer. Several members did not believe Dietrich, for it was well known that the SPD, in particular, had offered to help. Outside the major committees, Koch-Weser had been lobbying for list connections with the SPD. Rönneburg, supported by Konrad Schött, led off by demanding a list connection with the SPD; otherwise, he maintained, the results in the election would be catastrophic for the DStP. Rönneburg contended that while they might lose some support, they might gain as many as 671,000 votes. Several DDP leaders opposed this suggestion, including Heuss and Bäumer, close followers of the man who had wanted to forge a close working relationship with the SPD, Friedrich Naumann. Bäumer contributed a red herring—as she was inclined to do—by falsely contending that the SPD was not a fit partner because it was drawing closer and closer to the KPD. Heuss asserted that any list connection with the SPD would result in the loss of DStP seats in Baden and Württemberg. He also warned that all of the former DVP members would leave the DStP if it joined with the SPD even if it were only a "technical list connection," although in fact the DStP had attracted few former DVP members. Powerful voices from the business wing also opposed any ties with the hated socialists often blamed for the crisis; Fischer, Zeitlin, and Winschuh predicted disastrous consequences to the DStP. Outside of the committees, there had been an effort to thwart a SPD alliance as well. Mosich and Külz had been active in this. Mosich wrote to Gessler to organize a *Bürger* alliance against "socialism," which apparently included National Socialism.[9] An alliance with the Z party had even less backing than one with the SPD. Bäumer and the Baden wing of the party, where hatred of Catholics was especially strong, led the opposition. In concluding the *Geschäftsführender Vorstand* meeting, Dietrich summarized the majority sentiment, contending that without consensus for a list connection the DStP should go it alone.

In the *Gesamtvorstand*, a few more left-wing voices were present and heard. Lemmer, Barteld, and Maria Krause supported Rönneburg's demand for a list connection with the SPD. Heuss again led the opposition, seconded by Curt Platen, Reinhold, Fischer, and Höpker-Aschoff. Platen spoke for the Hamburg organization. Dietrich argued that the DStP had to represent the principles of *bürgerliche* and economic freedom and that the SPD would be detrimental to this stance. On the other hand, Barteld contended that the only way that democracy and freedom could be preserved was if the DStP worked with the SPD. Few rank-and-file members of the party probably would have accepted this; they still thought of the SPD as the enemy of freedom. On this occasion, they took a formal vote and defeated the list connection with the SPD twenty-nine to thirteen with six abstentions. As a result, the DStP entered the election battle alone.[10] The second order of business in the *Gesamtvorstand* was to formulate the *Reichslist*. This was always a bitterly contested struggle before every election, and July 1932 was no exception in spite of the puny size of the party. Bäumer cleared the way for another woman by announcing her withdrawal from an active political role. She suggested Ulich-Beil or Lüders to replace her in a top position on the *Reichslist*. In the end, Dietrich gained the first position, followed by Lemmer and Lüders, but it was not long before Lüders was demoted by the leadership to a lesser position.[11] Höpker-Aschoff moved up the list, followed by Barteld and Reinhold. Lüders received the top position in Düsseldorf-West, Erkelenz's old district, as compensation, but she refused to be consoled, and Dönhoff resigned in disgust as the head of the women's organization.

In the election of July 1932, the DStP sounded more like the old DDP than the confused and illiberal party which had fought the September 1930 election. It resolutely attacked the government of Papen, which had replaced the Brüning-Dietrich government at the end of May, and it attacked the Nazis in apocalyptic language. The most common theme of its electoral propaganda assailed dictatorship, whether Nazi dictatorship or Communist dictatorship. The DStP also bravely defended civil liberties and the principle of equal rights, although its defense of Jews was rather guarded. Once again, its message of moderation and warnings against extremes went unheeded. The DStP clearly knew a great deal more about the NSDAP by July 1932 than it had known earlier, in part because of the research and writing of Heuss, whose book *Hitlers Weg*, published in 1932, went through several printings.[12] Heuss found the strength of the Nazi movement in Hitler and the party's propaganda, but he also discovered that the NSDAP had succeeded in uniting people of various educational levels and classes in a mass movement with a common purpose. In many ways, it was a perceptive study, but its slightly mocking tone indicates that Heuss was incapable of taking the NSDAP seriously. He could not imagine that the NSDAP could actually govern Germany.

In the election, the DStP received about 372,000 votes and four seats, compared to 1.3 million votes and twenty seats in 1930. The NSDAP, on the other hand, gained about 13.7 million votes and 230 seats and became Germany's largest party, while the KPD received about 5.3 million votes and eighty-nine seats. Together, the two foremost enemies of liberal democracy in Germany had a majority of the seats. Was it any wonder that Constitution Day, a few weeks later, resembled a wake, and most people concluded that the German people wanted a dictator? The election results convinced most State party leaders that Papen's days as chancellor were numbered and that he would probably be replaced soon by General Kurt von Schleicher. There was also some perceptive speculation that if Schleicher did not succeed in forming a stable government after the next election, he would be replaced by Hitler.[13]

After the election, another familiar debate about the party's future occurred. Several of the realists favored immediate dissolution as the best course, but once again the party proved difficult to kill off. At the first significant party meeting following the election on 2 September, Dietrich, whose leadership was widely questioned, favored dissolving the party, but the Hamburg, Württemberg, and Baden organizations wanted it to continue.[14] Massive defection of some of the strongest supporters of left liberalism in the election seemed to indicate no hope for the party. As Dietrich often observed, the age of individualism was over. What hope was there for a party which stressed individual freedom? No one had any confidence in a *Bürger-Sammlung*. Nuschke, with his vested interest in the party's continuance, reminded the committee that only a party congress could dissolve it. He wished to poll the membership before any rash action was taken. On 11 September, the *Gesamtvorstand* met and went over the same ground.[15] Dietrich felt that the consensus was to dissolve the party, but others contested this, and the DStP fought two more national elections.

The wailing and recriminations for the failure in the July election of 1932 were scarcely over when preparations had to be made for a new election. The fate of parliamentary democracy was now the most important question. The possibility of a future *Bürger* party alliance seemed dim in view of the failures to conclude a *Bürger-Sammlung* for the July election. The unwillingness of the DVP to act with the DStP and Dietrich's reluctance to act without the DVP isolated the State party.[16] The local organizations had virtually disappeared. Baumgarten sketched a picture of his organization in 1932 which was probably typical of most of them.[17] Unable to secure allies, he had no helpers and no money. Those who had voted for the DStP in July refused to throw away their vote again. We are deluding ourselves, he advised the national headquarters, if we think we can accomplish anything without money or workers. Only in Baden and Württemberg were there still sufficient resources, human and monetary, to produce campaign literature and to campaign in the traditional ways. Many of the subgroups of the DStP had disintegrated. The Women's Committee seemed more interested in fighting old personal feuds than in working for the DStP.[18] Discontent with Dietrich's leadership continued, and Heuss attempted once again to undermine him, but Höpker-Aschoff refused to assume the leadership. Heuss felt that the only other possible leader was Walter Schreiber but admitted that Schreiber had few personal qualities which were politically attractive.[19] Heuss refused to consider becoming the leader because of the need to provide for his family. Actually, Dietrich seems to have made a strong effort in November 1932 to lead the party and to generate a major effort, but it could no longer respond. The only note of optimism in the campaign was the general feeling that the Nazis had peaked and would decline.

The election issue of *Deutscher Aufstieg*, on 30 October 1932, summarized the DStP's electoral message.[20] It was now the only national journal, aside from *Die Hilfe*, to support the DStP. The DStP, according to *Deutscher Aufstieg*, represented what it called the *Freiheitliche-Nationale Bürgertum*. It spent much time attacking the monarchical intrigues of Hugenberg, denounced the Nazi economic ideas, called for individual freedom, civic equality, and defense of private property. It was, as usual, opposed to dictatorship and reaction, and retained a taste for political doggerel:

> Volk ist erwacht,
> Nazi verkracht.
> Volk sei bedacht
> Wähl' Liste 8!

Meinecke contributed to this issue. He too seemed to fear a Hugenberg monarchical restoration more than a Nazi victory. He had little sympathy for an electoral alliance with the SPD or the Center party. The major political rally occurred early in October in Mannheim when Dietrich, Maier, and Petersen addressed a considerable crowd. Their speeches were later reproduced and published under the title *Der Weg der Nationalen Demokratie* (*The Way of National Democracy*). The DStP received only about 336,000 votes and only won seats for Heuss and Dietrich.

With the election over, the Democratic realists began trying to convince Dietrich and the Württemberg and Baden organizations to dissolve the party. Failing that, various individuals simply resigned. Lüders, Jaenicke, August Weber, Richthofen, Reinhold, and Meyer gave up, hoping their action would force the termination of the party, but Maier organized a meeting of the *Arbeitsausschuss* to discuss the party's future.[21] As he admitted, the Reichstag delegation of two was laughable and there were few chances to secure electoral allies, but he and others were still reluctant to give up. The *Arbeitsausschuss* met on 25 November, and the members discussed the now familiar alternatives.[22] In the end, they agreed to continue. They also passed a resolution condemning the "political reaction" in Prussia. Meanwhile, the crippled party continued to disintegrate. The Women's Committee seemed more interested in barring Lüders from the leadership than anything else, while the youth group had virtually expired. Only Württemberg seemed to have an organization with any spirit remaining. The party there sponsored its annual conference in January, and it still attracted audiences for the speakers. Maier was the principal speaker after Dietrich declined the invitation because of poor health. He sounded like Hellpach in his prime as he called for more authority for German democracy.

The *Gesamtvorstand* of the DStP met on 8 January 1933 with seventy-five members in attendance and with Dietrich still acting as chairman despite his earlier inclination to quit and the grumbling of Heuss and others about his failure as a leader.[23] Dietrich gave a short speech in which he indicated that he was still proud that 336,000 had remained true; he then left the meeting. After his departure, the session broke down in wrangling and complaining. The meeting concluded with the passing of a resolution which affirmed faith in the "middle course" and in the "national idea," which it still felt might rally supporters. The DStP seemed unaware of the fact that the Hitler-Hugenberg forces had appropriated the "national idea."

In the weeks that followed this meeting, Nuschke continued his lonely effort to maintain the organization. He attempted to raise money from old party friends to sustain a skeletal organization but with little success. Stolper's refusal was typical.[24] He indicated to Nuschke that, for some time, he had only really been a guest in the party. Moreover, he could not afford a contribution to the party. He would have resigned, he wrote, but he tried to avoid public declarations and did not want to appear to be abandoning a sinking ship. It was evident that he still bore a grudge against Dietrich and others for refusing to accept his advice on fiscal questions. Nevertheless, he hoped to remain friends and intended to remain close to the Berlin group. This was a characteristic sentiment of many Democrats. Despite their often bitter differences, they still enjoyed the social contacts of the DStP. They entertained each other in their homes or met at the Democratic Club. The shared political values and the intellectual stimulation they afforded each other, combined with their dread of political extremism, provided a firm bond which *Deutscher Aufstieg*, as well as *Die Hilfe* and the liberal urban press, furthered.

Hitler's chancellorship, which began on 30 January 1933, was soon followed by purges of civil servants, teachers, and academics. The harassment of Democratic municipal officials, which had existed for several years, increased. Democrats such as Külz, Luppe, and Friedensburg received threats. Despite this ominous atmosphere, the DStP pulled itself together sufficiently to wage another national campaign. Once again, the DStP discussed possible electoral allies and list connections. Nuschke, in particular, stressed the necessity for a list connection with the SPD, which was willing to help, as it had been in July 1932. Some still opposed this course; not even the threat of a Hitler-Hugenberg dictatorship would convince some members to ally with the SPD. The leadership finally determined to make a "technical list connection" with the SPD in the face of the opposition.[25] Even Heuss apparently approved of the list connection.

Several prominent members announced their resignations in opposition to this tactic despite Dietrich's efforts to explain the necessity for the action,[26] and the DVP attempted to win support for itself by attacking it. The Saxon organization fought the connection bitterly and made its own local arrangements. The formation of the *Reichslist*, as always, produced difficulties and bad feelings. The only prominent recruit from the WP, Otto Colosser, was lowered to second place on the Berlin list, which caused much anger in some quarters.

During an election campaign marked by Nazi and Communist violence, the DStP kept up its familiar attack against the extremists. Once again, its meetings were frequently interrupted or broken up by the Nazis. Maier seems to have been a special target of the NSDAP in Württemberg, where several of his electoral rallies were disturbed.[27] Although the DStP largely dropped the use of the term "State party" in this election and preferred to use the term "National Democrats," the *Aufruf* contained the hackneyed appeals of the past.[28] Once again, it stressed the economic issues favored by the middle classes and showed a special regard for the insecurity of the government officials and employees. In foreign policy it remained revisionist. It also again attacked the excesses of Nazi demagoguery and repudiated the NSDAP program in some detail. But few people were reading DStP propaganda, and even DStP members began to urge an accommodation with the Nazis.[29] Most of the local organizations of any importance campaigned under different names and with local allies, to the disappointment of the national leaders, who still hoped to prevent the party's disintegration. Although in the election the DStP received about 334,000 votes and five seats in the Reichstag, the slight improvement in its Reichstag strength was due solely to the list connection with the SPD. The results in Prussia, where there was also a tie to the SPD, were similar.

On the evening of 27 February 1933, the Reichstag building caught fire, and the Nazis used the "emergency" to crack down even harder on the extreme left and the Jews and to speed the exodus of "known democrats and republicans" from government service. The "coordination" of state governments was almost complete at the time of the election of the last Weimar Reichstag on 5 March 1933. Hitler immediately demanded the passage of an "enabling bill" to give him dictatorial power for four years. The KPD was barred from the Reichstag and most of the Communist leaders were either in hiding, in flight, or in concentration camps by the time the newly elected Reichstag met for its first meeting. The Nazis also threatened the SPD and several of its deputies, but it remained defiant in contrast to the attitudes of the bourgeois parties. The Center party, concluding that resistance was hopeless and that it was doomed, agreed to vote for the Enabling Bill, which gave Hitler and Hugenberg the necessary two-thirds majority. The DStP joined with the remaining middle-class parties to support the measure, isolating the SPD in opposition.[30] It proved to be the last action of any importance by the DStP. Hitler did not need the DStP's votes, but it gratuitously blessed his dictatorship in order to curry favor with the government. With this action the DStP betrayed everything left liberalism had once represented. In the discussion and debate in the Reichstag delegation which preceded the vote, Dietrich and Heuss wanted to vote against the bill, although Heuss seemed to have been the most unequivocal in his opposition. Lemmer and Landahl, regarded as members of the left wing of the DDP and the DStP, and Maier, a member of the right wing, argued that by supporting the Enabling Bill they would provide a legal limitation to Hitler's exercise of power. In four years he would be compelled to give up his emergency powers or become illegal! While this argument scarcely seems credible in the light of the Nazi actions in the preceding three years, Maier and his supporters apparently believed it at the time. Later, they offered other explanations for supporting Hitler's dictatorship, stressing that Hitler already had the votes he needed and to vote against him would only hurt DStP party members who were civil servants. Dietrich, in a letter to the former Progressive and DDP deputy Ablass, provided another explanation: the DStP could not be the only *Bürger* party to vote with the SPD.[31] Heuss and Dietrich were persuaded to vote with the majority of three, although in the past, on questions of conscience, members had usually voted as individuals. Maier spoke for the party in the brief debate which preceded the vote.[32] For the record, he voiced his—and his party's—apprehensions about the far-reaching nature of the grant of power in the bill. He also stressed the need to continue to protect the rights of civil servants, the independence of the courts, the principle of civic equality, as well as artistic, scientific, and intellectual freedom—all historic left-liberal concerns. Even though Maier must have known, in view of the Nazi record and the atmosphere in the Reichstag, that the Hitler-Hugenberg government would violate these principles as it had violated the rights of the KPD, the DStP supported the dictatorship anyway.

Shortly afterwards, the DStP deputies in the Prussian *Landtag* were removed, ostensibly because they had cooperated with the SPD in the election. In view of this, it seemed that the Reichstag delegation's future would most likely be curtailed soon, and the DStP soon received pressure to disband. During this same period, the Nazis forced several well-known Democrats in government service and academic life to retire early. A few controversial Jewish Democrats fled Germany for their lives. Most of the senior civil servants were terminated unceremoniously. Goetz's experience was exceptional; he enjoyed a dignified retirement dinner and an "appreciation night" in which Heuss was the principal speaker. Goetz also had an opportunity to make some comments about the work of the DDP/DStP and the achievements of the Republic. The Weimar democracy, he contended, began the dismantling of the peace settlement, and it had spread the "national idea" to the working classes, achieving the old Naumannite goal. He also defended the SPD but largely because of its struggle against the KPD and for its acceptance of the *"bürgerliche Demokratie"* of Weimar. Goetz asserted that they had done their work well in the DDP and the DStP, and that in the process they had forged a bond of friendship and a memory of having worked together which would endure. In his opinion, the greatest contribution of the DDP/DStP was its service to the fatherland. He felt that the Republic's successors would have difficulty matching its service to the nation.[33]

At the time of the DStP's vote on the Enabling Bill, no apparent opposition to the decision of the Reichstag delegation arose, although there was some curiosity about it. Only after 1945 were questions raised about the propriety and courage of the decision on the part of former DDP/DStP members. Thomas Dehler, an independent-minded and obstreperous member of the *Freie Demokratische Partei* (FDP), the successor of the DDP/DStP, sharply criticized the action in 1959 and implied that the members, and especially Maier, had lacked courage. The Württemberg *Landtag* investigated the assertions but reached no conclusion. The fact that all of the DStP members gained prominence in the postwar occupation governments and in the first years of the Federal Republic probably inhibited a critical investigation. While Maier and his colleagues had not behaved courageously, they had acted reasonably; and reasonable and orderly behavior has always been highly prized among German *Bürgern*.

Late in March 1933, Nuschke mailed a *Rundschreiben* to prominent members of the DStP in which he defended the action of the Reichstag delegation and expressed support for the government. The Hitler-Hugenberg government, he made clear, was the only legal government, and the DStP was a law-abiding party. Indeed, if the government found it necessary to dissolve all parties, the DStP would accept the decision without question. In addition, the DStP could be counted on to support the government's foreign policy—regardless of what that policy might be. "The struggle for German freedom and equality in the world is a nonpartisan concern, and we will support any government which can achieve foreign policy successes."[34] Meanwhile, Jewish Democrats were fleeing Germany for their lives, and non-Jewish former politicians and officials were being arrested and interrogated and jailed by the *Gestapo*. In mid-May, the *Gesamtvorstand* met to discuss the future of the party, a familiar enough subject but in a radically changed political environment.[35] This time, it met in the Hotel Prinz Albrecht in Berlin rather than in the familiar Democratic Club, now closed. Representatives from twenty-nine electoral districts and a scattering of others attended, some of whom had previously resigned from the party but now wanted to observe the last rites of left liberalism. Dietrich, Maier, and Petersen were not present, apparently intimidated by conditions "outside." Luppe, the beleaguered mayor of Nürnberg, however, made the long journey and was congratulated for his attendance. Goetz, a man of courage as well as liberal convictions, opened the meeting and Nuschke sketched the political situation to the gathering, which included figures such as Heuss, Lüders, Barteld, Rönneburg, Gerhard Vogt, Bartschat, Ehlermann, and Oscar Hofheinz—all veteran Democratic leaders. While both Ehlermann and Vogt called for the immediate dissolution of the party, the majority determined that it should continue despite the difficulties and the dangers. At the conclusion of the meeting, Heuss gave a speech on foreign policy which, though unfortunately not summarized, was cheered, and then the *Gesamtvorstand* approved a statement which asked the members to remain true to the state, the fatherland, and to the *"bürgerliche Freiheit."* These qualities, it was said, had built the sense of German national consciousness and had to be kept alive at all costs.

After this meeting, some political activity continued at the local level. The DStP, for example, participated in elections for the Hamburg *Bürgerschaft* and elected three members to it. The NSDAP, however, gained an absolute majority. It was common in these weeks of May and June 1933 to hear of the arrests or the flight of former Democrats and the purge of civil servants and teachers who had strongly supported the Republic. Some of the party leaders at this time received requests from their constituents to investigate the imprisonment of relatives.[36] In late June, the Reich government banned the DStP from any further political activity in Prussia,[37] and the DStP decided to dissolve itself before the government could take the same action it had taken in the case of the SPD.[38] Although the DStP Reichstag delegation later had the temerity to protest various illegal actions against the DStP and chided the government for its failure to respond positively to the assistance the DStP had given it by voting for the Enabling Bill, the delegation seemed most anxious to put some distance between itself and the SPD. While the party disbanded in confusion, losing much of the party's archives in the process, the individual members took different paths to personal survival.

The members most vulnerable to government retaliation and punishment were civil servants, Jews, teachers, and university professors. If they were clearly identified as party members—and hence strong supporters of Weimar—they were forced to retire on a reduced pension, far smaller than the one to which they were entitled and barely adequate to live on. If they were relatively young, they had to find employment in the private sector or in noncontroversial government positions unrelated to their previous positions. A few former DDP/DStP leaders had the temperament and the opportunity to collaborate with the Nazi regime and adjusted well to the new order. Rudolf Diels, for example, a Prussian police official who had been an active Democrat with many Democratic friends, became the first head of the *Gestapo*.[39] He contended, probably correctly, that he used his position to aid several former Democrats in 1933–1934. He soon transferred to the civil administration in Hannover, where he became the *Regierungspräsident*. He proved to be flexible enough to flourish under both the Nazis and the Federal Republic after 1949. Several other Democrats, most notably Stephan and Max Winkler, once a Prussian *Landtag* deputy of the DDP, not only retained their posts but received promotions and new responsibilities. Others were compelled to serve the government. Höpker-Aschoff, for example, was apparently conscripted for state service and worked for Winkler in administering expropriated properties.[40] Friedensburg, a reserve officer who was interned in the 1914–1918 war in Gibraltar, England, and Switzerland, used his training and talents as a geologist and writer to serve as a civilian employee of the army, while Wildemuth, a reserve colonel and a hero of the first war, commanded an infantry regiment and gained fame as the defender of Le Havre, where he was once again gravely wounded. Others found survival less hazardous. Heuss wrote for and edited *Die Hilfe* for several years and also wrote for the FZ under a pseudonym. Eventually, however, he was forced to give up his journalistic work and took refuge in historical research and in the writing of his great biographies of Naumann and Robert Bosch. Erkelenz had even less opportunity to earn his livelihood under the Nazis and lived in obscurity in Berlin until 1945 when marauding Russian laborers killed him. Bäumer wrote for *Die Hilfe* and *Die Frau* for several years and became a successful writer of historical fiction. Of all the prominent Democrats, she showed the most willingness to make her peace with the Nazi regime.[41] Lemmer became a correspondent for several foreign newspapers in Berlin and walked a narrow line between objective reporter and Nazi apologist.[42] Stephan, who had been in the Foreign Office between 1929 and 1933, transferred to Goebbels' Propaganda Ministry, where he became a well known press aide. While he clearly gave his services to the Nazi government, most recent students of the DDP have found his candor about his career in the Nazi years refreshing. He never attempted to deny his role or obfuscate his motives. Winkler became a specialist in managing and selling confiscated Jewish properties, including the major newspapers which had once supported the DDP/DStP. Heile, Korell, Baum, and dozens of others lived in relative poverty and some danger in the Nazi years. The *Gestapo* repeatedly arrested Heile, the family farmlands were seized, and he was unable for several years to secure any employment. Ironically, Schacht, his former party friend, rescued him at perhaps the low point in his life, while Schacht was minister of economics, by giving him a position as a translator at the *Reichsbank*, which enabled him to qualify for government assistance. Landahl, unable to teach, eventually found suitable employment in the private sector in a field related to education. Dietrich, who at first had some difficulties practicing law, built up a flourishing practice once again. Heuss-Knapp became the major breadwinner in the Heuss household by writing radio advertising until the Heusses were forced, late in the war, to take refuge in Heidelberg from the bombing of Berlin. Nearly all of the former Democrats, many of whom were quite elderly, suffered from the bombing raids, and Luppe was killed in one at the end of the war. Ulich-Beil's account of her life during the war is especially revealing.[43] Several Democrats were denounced by self-righteous guardians of Nazi purity, and Friedensburg, in particular, had a narrow escape after an eccentric female questioned his patriotism. Lüders was arrested and jailed, apparently the victim of a mistake, although such experiences were useful in advancing postwar political careers. Luppe, a marked man before 1933 because of his judicial encounters with Streicher, suffered mistreatment by the Nazis,[44] while Korell led a life of degrading poverty. After the attempt on Hitler's life on 20 July 1944, several former Democrats were detained and questioned, but they were too prominent or too harmless to be dispatched to concentration or death camps. The academic figures, including several historians, continued to research and write throughout the Nazi period, although they were forbidden to teach. After a lifetime of cautious behavior and commitment to the welfare of the state and nation, they succumbed to fear and threats, surviving under difficult and unpleasant conditions.

The fate of the Democrats who had Jewish ancestors or spouses was a marked contrast to those who did not. They generally felt compelled to leave Germany soon after 1933, and fortunately most of them had the means and opportunity to save themselves and their families. There were only two prominent Jewish Democrats who perished in Nazi hands: Wolff and Fritz Elsas, a prominent municipal official in Berlin. Wolff was a marked man in the Nazi litany of villains; he was on the Nazi death list as early as 1923. He left Germany in March 1933 for France, his second home, tarried there after seeing to the safety of his family, was rounded up by the *Gestapo* after the German invasion, and died in a Berlin hospital after mistreatment in several concentration camps. Bernhard Falk fled into Belgium, but his fate remains a mystery; Bernhard Weiss, a Prussian police official, found sanctuary in England. Cohnstaedt, Feder, and Georg Bernhard were also in the first group of emigrés. Feder went to France, where he pursued his journalistic work under great difficulties. He fled to Brazil in 1941 and continued writing and lecturing until he returned to Germany in 1957. Bernhard, too, first went to France and worked on an emigré resistance newspaper, but he once again became the center of a scandal in which his veracity was questioned and he departed for the United States. In America, he worked, apparently unhappily, for the Institute of Jewish Affairs until he died in 1944, his reputation ruined and his life shattered. Stolper, by contrast, adjusted well to America, wrote several well-regarded books and became a friend of and adviser to Herbert Hoover, whom he accompanied on his postwar survey of German conditions.[45] Koch-Weser moved to Brazil and established a cattle ranch even before Hitler came to power, aided by Böhme, the former head of the DBB, who had defected from the DDP in 1924. Koch-Weser made a trip back to Germany to acquire breeding stock in the late thirties and recontacted several of his colleagues in the DDP. Frankfurter also took refuge in South America, after a brief stay in Switzerland, while Meyer and Bonn moved to the San Francisco Bay area in the United States. Julie Meyer, the Nürnberg Young Democrat, taught at the New School in New York City. Several rank-and-file Democrats became prominent in American academic life, and the children of other Democrats achieved distinction in the field of modern German history.[46] August Weber, whose wife was Jewish, went to London with his family, where he pursued a vigorous anti-Nazi propaganda career in association with Hans Albert Kluthe, a Young Democrat. Kallmann, a prominent Young Democrat, escaped Europe through Spain and eventually reached America after a harrowing trip; Elsas, on the other hand, whose daughter later married the son of Theodor and Elly Heuss, chose to remain in Germany and perished in a Nazi death camp. Others, such as Gothein, whose father was Jewish, and Dernburg, whose parents were Christian converts, lived on in Berlin until their deaths by natural causes. Schiffer was placed, by influential friends, in the Jewish Hospital in Berlin after the outbreak of the war and managed to survive. Jaenicke, whose mother was Jewish but who was never apparently the target of radical anti-Semitic attacks, lived through the Nazi years in Germany without incident. Some Jewish converts with Gentile spouses, including Heinz Ullstein, lived in Nazi Germany under their own names without being harmed.[47]

Although most Democrats who remained in Germany between 1933 and 1945 thought of themselves as members of the resistance to Hitler, few of them were active in the physical resistance to Nazism. They were, for the most part, too old, too timid, and too nationalistic to become terrorists. Gessler and Bergsträsser knew some of the plotters in the 20 July 1944 attempt to kill Hitler, and they engaged in discussions and speculation about the government to follow the Hitler government. Only Eduard Hamm became so deeply implicated in the plot that he became a victim of Nazi retaliation.[48] He was the former minister of economics in the first and second Marx governments and the former Bavarian minister of trade. He had also been a prominent state secretary in the Reichs chancellory during the Cuno government. After he left government service, he became the leading Chamber of Commerce official in Germany and edited its newspaper. He had never been active in national DDP party affairs, but he retained many personal associations with leading conservative Democrats. It is thought that, somehow, he became implicated in the plot of 20 July, but, unlike his friend Carl Goerdeler, he remained so close-mouthed about his activities that it is uncertain how deeply involved he was. He was arrested in September 1944, taken to Berlin by the *Gestapo*, and imprisoned. He committed suicide, apparently before he was interrogated, in order to avoid implicating others. Several Democrats worked abroad in anti-Nazi resistance activities, largely limited to propaganda and carried on at a safe distance.

After the war, those who had remained in Germany, as well as several refugees who returned, proved ready and able to assist in the restoration of German democracy. Dietrich, Maier, Heuss, Jaenicke, Dehler, Eschenburg, Wildemuth, and Bergsträsser played leading parts in the American zone, while Höpker-Aschoff, Heile, Rönneburg, Hermann Schäfer, Gustav Heinemann, and Tantzen had responsible positions in the British zone and in the first years of the Federal Republic. In Berlin, Lüders, Lemmer, Friedensburg, Karl Brammer, and Walter Schreiber were noteworthy political figures in the Western sectors, while Nuschke, Külz, and Schiffer served first the Soviet zonal government and then the DDR. Most of the former Democrats active after 1949 were members of the FDP, although several, including Lüders, Heinemann, and Lemmer, joined the CDU (*Christlich-Demokratische Union*). Both Heuss and Heinemann, a rather obscure DDP member, served as presidents of the Federal Republic and made significant contributions to it. Höpker-Aschoff became a leading judicial official. In addition to the politicians, several former Democrats who were academics or journalists also had active postwar careers in building support for liberal democracy in Germany. They helped to demonstrate that Bonn was not Weimar. With the possible exception of Dehler, they all learned to moderate their differences with colleagues. They also softened most of their disagreements with like-minded parties, although some of them found it impossible to submerge their hostility to the SPD. Their hatred of communism and the German Democratic Republic remained unwavering. In many ways, the former Democrats made constructive contributions to the governance of Berlin and the Federal Republic, and they often showed their debts both to the Weimar and the Nazi experience. They helped provide continuity and stability in parliamentary democracy, which, together with the German Federal Republic's great economic accomplishments, secured the success of the new German democracy.

Conclusion
The Failure of Left Liberalism in the Weimar Republic

During the fourteen years of the Weimar Republic, the German Democratic party/State party participated in most of the national governments. In addition, it was a member of coalition governments in Prussia and several other *Länder* for several years. Many leading municipal officials were Democrats and hundreds of career officials at all levels of government belonged to the DDP. The Democratic party, as we have seen, also was largely responsible for the Weimar Constitution and several *Land* constitutions. Several of the most important commentaries on the Weimar Constitution were written by academics who were Democrats. The DDP undoubtedly had a closer relationship to the ideals and institutions of the Weimar Republic than any other political party. The DDP is generally credited with having brought over the educated middle class to the support of the Republic, and, for a time, the Naumann ideal to reconcile social classes, support parliamentary democracy, and combine democratic ideals with strong nationalism provided a powerful and compelling synthesis. The DDP also nourished and sustained a certain left-liberal political type—liberal, democratic, humane, tolerant—who strengthened the shaky hold liberal democracy had in the Weimar Republic and helped to relaunch liberal democracy after 1945. Leaders such as Koch-Weser, Preuss, Goetz, Erkelenz, Friedensburg, Lüders, and Heuss demonstrated the commitment to liberal-democratic ideals. The positive achievements and contributions of the DDP, however, were overshadowed by its failure: its decline from the third largest party in 1919 to a tiny splinter party after 1930.

The DDP has left the most voluminous store of party and private records of any Weimar party, and its members tended to be introspective. As a result, there are dozens of attempts by prominent party members to try to explain its failure.[1] Most Democrats in their analyses tended to blame the circumstances of the period, which were outside the party's control, usually stressing the Treaty of Versailles, the inflation, and the Great Depression. A few in the left wing of the party mentioned the familiar textbook explanation: the failure of Germany to undergo a profound revolution. Several party members from various wings blamed the political incapacity of the German people for the failure of the DDP. Another popular explanation was the "burden of responsibility" which the DDP assumed for statist reasons. Constitutional flaws made up another group of explanations: the multi-party sytem, worsened by proportional representation; the failure to achieve a true *Einheitsstaat*, which resulted in overlapping and needlessly expensive government; the impersonality of the list system and the overly large size of the electoral districts. The difficulty of achieving trust and cooperation within the Weimar Coalition and later among the bourgeois parties was also often cited. When Democrats turned to the flaws within the party to explain its demise, they generally agreed on certain causes, although they placed varying degrees of stress upon them: the confused ideological legacy of the party; the difficulties of trying to build a party above interests and class; the uninspiring leadership of the DDP; various organizational flaws. There were also a number of idiosyncratic explanations, such as Hellpach's claiming that the DDP was crippled by its name. Too many middle-class Germans, Hellpach contended, associated the word *democratic* with the Social Democratic party. Another popular explanation was the inability of the party to disassociate itself from the SPD. Some members concentrated on organizational weaknesses: inadequate finances; poor and unreliable press support; unpopular leaders. Others stressed the difficulties of attempting to achieve unity in such a heterogenous party. A few members noted the failure of the DDP to respond to the material grievances of sizable interest groups in the party such as the farmers or the *Mittelstand* members. There were also *sotto voce* references to the controversial relationship between the DDP and the Jewish community and especially its ties to certain controversial newspapers and individuals.

Some Democrats saw beneath the surface. Höpker-Aschoff, for example, in surveying the debacle of the DDP/DStP in 1930 attributed the party's decline to the effects of the war. The war had produced fundamental economic and social changes which disrupted the economic and social relationships for the middle classes, altering the structure of the middle classes and their psychology. He felt that the "possessing classes" had been proletarianized by the inflation, which he viewed as an outcome of the war, and this had radicalized them and turned them toward narrow interest groups and political extremists. Feder, also writing in 1930 when several members were burying the DDP, likewise placed the primary responsibility on the war. He felt that it had produced—along with technological changes—structural changes in the middle classes which had shrunk the size of the group the DDP relied on for supporters. He emphasized, as well, the failure of the "bridge approach," the DDP's attempt to unite the working class with the middle class in one political party. He and several other Democrats noted at this time the great weakness the DDP had compared to the SPD and the Center party: it lacked the kind of binding cement of religion, class loyalty, or a compelling ideology possessed by the great mass parties. Feder also noted lesser causes of the DDP's failure: errors in judgment by the DDP's leaders; indecisiveness; lack of courage. According to Feder, when the party lost the trust of the electorate, the leaders lost confidence in themselves. Erkelenz's letters and writings after his break with the DDP are filled with rationalizations and second-guessing to explain the party's collapse. In an article in *Vorwärts*, written after he joined the SPD, Erkelenz underlined the failure of the DDP to inject a stream of social consciousness into liberalism, although this had been an expressed goal of the party. He also emphasized how economic conditions had ruined the *Mittelstand* and caused the DDP to lose its mass support. In his article, Erkelenz felt that the DDP's greatest contribution had been to win the support of the educated middle class, but that this had been too small a base on which to build a party. Several authors of secondary accounts of the DDP have also stressed the weakness of its base as the fundamental cause of its failure. Many DDP writers bemoaned the inability of the party to attract women, young people, and newcomers as the most significant cause of its failure. Young Democrats, on the other hand, blamed the party's intimate ties to the HB and to other business groups, as well as repeated efforts to join the DDP to the DVP. Many young people also found liberalism an irrelevant ideology in the postindustrial era and in the circumstances of the Republic. Women found that they were not treated as equals and often were dismissed in a condescending manner. Outsiders found the DDP so ingrown and the leadership so unwilling to allow newcomers responsibility that the party appeared a closed circle.

Nearly all attempts to analyze the party's failure stress the confused image which the DDP presented to the voters, a factor undoubtedly important in its decline. How could one party appeal to pacifists, internationalists, strong patriots, and treaty revisionists? How could one party, given German political traditions and the atmosphere of the era, attract labor, farmers, the *Mittelstand*, public sector officials and employees, white-collar workers, great industrialists, bankers, businessmen large and small, department store owners, and small shopkeepers? And yet the DDP attempted to win the support of all these groups in nearly every election.

How could it develop a consistent program and a coherent ideology with constituencies so diverse and interests so contradictory? This effort flew in the face of deeply engrained class prejudices and social attitudes. In retrospect, it seems that the DDP should have jettisoned its labor and farm groups after 1924 and attempted to build an urban middle-class party composed largely of *Mittelstand* members, public sector officials and employees, white-collar and technician groups. Several leading members suggested such a course after 1924, but, by then, it was probably too late for such a change of direction. By 1926, the WP and other special interest groups were so well entrenched it was impossible to defeat them. Moreover, the DDP possessed too exalted an idea of its mission to become a party of artisans, lab technicians, and green grocers. It preferred to build castles on theoretical political abstractions or fanciful constitutional reforms rather than design a practical economic approach to politics. The DDP probably also should have driven out of the party the very wealthy men of commerce and banking, who traded financial contributions for a modicum of political influence but who gave to the party an aura of wealth and privilege which weakened its popular appeal. In the end, they deserted the DDP/DStP anyway. Lüders, whose sharp tongue and prickly personality made her unappreciated in the party, noted in 1928 the nature of the fundamental economic and social upheaval which had occurred since the war and called on the party to change its program and its organization or perish. She had attempted to get the DDP to promote the interests of the victims of inflation, but the right wing had rejected such moves as irresponsible. Bonn was another who realized the fundamental changes which were occurring and suggested various remedies, but he, too, was ignored. While the businessman's caution prevailed in the party, there were still a few members who complacently believed that the party's program and policies were correct and should be continued. The old Richter ideal of a small but pure party persisted. The Rhineland industrialist Gustav Dechamps, who would have been a DDP candidate in 1930 had the DStP not been formed, felt that the DDP course should not be altered or compromised; he gloried in being a member of a party which he regarded in the *avant-garde*, an observation which would have amused many of the DDP's rivals, who saw it mired in lethargy.

There seems little doubt that the DDP was hurt by sharing in the burden of responsibility for the government and by its partnership with the Center party and SPD in the Weimar Coalition. In 1919, it was forced to participate in controversial decisions on taxes and social policy which many of its voters abominated. The continued enforced close association with the SPD at most levels of government offended most Democrats. Although the DDP sometimes deserted the Weimar Coalition in order to remain close to the DVP, the partisan enemies of the DDP successfully linked it with the socialists, and conservative Democrats repeatedly called on the leadership to put more distance between itself and the SPD. Wiessner, for example, wrote to Koch-Weser in 1931, recalling that he had always felt that the DDP should have more clearly separated itself from the SPD. What, however, was the alternative? The only options were a Great Coalition, which the DDP preferred but DVP-SPD differences generally prevented, or a *Bürgerblock* government, which the DDP majority repeatedly rejected. The founders of the DStP were determined to show how little they had in common with the SPD, but their tactics only succeeded in driving many moderates from the party along with the offending left wing that was so difficult to distinguish from the SPD.

The DDP's ties to the Republic were also controversial. Few members of the middle class were fervent republicans even in 1919, but circumstances forced the DDP to become a stalwart defender of the constitution and "the system" against its extremist enemies. Although this became an eminently conservative policy, few of the party's middle-class supporters appreciated this tactic, and the party suffered accordingly. By 1924, the DDP found itself on the defensive because of its support for the Republic. The Republic's flag and its ceremonies, such as Constitution Day, received less and less support from Democrats themselves; by 1929, some Democrats began to look for alternatives to the Republic. At first they focused their hopes on the aged president and an increase in executive powers, but a few were looking for a strong man who might replace the Republic. The DDP's growing ambivalence toward the Republic may be seen in its changing attitude toward the *Reichsbanner Schwarz-Rot-Gold*. When the *Reichsbanner* was organized in 1924 as a paramilitary support for the Republic and republican parties, most leaders of the DDP joined it. The election of 1924 showed the dangers on the right. By 1929, however, only a small number remained active in the *Reichsbanner* because most Democrats perceived it as a SPD organization. While this did not unduly disturb figures in the left wing, including Lemmer, Cohnstaedt, or Erkelenz, or moderates like Haas, Luppe, or Hauff, it alarmed the right wing and leaders such as Koch-Weser and Stephan, who wished to merge the DDP with the DVP's left wing. Even such staunch republicans as Baumgarten refused to join it, ostensibly because of its paramilitary trappings, although he applauded its flaunting of the flag, which he saw as a symbol of class reconciliation. Others found other excuses to keep their distance from it, but the real reason was its connection to the SPD. In March, 1928, the *Vorstand* contended that the DDP's ties to the *Reichsbanner* hurt the party and, in December 1929, the Organization Committee, attempting to explain the party's setbacks in the communal elections in the autumn of 1929, blamed the *Reichsbanner* connection as well as a case of political corruption involving some Berlin Jews active in the DDP. Although the ties to the Center party were never as controversial as those with the SPD, especially after the death of Erzberger and the rapid slide of the Center party to the right, they did not enhance the popularity of the DDP, and in some places they probably hurt the Democrats.

From its founding, the DDP had fatal flaws in its organization. Historically, as we have noted, the liberal parties had been weak, poorly funded, locally based organizations. The Naumannites attempted to build a mass organization modeled on the SPD, but the DDP had only moderate success in establishing a large dues-paying membership and a strong *Zentrale*. The effort soon collapsed because of inadequate financial support and the legacy of deep-rooted traditions of political organization: when the plan to build a broadly based organization failed, local notables simply regained their prewar role in the organization. Increasingly, a few donors assumed much of the financial burden, and organizations such as the HB and the *Kuratorium* traded financial contributions to the party for political influence. In later years, candidates financed their own campaigns. The DDP's leadership worked hard to raise money for the party but without much success; by 1929, the DDP was unable to persuade members either to give money or to work for the party. As the money dried up and voluntary work diminished, the basis for the political organization disappeared. The young people and women who had done much of the voluntary work in the early years—the so-called "little tasks" of party work—apparently tired of being ignored or treated in a condescending manner, either turned to other parties or abandoned politics. The middle-aged male "establishment" of the DDP generally was too busy or felt too self-important to perform the minor tasks. As a result, the DDP's organization virtually disappeared.

In 1919, the DDP had well-known parliamentary leaders with major national reputations. It also included several beginners in national politics who seemed to have qualities which promised a supply of future leaders. In 1919, Naumann, Haussmann, and Fischbeck were the brightest lights among the parliamentary leaders, while Koch-Weser, Gerland, Schiffer, Luppe, Gessler, Heuss, Erkelenz, and Bäumer seemed promising newcomers. Unfortunately, several of the veteran leaders soon died or retired, while the new leaders never fulfilled their early promise, and by 1924 the party had no popular leader of great stature. Schiffer proved too conservative and duplicitous, while Koch-Weser lacked the charisma needed to endear him to the membership. Petersen, who succeeded Naumann as the party leader, could deliver long and emotional speeches and evoke pathos for the Naumann ideals, but he lacked organizational talent and intellectual rigor. Moreover, he was never able to achieve much success outside of Hamburg. Erkelenz was too far to the left and possessed too brusque a personality, while Bäumer had neither a common touch nor common sense and became increasingly illiberal. Hellpach, the party's choice as a presidential candidate in 1925, became an eccentric liability to the party, while Dietrich, who succeeded Koch-Weser as the party's leader in 1930, had a limited appeal in the right wing of the party. The party failed to attract outsiders with leadership talent or to promote young people quickly enough to retain them. In time, the younger leaders in the party such as Heuss, Landahl, Maier, Stolper, Lemmer, and Friedensburg might have developed as popular and effective leaders on the national scene, but there was too little time. While Haas had most of the qualities necessary to be a major concensus leader, he was a professed Jew and an emotional supporter of the Weimar Coalition and the Republic. As a result, he never received the leadership posts in the party he deserved, although he became the *Fraktion* leader in 1929–1930, shortly before he died.

The failure of the DDP to produce a nationally recognized and respected leader undoubtedly hurt it, but the struggle for power among the leaders damaged it even more. The ambitions of party leaders and their bitter differences over principles and policies produced an unedifying exhibition of pettiness and jealousy which strengthened the impression that the DDP was too divided to warrant public respect and popular support. The relations between Erkelenz and Koch-Weser, to cite only the most glaring example of the struggle between leaders, to some extent was the consequence of personal differences more than contrasting political philosophies. Erkelenz's hatred for Koch-Weser became paranoid and destroyed his health as well as his political career. Koch-Weser controlled his emotions better than Erkelenz, but he sometimes resorted to actions and used words against his left-wing opponents which cost him respect in the party. Hellpach, never a stable individual and always a lone wolf, became so embittered by the inadequacies of the party leadership that he resigned his mandate. Tantzen, another irascible personality, followed him out of the Reichstag *Fraktion* because of his opposition to the party's policies. The leadership of the party became increasingly angry and divided in 1929–1930. Figures such as Heuss and Petersen, who were amiable and polite and had a sense of humor, as a result were often seen as weak and vacillating. Because of the continual struggle of personalities, the style and tone of the leadership were sufficiently offensive to drive many from the party.

Other causes of the failure of the DDP were the reluctance of the leadership to promote younger figures to leadership positions and its inability to attract able outsiders to the party. In general, the leaders of the party refused to give young members or women positions commensurate with their contributions to the organization. To some extent, of course, this resulted from the local control of the nominating procedure by notables, but the national organization did not improve on the record of local organizations. The leadership bemoaned its failure to bring new talent into the party while clinging to every position of power. No wonder that women, younger people, and newcomers gained the impression that the party was controlled by a small, ingrown group.

Another factor that explains the failure of the DDP was its relationship to the Jewish community. I have dealt with this question in an article entitled "The German Democratic Party and the 'Jewish Problem' in the Weimar Republic," and it has been touched on throughout this book. Compared to the major external causes of the DDP's decline and many of the internal deficiencies, it was not a principal factor in the party's failure. Nevertheless, because it has been so commonly neglected in the memoir literature and in the secondary surveys by party members and party friends as well as by most German scholars, it needs to be reiterated. The relationship affected the unity and spirit of the party in subtle ways and contributed to personal feuds and misunderstandings. The presence of many Jews in the party and its reputation as the *Judenpartei* complicated various aspects of party life, but the presence in the party of so many moderate anti-Semites was a surprising discovery in a party which was allegedly philo-Semitic. The controversial association of the DDP with the large Jewish-owned and -staffed newspapers, on the other hand, is well known. Dozens of prominent defectors from the DDP associated their departure with the party's ties to these newspapers. From time to time, the latent anti-Semitism in the party broke through, as after the failure in the election of 1928, when several party leaders concluded that the association of the DDP with Jews had injured it at the polls. Even Lüders, who was not anti-Semitic, admitted that the prominence of Jews in the party in 1928 produced a kind of "ghetto atmosphere" which caused some non-Jews to shun party work.

Another cause of the DDP's failure was the inadequacy of liberalism as an ideology in the circumstances of the Weimar Republic. It was particularly inappropriate in economic and social questions. The attempt on the part of the followers of Naumann to create a social liberalism failed and traditional laissez-faire values had little appeal, although many in the DDP's right wing continued to believe in them. The left wing probably would have preferred something like the welfare states and mixed economies which have evolved since 1945, but it took time and bitter experiences before that blend evolved. Between the left and right wings of the DDP a kind of resigned consensus developed somewhat right of center, but it was too timid and responsible to win a hearing, let alone new voters. This is not to say that the party did not have an ideology, but only that the ideology was inappropriate for the circumstances. Left liberalism had little understanding of and few remedies for the terrible economic and social problems of the Weimar period. But did any ideology have the answers?

The DDP was also crippled by its association with Weimar parliamentary democracy. At the root of the failure was the ongoing economic crisis, which contributed to the ruin of many middle-class families and to a profound disillusionment about the political system. The DDP, which was irrevocably bound to defend the system, could not escape the effects of its decline. Democrats continued to cast about for some means to improve the machinery, such as changes in the electoral law, but they won little support for such efforts. When the DDP/DStP failed to win backing to adjust a valve here or fine-tune a piece of the mechanism there, many middle-class Germans began to look to a new machine or, short of that, to a reduction in parliamentary powers and an increase in the presidential powers. The German middle classes also began to see that they could only preserve a moderate voice in German politics by banding together in a *Sammlung*. Although the liberal parties made half-hearted efforts to co-operate with other moderate forces, the death of Stresemann ended whatever hope there had been for such an alliance. The middle-class parties proved unable to make the necessary concessions to pool their resources and members in a viable political organization. Some Democrats continued to make sincere if pathetic efforts to bring the "middle" together even late into 1932, but the public greeted this attempt with general indifference, and the middle-class parties seemed as paralyzed.

The final cause of the DDP/DStP's fall was the result of a failure of nerve or a lack of spirit among the liberal middle classes. The DDP never presented the image of a militant fighter. From the photographs of DDP gatherings that have survived, the protocols of the meetings, and the articles and books by Democrats, what emerges is a picture of a well-educated, moderate, inert group. The photographs show dark-suited, sober, middle-aged men and rather dowdy middle-aged women in dark dresses and old-fashioned coiffures. There are exceptions, of course, but what the party seemed to lack was youth, color, and vitality. It also lacked force and a combative spirit. The Nazis, who were the DDP's opposite in so many ways, ridiculed its gentility, and non-Nazi contemporary writers often noted its "academic nature." Its meetings recall the atmosphere of faculty meetings. Ernst Moering, a Lutheran pastor from Breslau, contended in 1928 that the DDP was damaged because of its pious, sober, responsible, and theoretical nature. Schacht later wrote that it lacked a fighting spirit, and Bernstoff felt it had no will to power.[2] Bernhard Guttmann, an editor of the FZ, had an even harsher judgment: he condemned it as a spineless party. It seems that this noncombative, passive spirit probably contributed to the members' lack of commitment. Increasingly the members refused to contribute money to the party or work for it; they felt no need to make a commitment to it or to the Republic. Increasingly, committee members refused to attend meetings, and the absentee record of the *Fraktion* was one of the worst in the Reichstag. Many of the people who gave to the party were those who expected something from it. Given the trail of electoral defeats, it is not surprising that many in the DDP became disheartened, and by 1929 even the most optimistic Democrats succumbed to the inescapable conclusion that the party was doomed. The rightist turn of the Württemberg organization early in 1930 is an important symbol of the increasing tendency for Democrats to reject left-liberal values. The DStP's formation confirmed this trend. How long can a political party endure that no longer believes in its professed values? In the case of the DDP/DStP it proved to be only a short time. In March 1930, Koch-Weser gave a speech in Berlin at the Democratic Club on the theme "Shall the Democratic Party Continue to Exist?" While he answered the question in the affirmative, he was already preparing to destroy the party. In its place, he and the right wing of the DDP erected the German State party, a tawdry parody of a left-liberal party. Such was the end of the bright hopes of the founders of the DDP. Failure was succeeded by disgrace.

Appendixes
Notes
Sources
Index

Appendix A: Organization

Membership

The paid membership of the DDP/DStP, as distinguished from its electoral support, represented the active Democrats who paid nominal dues and who often worked for the party without pay.[1] In July 1919, the membership totaled about 900,000, about one in six voters and too few, in the opinion of the party leaders, to build a viable party. By the autumn of 1919, the number of members declined to 800,000, and thereafter it dropped even more rapidly. By the summer of 1925, following the inflation and two debilitating elections in 1924, only 135,000 members were identified. In 1926–1927, the membership slipped as low as 113,300. After that and during the brief history of the DStP, membership totals were not publicized. Even the strongest DDP organizations suffered crippling losses. For example, one-fourth of the membership of the Greater Berlin DDP left the party in the mid-twenties, while Westphalia and Saxony lost 20 percent of their members. In 1928, the DDP's left wing was greatly reduced in size as a result of wholesale defections to the SPD, and then, in 1930, with the formation of the DStP, the left-liberal representative became a tiny splinter party. The DStP never released membership statistics.

The decline in membership paralleled the reduction in the number of local party organizations (*Ortsgruppen*). In April 1920, 2735 *Ortsgruppen* existed, but, by the autumn of 1925, there were only 1742 local groups. By the late twenties, this number was down to 1223. The commitment of individual members to work for the party also lessened. In 1919, about 16 percent of the DDP's voters performed some kind of party work, which testifies to the early enthusiasm for the DDP, but, by 1925, only 8 percent were discharging party tasks. Only a few local organizations still showed a high level of commitment. In Württemberg, where the party had a broad base which cut across socio-economic lines, 18 percent still worked for the party in some capacity in 1925.

The social composition of the membership also underwent considerable change from 1919 to 1933. In 1919, the DDP, while essentially an urban middle-class party, attracted considerable support from workers and farmers. By 1929, only a handful of either group remained, and most businessmen and professional men and women had also abandoned it. By then, it was largely a party of government officials and employees, teachers, and here and there representatives of the *Mittelstand*. A few businessmen and professional men and women remained as well. A disproportionately large number of academics, journalists, and intellectuals—few in number but relatively important in influence—still backed the DDP until 1930. According to Stephan's 1925 survey,[2] about 30 percent of the DDP backers were "officials," presumably mostly in the public sector. Another 30 percent were listed as "employees"—white-collar workers, clerks, technicians. He estimated that 30 percent were "employers," probably mostly small businessmen. The remaining 10 percent came from the "free professions"—law, teaching, medicine, engineering, architecture.

Party Committees

The DDP inherited its organizational structure from the prewar liberal parties. Even during the revolutionary period, when it improvised an organization, it was a clear descendent of the Progressive party. The initial self-appointed Executive Committee (*Der provisorische Geschäftsführende Ausschuss*—GA) provided the necessary, minimal national leadership, while the local organizations were built on either Progressive party or National-Liberal party foundations. Usually, they simply continued an older organization and often retained its name. The GA co-opted members into it and established the *Hauptvorstand* as a smaller leadership core. Initially, it seemed to overlap the GA and lacked a distinct mission. It only met once before the election of January 1919, but it became the true Executive Committee after the election, while the GA devoted itself largely to organizational questions. Before the first PT met in July 1919, the *Fraktion* of the National Assembly also became an important party institution. Following the first regular PT, the principal institutions of the DDP were the *Vorstand* (or *Hauptvorstand*), the *Parteiausschuss* (PA), the Review Committee (*Revisionsausschuss*), and, of course, the Party Congress (PT) itself. The *Fraktion* also helped determine party policy and usually worked closely with the *Vorstand*. In addition, there were several levels of regional and local party organizations. The PT was the highest organ in the party. Composed of delegates elected by various groups or appointed by major committees, it, in turn, elected a portion of the PA and the *Vorstand* as well as the *Revisionsausschuss*. The PT also elected the leader of the party, who served as the chairman of the PA.

From this core organization, many additional committees were formed. The Women's Committee (*Frauenausschuss*) and the Young Democrats (*Der Bund der Deutsch-Demokratischen Jugendvereine*; later, *Reichsbund der Deutschen Jungdemokraten*) antedated the first PT and met separately at the first PT. The other committees included a Press Committee, the Labor Committee (*Reichsarbeitnehmerausschuss*), an Officials' Committee (*Beamtenausschuss*), a *Mittelstandsausschuss*, a Reich Committee for Trade, Industry, and Business (*Reichsausschuss für Handel, Industrie, und Gewerbe*), a *Kultur* Committee, and, in time, an Agricultural Committee and a Committee for the Free Professions. Some of the committees had a continuous role through the history of the DDP/DStP, while others were only occasionally active or soon expired. Only a few of the committees were vital and hard-working, and even they only endured because of the dedication of a few individuals.

The DDP's organization proved most effective from November 1918 until the spring of 1919, when enthusiasm was still high and the threat of socialism gave the party a compelling mission. There was, in this period, a general agreement on abstract principles, and the special interest groups generally subordinated their material concerns to avoid dividing and weakening the party. The *Zentrale*, the party headquarters in Berlin over which the general secretary and business manager of the party presided, as well as the local organizations and major committees, were staffed at this period largely by seasoned veteran liberal organization figures in conjunction with a blend of enthusiastic newcomers to politics. As time went on, the supply of young and enthusiastic helpers diminished, and the repeated electoral defeats reduced the available funds and workers. In 1919, the DDP had adequate financial support and volunteers, but in later campaigns, despite the development of more sophisticated campaign methods, the organization became woefully deficient. The keys to a successful political organization were clearly money and member commitment, but these essentials were missing after the election of June 1920.

The leadership of the DDP planned its future organization in the spring of 1919 in anticipation of the first Party Congress. In May 1919, a draft of a party statute (*Satzung*) was completed which the PT later accepted almost without opposition. The leadership made minor changes in it in 1925 and again in 1930, largely to provide more input from the *Wahlkreis* organizations and to take into account the shrinking membership. Initially, the *Vorstand* had twenty-two members and forty in 1925. Usually, only about ten to fifteen members attended the meetings. It generally met nine times a year and during critical periods it sometimes convened once a week. It met less frequently during summer months. The *Vorstand* and the

Fraktion together made party policy in practice, although the PT and the PA originally were expected to be the major policy-forming bodies in the party. The PT and the PA, however, were too large and met too infrequently to be able to exercise control over the party. The PT usually had about 500 in attendance and met for only two to three days annually; the PA consisted of 155 members. In the history of the DDP, there were eight regular PT meetings and three special ones in eleven years. The DStP only had one PT meeting. The PA generally met three times a year.

The *Vorstand*, which represented all of the major constituencies of the party but was weighted toward the business wing, was the most important committee of the party. Left-wing members had only a minority of the seats on the major committees, while women, young people, and left-wing Jews suffered from discrimination. The *Vorstand* posts were at first hotly contested, and there was a continual struggle between right and left wings in it. In general, the protocols of the meetings are bland, and, in the late twenties, there were complaints that they were censored by the party leadership. Fortunately, there were always some members in both wings of the party who were highly verbal and blunt—figures such as Böhme and Gerland on the right before 1924 and Cohnstaedt and Frankfurter on the left wing. The most lively and critical committee of the DDP was the PA. The agenda and speakers' list never seemed to be as tightly controlled as it was in the *Vorstand* or the PT. With the exception of the first two PT meetings, the Party Congresses were generally sedate and dreary, but the PA meetings were often contentious. The sessions of the Review Committee (*Revisionsausschuss*) were seldom publicized, but they do not seem to have been very important.

The leader of the DDP also chaired the PA. The second leading figure in the party was the chairman of the *Vorstand*. Naumann became the recognized party leader at the first regular PT. Naumann's election was a great surprise because he had not sought the post. He was in poor health at the time of his election and soon died. Friedberg, the organizational leader of the NLP, first chaired the *Vorstand*, while three people—Payer, Schiffer, and Petersen—shared the *Fraktion* leadership post during the seventeen months of the National Assembly. Petersen succeeded Naumann, and the first special PT in December 1919 confirmed the decision. Petersen retired in 1924, and Koch (Koch-Weser after 1925) was elected in his place, serving as the DDP's leader until September 1930 when Dietrich became the leader of the DStP. Petersen, a loyal follower of Naumann, had had no national political experience. He had been prominent only in Hamburg city politics and his inexperience soon manifested itself. He assumed far too many party responsibilities and seemed unable or unwilling to delegate authority. For a time, he chaired the *Fraktion*, the PA, and the *Vorstand*. Many prominent members grumbled about his shortcomings, but he did not retire until he became Hamburg's mayor. Koch, who had been the mayor of Kassel, was a former NLP member who had been a member of Prussia's Upper House. He had also served as the head of Germany's League of Cities (*Städtetag*). He had been a candidate for the leadership in 1919 but chose not to contest Naumann aggressively. Petersen was elected by acclamation, so there was no chance for Koch to oppose him. By 1924, however, he wanted the leadership badly in order to revive the organization, which Petersen had allowed to decline. By this time, Koch had demonstrated his brilliance and energy in the National Assembly, the Reichstag, and in the party organization. After Friedberg died in 1920, Erkelenz succeeded him as chairman of the *Vorstand* in perhaps the most controversial election in the party's history.[3] To counter Erkelenz's alleged radical influence, the business wing installed Fischer, the party treasurer, as his deputy, and Fischer became one of the deputy party chairmen. Erkelenz and Fischer carried on a running feud until 1929, when Erkelenz retired because of illness. Erkelenz never achieved the prominence in the party which he thought his position deserved, and, in the late twenties, he and Koch-Weser became locked in a bitter struggle, one which Erkelenz could not win. Koch-Weser assumed the chairmanship of the *Vorstand* as well as the PA after that, although one of the deputy chairmen usually presided over the PA meetings. Fischer remained as treasurer until 1932. The *Fraktion* chairmen after Petersen were Koch-Weser, Haas, Meyer, and August Weber. Frankfurter, the chairman of the Organization Committee, a sub-group of the *Vorstand* which met separately, was another major organization leader of the DDP. His committee concentrated on organizational questions of all kinds, including finance, and worked closely with Fischer. Stephan viewed Frankfurter, a prominent attorney for the film industry and the Ullstein firm, as a dilettante, and he certainly was largely uninterested in many organizational details. He often wrote or polished the texts of party documents, although, from time to time, he made critical evaluations of the organization and suggested new and far-reaching reforms. He served briefly as a temporary replacement as a Reichstag deputy although he always aspired to a more active role and saw himself as a victim of anti-Semitism in the DDP.[4] There were several deputy chairmen in the party. Frankfurter, Bäumer, and Fischer were the most active and useful to the party. In general, about twenty people dominated the organization from its beginning until its demise, and many of them were also active in the DStP. Very little "new blood" came into the party, and hardly any new leaders appeared.

The *Parteitag* (PT)

The PT, theoretically the most important party institution, met for only a few days every year or so, and its agenda and speakers' list were tightly controlled by the party leadership. Unlike the major committees, which seldom met outside Berlin, it convened in Berlin, Leipzig, Nürnberg, Bremen, Elberfeld, Weimar, Berlin again, Breslau, Hamburg, Mannheim, and Hannover. The PT combined several functions. It mixed party business, a pep rally, speech making on important contemporary issues as well as abstruse political theory, and lastly social intercourse. The party leaders generally provided a political orientation, while others gave lectures on specialized topics of major importance to the Reichstag and the national leadership. Usually, there was a designated speaker (*Referent*) on foreign policy questions, another on economic and fiscal issues, and often one on *Kultur* questions. Prominent—and usually conservative—figures in the party gave these long lectures. They were followed by shorter speeches which commented critically on the *Referent*'s presentation. Generally, a brief discussion was then permitted, which sometimes produced some fireworks. Most of those who asked questions or gave short remarks of a critical nature were preselected, and they only received a few minutes for their presentations. Many in the left wing objected to this format and wanted greater freedom, but the leaders knew that in a party with as many articulate and trained people as the DDP it had to limit discussion. The DDP also had the usual collection of tiresome individuals who rode their hobbies in meeting after meeting. Generally, the PTs demonstrated a remarkable consensus, and they always granted the party leadership a renewed vote of confidence, but the liveliness of the first meetings was succeeded by torpor, except for the dedicated "organization men," for whom party politics remained exciting. The PTs of the local organizations of the DDP had more spontaneity and real debate, but even they tended to decline in relevance and spirit, which was understandable given the steady deterioration of the DDP's strength. The DDP always involved the local party in its Party Congress. The appearance of local dignitaries in the opening hours of the PT was as much a part of the routine of the meeting as honoring the memory of "party friends" who had died since the last PT. The local leaders were also generally involved in making the PT arrangements—finding hotels, restaurants, and meeting halls. The delegates to the PT were a good cross section of the active party members, overwhelmingly middle-class and highly educated. Many of them came away from the meetings refreshed and determined to continue the battle for the DDP and the Republic. They were often thrilled to meet the party leaders and to engage in the informal discussions in the corridors which characterize political—and professional—meetings. For a moment, many seemed to take heart and to see a future for the party. They also enjoyed themselves with congenial and compatible people—renewing old friendships and former associations, meeting new people, singing in groups, attending concerts, and engaging in social dancing. They also enjoyed much eating and drinking.

Other Important Committees

The Young Democrats and the Women's Committee

These organizations have been discussed previously. Like the DDP, they were rooted in prewar organizations and began with some promise, but, by 1920, they suffered the same devastating losses as the DDP itself. They also refused to dissolve and were still formally in existence when the DStP terminated itself in 1933. Few young people or women were attracted to these groups after 1924, but despite their small size, both interest groups made repeated demands for more power within the DDP organization. Although both groups had dedicated members who worked hard to overcome political apathy and win support for the DDP, young people, in general, found extremist groups more attractive, while many women thought the DDP to be too radical. Organizational leaders such as Stephan attempted to revitalize these organizations, but they failed.

The *Beamten* Committee

This committee also had a relatively long and active life and went over to the DStP in 1930. It represented government officials and employees from postal clerks and railroad employees to a few high-level civil servants. Railroad workers seemed particularly active in the DDP, and one of their number, Otto Schuldt, had a Reichstag seat from 1920 to 1930. There were successful subgroups of municipal employees and Prussian policemen. The committee was first chaired by Georg Graf, a professional engineer and an official of an employees' association, and then by Vogt, an officials' organization manager (*Beamtensyndikus*). Both had active roles in the DDP organization. The *Beamten* Committee published a national journal for several years, *Der Staatsbürger*; subsidized by the DDP, it also attracted subscribers from outside the party. While the committee only had 1245 members in 1926, the *Staatsbürger*, at one point, had well over 2000 subscribers. By 1930, however, its subscriptions fell to 1600. The failure of the DDP to support salary increases for government employees and its constant efforts to trim the cost of government in time alienated many government workers and crippled the work of the committee. The DDP always had been ambivalent about building a party on a base of teachers and other government employees, and after 1930, most of them turned elsewhere.

The Agriculture Committee

This committee was formed late and lasted only a short time. It originated as a defensive measure to halt the loss of farmers from the DDP, but the DDP's refusal to support high agricultural tariffs with any consistency doomed it. The fact that farmers saw the party as a party of Jews and of the city also contributed to the DDP's unpopularity among farmers and in rural districts.

The *Kultur* Committee

The *Kultur* Committee was organized to forward the traditional cultural program of liberalism. In the Weimar period, after church and state had been separated, this meant primarily establishing a uniform secular school system. The school compromise doomed the hopes of extreme anticlericals and clericals alike. The committee spent much of its time warding off Catholic efforts to reverse the compromise and to secure treaties between the Reich and the German *Länder* and the Vatican. The committee continued to fight to protect academic freedom and to reject censorship although, ironically, some of its most prominent members supported the Schund- und Schmutzgesetz in 1926, which established regional censorship offices to deal with "filthy literature." The committee was largely the instrument of Bäumer, who sought to use it to support her educational goals and anti-Catholic prejudices. Most Democrats, however, wished to work closely with the Center party to defend the Republic. This was particularly evident in Prussia where the Weimar Coalition prevailed until 1932.

The *Mittelstand* Committee; The Employers' Committee; The Labor Committee; The Committee of Trade, Industry, and Commerce

I have already alluded to these special interest committees. They were designed to represent the material interests of specific constituencies and to meet the competition of new special interest parties luring away many of the DDP's voters. Each group hoped to secure the DDP's backing for its special needs and to cooperate with other parties which also sought to support them. As conflicting interests within the DDP canceled each other out, businessmen and industrialists soon turned to the DVP and the DNVP, while workers and employees looked to the SPD and the Z. If the DDP had a natural constituency, it was the "little people" of the *Mittelstand*, whose needs had been ignored by the major parties before the war. The DDP, however, scorned this option and thereby contributed to the formation of the *Wirtschaftspartei* (WP) and other special interest parties. The DDP proved unwilling to abandon the Naumann vision of a national party representing all classes and interests. It was also reluctant to sacrifice its rich bankers and industrialists, not to speak of its sensitive academics and intellectuals, who would have been offended by the need to hustle voters by appealing to their material needs. Some leaders also still revered liberal principles. In short, the price to succeed as a *Mittelstand* party was too great.

Organization

The *Zentrale* (*Reichsgeschäftsstelle* and *Parteisekretäre*)

A small band of amateurs and several experienced liberal politicians organized the DDP as we have seen. It was soon necessary, however, to build on the existing liberal party organizations and to develop a central headquarters staff to coordinate the electoral campaign for the National Assembly. Naumann, particularly conscious of the acute weaknesses of the liberal organizations, wished to emulate the SPD's effective party organization. He wanted to build a mass membership who regularly paid party dues and a *Zentrale* and a local party secretariat to coordinate the party's propaganda and develop new methods of agitation. He and others also hoped that the *Zentrale*, together with the principal committees, would be able to select many candidates. Moreover, he aspired to develop a network of citizenship training institutions to remedy the shortcomings in German political education. In 1919, the *Zentrale* was relatively well funded and staffed and it played an important part in the electoral victories. But soon, by 1920, the old liberal party distrust of a *Zentrale* set in, and it became a constant struggle to force the local organizations to pay the agreed-upon dues to the *Zentrale*'s support. Only small amounts of the money owed to it were ever paid. As a result, the staff soon was greatly reduced in size and many of its organizational tasks had to be curtailed. Erkelenz, Koch-Weser, and Stephan continued the effort to maintain a strong central headquarters staff, but the financial problems of the DDP nullified their desires. The major committees passed numerous resolutions to provide the *Zentrale* with adequate funding, but there was no will to discipline the local organizations.

Hermann Schreiber, who first headed the *Zentrale*, proved—according to Stephan[5]—to be an able administrator, but he soon returned to his university work and abandoned partisan politics. Robert Jansen replaced him for a short time, but he resigned after he was elected to the Prussian *Landtag* and he, too, eventually drifted away from the DDP. Stephan, who succeeded Jansen in Bremen as the DDP's party secretary there, followed him as the DDP general secretary after he won much favorable attention for his part in the Bremen PT in 1921. He became an indispensable organization leader, the right-hand man of Erkelenz and Koch-Weser. When Erkelenz became ill and he and Koch-Weser quarreled, Stephan backed Koch-Weser. He instituted detailed questionnaires for local party organizations to complete and made systematic studies of the organization and elections. He also attempted to implement many of the organizational reforms sponsored by Erkelenz. Although Stephan knew far more than his predecessors about electoral behavior and party organization, he proved unable to halt the decline of the party and the weakening of the *Zentrale*, which increasingly was called the Business Office (*Reichsgeschäftsstelle*). The badly depleted and demoralized organization which he inherited after the crushing losses of 1920, compounded by the terrible effects of the inflation on the organization, made it impossible to recoup the earlier losses. He had only one reliable propaganda organ, *Der Demokrat*, although *Die Hilfe* and *Das demokratische Deutschland* (*Deutsche Einheit* after 1923) and dozens of other local journals often supported DDP positions on issues. The hundreds of newspapers which had backed the DDP in 1919 had been greatly reduced in number by 1924, but there was still impressive press support throughout the years of the Republic, and the DDP newspaper service (*Zeitungsdienst*), first managed by Weinhausen and then by Brammer, circulated news of the DDP and explained its positions on issues to many newspapers. There were also many newspapers and publications sponsored by local organizations and committees of the party.

Finance

There is a familiar figure in every western political party who assumes the tasks of party treasurer and who is continually forced to plead for members to fulfill their pledges. In the DDP, that person was Fischer, the party treasurer from 1919 to 1932, who sat on dozens of corporate boards and who was the president of the HB. His contacts were invaluable to the party for many years, but eventually even his sources of money dried up, which forced the DDP and the DStP to compel all members who held offices or positions on major committees to make large contributions to the party. So long as the DDP was unable to develop a large and regular dues-paying membership, Fischer's wealthy friends, from whom he collected personally and reported anonymously, provided a significant percentage of the party's national budget. His success, however, deterred the development of a tradition of small rank-and-file contributions to the national party. In the early years, the party had several other notable fund raisers: Kalkoff; Maximilian Kempner; Keinath; Schacht; Rathenau; Siemens; the Arnhold brothers. In Württemberg, Wieland, Bruckmann, Mück, and others performed important financial duties for the party. Every *Wahlkreis* had a few "angels" who were prepared to give money to certain individuals or for particular purposes, but raising money for the party became more and more difficult. As most of the DDP's major industrialists, bankers, and leading businessmen became disenchanted with its economic and social policies, and as the socialist threat diminished, the DDP's treasurer was reduced to making apocalyptic predictions about the future of the party. Indeed, as early as November 1920, in the wake of the electoral defeats of that year, Frankfurter, the chairman of the Organization Committee, predicted that unless the party radically improved its financial condition, it would suffer a catastrophic failure. The DDP's financial plight became a classic "Catch 22" situation. When not enough money was raised, the organization suffered and this then contributed to the DDP's defeat; as the DDP shrank in size and importance, people no longer contributed money to it.

The complaints about the financial circumstances of the party were heard in every major party gathering. In October 1922, for example, at the time of the Elberfeld PT, several speakers singled out finance as the root cause of the DDP's problems,[6] and leaders condemned the local organizations for their refusal to turn over to the *Zentrale* the money promised it. Reportedly only 20 percent of the party's expenses was being paid through small contributions from membership dues. In 1927, Stubmann, a major figure in the Hamburg organization and one of the editors of *Deutsche Einheit*, reported the widespread refusal of local organizations to pay the "head tax" to the national party. Although the tax only amounted to sixty *Pfennige* per member, the local organizations refused to pay it. At that time, Stubmann indicated that the head tax was producing only 12 percent of the party's income. Only in a few cities—Berlin, Hamburg, and Dresden—was the head tax adequate to finance the local organizations; most of the DDP's income came from a few wealthy donors or businesses, industries, banks, and special interest organizations. Even if the DDP had been well financed, it might not have been successful; without a proper financial base it was crippled. Other parties which emerged, such as the WP and the NSDAP, without recognized leaders or a "past," overtook the DDP in popularity, but they also attracted members who felt a deeper commitment to their party and sacrificed time and money to make it successful.

The Press

In 1919, as we have previously noted, the DDP was well served by several party publications and backed by hundreds of newspapers throughout Germany. Not only did they support the DDP editorially, they also publicized its party activities locally and occasionally printed leaflets and brochures gratuitously or at cost. The Ullstein and Mosse publishers in Berlin proved especially generous and occasionally made large contributions to the party. I have previously noted the importance of the FZ, the BT, and the VZ to the DDP, but there were dozens of regional newspapers which were identified with the DDP and which gave it important support. *Der Beobachter*, published by the Württemberg DDP in Stuttgart, the *Hamburger Fremdenblatt*, an independent paper which soon turned closer to the DVP, and the *Kieler Zeitung* are only a few examples of newspapers which generally supported the DDP.[7] Others, such as the *Münchener Neueste Nachrichten*, which strongly backed the DDP in 1919, soon were purchased by individuals who supported the DNVP. Hugenberg's firm purchased a number of former DDP newspapers which had been ruined by the inflation, but there were still many newspapers throughout Germany which remained close to the DDP and friendly to its values and positions. In 1925, Stephan reported that thirty of the thirty-five electoral districts had regional newspapers and/or journals sponsored by the DDP organization; he categorized twenty-five independent newspapers as "democratic," forty-six as "liberal," and 167 newspapers as "friendly" to the DDP.[8] After 1925, however, this base of support eroded. Even the giants had financial difficulties. Hermann Hummel, a prominent Democrat and an employee of I. G. Farben, did much to save Democratic newspapers. He established a German provincial press (*Deutscher Provinzverlag*), which set up a *Maternkorrespondenz* with 400 subscribers, mostly small newspapers. Later, Hummel was responsible for rescuing the FZ but at the price of I. G. Farben ownership. Although the FZ became somewhat more conservative, it maintained its editorial independence until Hitler came to power, and even then it continued as a token independent newspaper. Both Dietrich and Erkelenz attempted, without great success, to subsidize or buy newspapers which would support the DDP. The DDP also tried to organize a party press to publish books and pamphlets written by DDP leaders or supportive of DDP positions. Kalkoff organized the *Verlag Neuer Staat* and Erkelenz sought to maintain it, but it proved to be a costly failure as a business venture. Erkelenz's own works, such as the book of essays commemorating the DDP's tenth anniversary, *Zehn Jahre deutsche Republik*, were financial disasters. The DDP leaders often warned of the effects of the shrinking press support and criticized the failure of the leading newspapers which traditionally supported the DDP to give it their wholehearted backing in elections. They sometimes blamed the so-called "DDP press," which often proclaimed its independence and nonpartisan character, for its electoral failures. Koch-Weser lashed out at the "betrayal" of the BT in 1928, and Heuss and Bäumer became markedly hostile to the "Berlin press." It is true that after 1926 the DDP could no longer count on consistent support from the large urban newspapers, which were being forced by financial constraints to become more apolitical and nonpartisan. In many ways, the DDP's press supporters suffered from many of the same problems as the DDP. There were not enough committed liberals and democrats in Weimar Germany who were willing to subscribe to them or buy their advertising space. When the newspapers suffered financial reverses and acquired new leadership, they pulled away from the DDP.

Summer Schools

Although there is only a small amount of material available in the party records and *Nachlässe* about the DDP summer schools, they had some success in the period of 1924–1928, developing political education and training leaders. This was another facet of Naumann's emphasis on the need to train Germans in democratic government. The schools were usually held in scenic areas along the Neckar, in the Rhineland, the Harz Mountains, and in Mecklenburg, and participants combined a vacation for their families with political study. Although the seminar topics and lecture subjects seem rather heavy and forbidding, many recreational events were scheduled also—hikes, boat rides, games, and dancing. Most of the instructors, including Heuss and Martin and Dora Rade, were personally close to Naumann, but a wide variety of Democrats taught in these schools. In one summer, for example, conservative Democrats of the business wing, notably Dernburg and Meyer, shared the podium with Wilhelm Mommsen and labor officials such as Schneider and Paul Ziegler. The atmosphere of these gatherings resembled the Chautauqua camps in America, but apparently they only attracted the deeply committed members and, by 1929, they seem to have expired.

Social Life

Although the DDP often seemed rather stiff and formal to young people, the party sponsored social activities which appealed to the majority of its active members. In Berlin, its leading social institution was the Democratic Club,[9] which provided the setting for dinners, lectures, and political discussions from its founding in the spring of 1919 until its demise in late 1932. In October 1919, the members purchased a house on Viktoria Strasse, which opened in May 1920. Soon known for its fine restaurant, excellent wines, and dance facilities, it also had a library and reading room and several conference rooms where DDP committees often met. The club's first board included Bernstorff, who had taken a leading role in founding it; Siemens; Fischer, who was its treasurer as well as the DDP's; Gerland; Hans Carhe, prominent in the Mosse publishing firm and a cousin of Theodor Wolff; Keinath; Petersen; and Wieland. In 1919–1920, the club had over 1200 members, including many government officials and Berlin merchants. There were even a few army officers. Over 400 members lived outside Berlin, and they often made it their social headquarters while visiting. The club sponsored *Bierabende*, teas—"*mit Damen*"—debates, and good talk. Many of the most active members were Berlin Jews such as Feder, whose diary often notes the activities at the club. In the later years of the Republic, Eyck was its program chairman. Occasionally, the discussions were so heated that they provoked angry reactions from provincial members who soon dropped their memberships. The wives of leading Democrats often met there for tea or lunch and conversation and sometimes were invited to lectures.

Many upper middle-class members with educational and social connections belonged to other discussion groups. Some belonged to the *Deutsche*

Gesellschaft 1914, which had a rather conservative makeup, while others were members of the Wednesday Society, the Hans Delbrück Circle, the June Club, or the Tuesday Society. The Tuesday Society included Kessler, Heuss, Stolper, Kurt Riezler, Bernhard Wilhelm von Bülow, and Stresemann's successor, Curtius. Jäckh hosted political discussions, as did Solf, a colonial official and DDP Reichstag candidate, whose wife and daughters carried on the tradition after his death. Richthofen's house was a regular salon in Berlin, but it often featured people from the arts and the theatre. Dietrich, who after his first wife's death married the widow of Troeltsch, was also a prominent party giver in Berlin. On occasion, Koch-Weser also entertained. Many of the older members preferred more traditional and male forms of social life. Gothein, for example, preferred his *Stammtisch* with old Progressive colleagues, where he could eat, drink, and play skat. On occasion, the Reichstag *Fraktion* hosted a *Bierabend*, and major meetings of the DDP always featured music, dinners, and ballroom dancing. Koch-Weser was an enthusiastic dancer, who included among his partners the lively left-wing socialist Toni Sender. In 1928, when the planning committee met to discuss a party to celebrate the tenth anniversary of the DDP, it immediately determined that the party should include political speeches, dinner, and dancing. Unfortunately, there are no movies and only a few dim still pictures of these social occasions, so it is difficult to recreate the atmosphere.[10] Did Gertrud Bäumer dance the Charleston or Hermann Höpker-Aschoff the Black Bottom? It seems unlikely.

In the period of 1930–1932, the Democratic Club and the private clubs and houses continued to hold social functions, but much of the conviviality and fun had died away. The differences over issues and the political bitterness which still surrounded the formation of the DStP affected personal relations as well. The Democratic Club's financial picture resembled the party's. In April 1932, Fischer reported to Dietrich that he was attempting to raise, through his private sources, 5,000 M to save the club, but it was 40,000 M in debt.[11] Members found excuses—some of them financial—to drop their memberships. Diels, the police official, announced he was resigning because too many of the club's members were anti-Semitic. This provoked a retort from a Herr von Osten: "We could not be anti-Semitic; if we were half of our members would be excluded."[12] The "Jewish question" did produce frictions and misunderstandings, however, as in the estrangement of Stolper and Schacht, despite Stolper's desire to remain friends. The forming of the Papen government also produced splits at the Democratic Club. Figures such as Richthofen and Fischer supported the new government, while most members were repelled by it. After Hitler came to power, the Democratic Club expired, and the social life of former prominent Democrats seems to have been confined to small circles of friends they could trust. The kind of social life which had been embodied in the Democratic Club and the meetings of DDP organizations—open, tolerant, spirited—became impossible. The friendships which had been cultivated in the DDP, however, helped many members survive the ordeal of the Nazi years.

Appendix B:
The Elections of 1920, 1924, and 1928

DDP Vote Totals

	Vote Total	% Votes Cast	Seats
Election to the National Assembly 19 Jan. 1919	5,614,800	18.5	75
Reichstag Election, 6 June 1920	2,333,700	8.2	39
Reichstag Election, 4 May 1924	1,655,100	5.3	28
Reichstag Election, 7 Dec. 1924	1,919,800	6.3	32
Reichstag Election, 20 May 1928	1,505,700	4.9	25
Reichstag Election, 14 Sept. 1930	1,322,400	3.7	20*
Reichstag Election, 31 July 1932	317,800	1.0	5
Reichstag Election, 6 Nov. 1932	336,500	0.9	2
Reichstag Election, 5 March 1933	334,200	0.8	5†

*Included 6 *Volksnationalen*
†List connection with the SPD

The election statistics above illustrate the declining fortunes of left liberalism during the Weimar period.[1] After the aberrant great success in 1919, the DDP steadily declined. By 1928, it fell beneath the 5 percent standard established by the Federal Republic to eliminate splinter parties. After 1930, it lacked sufficient deputies to constitute a legal *Fraktion*. The electoral statistics for the *Land* and other local elections present a similar pattern. In the end, only the Hamburg and Württemberg organizations remained viable, but their strength was greatly reduced.

I have already analyzed the elections of 1919 and 1930 in some detail, but we should isolate the 1920, the two 1924 elections, and the 1928 election for additional study and also note the importance of some local elections, during the same period, which illustrate basic electoral trends. It is evident from the stark numbers that the election of 1920 proved crucial to the history of the DDP. In June 1920, and in later years, it was agreed that this first regular election was a decisive event, not only in the history of the DDP but in the history of the Republic.[2] It began the move away from the moderate center toward the extremes, which in the end brought down the "Weimar System." While the Weimar Coalition parties, and in particular the DDP and the SPD, lost heavily, the DVP, the DNVP and the Independent Socialists (USPD) made striking gains. The most serious consequence to any one party, however, was the terrible defeat of the Democrats. To contemporaries, the outcome showed that the former National Liberals had simply returned "home," but the DNVP as well as the DVP made dramatic advances in several districts, and, clearly, some of those who defected from the DDP voted DNVP. This was particularly evident in electoral districts in the northeast such as Mecklenburg, Pomerania, and East Prussia. The DDP suffered similar losses in *Land* and other local elections in 1920 and 1921. The extent of the DDP's defeat may be seen in examining the results in a variety of districts.

In Berlin, the DDP losses represented a shocking setback in what had been regarded as a left-liberal stronghold. In Greater Berlin, the DDP's vote total declined from about 480,000 votes to 230,000. In WK No. 2, which had backed the DDP heavily in 1919, the DDP vote dropped from about 178,000 to 72,000. In WK No. 13, Schleswig-Holstein, the most studied district in the Weimar period, the DDP slumped from slightly over 27 percent of the total vote to only 9.4 percent in 1921, when the election in the district occurred. The DVP, on the other hand, rose from 7.8 percent to 17.9 percent and the DNVP made similar gains. In the nearby district WK No. 14, Weser-Ems, where many of the same factors were present as in Schleswig-Holstein, the DDP declined from 24.5 percent of the votes cast to 8.6 percent, while the DVP increased its votes from 13 to 22 percent. In Hamburg, WK No. 34, to cite one more example, the DDP declined from 25.9 percent to 17.4 percent, while the DVP rose from 8.2 percent to 14.1 percent.

The DDP had expected to be defeated in June 1920, but the magnitude of the loss surprised everyone.[3] Ever since the election of January 1919, a steady flow of DDP supporters left the party, largely for the DVP. It quickly became evident that many had voted for the DDP in 1919 because they had hoped it might prevent a SPD majority. Others undoubtedly supported it because it represented the only *Bürger* party in tune with a democratic age. The realities of coalition government in a parliamentary democracy, however, soon disillusioned many. Apparently, not many voters had realized that the DDP would have to make far-reaching concessions on economic and social policy. Although the DDP left the government rather than sign the Treaty of Versailles, after the SPD and the Z signed it, the exodus continued. Many opposed the return of the DDP to the government in October 1919 and the acceptance of the socialization laws, tax legislation, and the Councils' Law. After the Kapp *Putsch* in March 1920, when the DDP felt compelled by coalition pressures to support the trade union position in favor of a general strike, the defections speeded up. The Erzberger-Helfferich trial also hurt the reputation of the Weimar Coalition. In rural districts such as Schleswig-Holstein, the association of the DDP with prominent and controversial Jews and with the Jewish-owned, "pacifist" newspapers such as the BT and the FZ damaged it. The press of the DVP and the DNVP waged a heavy hitting and damaging propaganda campaign linking the DDP with socialism, Jews, and the Treaty of Versailles. They repeatedly contended that the DDP was not a worthy defender of middle-class values and interests—a constant theme in subsequent elections—and weeks before the election of 1920, it seemed evident that the electorate would turn away from the Weimar Coalition. Many right-wing Democrats pressed unceasingly for a merger with the DVP to form a united liberal party, but the left wing rejected this. If anything, Stresemann and the DVP were more repugnant to them in 1920 than they had been in January 1919.

Considerable emotion and threats of violence from right and left marked the campaign. There were rumors of military coups, and the possibility of civil war was seriously entertained. "Unheard-of anti-Semitism" also characterized the 1920 election.[4] The DNVP and the DVP both used hatred of Jews to damage the DDP and both characterized it as the *Judenpartei*. Stresemann, whose wife stemmed from a baptized Jewish family and who had many Jewish friends and supporters, did not try to restrain the anti-Jewish agitation in the DVP until too late. Anti-Semitic Lutheran pastors also aided the DVP and the DNVP against the DDP in several districts. They tended to represent the DDP as godless and materialistic because of its desire to separate church and state.

The contemporary explanations for the DDP's smashing defeat generally agree with later scholarly analyses. It was felt in 1920 that the vote was directed primarily against the record of the Weimar Coalition since January 1919. The MNN, for example, contended that the voters had voiced their displeasure at the whole course of events since the revolution.[5] The FZ had a more complicated and variegated explanation.[6] It blamed underlying historic divisions in Germany—economic antagonism, class differences, religious divisions—as well as the political inadequacies of the German voter. In addition, the Entente powers were blamed for their imperialism and harsh actions, while the extreme Left was condemned because it frightened the middle classes. Weinhausen, a DDP publicist, censured the rightist turn of many of the women who had supported the DDP,[7] while Wilhelm Mommsen explained the disaffection of university students.[8] Some leaders, such as Gerland, Erkelenz, and Bergsträsser, focused on organizational flaws of the party and the absence of a true party press. Many prominent members felt the "individualism" of the DDP's press support hurt it in the election. This was a familiar refrain in subsequent elections. Some members of the left wing believed that the DDP placed too many representatives of interest groups on the *Reichslist*, while the business wing wanted even more business and industrial representatives in the Reichstag delegation. Apparently, the campaign was relatively well financed, for there were few specific complaints on that score compared to later elections when the leadership often singled out finances as a major factor in the DDP's defeats. Some DDP members arrived at explanations for the results which focused on one area only, excluding all others. Müller-Meiningen, for example, concentrated on the "national question" as the key to the DDP's loss.[9] According to him, the Weimar Coalition had affronted German nationalist sentiment by supporting the Investigative Committee to examine the causes of the German "collapse," by signing the Treaty of Versailles and accepting with it the stigma of "war guilt" and the burden of reparations.

Following the election, the leaders pooled their ideas about why the DDP had suffered such a striking loss. Erkelenz, who believed that the organization had been too complacent and tried to coast on its 1919 success, stressed the need for a renewed effort to improve the organization and to strengthen the central headquarters of the DDP in Berlin. He felt that the DDP should steer to the left toward a closer relationship with the SPD,[10] implying that socialism was the wave of the future and that the DDP should accommodate itself to this trend if it wished to have a major role in the Republic. This, however, was an unpopular view in the DDP even in 1920. Leaders such as Petersen, Fischer, Böhme, and Gerland preferred a closer relationship with the DVP, if not a merger, while Wolff and Koch were so shaken by the results of the election that it was some time before they could suggest necessary reforms. Wolff was bitter and depressed, and Koch felt that everything for which he had worked had collapsed. The *Vorstand* met on 10 June and the PA on 22 June to assess the situation.[11] The mood was gloomy and opinion divided on what the DDP's course should be. The left wanted to preserve the Weimar Coalition, while the right, including the leader, Petersen, felt that the only viable government was a coalition that would include the DVP. Koch, who was developing a talent for finding the middle position in every party debate, favored a government of the Weimar Coalition with the inclusion of some nonpartisan experts close to the DVP. Tax policy, which had provided the backdrop to many debates in the National Assembly, clearly influenced right and left positions and the choice of coalition partners. The PA, where the left wing was better represented and less intimidated than in the *Vorstand* or the *Fraktion*, attempted to forestall the DDP's entrance into the Fehrenbach *Bürger* government, but the motion lost 66 to 22. Bäumer, who was then in the left wing, advanced a motion to support a government coalition that would have favored the "republican-democratic state form" and an active social policy, but this, too, was defeated. The PA finally agreed on a motion which handed over the responsibility of coalition politics to the *Fraktion*, more conservative than ever since the election. With this action, the PA helped guarantee its own impotence in making major policies in the DDP. Henceforth, the *Vorstand* and the *Fraktion*, usually working together, made most of the DDP's basic policy decisions.

The period between June 1920 and May 1924, the date of the next election, was marked by many controversial decisions in foreign policy and the devastating inflation which encouraged the extremists to attempt to overthrow the government by force. The national government became more unpopular than ever, and the DDP's defeat in May 1924 was attributed to most of the same causes as the debacle of 1920.[12] Other *Bürger* parties again attacked the DDP for its cooperation with the SPD, and many of its middle-class followers were probably influenced by this propaganda. Foreign policy issues, however, were stressed even more heavily in this election. The DDP's *Bürger* rivals represented the Dawes Plan and the policy of fulfillment as shameful betrayals of Germany's national interests, and the DDP found it difficult to defend a rational foreign policy. The DNVP, which had a racist wing, once again flailed the DDP as unpatriotic and Jew-ridden, but the most flagrant Jew-hating party in the May 1924 election was the Racist party (*Deutsch-Völkische Freiheitspartei*—DVF), the forerunner of the NSDAP, which at this time made its first appearance in a national election and proved to be more popular than the DDP. The DNVP's vote climbed from 3.1 million and 44 seats in 1919 to 5.7 million votes and 95 seats in May 1924. The DVP also lost many seats; the electorate clearly rejected liberal parties and liberalism.

In the electoral post mortem, the DDP leaders developed a variety of explanations for its poor showing. Erkelenz blamed the outcome on three things: 1) the responsibilities of being a government party; 2) the desertion of many newspapers to rightist parties; 3) Poincaré and his vengeful colleagues.[13] Erkelenz's remarks to the *Vorstand*, of which he was chairman, also stressed the effects of the inflation.[14] Others—generally not those in the topmost leadership ranks—emphasized the many internal divisions within the DDP and the feuds among its leaders as important factors in its defeat. The organizational flaws and, in particular, the financial weaknesses of the party, also were frequently mentioned as causes of the party's serious setback.

The May election of 1924 settled nothing, and preparations were soon underway to fight another national election. Democratic supporters proved more alert to the dangers to the Republic, and they made a more militant defense of democracy than in the period preceding the May election. Jews especially were alarmed by the great increase in the DVF and DNVP vote.[15] Another effect of the election results was an increase in liberal unification talk, although the left wing of the DDP remained as opposed to a merger as the right wing of the DVP. The majority of the *Vorstand* and the *Fraktion* still opposed any cooperative relationship with the DNVP, although Fischer and Hummel thought it would be a good idea to hold talks with the DNVP to "learn their colors."[16] Although many leaders believed that the DDP's participation in the government had been the single most important cause of its losses, it nonetheless entered the government again. Gessler, Oeser, and Hamm assumed the same ministries which they had held in the previous government under Marx. The pressure to include the DNVP in the cabinet increased, and several prominent Democrats advocated this course. The principal committees of the DDP, however, opposed participation in any government which included the DNVP. As a result, several right-wing Democrats, the most notable of whom were Böhme, Schiffer, Gerland, and Keinath, resigned from the DDP.[17] They had become so alienated from the DDP's orientation on several issues that there was little chance, save for perhaps Schiffer, of their returning to the Reichstag. They expected to be welcomed into the DVP and perhaps to receive Reichstag seats, but this did not occur in 1924. Only a few members seem to have followed them out of the DDP, although their defection proved to be a more serious setback to the DDP than the party leadership indicated.

Between the two national elections in 1924, a few *Land* elections took place, but the results were generally inconclusive. In Hamburg, the DDP lost nearly 10,000 votes and 2 seats in the *Bürgerschaft*. The DVP and the DNVP also suffered losses there. Early in December, the DDP received a needed boost to its morale when it scored a victory in the tiny state of Anhalt. Its vote jumped from 6181 to 13,001. Dessau had a DDP mayor, Fritz Hesse, and a well-established left-liberal tradition, but whatever the causes of the victory in Anhalt, it did not herald a major recovery for the DDP. The DDP's leadership sought to turn the "good news of Anhalt" and the defection of a solitary WP local organization to the DDP into a tidal wave of Democratic enthusiasm, but, alas, it was only a ripple.

In November, the DDP held a PT in Berlin, and 20,000 attended an election rally in the *Sportspalast*.[18] The meeting showed a spirited fighting mood, but the speakers' list contained only the usual familiar names and the speeches were, for the most part, interchangeable with DDP speeches in earlier elections. The prevailing theme was the denouncing of the rightist parties. Koch gave a powerful speech castigating the Right, while Heuss and Hamm made speeches in support of the Republic. Despite the tone of this meeting, the *Reichslist* and the candidates in the various districts appeared to be more conservative than ever, and several left-wing candidates failed to secure high enough list positions to receive seats.

Wolff and Erkelenz, for example, attempted to secure a favorable list position for the ardent republican and pacifist Deimling. He received the no. 11 position on the *Reichslist*, and only nine were elected. This election also saw several conservative establishment figures publicly campaign for the DDP, despite the defections of Schiffer and others. Delbrück, who addressed the Party Congress in Berlin, Count Max Montgelas, Schacht, as well as several academics, supported the DDP largely on foreign policy grounds. The DDP traded heavily on the doubtful premise that Schacht had "saved the mark," and he enjoyed great success in Dessau, where he addressed a large and enthusiastic Democratic rally.

On the eve of the election, Koch, as usual, was optimistic.[19] He based his estimate on greater internal unity in the party, more money available for the organization and several organizational reforms. The *Reichsbanner*, which had recently been formed, also provided a more secure atmosphere for party rallies because the rightist enemies of the DDP, including its later ally, the *Jungdo*, could no longer terrorize its members and guests. Attendance at DDP meetings was reported much higher than in May, and, even in districts such as Schleswig-Holstein, circumstances looked more favorable. Local organization figures, however, were often unduly optimistic. Nonetheless, many felt that the antirightist and prorepublican campaign had proved popular and it had given the campaign a unifying theme. Ludendorff, whom Koch had attempted to protect in May, received heavy criticism in December. The DDP's press support also seemed more unified and lively. While the results represented a slight improvement, they were not as favorable as the leaders had hoped. Still, they were able to crow: "We are not dead after all, despite the premature funeral orations."[20] Later analyses of the results and critiques of the campaign showed that the party had not been able to attract new voters or to win youthful workers. The DDP had become essentially what the Progressive party had been before 1918: a party of *Bildung und Besitz*, with a scattering of business and professional men and women, middle-grade government officials, Jews, teachers, and tiny groups of workers, farmers, and *Mittelstand* elements. The hopes entertained in 1918–1919 for a mass party representing all classes expired for all but interest group leaders in the DDP, who continued to contend that they represented significant numbers of actual or potential DDP voters.

Although the complexities and the arid ground of coalition government politics between 1924 and 1928 are beyond the scope of this study,[21] the DDP was in the government about half the time in these four years and in the opposition in the remaining years. It refused to serve in governments which included the DNVP, although Gessler served anyway. While these were years in which the German economy revived somewhat and Stresemann had several successes in foreign policy, too many Germans were still unemployed and too few benefited from Stresemann's achievements.

These were years also in which the DDP exposed its several internal contradictions on a variety of issues: the presidential election of 1925; the referendum to expropriate the property of the princes; the *Schund- und Schmutzgesetz* controversy. The DDP also alienated several important interest groups at this time by failing to support agricultural tariffs, a radical reevaluation effort to aid the victims of the inflation, or salary boosts for government officials and employees. There was a steady drain of members from the DDP during this period in which the Republic was supposedly consolidating itself and the economy was reviving. The DDP leadership grew acutely aware of its organizational weaknesses and made an effort to improve the organization through systematic study, but a flurry of organizational seminars brought only petty changes. Meetings, speeches, still more pamphlets, new committees, and new programmatic statements failed to halt the rot. Local elections, notably those in Saxony in October 1926 and the communal elections in November 1926, showed that not only the DDP but the DVP and the DNVP as well were rapidly losing supporters. In addition, two more prominent DDP leaders, Wolff and Schacht, left the party. Wolff resigned because the party's position on "filthy literature" was too ambiguous; Schacht left because he felt the DDP had not supported the principle of private property strongly enough in the referendum on princely property.

There were two national party congresses in the years between 1924 and 1928, one in Breslau in December 1925, concentrating largely on foreign policy issues,[22] and the other in Hamburg in April 1927, where the leaders swept most of the basic and divisive issues under the rug and emphasized relatively trivial topics.[23] They made an attempt to push Koch-Weser's "decentralized unitary state" as a panacea issue. This proposal was supposed to unify the party, to heal the difficulties between the Reich government, *Länder*, and cities, and to pave the way for an electoral law reform which would prevent the continued fragmentation of the party structure. The PT also stressed *Kultur* issues as unifying themes as well as the fight against the Center party's campaign to secure a clerical national educational law and a concordat. Some members also saw this effort as a way to cooperate with the DVP. Plans were made at Hamburg to formulate an economic program, although this never materialized, but an agriculture program was announced—too late, however, to retain the farmers. For the most part, the DDP leadership dodged any firm stand on significant economic and social questions for fear of splitting and weakening the party.

In the period of 1924–1928, several right-wing Democrats, including Hellpach and Meinecke and new converts to pessimism such as Alfred Weber, began to despair about the future of parliamentary democracy in Germany.[24] In general, they wanted to strengthen the executive at the expense of the Reichstag and the president's office at the expense of the cabinet. While some agonized about these large and fundamental concerns, other Democrats myopically focused on the importance of card files and organized letter campaigns to members of various interest groups. To all but the inner core of active Democrats, the DDP seemed increasingly irrelevant. The United States' consulate in Frankfurt a/M, in commenting on a local election, noted: "It is frequently asserted by its enemies that the Democratic Party is a strange growth in Germany, and that its election slogans do not appeal to the German way of thinking. It is, in fact, a small band of liberal intellectuals."[25] Some members began to think of organizing a new party to replace the DDP. Wolff, a superb editor but an inept politician, attempted, in 1928, to form a new Republican party which, he hoped, would attract youth and rejuvenate democratic liberalism. It failed. It was also in 1928 that the volume edited by Erkelenz, *Zehn Jahre Deutsche Republik*, appeared. It intended to memorialize the DDP's achievements, but not even the most active Democrats purchased a copy. In his introduction, Erkelenz asserted that the DDP was not dead and that it remained flexible and adaptable, although new members were needed and difficult tasks lay ahead. He also unconsciously wrote the DDP's epitaph: "Seldom has a party with so few voters had so much influence as we have had." While this was probably true, it was of little solace to those attempting to breathe life into the organization for another national election.

Several *Land* and local elections as well as the first national election in forty months demonstrated the DDP's protracted failure. The organization was beyond hope and the party had never been so unpopular. Despite these cold realities, however, the leadership professed to see a revival of spirit in the party, and there was the usual optimistic moonshine about the DDP's chances in the weeks before the May election of 1928. Indeed, reading the DDP's propaganda, one would think that all parties but the DDP were in deep trouble. There were, as always, some large and enthusiastic party rallies; even though the number of DDP members was not large, they were probably more willing to attend political meetings than most Germans. Koch-Weser once again found some hopeful signs of organizational recovery. On the other hand, the bitter haggling over list positions recurred, and candidates had little money except what they raised or donated themselves. And the party did not generate any fresh ideas or issues either. With a few exceptions, it presented the same candidates as in earlier elections. Behind the election in December 1924 was "the good news of Anhalt," but, in 1928, the voters halved the DDP's vote in Anhalt. In Silesia and Königsberg, old Progressive strongholds, the DDP suffered devastating losses, mostly to the WP and local interest parties, but the best-documented trend was the decision of hundreds of thousands of Democrats to support the SPD. Many in the left wing and most of the remaining Young Democrats concluded that the SPD best safeguarded German democracy, although many Democrats still found it impossible to join the SPD or vote for it. Left-wing figures such as Wolff, Friedensburg, Feder, and Cohnstaedt, for example, continued to be repelled by the SPD's Marxism and its trade union ties.

The DDP campaign in 1928 stressed new electoral technology more than ever—records, films, radio—but it could not overcome the party's basic unpopularity. The DDP also made its usual belated appeals to various interest groups that had once supported left-liberal parties. It also wrote moving appeals to women and families about child care, housing, and other social issues about which it had been little concerned before the campaign. And, as usual, the DDP pledged tax cuts on everything from matches to rents, a position more in line with its voting record in the four years preceding the election. Although Berlin was no longer a vital DDP center, the party held another giant rally in the *Sportspalast*, and once again hundreds of undoubtedly sincere DDP speakers made thousands of speeches throughout the Reich. The party made a determined effort to recruit new adherents, and the FZ found at least one to boast about: the mayor of Kaiserstuhl.[26] While the cheers of the few party faithful could still gladden the hearts of the leaders, the party rallies and the applause could not disguise the fact that the DDP was a moribund organization.

When the votes were added up, only one big winner emerged in the 1928 elections: the SPD. While this heartened a few Democrats, most members still saw the SPD more as a threat than as an ally or a friend. Once again the leadership conducted a post mortem, and there were many confident analyses of the causes of the DDP's poor showing. The most important critique took place in the *Vorstand* meeting of 14 June, about three weeks after the election.[27] Stubmann, coeditor of *Deutsche Einheit* and an important organizational figure in Hamburg, made the most telling judgment. In his opinion, the DDP lost and the SPD won because of economic factors. The SPD, he felt, had identified itself with the material needs of the "little people," while the DDP had ignored them. The basic failure of the DDP, as he saw it, was its unwillingness to identify itself with the most pressing needs of the people. He felt that the only future for the DDP was to transform itself into a radical *Bürger* party which would emphasize the social question. The prevailing mood, however, dictated that the DDP separate itself from the SPD and the social question. Frankfurter, who, from time to time, had advocated that the DDP become a *Mittelstand* interest party, belabored Koch-Weser's unwillingness to move the party in that direction, which he felt opened the door for the WP. Nearly everyone bemoaned the inability of the DDP to attract young people, but they were the same leaders who were seldom willing to listen to young people or to give them opportunities to run for office. Further division occurred when the left wing attacked Koch-Weser because of his active support of the *Liberale Vereinigung* and argued that his position had seriously divided the party. Wachhorst de Wente, the farmers' leader, cited another source of division in the DDP: its intimate association with the Jewish community. Stephan attributed the defeat to the exodus of large numbers of self-employed *Mittelstand* members and *Angestellten*. Dietrich disparaged the importance of the Jewish question in this election and the organizational weaknesses, agreeing with Stubmann that the results were largely attributable to material considerations. He felt that the inflation had destroyed the independence of the middle classes (*Mittelschichten*), causing large numbers of them to leave the DDP for the WP and peasant parties. Dietrich dismissed the importance of the press, which Koch-Weser often blamed for the DDP's setbacks. For Koch-Weser, the defeat was a surprise, a devastating blow to him personally as well as to his judgment as a leader. He admitted that there had been some signs that the party was in trouble—attendance at election meetings was not as great as in earlier elections. He complained that in the four previous years he had seldom received constructive criticism about the course of the DDP or its program, but now everyone wanted to blame the defeat on him. He admitted that constitutional reforms and the school question had not been attractive to voters and that economic factors had indeed been the determining consideration in the election, but he warned that if politics became only a naked struggle between economic interests and classes, democracy in Germany could not endure. If one reads between the lines, it seems probable that Koch-Weser and others were looking toward the left wing of the DVP and other groups to form a new party; the DDP alone was no longer viable.

On the following day, 15 June, the speeches and post-election analysis continued in the *Vorstand*, although few new points were made.[28] Hellpach also stressed the centrality of material questions, but rather than to turn left, as Stubmann wished, he preferred to try to attract more businessmen and industrialists. We cannot be a party of *Beamten* and *Angestellten* only, he contended. He hoped that the DVP and the DDP might finally merge and joined the chorus demanding an economic program for the party. Lemmer, on the other hand, remained skeptical about an economic program. How, he asked, could we ever agree on one? He felt, moreover, that the general perception of the DDP as a party of big capitalists had harmed it. He vigorously opposed fusion with the DVP; he felt that the DDP and the DVP were still fundamentally incompatible and that it was unrealistic to discuss a merger.

On 19 July, the Organization Committee met, and the gloom was so thick that Frankfurter suggested that it was perhaps time to dissolve the party.[29] He pointed out that nineteen districts no longer had a DDP Reichstag deputy and that without money and press support it was unlikely that the organization could be maintained much longer. Only a few local organizations still had a paid political secretary. Election results in Berlin showed that the DDP had again suffered a terrible loss; one by one the electoral strongholds were falling.

The PA met in October for the first time since the election and once again rehashed the election results.[30] The consensus was that the SPD and the WP were indeed the most significant winners and that material factors and the general unpopularity of the DDP explained its defeat. Vogt, a prominent *Beamten* Committee member, reported that hundreds of thousands of DDP members, many of whom were government officials and employees, had defected to the SPD and that the DDP had little chance of winning them back. It was apparent that there were no easy solutions or explanations. Dietrich once again dismissed the importance of the press in the outcome, and Stephan contended that not even more money would have changed the results.

In the light of Frankfurter's pessimism and general ineffectiveness and the illness of Erkelenz, it became imperative to change the organization's leadership. Although Koch-Weser was personally unpopular and his electoral tactics had failed, there was no move to unseat him. Indeed, he soon assumed additional responsibilities, becoming chairman of the *Vorstand* as well as of the PA. Stephan replaced Frankfurter as chairman of the Organizational Committee, but he soon resigned as business manager and general secretary of the organization. On the surface, the DDP continued to exist and occasional meetings of the major committees occurred, but several members, including Koch-Weser, began to meet with left DVP members, *Jungdo* representatives, and others from various splinter parties to discuss cooperation in order to save a place in German politics for the moderate middle classes. Out of these talks came the DStP, the DDP's successor, which was thrown together in time for the elections of September 1930. Most of the DDP realists concluded, after the 1928 election, that no hope remained for halting its decline. Only a new party could save a political role for the "state-supporting middle classes."

Notes

Introduction

1. For the electoral statistics which illustrate the DDP's decline from a major party to an insignificant splinter party, see Appendix B, p. 223.
2. For a recent discussion of many of the issues which concern students of German liberalism, including exceptionality, see Geoff Eley, "James Sheehan and the German Liberals: a Critical Appreciation." *Central European History* 14, no. 3 (Sept. 1981): 273–88.

1. German Left Liberalism before 1918

1. For the history of German left liberalism before 1914, see James J. Sheehan, *German Liberalism in the Nineteenth Century* (Chicago, 1978); John L. Snell, *The Democratic Movement in Germany, 1789–1914*, ed. and comp. Hans A. Schmitt (Chapel Hill, NC, 1976); Wolfgang J. Mommsen, Konstanze Wegner, et al., articles on liberalism, in *Geschichte und Gesellschaft*, (1978) 4: 77–90, 120–37, and *passim*. Lotha Gall, ed., *Liberalismus* (Cologne, 1976); Leonard Krieger, *The German Idea of Freedom* (Boston, 1957); Theodor Schieder, "Die Krise des bürgerlichen Liberalismus," from his *Staat und Gesellschaft im Wandel unserer Zeit* (Munich, 1958); Gustav Seeber, *Zwischen Bebel und Bismarck. Zur Geschichte des Linksliberalismus in Deutschland 1871–1892* (Berlin, 1965); Ludwig Elm, *Zwischen Fortschritt und Reaktion* (Berlin, 1968); Karl Holl and Günther List, eds., *Liberalismus und imperialistischer Staat* (Göttingen, 1975); Konstanze Wegner, *Theodor Barth und die Freisinnige Vereinigung* (Tübingen, 1968); Peter Gilg, *Die Erneuerung des demokratischen Denkens im Wilhelminischen Deutschland* (Wiesbaden, 1965); James Clark Hunt, *The People's Party in Württemberg and Southern Germany, 1890–1914* (Stuttgart, 1975).
2. For an extended analysis of the left-liberal electorate, see Lothar Albertin, *Liberalismus und Demokratie am Anfang der Weimarer Republik* (Düsseldorf, 1972), pp. 106–38; Hunt, *The People's Party*, pp. 45–59.
3. Electoral data used in this study are primarily based on Alfred Milatz, *Wähler und Wahlen in der Weimarer Republik* (Bonn, 1965).

235

4. This familiar refrain in liberal programmatic statements was repeated in the DDP program of 1919–1920. DDP, *Bericht über die Verhandlungen des zweiten ausserordentlichen Parteitags in Leipzig. 13. bis 15. Dezember 1919* (Berlin, 1919), p. 248. Hereafter cited as first special PT *Bericht*.

5. See V. R. Berghahn, *Germany and the Approach of War in 1914* (New York, 1973); Fritz Fischer, *War of Illusions. German Policies from 1911 to 1914*, trans. from the German (New York, 1975); Immanuel Geiss, *German Foreign Policy. 1871–1914* (London, 1976); Wolfgang J. Mommsen, "Domestic Factors in German Foreign Policy before 1914," *Central European History (CEH)* 6, no. 1 (March 1973): 3–43.

6. NL Gothein.

7. Hans Peter Hanssen, *Diary of a Dying Empire*, trans. from the Danish, 3–4 Aug. 1914 (Bloomington, IN, 1955), p. 31.

8. Naumann's address on "World Politics and Peace," was the principal speech on foreign affairs. *Der zweite Parteitag der Fortschrittlichen Volkspartei zu Mannheim, 5. bis 7. Oktober 1912* (Berlin, 1912), pp. 77–80.

9. Ibid.

10. Quoted in Roger Chickering, *Imperial Germany and a World without War. The Peace Movement and German Society 1892–1914* (Princeton, 1975), pp. 247–48.

11. Gothein, "Aus meiner politischen Arbeit," p. 389. Hereafter cited as NL Gothein, no. 12.

12. Ibid., p. 119.

13. Naumann, *Werke*, ed. Theodor Schieder (Cologne, 1964), 5:501–15.

14. This is forcefully asserted in Stuart T. Robson's "Left Liberalism in Germany, 1900–1919", unpublished Ph.D. thesis (Oxford University, 1966), and in Beverly Heckart, *From Bassermann to Bebel. The Grand Bloc's Quest for Reform in the Kaiserreich, 1900–1914* (New Haven, CT, 1974). For refutations of this optimistic evaluation of the course of German parliamentarization, see (in addition to the author's judgment) material in Snell, *The German Democratic Movement*; Hunt, *The German People's Party*; Klaus Epstein, *Matthias Erzberger and the Dilemma of German Democracy* (Princeton, 1959); and, most recently, Gordon Craig, *Germany 1866–1945* (New York, 1980).

15. Anti-Catholic sentiments ran very deep among left liberals. For the views of a "liberal Protestant" see Otto Baumgarten, *Meine Lebensgeschichte* (Tübingen, 1929), pp. 228–29 and p. 247. Baumgarten was one of the Naumann circle and a cousin of Max Weber, but his anti-Catholic attitudes were traditional. The Center party was usually linked to the Conservative party by German liberals.

16. The most valuable secondary account of the Progressive party during the war is Robson's "Left Liberalism in Germany."

17. Hanssen, *Diary*, 4 August 1914, pp. 26, 31–32; Conrad Haussmann, *Schlaglichter, Reichstagsbriefe und Aufzeichnungen*, ed. Ulrich Zeller (Frankfurt a/ M, 1924). Haussmann often felt the same sense of isolation.

18. Werner Stephan, *Aufstieg und Verfall des Linksliberalismus 1918–1933* (Göttingen, 1973), p. 42. On German war goals plans see Fritz Fischer, *Germany's Aims in the First World War*, trans. from the German (New York,

1967), and Hans W. Gatzke, *Germany's Drive to the West* (Baltimore, 1950). For a general description of the left-liberal position on war aims see Leo Haupts, *Deutsche Friedenspolitik 1918–1919* (Düsseldorf, 1976), pp. 100–38.

19. The protocol of the 11 July 1915 meeting at Eisenach is in NL Payer, no. 10.

20. The most notable Progressives were Pius Dirr, a veteran Bavarian left liberal, and Marie-Elisabeth Lüders. Her papers are now in the Bundesarchiv Koblenz. Hereafter cited as NL Lüders. Lüders, *Fürchte dich nicht* (Cologne, 1964), p. 63. See also Dorothee von Velsen, *Im Alter die Fülle* (Tübingen, 1956), pp. 143–73. Von Velsen also served in the Ukraine, pp. 197–232.

21. For the text of the papal note, see Herbert Michaelis and Ernst Schraepler, eds., *Ursachen und Folgen. Vom Deutschen Zusammenbruch 1918 und 1945 bis zur staatlichen Neuordnung Deutschlands in der Gegenwart* (Berlin, 1961), 2:73–76. Hereafter cited as *Ursachen und Folgen*.

22. Erich Matthias and Rudolf Morsey, eds., *Der Interfraktionelle Ausschuss 1917/1918, Erster Teil* (Düsseldorf, 1959), pp. 128–32, and 151–155. Hereafter cited as *Der Interfraktionelle Ausschuss, Erster Teil*; *Ursachen und Folgen* 2:30–35.

23. Haussmann, *Schlaglichter*, p. 170; Hanssen, *Diary*, 13 March 1918, p. 267.

24. Quoted in Gatzke, *Germany's Drive*, p. 252.

25. The Memorandum was dated 27 July 1915; Werner Schiefel, *Bernhard Dernburg, 1865–1937 Kolonialpolitiker und Bankier im Wilhelminischen Deutschland* (Zurich, 1974), pp. 149–61. Hereafter cited as Schiefel, *Bernhard Dernburg*.

26. Ralph H. Lutz, ed., *Fall of the German Empire*, 2 vols., trans. from the German. (Stanford, CA, 1932), 1:181. Hereafter cited as Lutz, *Fall of the German Empire*; Konrad H. Jarausch, *The Enigmatic Chancellor. Bethmann Hollweg and the Hubris of Imperial Germany* (New Haven, CT, 1973), pp. 264–307.

27. Haussmann, *Schlaglichter*, pp. 64–66. Fischer, *Germany's Aims*, p. 172; Jarausch, *The Enigmatic Chancellor*, p. 307.

28. Robson, "Left Liberalism in Germany," p. 192; Peter de Mendelssohn, *Zeitungsstadt Berlin* (Berlin, 1959), pp. 204–5.

29. Georg Gothein, *Warum verloren wir den Krieg?* (Berlin, 1919), p. 165.

30. Friedrich Naumann, *Central Europe*, trans. from the German (New York, 1917), pp. 12, 33–34.

31. NL Gothein, no. 12, p. 177.

32. Meinecke to Goetz, 6 May 1915. Meinecke, *Ausgewählter Briefwechsel. Werke* (Stuttgart, 1962), 6:56–60.

33. Fischer, *Germany's Aims*, p. 172.

34. Naumann, *Werke*, 4:480–84; Naumann in the Inter-Party Committee, 2 January 1918, *Der Interfraktionelle Ausschuss, Erster Teil*, pp. 59–60; Gerhard Ritter, *The Sword and the Scepter. The Problem of Militarism*, trans. from the German. (Coral Gables, FL, 1972), 3:94–96.

35. Inter-Party Committee, 6 Nov. 1917, *Der Interfraktionelle Ausschuss, Erster Teil*, p. 511.

36. For a typical Fischbeck performance see ibid., 1 Jan. 1918, pp. 40–43, in

which he straddled every issue presented. Hanssen, *Diary*, 3 Jan. 1918, p. 245.

37. *Der Interfraktionelle Ausschuss, Erster Teil*, 20 Dec. 1917, p. 218. Gothein wrote several memoranda on Poland, which are in his papers. They are summarized in Robson, "Left Liberalism in Germany," pp. 175–83, and in Elm, *Zwischen Fortschritt und Reaktion*, p. 242. Also see Gothein, *Warum verloren wir den Krieg?* p. 181.

38. *Der Interfraktionelle Ausschuss, Erster Teil*, 21 July 1917, p. 107 fn. 3; ibid., 20 Dec. 1917, p. 642.

39. Erich Matthias and Eberhard Pikart, eds., *Die Reichstagsfraktion der deutschen Sozialdemokratie 1898 bis 1918* (Düsseldorf, 1966), 19 Feb. 1918, p. 373, and 23 Sept. 1918, p. 432. Hereafter cited as *Die Reichstagsfraktion der deutschen Sozialdemokratie*.

40. The mood of uncritical optimism was captured by the Naumann follower, Carl Petersen, in a letter to Gothein in March 1918, when he predicted that England would soon have to give up and the blood letting would come to an end. NL Gothein, no. 28. Also see Fischer, *Germany's Aims*, p. 472, fn. 4; Robson, "Left Liberalism in Germany," p. 302.

41. Inter-Party Committee, 23 Sept. 1918, *Der Interfraktionelle Ausschuss, Erster Teil*, pp. 690–91.

42. Lutz, *Fall of the German Empire*, 2:135–36.

43. Inter-Party Committee, 14 Aug. 1917, *Der Interfraktionelle Ausschuss, Erster Teil*, p. 119; ibid., 20 Aug. 1917, p. 122; Naumann, *Werke*, 5:591–96. The need for immediate action on Alsace-Lorraine was not perceived in Progressive circles until Haussmann's return from Switzerland in Feb. 1918, after he had talks with the American agent of Wilson, George Herron. Inter-Party Committee, 22 Feb. 1918, *Der Interfraktionelle Ausschuss, Erster Teil*, p. 280.

44. Payer's speech in the Reichstag on 6 April 1916, in Lutz, *Fall of the German Empire* 1:216–18.

45. Lutz, *Fall of the German Empire* 1:259. This was also the day on which the Reichstag created a Constitution Committee to consider constitutional reforms. Scheidemann was designated the chairman of the committee. Haussmann to Gothein, 7 April 1917, NL Gothein, no. 22, cited in Robson, "Left Liberalism in Germany," p. 205.

46. *Ursachen und Folgen* 1:320–21.

47. Ibid., pp. 318–20.

48. Report of the Progressive party *Parteitag*, June 9–10, 1917, in *Die Hilfe* 23, no. 23 (June 14, 1917): 397–98. See the letter of the Pomeranian Progressive party (Ranke) to the national headquarters of the Progressive party, 23 May 1917, NL Gothein, no. 20, p. 68. Carl Hermann Kreuser to Bruno Marwitz, NL Marwitz, no. 303–13. Marwitz was a prominent young National Liberal who joined the DDP in 1918 and defected in 1920.

49. Paul Rohrbach in *Deutsche Politik* 2, no. 27 (6 July 1917): 199.

50. Hanssen, *Diary*, 5 July 1917, p. 199. Gothein's question was asked in the main committee on 4 July 1917. Haussmann's *Schlaglichter*, pp. 95–140.

51. Haussmann to Under State Secretary Arnold von Wahnschaffe, 25 Oct. 1920, NL Haussmann, no. 117; Hanssen, *Diary*, p. 211; Gothein, *Warum verloren*

wir den Krieg? pp. 166–77; *Ursachen und Folgen* 2:3–7; Lutz, *Fall of the German Empire* 2:285–90; Epstein, *Erzberger*, p. 192.

52. For meetings of the Inter-Party Committee in late August and October 1917 see *Der Interfraktionelle Ausschuss, Erster Teil*, pp. 128–32, 133–34, 138–46, 217–18.

53. See the memo of Haussmann and quotations from his Reichstag speech of 10 Oct. 1917 in ibid., pp. 584–96. The Memo deals with the "Chancellor Crisis" of Sept. 1917.

54. The committee documents are in Erich Matthias and Rudolf Morsey, eds., *Die Regierung des Prinzen Max von Baden* (Düsseldorf, 1962). Hereafter cited as *Die Regierung des Prinzen Max von Baden.*

55. Klaus Epstein, "Wrong Man in a Maelstrom: The Government of Max of Baden," *The Review of Politics* 26, no. 2 (April 1964): 215–43. Epstein's article is a review of the document collection cited in fn. 54, but he also had some telling judgments to make about Max of Baden. Also see Prince Max of Baden, *Erinnerungen und Dokumente*, new ed. (Stuttgart, 1968).

56. Theodor Heuss, "Versailles," reprinted in Modris Eksteins, *Theodor Heuss und die Weimarer Republik. Ein Beitrag zur Geschichte des deutschen Liberalismus* (Stuttgart, 1969), pp. 133–36. Hereafter cited as Eksteins, *Theodor Heuss.* The most politically sophisticated Progressives immediately perceived in Wilson's note of 14 October a contrast with what they had earlier seen in Wilson. Haussmann to his daughter on 15 Oct. 1918, *Schlaglichter*, p. 253; *die Regierung des Prinzen Max von Baden*, pp. 210–11; Epstein, *Erzberger*, pp. 260–61.

57. See the observation of Hermann Luppe, 5 Oct. 1918, in *Die Regierung des Prinzen Max von Baden*, p. 75, also p. 377; Haussmann, *Schlaglichter*, pp. 261–62; Gotthart Schwarz, *Theodor Wolff und das 'Berliner Tageblatt.' Eine Liberale Stimme in der deutschen Politik 1906–1933* (Tübingen, 1968), pp. 75–76. Hereafter cited as Schwarz, *Theodor Wolff.*

58. Walther Rathenau, *Tagebuch 1907–1922*, ed. Hartmut Pogge von Strandmann (Düsseldorf, 1967), p. 226; *Ursachen und Folgen* 2:381–82; Moritz Julius Bonn, *Wandering Scholar* (New York, 1948), p. 193; Friedrich Meinecke, *Strassburg/Freiburg/Berlin 1901–1919. Erinnerungen* (Stuttgart, 1949), pp. 270–71; Meinecke to L. Aschoff, 21 Oct. 1918, *Werke* 6:95–98.

2. The German Democrats and the November Revolution

1. The literature on the German Revolution is now enormous, but many of the specialized studies ignore the middle-class parties. The following works have been particularly useful: Gerhard Schulz, *Revolutions and Peace Treaties, 1917–1920*, trans. from the German (London, 1972), pp. 105–23; F. L. Carsten, *Revolution in Central Europe. 1918–1919* (Berkeley, 1972); Charles B. Burdick and Ralph H. Lutz, *The Political Institutions of the German Revolution. 1918–1919* (Stanford, CA, 1966); Susanne Miller and Gerhard A. Ritter, eds., *Die deutsche Revolution 1918–1919. Dokumente* (Frankfurt a/ M, 1968); Susanne Miller, *Die Bürde der Macht. Die deutsche Sozialdemok-*

ratie 1918–1920 (Düsseldorf, 1978); A. J. Ryder, *The German Revolution of 1918* (Cambridge, 1967); Gerhard A. Ritter, "Die sozialistischen Parteien in Deutschland zwischen Kaiserreich und Republik," in Werner Pöls, ed., *Staat und Gesellschaft im politischen Wandel* (Stuttgart, 1979), pp. 100–54.

2. On the armistice see Harry Rudin, *Armistice. 1918* (New Haven, CT, 1944); Barrie Pitt, *1918. The Last Act* (New York, 1963).

3. Albertin, *Liberalismus und Demokratie*, p. 46 fn. 82; Hartmut Schustereit, *Linksliberalismus und Sozialdemokratie in der Weimarer Republik* (Düsseldorf, 1975), pp. 31–32; Ludwig Luckemeyer, *Die Deutsche Demokratische Partei von der Revolution bis zur Nationalversammlung 1918–1919*, published inaug. diss. (Giessen, 1975), p. 136.

4. Max Weber abandoned the monarchy in mid-October. Theodor Heuss, *Friedrich Naumann. Der Mann. Das Werk. Die Zeit*, 2nd ed. (Stuttgart, 1948), pp. 437–38. The FZ called for Wilhelm II's abdication as early as 25 Oct. Ernst Portner, *Die Verfassungspolitik der Liberalen 1919* (Bonn, 1973), p. 16. The cabinet and Inter-Party Committee discussions are presented in Matthias, ed., *Die Regierung des Prinzen Max von Baden*, pp. 487 and 502.

5. Hanssen, *Diary*, 5 Nov. 1918, p. 340.

6. Matthias, ed., *Die Regierung des Prinzen Max von Baden*, p. 595; Haussmann, *Schlaglichter*, p. 268; Hanssen, *Diary*, 9 Nov. 1918, pp. 347–49. Erich Koch, Diary, 9 Nov. 1918, in Koch (Koch-Weser) *Nachlass*, no. 15, p. 209. Hereafter it will be referred to as the NL KW.

7. NL Gothein, no. 12, p. 75; Robson, "Left Liberalism in Germany," p. 378.

8. Paul Rohrbach in *Die Hilfe* 24, no. 27 (21 Nov. 1918): 557–58.

9. Richard A. Comfort, *Revolutionary Hamburg* (Stanford, CA, 1966), pp. 39–57.

10. NL KW, no. 15; Fritz Hesse, *Von der Residenz zur Bauhausstadt*, (Bad Pyrmont, 1964), 1:96–101. This is the first volume of Hesse's memoirs. He was the mayor of Dessau. Also see the papers and unpublished autobiography of Wilhelm Külz, the mayor of Dresden. Külz's NL is in the BA Koblenz. Hereafter cited as NL Külz.

11. NL KW, no. 15. Diary, 12 Nov. 1918, p. 245.

12. Cited in Kurt Sontheimer, "The Weimar Republic—Failure and Prospects of German Democracy," in E. J. Feuchtwanger, ed., *Upheaval and Continuity. A Century of German History* (London 1973), pp. 103–4. Many Democrats found themselves in the position of the Bavarian liberal professor Siegmund Günther, who declared in a meeting of Bavarian Progressives: "When I was a democrat, Conservatism was trump; when democracy triumphed I found myself a conservative." Joachim Reimann, *Ernst Müller-Meiningen Senior und der Linksliberalismus in Seiner Zeit.* (Munich, 1968), pp. 217–18. For more information on the Bavarian left liberals, see Joachim Reimann, "Der politische Liberalismus in der Krise der Revolution," in Karl Bosl, ed., *Bayern im Umbruch. Die Revolution von 1918* (Munich, 1969), pp. 165–99. The desire to retain the monarchy, which was especially strong in Bavaria, often combined with the hatred of socialism to determine the attitude of older left liberals.

13. Conservative Democrats such as Gessler, Meinecke, or Dominicus display much nostalgia for the empire in their memoirs, but there were few attempts

to defend the kaiser or the political system, which had failed the test of war. Others, such as Schiffer, a converted Jew, or Gothein, a Christian "half-Jew" with radical "internationalist" views, show no nostalgia for the *Kaiserreich*. Many Democrats were excited and joyful about the new day dawning and greeted the changes with enthusiasm. For example, see the letter of the Kiel left-liberal organization, signed by Ferdinand Hoff, 24 Oct. 1918, cited in Luckemeyer, *Die Deutsche Demokratische Partei*, p. 135, or the position of the FZ toward the Revolution.

14. There is, of course, a vast literature on Max Weber, most of which concentrates on his intellectual importance. Few books have paid much attention to his political career, but see Wolfgang J. Mommsen, *Max Weber und die deutsche Politik 1890–1920* (Tübingen, 1959); Marianne Weber, *Max Weber: Ein Lebensbild* (Tübingen, 1926); Karl Loewenstein, *Max Webers Staatspolitische Auffassungen in der Sicht unserer Zeit* (Frankfurt a/M, 1965); Ilse Dronberger, *The Political Thought of Max Weber: In Quest of Statesmanship* (New York, 1971); Bruce B. Frye, "Max Weber: The German Professor in Politics," *The Rocky Mountain Social Science Journal* 8, no. 1 (April 1971): 1–10.

15. For example, in Eugen Schiffer, *Ein Leben für den Liberalismus* (Berlin, 1951), p. 214.

16. Mommsen, *Max Weber*, p. 300.

17. Schwarz, *Wolff*, p. 124.

18. Ibid.

19. See the remarks of Payer in the National Assembly, in Eduard Heilfron, ed., *Die deutsche Nationalversammlung im Jahre 1919/1920 in ihrer Arbeit für den Aufbau des neuen deutschen Volksstaates*, 7 vols. (Berlin, 1919–1920), 4:2289. Hereafter cited as Heilfron, *Die deutsche Nationalversammlung*.

20. Gothein, *Warum verloren wir den Krieg?* p. 236; Carl Petersen in the meeting of the *Parteiausschuss*, 28 Sept. 1919, cited in Stephan, *Linksliberalismus*, p. 135; Heuss at the DDP's second regular *Parteitag*, in Dec. 1920, cited in Jürgen C. Hess, *Theodor Heuss vor 1933: Ein Beitrag zur Geschichte des demokratischen Denkens in Deutschland* (Stuttgart, 1973), p. 59.

21. Undated clipping from the *New York Herald Tribune*, preserved in the Stresemann Papers. NL Stresemann, 3150/7380/H168406. Microfilmed records filmed by the United States Department of State.

22. Naumann raised funds to help Eduard Stadtler's League to Combat Bolshevism, while Rathenau organized a *Demokratische Volksbund* which lasted only two weeks. It seems to have complemented the Stinnes-Legien arrangements to secure industrial peace. Albertin, *Liberalismus und Demokratie*, p. 29; Heuss, *Naumann*, pp. 453–54; Harry Kessler, *Walther Rathenau*, trans. from the German, (New York, 1928), p. 248; Eduard Stadtler, *Lebenserinnerungen. Als Antibolschewist 1918/1919* (Düsseldorf, 1936), 3:13. On the *Volksbund*, see *Mitteilungen für die Mitglieder der Deutschen Demokratischen Partei*, available as a Society Publication at the Hoover Institution. The first third of the volume consists of materials published by the *Volksbund für Freiheit und Vaterland*.

23. NL Goetz, nos. 36, 61, 62. Goetz, *Historiker in meiner Zeit* (Cologne, 1958); pp. 55–56; NL Wildemuth, no. 61. Hermann Hummel, a major DDP leader

and also a returned officer with much combat experience, organized and led a military group in Baden. In Kassel, a *Bürgerwehr* was organized. NL KW, Diary, 7 Nov. 1918, p. 191; 16 Nov. 1918, p. 277.

24. Armin Behrendt, *Wilhelm Külz. Aus dem Leben eines Suchenden* (Berlin, 1968), pp. 56–60; NL KW, no. 15; Paul Müller, *Alexander Dominicus. Ein Lebensbild* (Berlin, 1957), pp. 82–85. The mayor of Esslingen on the Neckar to Payer, 16 Nov. 1918, NL Payer, no. 11, p. 175. The mayor urged Payer to work to "place a cap on the volcano or all hell will break loose."

25. See Wolfgang Elben, *Das Problem der Kontinuität in der Deutschen Revolution* (Düsseldorf, 1965); Arnold Brecht, *Lebenserinnerungen*, 2 vols. (Stuttgart, 1966–1967), 1:200ff.

26. Burdick and Lutz, *Political Institutions of the German Revolution*, p. 100.

27. Ernst Troeltsch, *Spektator Briefe* (Tübingen, 1924); Max Weber, *Gesammelte politische Schriften* (Munich, 1921); Hugo Preuss, *Staat, Recht und Freiheit* (Tübingen, 1926).

28. *BT* (14 Nov. 1918); Miller and Ritter, *Dokumente*, pp. 292–95; the DDP *Aufruf* which was published 16 Nov. also stressed this. *Ursachen und Folgen* 3:173–75.

29. *Kölnische Volkszeitung*, 14 Nov. 1918, clipping in the papers of Karl Bachem, Cologne *Stadtarchiv*. *Die Hilfe* 24, no. 47 (21 Nov. 1918): 563–64. The Hirsch-Duncker unions and the Catholic unions also emphasized this.

30. *Ursachen und Folgen* 3:39–43; Miller and Ritter, eds., *Dokumente*, p. 300.

31. NSDAP *Hauptarchiv*, 36/720. Microfilm edited by the Hoover Institution.

32. Max Wiessner to Anton Erkelenz, 10 Jan. 1919, NL Erkelenz, no. 13.

33. Reimann, *Müller-Meiningen*, p. 219; Theodor Boehm to Stresemann, 6 Nov. 1918, NL Stresemann, 3068/6889/H133660-61; Phillip Wieland to Stresemann, 13 Nov. 1918, ibid., 3069/6894/H134519; Kurt Riezler to Haussmann, 14 Nov. 1918, NL Haussmann, no. 116; Wolfgang Hartenstein, *Die Anfänge der Deutschen Volkspartei* (Düsseldorf, 1962), pp. 9–10.

34. Otto Hugo to Stresemann, 18 Nov. 1918, NL Stresemann, 3069/6896/H134545-48.

35. Stresemann to H. Binder, 16 Oct. 1918, ibid., 3077/6910/H135859-61; Stresemann to Frau Margarethe Dammann, 15 Nov. 1918, ibid., 3069/6896/H134533.

36. NL Richthofen, no. 15.

37. Payer to Fischbeck, 13 Nov. 1918, NL Payer, no. 11, p. 173.

38. NL Stresemann, 3131/7353/H166100.

39. Stresemann to Wieland, 15 Nov. 1918, NL Stresemann, 3069/6896/H134556.

40. Stresemann, *Deutsche Stimmen* 31, no. 5 (2 Feb. 1919): 71; Henry Ashby Turner, Jr., *Stresemann and the Politics of the Weimar Republic* (Princeton, 1963), pp. 14–15. Years afterwards, conservative Democrats were still bitter over "*die Herren Demokraten*," who had prevented liberal unification. Julius Kopsch to Hermann Dietrich, 11 Aug. 1930, NL Dietrich, no. 121.

41. The most reliable version of the first gathering is in an essay by Frankfurter, which is in the NL Haussmann, no. 100. Ten years afterwards, Frankfurter called most of the participants together for a celebration which the racist press noted. *Hammer* 38, no. 637 (March 1929): 135. For Wolff's account,

see Theodor Wolff, *Through Two Decades*, trans. from the German (London, 1936), pp. 141–42.

42. Vogelstein's sister, Julie Braun-Vogelstein, *Was niemals stirbt* (Stuttgart, 1966), pp. 51–55, has some personal information about him.

43. Alfred Weber was a sociologist at Heidelberg, as was his more famous brother Max. According to Max, Alfred was a socialist. Bruce B. Frye, "A Letter from Max Weber," *The Journal of Modern History* 39, no. 2 (June 1967): 119–25. For Alfred Weber's complaints about the generally conservative policies of the Max of Baden government see *BT*, no. 568, (6 Nov. 1918). Gerland was a judge who became a law professor at Jena. He, as well as Alfred Weber, was stationed in the army in Berlin at the end of the war.

44. Gothein to Haussmann, 13 Nov. 1918, NL Haussmann, no. 114.

45. *BT*, no. 587 (16 Nov. 1918); *Ursachen und Folgen* 3:173–74; Hartenstein, *Anfänge der Deutschen Volkspartei*, p. 57.

46. Heuss, *Naumann*, p. 453. Naumann described the founding of the DDP as a *Staatsstreich* directed by the BT. Also see Phillip Wieland to Haussmann, 21 Nov. 1918, NL Haussmann, no. 101; Klaus Simon, *Die württemberger-ischen Demokraten* (Stuttgart, 1969), pp. 204–8.

47. For examples of Stresemann's response to the news, see Stresemann to Admiral Dick, 15 Nov. 1918, 3068/6889/H133666; Stresemann to Theodor Boehm, 15 Nov. 1918, 3068/6889/H133622; Stresemann to Peter Stubmann, 15 Nov. 1918, 3068/6896/H134553; Stresemann to Paul von Schwabach, 17 Nov. 1918, 3069/6896/H134563-65.

48. Stresemann to Hugo, 18 Nov. 1918, 3069/6896/H144572-74.

49. Stresemann to Brües, 25 Nov. 1918, 3069/6896/H134605-09.

50. *BT*, no. 595 (21 Nov. 1918).

51. *Ursachen und Folgen* 3:183–84.

52. Stresemann, *Deutsche Stimmen* 31, no. 5 (1919): 71–72; also see Stresemann's obituary of Friedberg, ibid., 32, no. 26 (1920): 424–29.

53. Telegram from Haussmann to the Executive Committee, 26 Nov. 1918, NL Haussmann, no. 102. Haussmann also sought to try to persuade certain individuals whom he thought suitable to accept nominations to the Executive Committee. Haussmann to Max Warburg, 26 Nov. 1918, ibid., no. 117.

54. Fischbeck to Haussmann, 1 Dec. 1918, ibid., no. 114.

55. For an attempt by a moderate newspaper to try to emphasize the similarities, see the *Hamburger Fremdenblatt*, no. 331, 29 Nov. 1918.

56. *BT*, no. 615 (2 Dec. 1918); *Demokratische Partei Korrespondenz* (DPK), 2 Dec. 1918; *MNN*, no. 609 (2 Dec. 1918).

57. *BT*, no. 631 (10 Dec. 1918). In the executive committee only Weber's friend Gerland, defended him.

58. Gothein to Haussmann, 25 Nov. 1918, NL Haussmann, no. 114.

59. NL Gothein, no. 12, p. 325.

60. Heuss to Haussmann, 13 Dec. 1918, NL Haussmann, no. 114. For a similar judgment about the same time, see Walther Schotte, an important figure in the DDP *Zentrale* at this time, to Richard von Wettstein, 18 Dec. 1918, in NL Stolper, no. 4. Two of Weber's students conclude that he was too theoretical, too abstruse, and lacked clarity. Rosie Goldschmidt Graefenberg, *Prelude to the Past* (New York, 1934), p. 90; Hugo Marx, *Werdegang eines*

jüdischen Staatsanwalts und Richters in Baden 1892–1933 (Villingen, 1965), p. 62.

61. Otto Nuschke's sketch of the early party history in Anton Erkelenz, ed. *Zehn Jahre Deutsche Republik* (Berlin, 1928), p. 28. Eugen Leidig reconstructed the negotiations later on, and Stresemann relied on these for his history of the founding of the DVP. Leidig in NL Stresemann, 3069/6895/H134436-37. Stresemann's account was published as *Entstehung der Deutschen Volkspartei* (Berlin, 1920).

62. Stresemann's account of this is crossed out in a draft of his *Entstehung*, NL Stresemann, 3069/6895/H133459-60.

63. *DPK*, no. 3 (5 Dec. 1918); *FZ*, no. 336 (4 Dec. 1918).

64. Stresemann in *Deutsche Stimmen* 31, no. 5 (2 Feb. 1920): 72–73; Hartenstein, *Anfänge*, pp. 30–32.

65. See Stresemann's *Entstehung der Deutschen Volkspartei* and Nuschke's article in Erkelenz, ed., *Zehn Jahre*, pp. 24–41.

66. For example, Stresemann to Wolff, 3 Feb. 1920, NL Stresemann 3091/6935/H140091; Stresemann to Fischbeck, 4 July 1921, ibid., 3110/7013/H143864; Stresemann to Fischbeck, 2 May 1925, ibid., 3143/7313/H158916. After 1945, Alfred Weber and Richthofen attempted to establish objectively the circumstances which led to the exclusion of Stresemann. Weber wrote a long memorandum on the subject, which Felix Hirsch has included in his biography of Stresemann. Felix Hirsch, *Gustav Stresemann. Patriot und Europäer* (Frankfurt a/M, 1964), pp. 42–43. See Richthofen's memorandum of March 1947, NL Richthofen, no. 21. Richthofen maintains that he tried to persuade Stresemann in mid-December to enter the DDP on more favorable terms than he had been offered on 2 December, but Stresemann rejected the offer because he was too strong a monarchist and because the "Jewish press" had too much influence in the DDP.

67. Haussmann to Wieland, 23 Nov. 1918, NL Haussmann, no. 110.

68. See the discussion of Stresemann by General Wilhelm Groener and Koch, in NL KW, *Diary*, 12 Dec. 1918, no. 14, p. 191; Johannes Junck to Richthofen, 24 Dec. 1918, NL Richthofen, no. 17.

3. The Election of the National Assembly

1. Summaries of these meetings are available in the NSDAP *Hauptarchiv*, Roll 36. Fourteen of the notes of these meetings are reproduced in Lothar Albertin and Konstanze Wegner, eds., *Linksliberalismus in der Weimarer Republik: Die Führungsgremien der Deutschen Demokratischen Partei und der Deutschen Staatspartei 1918–1933* (Düsseldorf, 1980), pp. 3–10 and 12–22. Hereafter cited as Albertin, ed., *Führungsgremien*.

2. NSADP *Hauptarchiv*, 36/723. Albertin, ed., *Führungsgremien*, p. 11.

3. Stephan, *Linksliberalismus*, pp. 34–50.

4. See Naumann's article "Organisation," in *Das demokratische Deutschland* 1, no. 1 (14 Dec. 1918): 18–19.

5. Nipperdey, *Die Organisation der Parteien in Deutschland vor 1918* (Düsseldorf, 1961), p. 235.

6. Ibid.; Bertram, *Die Wahlen. . . .vom Jahre 1912*, p. 193.

7. While this was never publicized in the DDP, it may be ascertained from the private papers of several Democrats as well as the membership of the major financial committee, the *Kuratorium*. The Külz papers, in particular, illustrate this. The HB also had a disproportionate Jewish membership.

8. Richthofen to the Hannover DDP, 10 Dec. 1918, NL Richthofen, no. 17; Stephan, *Linksliberalismus*, p. 42; Luckemeyer, *Die Deutsche Demokratische Partei*, pp. 263–67.

9. Albertin, *Liberalismus*, pp. 167–95; Behrendt, *Külz*, p. 62; Hans Jaeger, *Unternehmer in der deutschen Politik 1890–1918* (Bonn, 1967), p. 125.

10. Bruckmann to Haussmann, 25 Dec. 1918, NL Haussmann, no. 104.

11. Bernhard Falk, "Aufzeichnungen," p. 109, BA Koblenz.

12. Among them were Maximilian Harden, the editor of *Zukunft*, who was attracted to the DDP in November 1918 but, by February 1919, saw it as a middle-class protective association. Also see Hugo Marx, *Werdegang eines jüdischen Staatsanwalts und Richters in Baden 1892–1933*, pp.128–29.

13. Elly Heuss-Knapp, *Bürgerin zweier Welten*, ed. Margarethe Vater (Tübingen, 1961), p. 171.

14. See the *Aufruf* of former NLP members supporting the DDP, *Ursachen und Folgen* 3:177. Also see the announced decision of former Young Liberals to support the DDP, DPK, 3 Jan. 1919, p. 1.

15. Stresemann to Biermann, 27 Dec. 1918, NL Stresemann 3068/6891/ H133867.

16. The ideology of the DDP is best seen in the election *Aufruf* of 15 Dec. 1918, *Ursachen und Folgen* 3:180. It combines election appeals, slogans, and fundamental political, economic, and social values.

17. The DDP took great pains to define its terms and to explain its values, sometimes with maddening didactic persistencey. For an example see Paul Hoffmann, *Soziale oder Sozialistische Republik* (Berlin, Dec. 1918); Otto Nuschke, "Die neue Demokratie," *Das demokratische Deutschland* 1, no. 1 (14 Dec. 1918). Democrats often defined what kind of Democrats they were by the stress they placed on terminology. The traditional left liberals persisted in the prominence of *liberal*. The Naumann followers regarded the term as irrelevant or anachronistic and stressed *democracy* and *social*. See the report of a speech by Carl Petersen on "national feeling as the leitmotif of the DDP." *Der Democrat* 1, no. 10 (28 Oct. 1920), p. 359.

18. GA, 28 Dec. 1918, NSDAP *Hauptarchiv*, 36/722. Albertin, ed., *Führungsgremien*, pp. 8–9.

19. See the *Flugblatt* issued by the local church in Greifswald, which attacked the DDP as an enemy of middle-class concerns and of the Christian faith. NSDAP, 37/731.

20. DDP *Flugblatt* published and distributed by the Bavarian DDP, in the Hoover Institution collection. In Bavaria, the DDP and the SPD worked more closely together because they had common enemies in the USPD and the BVP.

21. DDP *Flugblatt* published and distributed by the local DDP in Pomerania, Jan. 1919. NSDAP *Hauptarchiv*, 37/731.

22. See the report of a Petersen speech at a Berlin rally, in the *Hamburger Fremdenblatt*, no. 10, 6 Jan. 1919.

23. GA meetings, 23 Dec. and 28 Dec. 1918. NSDAP *Hauptarchiv*, 36/722. Albertin, ed., *Führungsgremien*, pp. 7–9; NL Erkelenz, no. 13.
24. Böhme made repeated attacks on the "Berlin press," the *Tageblatt* group and Berlin's "asphalt culture," all of which had anti-Semitic connotations in the Weimar period. An old associate with sterling democratic credentials, Ferdinand Friedensburg, who worked for Böhme and who was a close friend for many years, claims he was not an anti-Semite. Friedensburg, *Lebenserinnerungen* (Frankfurt a/M, 1969), p. 36.
25. Kopsch at first joined the DVP. During the campaign for the National Assembly he made some speeches which revealed him as a monarchist and an extreme nationalist. He was also apparently an anti-Semite, but he was nonetheless chosen by a Silesian district to represent it on the DDP ticket in 1920 and was elected.
26. Both were offered their old Reichstag district seats, but for personal reasons they chose districts which were closer to their homes and more compact. NL Gothein, no. 12, pp. 75 and 325; Luckemeyer, *Die Deutsche Demokratische Partei*, pp. 175, 269–71.
27. *Hauptvorstand* Meeting, 7 Jan. 1919, NSDAP *Hauptarchiv*, 36/723. Albertin, ed., *Führungsgremien*, pp. 11–22.
28. For a summary of the debate on list connections, see *Hauptvorstand*, 7 Jan. 1919, NSDAP *Hauptarchiv*, 36/723; GA, 30 Dec. 1918, ibid., 36/722. Albertin, ed., *Fuhrungsgremien*, pp. 9–22; Wilhelm Ziegler, *Die deutsche Nationalversammlung 1919/1920 und ihr Verfassungswerk* (Berlin, 1932), p. 68.
29. For a summary of Max Weber's political bid and his failure, see Bruce B. Frye, "Max Weber: The German Professor in Politics," *The Rocky Mountain Social Science Journal* 8, no. 1 (April 1971): 1–10; Marianne Weber, *Lebenserinnerungen* (Bremen, 1948), p. 85; Marie Baum, *Rückblick auf mein Leben* (Heidelberg, 1950), p. 219; René König and Johannes Winckelmann, eds., *Max Weber zum Gedächtnis* (Cologne, 1963), pp. 18, 71–73, 116–25.
30. Wolff to Gothein, 3 Jan. 1919, NL Gothein, no. 35, p. 55; GA, 4 Jan. 1919, NSDAP *Hauptarchiv*, 36/722. Albertin, ed., *Führungsgremien*, p. 10; Albertin, *Liberalismus*, pp. 281–87.
31. Hjalmar Schacht, *My First Seventy-Six Years*, trans. from the German (London, 1955), pp. 148–54; Luckemeyer, *Die Deutsche Demokratische Partei*, p. 262ff.
32. Peter Bruckmann to Haussmann, 24 Dec. 1918, NL Haussmann, no. 104.
33. Heuss to Haussmann, 13 Dec. 1918, NL Haussmann, no. 114; for Haussmann's reply, 15 Dec. 1918, ibid., no. 115.
34. The basic biographical data on the *Fraktion* may be found in the Reichstag *Handbücher*. There are good analyses of the *Fraktion* in Hartenstein, *Die Anfänge der Deutschen Volkspartei* and in Regina Getreuer Gottschalk, "Die Linksliberalen zwischen Kaiserreich und Weimarer Republik," unpubl. Ph.D. diss. (Tübingen, 1969).
35. In Württemberg, where the artisans were numerous and well organized, a secretary of an artisans' association, Karl Hermann, gained a seat in the National Assembly, much to the dismay of Heuss and other Naumannites. Payer and Haussmann, the grand old men of Württemberg democratic poli-

tics won the top two spots. Phillip Wieland, a prominent National Liberal, the third. The fourth slot went to Hermann. There was a total of seventeen names on the list, and most represented some kind of a constituency. Simon, *Die württembergischen Demokraten*, p. 215; the list of DDP candidates is in *Das demokratische Deutschland* 1, no. 5 (11 Jan. 1919): 114–18.

36. Richthofen to Wilckens, 18 Dec. 1918, NL Richthofen, no. 17. Haussmann was not only interested in finding places for worthy candidates—preferably outside Württemberg—but also sought to police the party's ban on extreme annexationists. He was one of the few DDP leaders who seemed to care about it, however. Haussmann to the *Zentrale*, 3 Dec. 1918, NL Gothein, no. 22, p. 85.

37. Lüders, *Fürchte dich nicht*, p. 76; Baumgarten, *Meine Lebensgeschichte*, pp. 35–37.

38. There is a graphic account of one of Külz's party helpers, who accompanied him on the campaign trail, in Behrendt, *Külz*, pp. 63–67.

39. Heuss-Knapp, *Bürgerin Zweier Welten*, p. 171; Velsen, *Im Alter die Fülle*, pp. 234–37.

40. Wolff, *Two Decades*, pp. 147–49.

41. Willy Hellpach, *Wirken in Wirren. Lebenserinnerungen*, 2 vols., (Heidelberg, 1948/1949), 2:112–13. Hereafter cited as Hellpach, *Lebenserinnerungen*. KW Diary, 3 Jan. and 8 Jan. 1919, NL KW, no. 14, p. 212; ibid., no. 15, p. 323; Hesse, *Erinnerungen* 1:107–10; NL Gothein, no. 12, p. 236.

42. Max Wiessner to Payer, 27 Dec. 1918, NL Payer, no. 11; KW Diary, 22 Jan. and 28 Jan. 1919, NL KW, no. 14, pp. 215 and 217.

43. The official publications of the party included a series called *Mitteilungen*, which was distributed primarily to party workers, *Das demokratische Deutschland*, a party journal, and *Deutsche Partei-Korrespondenz*. *Die Hilfe* was also, in effect, a party organ at this time. Richard Bahr's *Nationalliberale Beiträge* also supported the DDP in exchange for a subvention.

44. Ernst Portner, "Der Ansatz zur Demokratischen Massenpartei im deutschen Linksliberalismus," *Vierteljahrshefte für Zeitgeschichte (VZG)* 13, no. 2 (April 1965): 150–61.

45. Verses such as the following were also a popular device: "Die beste Liste, die Du lobst, heisst Gothein-Schmidthals-Heilberg-Obst."

46. Local organizations soon called for help against the DVP/DNVP attacks. For example, DDP Ortsgruppe Göttingen to Richthofen, 17 Jan. 1919, NL Richthofen, no. 18.

47. Otto Erbslöh to Erkelenz, 14 Dec. 1918, NL Erkelenz, no. 12; DPK, 3 Jan. 1919, p. 2; Baumarten, *Lebensgeschichte*, p. 368.

48. Martin Wenck, in *Das demokratische Deutschland* 1, no. 7 (25 Jan. 1919): 145, evaluates the victory. Erkelenz sought to assess the sources of the DDP's electorate in an article in *Die Hilfe*. He estimated that of the total vote of 5.6 million, about 2 million came from the *Angestellten* and *Arbeitern*, with 400,000 from the latter and 1.6 million from the former. One million votes came from the ranks of artisans, merchants, and middle-class people in industry. In addition, one million farmers and another million officials, lawyers, teachers, and other professionals gave the DDP their votes. *Die Hilfe* 25: 692, cited in Günther Fischenberg, "Der deutsche Liberalismus und die

Entstehung der Weimarer Republik," Ph.D. diss. (Münster, 1958), p. 176. Erkelenz's estimate was not based on any scientific polling techniques, of course, but it was probably a shrewd approximation.

4. The Configuration of DDP Politics

1. Hagen Schulze, ed., *Das Kabinett Scheidemann. Akten der Reichskanzlei* (Boppard, 1971), p. xxiv; *Hauptvorstand*, 4 Feb. 1919, NSDAP *Hauptarchiv*, 36/723. Albertin, ed., *Führungsgremien*, pp. 23–38; NL Carl Petersen, no. 18; Stephan, *Linksliberalismus*, pp. 49–50.
2. Koch, "*Aufzeichnungen* vom 13 Feb. 1919," ed. and introd. Günter Arns, in *VZG* 17, no. 1 (Jan. 1969): 96–115.
3. Rudolf Morsey, *Die Deutsche Zentrumspartei 1917–1923* (Düsseldorf, 1966), pp. 165–72.
4. Stephan, *Linksliberalismus*, pp. 47–48 and 51–53.
5. Ibid., pp. 183–84.
6. See Erkelenz's article in the DN, 11 Feb. 1919, in NL Erkelenz, no. 84, p. 46.
7. NL Petersen, no. 18.
8. Friedrich von Payer, *Autobiographische Aufzeichnungen und Dokumente*, ed. Günther Bradley. (Göppingen, 1974), pp. 228–30; Koch, "*Aufzeichnungen*, 13 Feb. 1919," *VZG*, 17, no. 1 (Jan. 1969): 109–10.
9. Naumann died at the age of 59 in the summer of 1919, while Haussmann was ill and often out of action but lived until 1922. Payer retired because of old age in 1920, although he lived until 1931. Max Weber and Troeltsch, two of the party's most prominent intellectuals, died in their early fifties in 1920, and Haas, who was 44 in 1919, died in 1930. Fischbeck, 53 in 1919, was often ill, while Gothein, 62 in 1919, frequently complained about his ill health and his advanced age. Erkelenz, only 41 in 1919, was a physical and mental wreck by 1930. Only Koch seemed to have the health and mental toughness to remain in the leadership ranks throughout the period. Dietrich's poor health greatly weakened his leadership potential in the DStP after 1930. No one can say, of course, what effects the loss and illness of so many of its leaders had on the fortunes of the DDP, but the feeling existed among many prominent members that the party had lost its "best and brightest" by 1924.
10. The delegation included Schücking, Carl Melchior, a Hamburg banker and active Democrat, as well as Walter Simons and Brockdorff-Rantzau, who were "close" to the DDP both ideologically and personally.
11. Erkelenz, DN, 12 May 1919, NL Erkelenz, no. 84, p. 92; ibid., 27 May 1919, p. 102; Naumann, "Was soll geschehen?" *Die Hilfe*, vol. 25, no. 21 (22 May 1919): 251–52.
12. Heilfron, ed., *Die deutsche Nationalversammlung* 4: 2666–73.
13. Ibid., pp. 2683–86.
14. Ibid., pp. 2707–13.
15. Hagen Schulze, ed., *Akten der Reichskanzlei. Das Kabinett Scheidemann.* 12 May 1919, pp. 314–15.
16. *Die Hilfe* 25, no. 20 (15 May 1919): 244–45.
17. NL Erkelenz, no. 84, p. 92.

18. NSDAP *Hauptarchiv*, 36/723. Albertin, ed., *Führungsgremien*, pp. 65–72.
19. *Bericht über die Verhandlungen des 1. Parteitages der Deutschen Demokratischen Partei abgehalten in Berlin vom 19. bis. 22. July 1919* (Berlin, n.d.), pp. 64–65. Hereafter cited as first party congress *Bericht*.
20. Payer, *Aufzeichnungen*, p. 230; Friedrich von Payer, *Von Bethmann Hollweg bis Ebert. Erinnerungen und Bilder*. (Frankfurt a/M, 1923), pp. 299–300. For Richthofen, it was clear that the days of costly heroics were over. Richthofen to Frau Bonza, 23 June 1919, NL Richthofen, no. 16. See Haussmann's notes on the *Fraktion* meeting of 22 June. NL Haussmann, no. 25. Richthofen and Naumann debated their differences at the first party congress. First party congress *Bericht*, pp. 59, 64–65, 73. Most of the Naumann group fought acceptance. For an evaluation of Württemberg opinion by one who supported Haussmann against signing and opposed Payer see Friedrich Mück to Heuss, 27 June 1919, NL Heuss, no. 269. Several *Fraktion* members had a difficult time making up their minds. Erkelenz, along with the labor group in the DDP, opposed leaving the government, but he also opposed the treaty. In the end, he voted with the majority against acceptance to maintain the authority and discipline of the *Fraktion*.
21. Baum, *Rückblick auf mein Leben*, p. 220.
22. There is a good selection of press clippings of the major DDP newspapers in the file kept by the U.S. State Department. See *Records of the Department of State relating to the internal affairs of Germany 1910–1929*, Microcopy 336, roll 141. Hereafter cited as U.S. State Department, *Germany 1910–1929*. Also see the British publication *Daily Review of the Foreign Press* for June 1919.
23. Hagen Schulze, ed., *Akten der Reichskanzlei. Das Kabinett Scheidemann*, pp. 417–420; Epstein, *Erzberger*, p. 318.
24. Alma Luckau, "Unconditional Acceptance of the Treaty of Versailles by the German Government/June 22–28, 1919," *JMH* 17, no. 3 (Sept. 1945): 216.
25. *Ursachen und Folgen* 3:379; KW Diary, 23 June 1919, no. 16, p. 181.
26. *Das demokratische Deutschland*, vol. 1, no. 28, (21 June 1919): 649–50.
27. Heilfron, ed., *Die deutsche Nationalversammlung* 4 (22 June 1919): 2731–37. See Haussmann's notes on the *Fraktion* Meeting of 22 June 1919, NL Haussmann, no. 25.
28. Albertin, *Liberalismus*, p. 344; Stephan, *Linksliberalismus*, p. 56. The critique of Fritz Elsas, an important communal official first in Stuttgart and then in Berlin, supports the idea that it was the DDP's fiscal and economic views which were the real issue. First party congress *Bericht*, p. 75. Petersen denied this. Ibid., p. 24.
29. Matthias Erzberger, *Erlebnisse im Weltkrieg* (Stuttgart, 1920), pp. 382–83; Heuss, *Naumann*, p. 494.
30. Wolff, *Two Decades*, pp. 279–80.
31. First party congress *Bericht*, pp. 59–60, 73–74. Haussmann and Payer also had a falling out. Haussmann to Johannes Hieber, 20 June 1919, NL Haussmann, no. 115; Haussmann to Naumann, 30 June 1919, NL Haussmann, no. 116.
32. Jürgen C. Hess, *"Das ganze Deutschland soll es sein." Demokratischer Na-*

tionalismus in der Weimarer Republic (Stuttgart, 1978), p. 111. Hereafter cited as Hess, *Das ganze Deutschland*.

33. Portner, *Die Verfassungspolitik der Liberalen 1919*; Erich Eyck, *A History of the Weimar Republic*, 2 vols. trans. from the German (Cambridge, MA, 1962–1963), 1:64–79; Hajo Holborn, *A History of Modern Germany*, 3 vols. (New York, 1969), 3:540–57.

34. For *Reich-Länder* relations throughout the Republic, see Gerhard Schulz, *Zwischen Demokratie und Diktatur* (Berlin, 1963).

35. NL Haussmann, no. 25; GA, 17 Jan. 1919, NSDAP *Hauptarchiv* 36/722. Albertin, ed., *Führungsgremien*, pp. 22–23; *Hauptvorstand*, 5 Feb. 1919, NSDAP *Hauptarchiv*, 36/723. Albertin, ed., *Führungsgremien*, pp. 25–38; Payer to von Hermann-Reutti, 28 Jan. 1919, NL Payer, no. 12, p. 211; Schulz, *Zwischen Demokratie und Diktatur*, pp. 116–23.

36. For DDP reactions to this threat to Prussia see Carl Kundel, *Liberal Correspondenz*, 30 Jan. 1919, in NL Schücking, no. 52, which indicates that an overwhelming number of Prussian Democrats rejected Preuss's proposal; Albertin, *Liberalismus*, pp. 281–87.

37. Portner's *Verfassungspolitik* finds most of the harsh evaluations of Preuss to be unjustified. For a contemporary defense see Cohnstaedt in the first party congress *Bericht*, pp. 53–54.

38. DN, 5 July 1919, NL Erkelenz, no. 84, p. 160.

39. Erich Koch-Weser, *Einheitsstaat und Selbstverwaltung* (Berlin, 1928). This topic was a major subject at the seventh regular party congress in Hamburg in April 1927. NSDAP 37/740. Also see the *Vorstand* meeting, 27 Nov. 1926, ibid., 38/760. Albertin, ed., *Führungsgremien*, pp. 402–3.

40. Richard W. Sterling, *Ethics in a World of Power. The Political Ideas of Friedrich Meinecke*. (Princeton, 1958) p. 178. *Ausgewählter Briefwechsel*, pp. 138–39. Max Weber's ideas have been analyzed in depth by Wolfgang J. Mommsen and others. Eduard Baumgarten, *Max Weber. Werk und Person* (Tübingen, 1964), pp. 549–51; Albertin, *Liberalismus*, p. 250ff.; Reinhard Opitz, *Der deutsche Sozialliberalismus 1917–1933* (Cologne, 1973), pp. 67–78.

41. This has been suggested by Wolfgang J. Mommsen. Also see Opitz, *Der Deutsche Sozialliberalismus*, p. 77.

42. *Das demokratische Deutschland* 1, no. 4 (4 Jan. 1919): 83–86; *Der Demokrat* 1, no. 29 (21 July 1921).

43. Heilfron, ed., *Die deutsche Nationalversammlung*, 7: 432–35; Hermann Hanschel, *Oberbürgermeister Hermann Luppe* (Nürnberg, 1977), p. 20; Reinold Issberner, *Demokratische ABC Buch* (Berlin, 1920), p. 149; Ernst Christian Helmreich, *Religious Education in German Schools* (Cambridge, MA, 1959), pp. 109–11 and 117; Jutta Stehling, *Weimarer Koalition und SPD in Baden* (Frankfurt a/M, 1976), pp. 27–30. The relevant articles in the Weimar Constitution were articles 146–49.

44. Günther Grünthal, *Reichsschulgesetz und Zentrumspartei* (Düsseldorf, 1968); Ellen L. Evans, "The Center Wages Kulturpolitik: Conflict in the Marx-Keudell Cabinet of 1927", *CEH* 2, no. 2 (June 1969): 139–58.

45. Johannes Hieber to Schiffer, 6 June 1919, NL Schiffer, no. 6. Hieber, like Schiffer a former member of the NLP, sought to instruct Shiffer on Württem-

berg traditions and the position of Payer and Haussmann on the flag question. As he explained it, the black-red-gold colors were inseparably associated with the history of democracy in Germany and this was a passionate cause for them.

46. Stanley Suval, *The Anschluss Question in the Weimar Era. A Study of Nationalism in Germany and Austria 1918–1932* (Baltimore, 1974), p. 25.

47. In 1934, Carl Petersen's widow, following a family discussion, wrote to Heuss to learn how the Naumann followers voted on the flag question. According to Heuss, they had all voted for the old flag, including Petersen. Heuss overlooked Erkelenz, an ardent if not slavish follower of Naumann and never a favorite of Heuss. Heuss to Frau Petersen, 30 Nov. 1934, NL Petersen.

48. Gerhard Vogt discusses the formation of the *Reichsbanner* organization in *Der Demokrat* 5, no. 32–33 (9 Oct. 1924): 269–70; Karl Rohe, *Das Reichsbanner Schwarz-Rot-Gold* (Düsseldorf, 1966). The only prominent Democrats who remained active in the *Reichsbanner* were Haas and Erkelenz.

5. Left, Right, and Center in the DDP

1. See Rennie W. Brantz, "Anton Erkelenz, the Hirsch-Duncker Trade Unions, and the German Democratic Party," unpublished Ph.D. diss. (Ohio State Univ., 1973).

2. Gustav Schneider led the GDA. Its membership varied from about 300,000 to 385,000 from 1920 to 1930. Schneider was a Reichstag deputy after 1924 and a vigorous defender of the rights of employees. See his *Briefe aus dem Reichstag* (Berlin, 1927), which give a good picture of his activities. Dieter Fricke, ed., *Die bürgerlichen Parteien in Deutschland*, 2 vols., (Leipzig, 1968–1970), 2:177–82.

3. The *Gewerksschaftsring* was founded in 1920 and had 700,000 members at one time. It was committed to the Weimar Constitution, social reform, and a democratization of the economy. Erkelenz delivered the keynote address at its founding and retained an active interest in its activities. Ernst Lemmer became its director and was also general secretary of the Hirsch-Duncker unions after 1924.

4. The *Reichsbund demokratischer Jugend* published a journal, *Echo der Jungen Demokratie*, and several regional organizations also published journals. They are the most important source for its activities. Hans Otto Rommel wrote a dissertation on the organization and from this has published an article, "Die Weimarer Jungdemokraten," *Liberal* 13 (Bonn, 1971): 215–24. There are scattered materials in the NSDAP *Hauptarchiv* records and in the papers of DDP leaders. Fairly recently, the papers of two prominent Young Democrats, Eberhard Wildemuth and Hans Albert Kluthe, have been deposited in the Koblenz BA, but they contain little of importance about the Young Democrats. There is also some information in Erich Lüth, *Viele Steine lagen am Weg* (Hamburg, 1966). Lemmer is almost silent on the Young Democrats in his memoirs, although he was the organization's leader in the late twenties.

The Young Democrats met with the DDP at the first PT and a protocol of their meeting is attached to the *Bericht*, pp. 348–63.

5. The committee's records are scattered throughout the DDP materials in the NSDAP *Hauptarchiv*. In addition, a number of the major female members of the DDP who were active in the committee wrote memoirs and/or have left papers. The most helpful secondary works are Richard J. Evans, *The Feminist Movement in Germany. 1894–1933* (London, 1976) and Werner Huber, "Gertrud Bäumer. Eine politische Biographie," inaug. diss. (Munich, 1970), which has an extensive bibliography of Bäumer's publications.

6. There is now a rather extensive literature on the left-liberal press. The best general reference is Kurt Koszyk, *Deutsche Presse 1914–1945*, 3 vols. (Berlin, 1972). For specific works on the DDP press, see Modris Eksteins, *The Limits of Reason: The German Democratic Press and the Collapse of Weimar Democracy* (London, 1975); Becker, "Demokratie des sozialen Rechts," and autobiographical accounts of Wolff, Feder, Bernhard, and others. Schwarz, *Wolff*, is a valuable work. Also see Werner Schneider, *Die Deutsche Demokratische Partei, 1924–1930* (Munich, 1978), pp. 237–44.

7. On Bäumer, see her *Lebensweg durch eine Zeitenwende* (Tübingen, 1933); *Grundlagen demokratischer Politik* (Karlsruhe, 1928). For an analysis of this work, see Robert A. Pois, *The Bourgeois Democrats of Weimar Germany* (Philadelphia, 1976), pp. 62–64. There are some interesting personal comments about Bäumer in Velsen, *Im Alter die Fülle*, pp. 266–70 and *passim*; also see Huber's "Gertrud Bäumer."

8. On Erkelenz, see Brantz, "Anton Erkelenz, the Hirsch-Duncker Trade Unions"; A. A. Chanady's "Anton Erkelenz and Erich Koch-Weser. A Portrait of Two German Democrats," *Historical Studies: Australia and New Zealand* 12 (1965–1967): 491–505, was published before the NL Erkelenz was available. Erkelenz's papers are second in importance only to Koch-Weser's as a source for the history of the DDP.

9. *Bericht über die Verhandlungen des 3. ordentlichen Parteitages der Deutschen Demokratischen Partei* in Bremen, 12–14 Nov. 1921, ed. Reich Business Office. Hereafter cited as third regular PT (Bremen) *Bericht*; Brantz, "Anton Erkelenz, the Hirsch-Duncker Trade Unions," p. 153; Stephan, *Linksliberalismus*, pp. 220–21.

10. Erich Lüth, *Bürgermeister Carl Petersen* (Hamburg, 1971); I am indebted to Eduard Rosenbaum for a long and candid letter about Petersen's qualities and personality. Eduard Rosenbaum to the author, 14 Oct. 1967. Rosenbaum at the time he knew Petersen was an employee of the Hamburg Chamber of Commerce and often saw Petersen in action. Judge Edgar Petersen discussed his uncle with me in 1964 and brought him to life for me. Stephan, *Linksliberalismus*, pp. 142, 224–25.

11. His flabby leadership of the DDP was frequently criticized privately by Koch and Heinrich Gerland. For example, Gerland to (?Georg) Bernhard, 10 Nov. 1921, NL Gerland, no. 6. Also see the PA meeting, 11 Nov. 1921, NSDAP *Hauptarchiv*; 38/745. Albertin, ed., *Führungsgremien*, pp. 216–28.

12. The mountain of material on and by Heuss can only be suggested here. His papers are an important supplement to his autobiographical works. For the Weimar period, his *Erinnerungen. 1905–1933* (Tübingen, 1963) is the ap-

propriate work, but it is disappointing. The earlier volume, *Vorspiele des Lebens. Jugenderinnerungen*, 2nd ed. (Tübingen, 1954), on the other hand, is a fascinating work. It chronicles Naumann's influence in his early years.

13. For an extended discussion of the "community of August," in which Bäumer's views are often cited, see Erich J. Leed, *No Man's Land. Combat and Identity in World War I* (Cambridge, England, 1979), pp. 39–72.

14. Erkelenz to Gustav Stockinger, 20 Jan. 1927, NL Erkelenz, no. 42, p. 66.

15. Goetz, *Historiker in meiner Zeit*, p. 66.

16. Statement of the Hamburg Young Democrats (Lüth), 8 Nov. 1928, In NL Dietrich, no. 228. The Rhineland Young Democrats, by the spring of 1930, opposed continued membership in the Brüning government. BT, no. 199, 28 April 1930.

17. Mück to Heuss, 5 April 1929. NL Heuss, no. 269; PA meeting, 21 Oct. 1928, NSDAP *Hauptarchiv*, 37/731. Albertin, ed., *Führungsgremien*, pp. 473–78.

18. Heuss to Koch-Weser, 18 Dec. 1924, NL Heuss, no. 58.

19. NL Lüders, nos. 99 and 100; KW Diary, 22 March 1924, NL KW, no. 30, p. 1; Lilo Linke, *Restless Days: A German Girl's Autobiography* (New York, 1935), p. 301.

20. Linke, *Restless Days*, has several observations which bear this out; also see Katherine Thomas, *Women in Nazi Germany* (London, 1943), pp. 20–21.

21. Heuss to Hugo Wendorff, 24 May 1928, NL Heuss, no. 103; Friedrich Mück to Heuss, 25 Jan. 1925, NL Heuss, no. 269; Bäumer to Koch-Weser, 8 Feb. 1927, NL KW, no. 36, p. 67.

22. Feiler's contributions to the FZ are identified in Becker's "Demokratie des sozialen Rechts." Also see Alexander Böker, "Arthur Feiler and German Liberalism," *Social Research* 10 (1943): 455–79. Feiler Papers.

23. NL Dietrich, no. 294; Larry Eugene Jones, "Inflation, Revaluation, and the Crisis of Middle-Class Politics: A Study in the Dissolution of the German Party System, 1923–1928," *CEH* 12, no. 2 (June 1979): 143–68; David B. Southern, "The Impact of the Inflation: Inflation, the Courts and Revaluation," in Richard Bessel and Edgar J. Feuchtwanger, eds., *Social Change and Political Development in Weimar Germany* (London, 1981), pp. 56–76.

24. In addition to Friedenburg's valuable NL and his memoirs previously cited see his autobiographical work for the post–1945 period: *Lebenserinnerungen; Es ging um Deutschland* (Berlin, 1971). Also see the collection of articles, some from the Weimar period, *Politik und Wirtschaft. Aufsätze und Vorträge* (Berlin, 1961).

25. See his NL, his autobiography, *Mein Leben* (Nürnberg, 1977), and an excellent biography by the editor of his memoirs, Hermann Hanschel, *Oberbürgermeister Hermann Luppe*.

26. There is a notable example in Milton Mayer's *They Thought They Were Free* (Chicago, 1955).

27. NSDAP *Hauptarchiv*, 37/740.

28. Harry Kessler, *In the Twenties. The Diaries of Harry Kessler*, trans. from the German (New York, 1971).

29. This was particularly true of Gerland. Goetz, on the other hand, whose scholarly achievements were far greater than Gerland's, emerges as a gentleman

and scholar and a decent human being. At Heidelberg, Alfred Weber stood in marked contrast to the arrogant Hellpach.

30. On the HB see Siegfried Mielke, *Der Hansa-Bund für Gewerbe, Handel und Industrie 1909–1914* (Göttingen, 1976). Erkelenz early saw the HB as the chief adversary of the DDP's left wing. *Die Hilfe* 25, no. 5 (29 Jan. 1920); Max Schmidt to Erkelenz, 18 Feb. 1920, NL Erkelenz, no. 14, pp. 44–45. The HB often published statements of its position on issues affecting the economy. For example, see FZ, no. 893, 29 Nov. 1924; *BBZ*, no. 147 (27 March 1928); FZ, no. 438, (15 June 1930); "Wahlaufruf des Hansa-Bundes," *Hamburger Fremdenblatt*, no. 212, 2 Aug. 1930. Three of the leaders in 1930—three of six—were prominent Democrats who went over to the DStP: August Weber, Fischer, Mosich. Whatever liberal or political impulses the HB might have had had been largely overcome, by 1928, by material concerns.

31. Fischer was a reserve officer and an active "old boy" in his fraternity. Fischer to Friedensburg, 22 Aug. 1928, NL Friedensburg, no. 6. His conservative social values were compatible with his economic views, but his political views were sometimes relatively radical in the *Fraktion*. Fischer was often used by the DDP *Fraktion* as a speaker. Late in 1927, for example, it chose him to criticize the Köhler finance plan, which included long overdue raises for public officials. *BT*, 2 Nov. 1927, in Lüders, NL, no. 225.

32. The Liberal Association (*Liberale Vereinigung*) was formed in 1924 by dissident Democrats to produce a united liberal party. The DVP, however, proved largely uninterested, and it had a shaky existence until 1928. Fricke, ed., *Die bürgerlichen Parteien in Deutschland* 2:322–24.

33. Dietrich, a widower when he married the widow of Troeltsch, inherited a considerable fortune from his first wife, which he increased by shrewd management. His papers are extensive and well organized and reveal much about his personal affairs. There is a good if rather uncritical biography of him based on his papers. Adelheid von Saldern, *Hermann Dietrich. Ein Staatsmann der Weimarer Republik* (Boppard, 1966). His friends were the arch-conservatives of the party, figures such as Gothein, Falk, Hellpach, and Fischer.

34. This is evident in most budget debates. For example, see the speech of Fischer, *Reichstag Verhandlungen* 387 (30 July 1925): 3733–41; Dietrich in ibid., (31 July 1925): 3762; Wieland, ibid., 395 (8 March 1928): 1328ff. One of the most persistent efforts was to reduce the business turnover tax. Oswald Riedel, ed., *ABC Buch* (Brandenburg, 1927), pp. 208–9.

35. See his statement before the DIHT steering committee, reacting against the emergency decree of 5 June 1931. David Abraham, *The Collapse of the Weimar Republic: Political Economy and Crisis* (Princeton, 1981), p. 267.

36. Stephan, *Linksliberalismus*, p. 223. In Bavaria, Müller-Meiningen and Fritz Gerlich, the editor of the MNN, continued the Richter tradition. Gerlich made a notable appearance at the PT in December 1919. First special PT *Bericht*, pp. 52–54. For a characteristic *Denkschrift* by Mosich dated mid-Nov. 1920 see NL Schücking, no. 50. Among other things, it prized the central importance of the individual, praised and defended capitalism on "ra-

tional principles," attacked socialism, and called for the end of wartime controls and regulations.

37. See, in particular, the books and articles of Heinrich August Winkler, especially his *Mittelstand. Demokratie und Nationalsozialismus* (Cologne, 1972), and "From Social Protectionism to National Socialism. The German Small Business Movement in Comparative Perspective," *JMH* 48, no. 1 (March 1976): 1–18. Also, see Hermann Lobovics, *Social Conservatism and the Middle Classes in Germany. 1914–1933* (Princeton, 1969). The DDP *Mittelstand* spokesmen were not voluble, but occasionally their words were reported. FZ, no. 484, 12 Nov. 1924, reports a speech of Wilhelm Kniest. Also see the report of the DDP's *Mittelstandtag*, NSDAP *Hauptarchiv*, 38/759. For a defense of the DDP's *Mittelstand* record, see *Der Demokrat*, no. 19 (1 Nov. 1926), in ibid., 38/760; also other *Mittelstand* materials in NSDAP *Hauptarchiv*, 38/761.

38. Larry Eugene Jones, "The Dissolution of the Bourgeois Party System in the Weimar Republic," in Bessel and Feuchtwanger, eds., *Social Change*, pp. 268–88.

39. Büll to Stolper, 23 Aug. 1930, NL Stolper, no. 44.

40. On the WP, see Martin Schumacher, *Mittelstandsfront und Republik. Die Wirtschaftspartei-Reichspartei des deutschen Mittelstandes 1919–1933* (Düsseldorf, 1972); Martin Schumacher, ed., *Erinnerungen und Dokumente von Johann Victor Bredt 1914–1933* (Düsseldorf, 1970); "Zehn Jahre Wirtschaftspartei," *Deutsche Mittelstands-Zeitung* 7, no. 6 (3 Feb. 1929).

41. BT, no. 206, 4 May 1920.

42. For some examples of DDP reactions to the threat of the WP, see Fischbeck's comments in the *Vorstand*, 26 Feb, 1921, NSDAP *Hauptarchiv*, 36/737. Albertin, ed., *Führungsgremien*, pp. 163–65; also see Hugo Wolf to Gothein, 9 May 1924, NL Gothein, no. 18, p. 90. See Erkelenz's warning at the *Vorstand* meeting, 6 Nov. 1926, NSDAP *Hauptarchiv*, 37/730. Albertin, ed., *Führungsgremien*, pp. 400–2 has an inadequate, abbreviated account of this meeting. For the WP's attempts to smear the DDP as a party of big business and bankers, see the WP's *Wahl-Katechismus für die Kommunal-Wahlen Herbst 1925* (Berlin, 1925), in which it alleged that banking and stock market capital dominates the "so-called Democratic Party." The DDP, it contended, "marches shoulder to shoulder with Big Industry and Trade."

43. This question and related organization problems were aired at a meeting devoted to organizational questions at Bad Eilsen in September 1927. *Vorstand* meeting, 3 Dec. 1927, in Albertin, ed., *Führungsgremien*, pp. 431–32. This was part of a plan to revamp the organization in time for the 1928 election. Stephan, *Linksliberalismus*, pp. 366–69. Frankfurter to Erkelenz, 27 Aug. 1927, NL Erkelenz, no. 44, pp. 155–57 reveals Frankfurter's fears of the "rightist yearnings" and apathy in the German middle classes.

44. *Vorstand* meeting, 29 Oct. 1928, NSDAP *Hauptarchiv*, 37/730. Albertin, ed., *Führungsgremien*, pp. 470–71. After the *Mittelstand* had abandoned the DDP, there were several perceptive retrospective analyses of the future of the party without *Mittelstand* supporters. See, for example, the article of Bonn in the *BT*, no. 208 (4 May 1930). Erkelenz to Carl von Voss, 7 May 1930, NL Erkelenz, no. 58, pp. 33–36.

45. For studies of agriculture in Germany and the relationship of agriculture to politics, see Alexander Gerschrenkron, *Bread and Democracy in Germany* (Berkeley, 1943); John Bradshaw Holt, *German Agricultural Policy. 1918–1934* (Chapel Hill, NC, 1936); Rudolf Heberle, *Landbevölkerung und Nationalsozialismus* (Stuttgart, 1963); Klaus Schapp, *Die Endphase der Weimarer Republik im Freistaat Oldenburg, 1918–1933* (Düsseldorf, 1978); Dieter Hertz-Eichenrode, *Politik und Landwirtschaft in Ostpreussen 1919–1930* (Cologne, 1969); Dieter Gessner, *Agrarverbände in der Weimarer Republik* (Düsseldorf, 1976); "The Dilemma of German Agriculture during the Weimar Republic," trans. from the German, in Bessel and Feuchtwanger, eds., *Social Change*, pp. 143–54.

46. The DDP's insensitivity to the feelings of the *Mittelstand* was equaled by its indifference to the prejudices of farmers. In 1925, for example, the *Fraktion* leadership chose Dernburg, a wealthy Berlin banker with well-known Jewish ancestors, to lead its opposition to protective tariffs desired by most farmers. Reichstag *Verhandlungen* 388 (26 Nov. 1925): 4592.

47. I have puzzled more over Koch-Weser's character than any leader of the party, and I have vacillated about my interpretation over the years. Was he a man of principle or an opportunist? Part of the difficulty stems from reading his diary and correspondence. He could be arrogant, petty, and mean. His "party friends" found him difficult to like; he lacked warmth and compassion. On the other hand, the DDP was an impossible party to lead and most of his party enemies were less admirable than he was. He devoted himself to the party and German democracy, and he never received credit relative to the abuse he received. He consistently received overwhelming votes of approval from the party congresses and the major committees; of the party leaders, only Erkelenz attempted to challenge Koch-Weser's leadership, and he failed miserably. Nonetheless, when the *Staatspartei* lost heavily in September 1930, enemies emerged who heaped the blame for the disaster on Koch-Weser and forced his retirement from politics.

48. See the remarks of Goldschmidt, PA meeting, 28 April 1929, NSDAP *Hauptarchiv*, 39/770. Albertin, ed., *Führungsgremien*, pp. 495–507; Erkelenz to Feiler, 25 Feb. 1929, NL Erkelenz, no. 51, pp. 188–89.

49. Mosich to Stolper, 21 March 1929, NL Stolper, no. 44.

50. PT Mannheim, 5 Oct. 1929, NSDAP *Hauptarchiv*, 37/731. It was later published as a 44-page pamphlet entitled *Die wirtschaftliche-soziale Weltanschauung der Demokratie* (Berlin, 1929). Also see Toni Stolper, *Ein Leben in Brennpunkten unserer Zeit. Wien, Berlin, New York, Gustav Stolper 1888–1947* (Tübingen, 1964), pp. 233–37.

51. Bernhard to KW, 11 Oct. 1929, NL Stolper, no. 44.

52. Stolper to M. J. Bonn, 21 Oct. 1929, NL Stolper, no. 44.

53. Erkelenz, ed., *Zehn Jahre Deutsche Republik*; the first *ABC Buch* was published in 1920 and the second in 1927. The first was edited by Reinold Issberner and the second by Oswald Riedel.

54. Portner, *Verfassungspolitik der Liberalen 1919*, pp. 180–89.

55. *Bericht*, pp. 77–90. He retreated somewhat toward the end of his speech, indicating that there was no way one could tell how well the mines might have done under private ownership.

56. For example, *Ortsgruppe* Breslau to Gothein, 7 March 1919, NL Gothein, no. 18, p. 79.

57. Portner, *Verfassungspolitik der Liberalen 1919*, p. 189; Schustereit, *Linksliberalismus und Sozialdemokratie*, pp. 53–59. The threatening revolutionary atmosphere in Berlin at this time, which certainly influenced the DDP's majority to make concessions, is portrayed in a letter from Gerland to his sister, Cornelie, 12 March 1919, NL Gerland, no. 45.

58. *Hauptvorstand* meeting, 12–13 April 1919, NSDAP *Hauptarchiv* 36/723. Albertin, ed., *Führungsgremien*, pp. 47–62.

59. *Vorstand* meeting, 10 Nov. 1921, and PA meeting, 11 Nov. 1921, in Albertin, ed., *Führungsgremien*, pp. 213–28; Schustereit, *Linksliberalismus und Sozialdemokratie*, pp. 53 and 56–61; Morsey, *Zentrumspartei*, pp. 221–26.

60. Epstein, *Erzberger*, pp. 328–48; Eyck, *A History of the Weimar Republic* 1:123–33.

61. First special *Parteitag* in Leipzig, Dec. 1919, *Bericht*, p. 108.

62. Heilfron, ed., *Die Deutsche Nationalversammlung* 5, (9 July 1919): 3403–31 and 7 (12–13 Aug. 1919): 609–10.

63. First special *Parteitag* in Leipzig, Dec. 1919, *Bericht*, p. 108.

64. The most notable defenders were Erkelenz and Haas. They even defended the capital levy. *Die Hilfe* 35, no. 1 (1 Jan. 1920); ibid., No. 5 (29 Jan. 1920): 66–67.

65. Abraham Schuchman, *Co-determination: Labor's Middle Way in Germany* (Washington, D. C., 1957); Eyck, *A History of the Weimar Republic* 1:133–34; Portner, *Die Verfassungspolitik der Liberalen 1919*, pp. 190–93.

66. See Naumann's supportive speech in the National Assembly. Heilfron, ed., *Die Deutsche Nationalversammlung* 7 (31 July 1919): 444.

67. See the article by Gothein and Petersen in the BT, no. 496, 20 Oct. 1919, no. 514, 30 Oct. 1919; for the HB's reaction, see its statement of 26 July 1919. NL Richthofen, no. 16. Dresden Bank to Payer, 9 Sept. 1919, NL Payer, no. 12, p. 565. The industrialists in the party placed great pressure on the organization at this time to oppose the Factory Councils Law. In Württemberg, the DDP's industrialists were divided, with Peter Bruckman favoring it. Mück to Heuss, 31 Oct. 1919, NL Heuss, no. 269. The general policy of the DDP was explained by Friedrich Weinhausen in *Die Hilfe* 15, no. 49 (4 Dec. 1919): 690–92.

68. The text of the law is in *Ursachen und Folgen* 3: 375–78. Erkelenz explained its mechanics in a trade union publication, *Wegweiser für das werktätige Volk* 2, no. 7 (Feb. 1920), in NL Erkelenz, no. 85, p. 22.

69. See Dietrich's article on this theme in BT, no. 457, 28 Sept. 1931.

70. She wrote several letters, including one to Erkelenz, to ask her friends about whatever second thoughts they might have had on economic policy during the Depression. Erkelenz indicated he favored deficit financing and mildly inflationary policies. Erkelenz to Bäumer, 3 Feb. 1934, NL Heuss, no. 77.

71. Robert A. Gates, "German Socialism and the Crisis of 1929–1933," *CEH* 7, no. 4 (Dec. 1974): 332–59. For a discussion of the impact of the economic crisis on the Center party, see Evans, *The German Center Party 1870–1933* (Carbondale, IL, 1981), pp. 335–74.

6. The DDP and the "National Questions"

1. *Akten der Reichskanzlei. Weimarer Republik. Das Kabinett Wirth*, ed. by Ingrid Schulze-Bidlingmaier, 2 vols. (Boppard, 1973), 1: xix–xxi; KW Diary, 9 May 1921, NL KW, no. 28; *Vorstand* meeting, 9 May 1921, NSDAP *Hauptarchiv*, 36/727. Albertin, ed., *Führungsgremien*, pp. 181–82; *Das demokratische Deutschland* 2, nos. 13 and 19–20 (3 April 1921 and 15 May 1921); Ernst Laubach, *Die Politik der Kabinette Wirth 1921/1922 (Lübeck, 1968), pp. 9–19.*

2. *Laubach, Die Politik der Kabinette Wirth*, is especially valuable for showing the relationship between tax policy and the problems of the Wirth governments; Lothar Albertin, "Die Verantwortung der Liberalen Parteien für das Scheitern der Grossen Koalition im Herbst 1921," *Historische Zeitschrift (HZ)* 205, no. 3 (Dec. 1967): 566–627.

3. The debate within the DDP on the tactics of fulfillment was reduced to a two-man confrontation in the correspondence between Gerland and R. K. Frankfurter. Gerland opposed fulfillment and Frankfurter defended it. For example, Gerland to Frankfurter, 13 May 1921 and Frankfurter's reply, 21 May 1921, in NL Gerland, no. 31. For a rather typical justification of fulfillment, see Erkelenz to Karl Dinger, 6 Sept. 1921, NL Erkelenz, no. 17, p. 22.

4. For an example of Rathenau's arguments, see his long speech in defense of the need for realism in a gathering of party leaders, 13 Oct. 1921, NSDAP *Hauptarchiv*, 38/745. Albertin, ed., *Führungsgremien*, pp. 196–212; FZ, no. 847, 13 Nov. 1921.

5. *Der Demokrat* 2, no. 11 (7 April 1921): 261–62; Friedrich Weinhausen, *Demokraten und Oberschlesische Krisis* (Berlin, 1921); NL Erkelenz, no. 15, p. 5; NL Jaenicke, no. 5.

6. Rathenau to Koch-Weser, 31 Oct. 1921, NL Koch-Weser, no. 74, p. 37; PA meeting, 11 Nov. 1921, NSDAP *Hauptarchiv*, 38/745. Albertin, ed., *Führungsgremien*, pp. 216–26; Haussmann to Rathenau, 29 Dec. 1921, NL Haussmann, no. 116; *Das demokratische Deutschland* 3, no. 45 (11 Nov. 1921): 989–96.

7. Becker, "Demokratie des sozialen Rechts," pp. 127–43.

8. Hess, *Das ganze Deutschland*, pp. 142–43; also see Alfred Weber's Memorandum, 11 Jan. 1930, in NL Stolper, no. 44.

9. *Das demokratische Deutschland* 1, no. 45 (19 Oct. 1919).

10. Haussmann to Walter Simons, 15 Oct. 1920, NL Haussmann, no. 117.

11. Karl Dietrich Erdmann, "Deutschland, Rapallo und der Westen," *VZG* 11, no. 2 (April 1963): 105–65; Hermann Graml, "Die Rapallo-Politik im Urteil der westdeutschen Forschung," *VZG* 18, no. 4 (Oct. 1970), 366–91; Laubach, *Die Politik der Kabinette Wirth*, pp. 190–223; Eyck, *History of the Weimar Republic* 1:203–12. Hartmann Pogge von Strandmann, "Rapallo—Strategy in Preventive Diplomacy, New Sources and New Interpretations," in Volker R. Berghahn and Martin Kitchen, eds., *Germany in the Age of Total War* (London and Totowa, New Jersey, 1981), pp. 123–46.

12. Koch-Weser to Rathenau, 6 May 1922, NL KW, no. 74, p. 41.

13. PA meeting, 28 May 1922, NSDAP *Hauptarchiv*, 38/748. Albertin, ed., *Führungsgremien*, pp. 240–56.

14. *Reichstag Verhandlungen* 355 (30 May 1922): 7729–30.
15. *Vorstand*, 11 July 1922, NSDAP *Hauptarchiv*, 38/756. Albertin, ed., *Führungsgremien*, pp. 259–67; Gerland to Frankfurter, 4 Aug. 1922, NL Gerland, no. 7.
16. Hess, *Das ganze Deutschland*, p. 171.
17. See KW's speech at the sixth regular Party Congress in Breslau, December 1925, NSDAP *Hauptarchiv*, 37/739; Heile later saw this phrase as a symbol of the shallowness of Stresemann's conversion to internationalism, NL Heile, no. 18.
18. For example, Sally Marks, *The Illusion of Peace*, pp. 74–107.
19. *Akten der Reichskanzlei. Weimarer Republik, Das Kabinette Cuno*, ed. by Karl-Heinz Harbeck (Boppard, 1968); Hermann J. Rupieper, *The Cuno Government and Reparations 1922–1923* (The Hague, 1979); Alfred E. Cornebise, *The Weimar Republic in Crisis* (Washington, D.C., 1977).
20. *Vorstand*, 27 Jan. 1923, NSDAP *Hauptarchiv*, 36/729. Albertin, ed., *Führungsgremien*, pp. 285–88.
21. See the article of Wieland in *Das demokratische Deutschland* 5, no. 7 (17 Feb. 1923): 156–60. Some of the private communications of Democrats were less defiant and more pessimistic. Heuss's friend Friedrich Mück predicted that in six weeks Germany would be without food or coal and the French would have the Rhine-Ruhr state which they had always wanted. Mück to Heuss, 18 Jan. 1923, NL Heuss, no. 269.
22. This story along with a host of interesting clippings on the Ruhr Invasion is in U.S. State Department, Decimal File, 336/Roll 18.
23. PA meeting, 8 March 1923, NSDAP *Hauptarchiv*, 38/749. Albertin, ed., *Führungsgremien*, p. 289.
24. NL Richthofen, no. 19 (April 1923); Erkelenz in *Die Hilfe* 31, no. 7 (1 April 1923); Anton Erkelenz, *Junge Demokratie. Reden und Schriften* (Berlin, 1925), pp. 111–17.
25. *Vorstand*, 22 Sept. 1923, NSDAP *Hauptarchiv*, 36/729. Albertin, ed., *Führungsgremien*, p. 299. To illustrate the mad scale of the inflation: Erkelenz received a check for 35 billion M as an honorarium for ten book markers at 35 million M apiece. 29 Sept. 1923, NL Erkelenz, no. 28, p. 98; in mid-October, Theodor Wolff sent Gothein an honorarium of 25 billion M, which was then worth about a half dollar. Gothein regarded this as too little, and Wolff raised the amount to 225 billion. Wolff to Gothein, 15 Oct. 1923, NL Gothein, no. 35.
26. Among the most notable defectors at this time were Schiffer, Gerland, Keinath, Böhme, and Dominicus. Gerland's departure is well documented. See his letter to his sister, Betty, 24 Oct. 1924, NL Gerland, no. 45. Also see NL KW, no. 87, pp. 63 and 75. The party leadership tried to make light of the defections. *Der Demokrat* 5, nos. 34/35 (23 Oct. 1924): 284–85; Heuss to Koch-Weser, 29 Oct. 1924, NL Heuss, no. 58; Schiffer to Gerland, 31 Oct. 1940, NL Gerland, no. 21; Friedensburg-Böhme correspondence, NL Friedensburg, no. 17.
27. Manfred J. Enssle, *Stresemann's Territorial Revisionism. Germany, Belgium, and the Eupen Malmédy Question 1919–1929* (Weisbaden, 1980), pp. 51–79; Robert P. Grathwol, *Stresemann and the DNVP. Reconciliation and Re-*

venge in German Foreign Policy 1924–1928. (Lawrence, KS, 1980), pp. 42–57.

28. PA meeting, 16 Aug. 1924, NSDAP *Hauptarchiv*, 38/749. Albertin, ed., *Führungsgremien*, p. 328.

29. During the course of the debate, Erkelenz, Bernstorff, Schiffer, and two DDP cabinet officers, Hamm and Oeser, spoke. *Reichstag Verhandlungen* 381 (25 Aug. 1924): 847–55; ibid., (26 Aug. 1924): 903–5; ibid., (28 Aug. 1924): 1045–49.

30. Second special party congress, Berlin. 2 Nov. 1924, NSDAP *Hauptarchiv*, 37/738; Dernburg's article in the FZ, no. 911, 6 Dec. 1924.

31. Jon Jacobson, *Locarno Diplomacy* (Princeton, 1972), deals with the period from Locarno through the Young Plan in 1929.

32. *Reichstag Verhandlungen* 388 (24 Nov. 1925): 4524–30. Heuss always stressed that Locarno was a "security pact." Newspaper articles in 1925, NL Heuss, no. 38.

33. Sixth regular party congress in Breslau, Dec. 1925, NSDAP *Hauptarchiv*, 37/739, pp. 1–210. Oswald Riedel, a significant leader of the Prussian DDP, summed up the feeling of many Democrats when he hailed the new opportunities which now existed to "free the East." "The German East is for us a bridge to the *grossdeutsche Einheitsstaat*." Ibid., p. 210. For a summary article on the DDP and Locarno see *Der Demokrat* 7, no. 2 (21 Jan. 1926): 27–28.

34. Also see NL Brönner-Höpfner.

35. Suval, *The Anschluss Question in the Weimar Era*, pp. 24–29; Hess, *Das ganze Deutschland*, pp. 203 and 206–7.

36. Among DDP politicians and publicists apparently only Wolff opposed it. Heuss continued to press for *Anschluss* throughout 1931. *Jenauer Volksblatt* (25 March 1931), NL Heuss, no. 44.

37. First regular PT *Bericht*, p. 64.

38. Erich Koch-Weser, *Germany in the Post–War World*, trans. from the German (Philadelphia, 1930), p. 207.

39. See, for example, Wilhelm Scheffen's article, "Der Deutsche im Ausland," in Erkelenz, ed., *Zehn Jahre*, pp. 526–33. Scheffen even spoke wistfully of the "lost Germans" in America, but it was more common to concentrate on the "enslavement" and "oppression"—the terms were almost obligatory—of the ethnic Germans in eastern Europe. The most active Democrats in *Auslandsdeutsche* organizations were Dietrich, Brönner-Höpfner, Külz, Petersen, Heuss, Rohrbach, and Korell.

40. Hess, *Das ganze Deutschland*, pp. 232–33; Heuss, *Erinnerungen. 1905–1933*, pp. 336–39.

41. F. Gregory Campbell, *Confrontation in Central Europe. Weimar Germany and Czechoslovakia* (Chicago, 1975), pp. 212–13.

42. Huber, "Gertrud Bäumer," pp. 286–87.

43. See Enssle's *Stresemann's Territorial Revisionism*, which concentrates on this theme.

44. Even the cool, sophisticated DDP urban newspapers were carried away by this occasion, and the DDP press contained dozens of stories from all over

Germany, but particularly in the Rhineland, of the "liberation." There are some clippings in NL Lüders, no. 323, as well as in the NL Korell.

45. Cited in Schneider, *Die Deutsche Demokratische Partei*, p. 134; von Salder, *Dietrich*, pp. 84–86.

46. There is a small collection of Korell's papers and newspaper clippings on his career at Darmstadt (Hesse-Darmstadt *Staatsarchiv*).

47. NL Külz, no. 30, for materials on the colonial question.

48. These examples are drawn from the clipping collection of the U.S. State Department, Decimal File, No. 336, and from the article of Mary E. Townsend, "The Contemporary Colonial Movement in Germany," *Political Science Quarterly*, 43 (1928): 64–75.

49. Bernstorff, as early as 1919, saw that the League could be used as a revisionist instrument. First regular party congress *Bericht*, pp. 43–44. Heuss, in 1926, could only justify Germany's entrance into the League on revisionist grounds. *Reichstag Verhandlungen* 388 (27 Jan. 1926): 5178–79. There is some material in the NL Heile, no. 34, on the *Deutsche Liga für Völkerbund* (German League for the League of Nations), one of the several international organizations for which Heile managed a subsidy from the government. See Wilhelm Heile, *Nationalstaat und Völkerbund* (Halberstadt, 1926). He continued to try to reconcile German national goals with international organizations. Following 1945, Heile chided Heuss that, while he had been a true internationalist, Stresemann and Heuss had been wedded to traditionalist and narrow nationalistic views. Heile to Heuss, 4 Sept. 1951, NL Heile, no. 129.

50. NL Gothein, no. 12, p. 186. The literature on the German pacifist movement is largely on the pre–1918 movement. Chickering, *Imperial Germany and a World Without War*; Karl Holl, ed., *Der deutsche Pazifismus während des Weltkrieges 1914–1918. Ludwig Quidde* (Boppard, 1979). Also see the NL Schücking.

51. Schoenaich wrote several volumes of memoirs: *Zehn Jahre Kampf für Frieden und Recht* (Hamburg, 1929); *Mein Damaskus. Erlebnisse und Bekenntnisse*, 2nd ed. (Hamburg, 1929); *Mein Finale* (Flensburg and Hamburg, 1947); Lüth, *Viele Steine lagen am Weg*.

52. Hellmut von Gerlach, *Von Rechts nach Links*, ed. Emil Ludwig (Zurich, 1937); Karl Holl and Adolf Wild, eds., *Ein Demokrat kommentiert Weimar* (Bremen, 1973). This volume consists of Gerlach's reports to the Carnegie Foundation, 1922–1930.

53. Berthold von Deimling, *Aus der Alten in die neue Zeit. Lebenserinnerungen* (Berlin, 1930).

54. Else Ulich-Beil, *Ich ging meinen Weg* (Berlin, 1961).

55. Both the Gessler NL and the Heuss NL contain many letters of Heuss to Gessler. Much of Heuss's enmity toward the FZ, the BT, and the VZ seemingly stemmed from their attacks on Gessler and the *Reichswehr*. Heuss's party enemies were, for the most part, Gessler's enemies. See, for example, Heuss to Koch-Weser, 29 Oct. 1924, NL Heuss, no. 58, in which he attacks the antimilitary group in the party, including Preuss, Tantzen, Feder, Bernhard, and Cohnstaedt. Heuss to Eberhard Wildemuth, 27 Jan. 1925, NL Heuss, no. 61, in which he assails the FZ (Cohnstaedt) for its attacks on Gessler. See the exchange of correspondence between Heuss and Gessler in

NL Heuss, no. 79. In his letter to Gessler on 29 Oct. 1924, Heuss urges Gessler to remain a member of the DDP *Fraktion*. He makes light of the flying of the "old flag" by a *Kasino* party of *Reichswehr* officers and dismisses the importance of the "so-called black *Reichswehr*." Heuss to A. Hopf, 30 Jan. 1924, NL Heuss, no. 57, in which he indicates that he supports Gessler for party leader because of his nationalist and statist reputation. According to Heuss, the DDP could only succeed by being "national."

56. The relevant material is in NL KW, no. 96. The *Hilfe* article immediately produced a letter of protest from Gessler. Gessler to KW, 29 Aug. 1927 and KW's reply, 6 Sept. 1927; KW to Erkelenz, 6 Sept. 1927; Erkelenz to KW, 8 Sept. 1927. Haas and several provincial DDP newspapers also jumped in on the attack on Erkelenz. In his letter to KW, Erkelenz showed the extent of the DDP's "cover-up" of the black *Reichswehr* and Gessler's duplicity.

57. Cohnstaedt to KW, 12 Dec. 1927, NL Erkelenz, no. 46, p. 193. The commendation was published in *Der Demokrat* 8, no. 24 (22 Dec. 1927): 568.

58. Lüth helped convey the impression that the Young Democratic organization was pacifistic. See NL KW, no. 100, p. 25 (24 August 1929); *FZ*, no. 380 (23 May 1930); Lüth, *Viele Steine*, p. 61. He was doubly offensive as a pacifist and an economic radical. *BBZ*, no. 243 (23 May 1930).

59. For a general survey of the DDP's defense policies, see Hartmut Schustereit, "Unpolitisch-Überparteilich-Staatstreu, Wehrfragen aus der Sicht der Deutschen Demokratischen Partei: 1919–1933," *Militärgeschichtliche Mitteilungen* 16:131–72 (With Documents). Many Democrats wrote on the theme of the "new army" or the "republican army," but the party seldom went beyond words to try to secure a true republican army. Their timid efforts paralleled their equally ineffectual attempt to democratize the civil bureaucracy. For examples of the DDP's rhetoric about a republican army, see Haas in *Reichstag Verhandlungen* 391 (10 Nov. 1926): 8018ff; Richthofen, ibid. 393 (28 March 1927): 10058–67.

60. Wieland to Payer, 19 March 1921, NL Payer, no. 15, protesting the FZ's attitude toward the *Reichswehr*; Emile Deines to Dietrich, 17 April 1922, NL Dietrich, no. 67, p. 227; Heuss to Koch-Weser, 24 June 1926, NL Koch-Weser, no. 34, p. 265.

61. KW to Erkelenz, 12 Sept. 1927, NL KW, no. 96, p. 109; KW Diary, 4 Feb. 1928, NL KW, no. 37, p. 35. Koch-Weser's second wife was the daughter of his regimental commander, a Prussian general, and he was proud of his reserve commission. He found it difficult to criticize the *Reichswehr* and Gessler and was also close to several naval officers.

62. *CVZ* 4 (17 April 1925): 285.

63. *Reichstag Verhandlungen* 395 (14 March 1928): 13400ff.

64. Haas to KW, 4 Nov. 1924, NL KW, no. 87, p. 77ff; KW to Haas, 7 Nov. 1924, ibid., p. 87. Telegram, Stephan to Erkelenz, 7 Nov. 1924, NL Erkelenz, no. 22, p. 230. Richard Bahr, a veteran liberal publicist and DDP member, tried to end his political career in Baden. Bahr to Dietrich, 15 Nov. 1924, NL Dietrich, no. 68, cited in Koszyk, *Deutsche Presse 1914–1945*, p. 260. Bahr felt that the Jews already had too much influence in the DDP. For the plight of the Jewish deputy who repeatedly had to endure racist attackers see Haas's article, *CVZ* 3, no. 23 (1 June 1924): 340–41. Haas's activities in

the *Republikanische Union*, where he worked closely with Joseph Wirth and Paul Löbe, a Social Democrat, received little publicity in the DDP. Herbert Gottwald and Günter Wirth, "Republikanische Union," in Fricke, ed., *Die bürgerlichen Parteien in Deutschland* 2: 636–40.

65. For Gessler see his NL, his autobiography, *Reichswehrpolitik in der Weimarer Zeit* (Stuttgart, 1958), as well as the standard works on the *Reichswehr*, where he is generally depicted as a dupe.

66. Albertin, *Liberalismus*, p. 383.

67. In time, Gessler's defense became less convincing to Erkelenz, Tantzen, and the left-wing journalists, and they became immune to his charms. Nonetheless, a large majority of Democrats had confidence in Gessler to the end of his tenure. For examples of his defense and DDP relations to Gessler, see PA, 23 Sept. 1923, NSDAP *Hauptarchiv*, 38/757. Albertin, ed., *Führungsgremien*, pp. 403–19; Tantzen to Erkelenz, 30 Jan. 1925, NL Erkelenz, no. 90, p. 179; Erkelenz to W. Dürr, 8 Aug. 1927; Ibid., no. 44, p. 96.

68. Heuss and Goetz are good examples of close friends of Gessler, whose national feelings sometimes overcame their democratic and liberal values. Heuss sought to explain his position in 1924: "I am no jackass (*Esel*) who derives joy from war or war leaders, and I am free of nationalist hatred. I felt isolated before 1914 because of this. I have done everything, however, to win support for my country and to advance its interests." Heuss to W. Hartmann, 6 Nov. 1924, NL Heuss, no. 56. Heuss's brother, Ludwig, felt that Theodor had become more reactionary because of his friendship with Gessler. Mück to Heuss, 27 July 1927, NL Heuss, no. 269. The attacks on Gessler by the "Jewish press" of the DDP sometimes produced anti-Semitic outbursts from the friends of Heuss.

69. Cohnstaedt to Payer, 21 Nov. 1925, NL Payer, no. 15; KW Diary, 16 Nov. 1925, NL KW, no. 32, p. 153; KW blamed Luppe for the controversy and called it the "Luppe affair." The FZ, on the other hand, condemned Gessler and defended Luppe. Haas sought to soothe Gessler's ruffled feelings: "If you only knew how often we do battle for you." Haas to Gessler, 22 Nov. 1925, NL Gessler, no. 18. For a party debate on the controversy see PA, 4 Dec. 1925, NSDAP *Hauptarchiv*, 37/758. There is a greatly abbreviated coverage of this meeting in Albertin, ed., *Führungsgremien*, pp. 356–57.

70. PA, 24 Jan. 1926, NSDAP Hauptarchiv, 38/759. Albertin, ed., *Führungsgremien*, pp. 362–76.

71. FZ, no. 746 (7 Oct. 1926); no. 747 (7 Oct. 1926); PA, 28 Nov. 1926, NSDAP *Hauptarchiv*, 37/760. Albertin, ed., *Führungremien*, pp. 403–19; Haas in the *Reichstag Verhandlungen* 391 (10 Nov. 1926): 477–79, in which he mixed criticism of the monarchical character of the *Reichswehr* with condemnation of SPD criticism of it.

72. KW Diary, 30 March 1924, NL KW, no. 30, p. 3.

73. KW Diary, 3 Dec. 1926, NL KW, no. 34, p. 379ff; Erkelenz in the BT, no. 598 (19 Dec. 1926). There was anger in some quarters of the DDP that it had been the urban newspapers and Young Democrats which were most responsible for Gessler's problems. "If Gessler is ousted thanks to the work of *Berliner Judenjungen* then we will have mass defections." Ludwig Heuss to Theodor Heuss, 24 Jan. 1927, document no. 5 in Schustereit, "Unpolitisch-

Überparteilich-Staatstreu," pp. 155–56. Mück to Heuss, 27 July 1927, NL Heuss, no. 269. Keith W. Bird, *Weimar, the German Naval Officer Corps and the Rise of National Socialism* (Amsterdam, 1977), pp. 162–63. KW Diary, 4 Feb. 1928, NL KW, no. 37, p. 35; F. L. Carsten, *Reichswehr and Politics, 1918–1933* (Oxford, 1966), pp. 284–90.

74. *The Times* (London, 9–10 Aug. 1927); Gessler to KW, 29 Aug. 1927, NL KW, no. 96, p. 1; KW to Gessler, 6 Sept. 1927, ibid., p. 4; KW to Erkelenz, 6 Sept. 1927, ibid.; Haas to KW, 10 Sept. 1927, ibid., pp. 122–23. KW to Erkelenz, 22 Sept. 1927, NL Erkelenz, no. 45, p. 65. Haas and KW were most anxious to protect the DDP's reliability on the "national questions," although they also doubted the authenticity of the documents.

75. Wolfgang Wacker, *Der Bau des Panzerschiffs 'A' und der Reichstag* (Tübingen, 1959); Andreas Dorpalen, *Hindenburg and the Weimar Republic* (Princeton, 1964), pp. 149–51. The DDP summarized its opposition in *Der Demokrat* 9, no. 5 (8 March 1928); Haas spoke for the *Fraktion* in the *Reichstag. Verhandlungen* 395 (14 March 1928): 13400–43. It would be better, he contended, for Germany to disarm, not rearm. "We should not abandon the search for agreement and conciliation." The DDP's *Fraktion* divided. Dietrich, for example, voted *for* the *Panzerschiff* which he boasted about in the May 1928 campaign. Eyck, *History of the Weimar Republic* 2:192. Mück, Heuss's political confidant, thought the *Fraktion*'s position incorrect and unclear. He suspected any situation in which the FZ ended up supporting the *Fraktion* majority. When this happens, he contended, "something is rotten in Denmark." Mück to Heuss, 28 March 1928, NL Heuss, no. 269.

76. *Der Demokrat* 9, nos. 17/18 (20 Sept. 1928): 414–15.

77. PA, 20 Oct. 1928, NSDAP *Hauptarchiv*, 39/768. Albertin, ed., *Führungsgremien*, pp. 471–72.

78. *Reichstag Verhandlungen* 423 (16 Nov. 1928): 358ff; Ernst Lemmer, *Manches war doch anders. Erinnerungen eines deutschen Demokraten* (Frankfurt a/M, 1968), p. 141ff; Eyck, *History of the Weimar Republic* 2:163–64.

79. Erkelenz to Bäumer, 29 Nov. 1928, NL Erkelenz, no. 50, p. 242; Erkelenz to Bäumer, 30 Nov. 1928, ibid., p. 246; Bäumer to Erkelenz, 4 Dec. 1928, ibid., p. 269.

80. NL Külz, no. 129 (Feb.–Apr. 1929); Behrendt, *Külz*, p. 93; *Vorstand*, 12 Feb. 1929, NSDAP *Hauptarchiv*, 37/732. Albertin, ed., *Führungsgremien*, pp. 479–85; *Vorstand*, 23 March 1929, ibid.; *Der Demokrat* 10, no. 7 (5 April 1929): 193ff; Erkelenz to Bäumer, 24 Feb. 1929, NL Erkelenz, no. 51, pp. 173–74; Erkelenz to Bäumer, 25 Feb. 1929, ibid., p. 192; Robert Kauffmann to Lüders, 22 Feb. 1929, NL Lüders, no. 109. Kauffmann, a member of the *Vorstand* and a Berlin attorney and city official, opposed the defense program, contending that Külz, and perhaps Meyer, were the only supporters of the military in the party.

81. *Gesamtvorstand*, 14–15 March 1931, NSDAP *Hauptarchiv*, 39/776. Albertin, ed., *Führungsgremien*, pp. 636–37.

82. Bäumer was the most indiscreet after 1933. She could be carried away on flights of romantic nationalism, but she was also something of a bellwether in the DDP/DStP. Elly Knapp-Heuss also cheered the success of the German

armies in the first years of World War II, and most former Democrats repeatedly demonstrated their patriotism in various forms of service.

83. For example, Erich Koch-Weser, *Und dennoch Aufwärts! Eine deutsche Nachkriegsbilanz* (Berlin, 1933), pp. 217–22; Hermann Dietrich, *Auf dem Wege zum neuen Staat. Die Deutsche Aufgabe* (Stuttgart, 1951), p. 18; Meinecke to W. Lenel, 7 May 1933, Meinecke, *Ausgewählter Briefwechsel*, pp. 138–39.

7. Divisive Domestic Issues during the Years of Party Crisis, 1925–1929

1. Hugo Stehkämper, ed., *Der Nachlass des Reichskanzlers Wilhelm Marx*, 4 vols. (Cologne, 1968), 1:374–77; PA meeting, 1 March 1925, NSDAP *Hauptarchiv* 38/758. Albertin, ed., *Führungsgremien*, pp. 336–40; Eyck, *A History of the Weimar Republic* 1:324–40.

2. Stresemann to Gessler, 11 March 1925 (corrected draft), NL Stresemann, 3166/7311/H158433-34; KW Diary, 7 March 1925, NL KW, no. 32, p. 53; Heuss, "German Grotesque," *Stuttgarter Neues Tageblatt* (16 March 1925), NL Heuss, no. 38; Turner, *Stresemann*, pp. 192–93.

3. NL Marx, vol. 5.

4. Karl Holl, "Konfessionalität, Konfessionalismus und demokratische Republik—Zu einigen Aspekten der Reichspräsidentenwahl von 1925," *VZG* 17, no. 3 (July 1967): 254–75; PA, 5 April 1925, NSDAP *Hauptarchiv* 38/749. Albertin, ed., *Führungsgremien*, pp. 342–49; Baumgarten, *Meine Lebensgeschichte*, pp. 464–65; Heuss, "Hindenburg oder Marx?" *Stuttgarter Neues Tageblatt* (25 April 1925), NL Heuss, no. 38.

5. *Der Demokrat* 6, no. 9 (7 May 1925): 225–27.

6. Hellpach, *Lebenserinnerungen* 2:258–64; NL Heuss, no. 38; Heuss, *Erinnerungen*, p. 327; Erkelenz to Hellpach, 10 Jan. 1929, NL Erkelenz, no. 47, pp. 85–102, in which he recapitulates the 1925 campaign and Hellpach's later transgressions, particularly his persistent criticism of German democracy.

7. *Akten der Reichskanzlei. Das Kabinette Luther I and II (Jan. 1925–Oct. 1925)*, ed. Karl-Heinz Minuth (Boppard, 1977), 2:1334, 1345, 1349–50, 1358, 1363, 1367. See KW's Diary, 1–6 May 1926 and a long KW memorandum on the crisis, NL KW, no. 34, pp. 173–215; *Vorstand*, 10 May 1926, NSDAP *Hauptarchiv* 38/759. Albertin, ed., *Führungsgremien*, pp. 387–95; DDP *Reichsgeschäftsstelle*, 21 May 1926, NSDAP *Hauptarchiv* 38/759; Stehkämper, ed., *Der Nachlass des Reichskanzlers Wilhelm Marx* 1:415–16 (from Marx's autobiography).

8. *Verhandlungen des Reichstages* 390 (12 May 1926): 7191–96; Bergsträsser in *Deutsche Einheit* 8, no. 20 (15 May 1926); *Der Demokrat* 7, no. 11 (3 June 1926): 231–34; KW Diary, 18 Dec. 1925, NL KW, no. 32, Cited in Minuth, *Luther* 1:1009.

9. Mück to Heuss, 15 May 1926, NL Heuss, no. 269; Heuss, "Misstrauensvotum oder Stimmenthaltung," distributed by the *Demokratischer Zeitungsdienst*, 29 Jan. 1925, in NL Heuss, no. 38.

10. NL Marx, no. 5; *Der Demokrat* 7, no. 11 (3 June 1926): 234.

11. See the confidential briefing on the controversy by the DDP *Geschäftsstelle*, 6 Feb. 1926, NL Erkelenz, no. 112; NSDAP *Hauptarchiv* 38/759; KW Diary, 5–6 March 1926, NL KW, no. 34, pp. 41–45; PA meeting, 10 March 1926, NSDAP *Hauptarchiv*, 37/731. Albertin, ed., *Führungsgremien*, pp. 376–87. In the debate in the Reichstag, Richthofen spoke for the *Fraktion*. Reichstag *Verhandlungen* 390 (28 April 1926): 691ff. *Reichsgeschäftsstelle*, 12 March 1926, 17 April 1926, 21 May 1926, 16 June 1926; NSDAP *Hauptarchiv* 38/759; Lüders, "Zur Fürstenabfindung," *Der Beobachter* (Stuttgart, 20 Feb. 1926), NL Lüders, no. 269; Ulrich Schüren, *Der Volksentscheid zur Fürstenenteigung 1926* (Düsseldorf, 1978).

12. Bahr to Meinecke, 23 May 1926, NL Meinecke, no. 2; NL Gothein, no. 18, p. 95; *Vorstand* meetings, 10 May and 20 May 1926, NSDAP *Hauptarchiv* 38/749. Albertin, ed., *Führungsgremien*, pp. 387–99; Schüren, *Der Volksentscheid*, p. 223.

13. KW Diary, 12 June 1926, NL KW, no. 34, p. 240.

14. For Schacht's letter to Koch-Weser and the DDP's explanation for his resignation see *Der Demokrat* 7, no. 12 (17 June 1926): 25. KW Diary, 24 June 1926, NL KW, no. 34, p. 265. Peter Stubmann, "Partei und Staat," *Deutsche Einheit* 8, no. 32 (7 Aug. 1926): 745ff.

15. DVP *Wahlhandbuch* (Berlin, 1928).

16. NL Marx, 3:375ff; Ernst Feder, *Heute sprach ich mit . . . Tagebücher eines Berliner Publizisten 1926–1932*, ed. C. Lowenthal-Hensel and Arnold Paucker, 29 June 1928 (Stuttgart, 1971), p. 195. Hereafter cited as Feder, *Diary*; Eksteins, *Heuss*, pp. 76–77; PA meeting, 28 Nov. 1926, NSDAP *Hauptarchiv* 38/760. Albertin, ed., *Führungsgremien*, pp. 403–18; FZ, no. 848, 13 Nov. 1926; Heuss, "Von 'Schund und Schmutz,'" *Weserzeitung* (16 June 1926), in NL Heuss, no. 38; Heuss, *Erinnerungen*, p. 342; Bäumer, *Lebensweg*, pp. 416–17.

17. *Der Demokrat* 7, no. 23 (28 Nov. 1926); FZ, no. 903 (4 Dec. 1926). Twelve Democrats voted for the law, fifteen against, four abstained. The law passed with a majority of 250 to 158.

18. KW Diary, 4 Dec. 1926, NL KW, no. 34, p. 361; KW to Wolff, 8 Dec. 1926, ibid., p. 363; KW to Wolff, 14 Dec. 1926, ibid., p. 375; Wolff to KW, 10 Dec. 1926, ibid., p. 373. There are four letters of Wolff which were written in 1926 in the NL Wolff. Feder, *Diary*, 7 Dec. 1926, p. 90; *Der Demokrat* 7, no. 23 (9 Dec. 1926): 393–95; ibid., no. 24 (23 Dec. 1926): 411–13; Schwarz, *Wolff*, pp. 216–18.

19. Erkelenz to Tantzen, 10 Dec. 1926, NL Erkelenz, no. 41, pp. 153–54; KW Diary, 13 Dec. 1926, NL KW, no. 34, p. 379; Erkelenz to Franz Ullstein, 3 Jan. 1927, NL Erkelenz, no. 42; Erkelenz to Walther Schreiber, 24 Jan. 1927, NL Erkelenz, no. 42; *Vorstand* meeting, 12 Feb. 1927, NSDAP *Hauptarchiv* 37/720. Albertin, ed., *Führungsgremien*, pp. 419–23. Both Bäumer and Heuss were outraged that they had been singled out for attack by the "Berlin press." Bäumer charged that the *Fraktion* had capitulated before the "Jewish-Liberal" Berlin circle. Bäumer to Koch-Weser, 17 Feb. 1927, NL KW, no. 36, p. 53. She threatened to resign and Koch-Weser pleaded with her to remain. "Do you wish for me to turn over the party to Grossmann and Feder?" Koch-Weser to Bäumer, 10 Feb. 1927, NL KW, no.

36, p. 71. By mid-February, Koch-Weser noted in his diary that "all hell was breaking loose" over the implementation of the S and S Law in the theatre. Artists and intellectuals were forming committees to fight it. KW Diary, 17 Feb. 1927, NL KW, no. 36, p. 53. Despite Bäumer's threat to resign, she retained her party offices and Reichstag seat.

20. The background for the Center party's clerical push in this period can be found in Morsey, *Deutsche Zentrumspartei*; Evans, *The German Center Party*; Helmreich, *Religious Education in German Schools*; Rudolf Morsey, ed., *Die Protokolle der Reichstagsfraktion und des Vorstandes der Deutschen Zentrumspartei 1926–1931* (Mainz, 1969). References to appropriate materials in the Marx NL may be found in Stehkämper: Bavarian concordat 1:353–54; Prussian concordat 2:354–58; scattered materials on the school question and S and S Law. See especially the drafts of the national school law 2:433–62.

21. On the Bavarian concordat see two articles by the Hamburg school administrator, Emmy Beckmann, in *Deutsche Einheit* 7, no. 2 and 3 (10 and 17 Jan. 1925).

22. See Marx's unpublished autobiography. Chap. 2, p. 35 in NL Marx II, 1.

23. Mück to Heuss, 8 Feb. 1929, NL Heuss, no. 269.

24. Heuss, "Um ein Konkordat," *Deutsche Einheit* 9, no. 16 (23 April 1927): 390–91.

25. Bäumer, "Religion und Bekenntnisschule," *Die Hilfe* 31, no. 19 (1 Oct. 1925): 404–6; Georg Wolff, "Der neue Reichsschulgesetzentwurf," ibid., pp. 406–8; PA meeting, 20 Sept. 1925, NSDAP *Hauptarchiv* 38/758. Albertin, ed., *Führungsgremien*, p. 352. Bäumer wrote a book on the subject: *Deutsche Schulpolitik* (Karlsruhe, 1928). Several *Rundschreiben* from the *Reichsgeschäftsstelle* enabled party leaders to stay abreast of the committee hearings in the Reichstag in 1927 and 1928. They are in NSDAP *Hauptarchiv* 39/764–765.

26. Erkelenz, "Die Demokratische Partei und das Konkordat," *Demokratischer Zeitungsdienst* (19 March 1927), in NL Erkelenz, no. 93, p. 35.

27. NSDAP *Hauptarchiv*, 37/739, 4 Dec. 1925.

28. Otto Braun, *Von Weimar zu Hitler*, 2nd ed. (New York, 1940), pp. 274–80; KW Diary, 5 July 1929, no. 39, p. 57; *Vorstand* meeting, 3 June 1929, NSDAP *Hauptarchiv* 37/732. Albertin, ed., *Führungsgremien*, pp. 507–12. Helga Timm, *Die deutsche Sozialpolitik und der Bruch der Grossen Koalition im März 1930* (Düsseldorf, 1952), p. 119; Michael Stürmer, *Koalition und Opposition in der Weimarer Republik 1924–1928* (Düsseldorf, 1967), p. 198.

29. See the correspondence between Bäumer and Erkelenz, 14 and 19 June 1929, NL Erkelenz, no. 52, p. 233.

30. Georg Schreiber, *Zwischen Demokratie und Diktatur* (Regensberg, 1949), pp. 124–35. There is much correspondence in the NL Marx which shows this growing enmity. The BVP's *Wahlhandbuch* for the 1928 election attacked the DDP as an advocate of an *Einheitsstaat* (the party of Preuss), an opponent of a Christian *Kulturpolitik*, protective tariffs, and described it as "Berlin-oriented." U.S. State Department, no. 336, roll 28.

31. This pessimism can be seen in the diary of Koch-Weser and in Anton Erke-

lenz, "Die Krise der Weimarer Koalition," *Die Hilfe* 33, no. 16 (15 Aug. 1927).

8. The Formation and Breakup of the *Deutsche Staatspartei*

1. Attila Chanady, "The Dissolution of the German Democratic Party in 1930," *The American Historical Review* 73, no. 5 (June 1968): 1433–53; *Vorstand* meeting, 13 Dec. 1929, NSDAP *Hauptarchiv* 37/732. Albertin, ed., *Führungsgremien*, pp. 519–21; FZ, no. 739, 4 Oct. 1929; Koch-Weser to Lemmer, 17 April 1930, NL KW, no. 191, p. 161; ibid., no. 101 and NL Dietrich, no. 222.

2. Willy Hellpach in *Der Beobachter* (Stuttgart, 1 Feb. 1930); Hopf (the Württemberg organization leader) to Heuss, 8 Nov. 1929, NL Heuss, no. 57; Hopf to Heuss, 27 Jan. 1930, ibid.; August Weber to Jaenicke, 1 Nov. 1929, NL Jaenicke, no. 18; Hans Otto Rommel, "Aufbau und Zusammenbruch der Demokratie in Württemberg," in Paul Rothmann and Erhard W. Wiehn, eds., *Die FDP/DVP in Baden-Württemberg und ihre Geschichte* (Stuttgart, 1979), pp. 131–64.

3. Stresemann to Koch-Weser, 17 Sept. 1929, NL Stresemann 3178/7393/H171118-119; August Weber in the *Kölnische Zeitung*, no. 566a, 20 Oct. 1929; KW Diary, 5 July 1929, NL KW, no. 39, p. 57. Stresemann's son, Wolfgang, became an active supporter of the DStP after its formation and turned against Scholz. See Artur Mahraun, "Stresemann und die Staatspartei," *KZ*, no. 422 (4 July 1930); "Wolfgang," in the *BBZ*, no. 382 (6 Aug. 1930); and an article by Wolfgang Stresemann, *KZ*, no. 416 (1 Aug. 1930). Larry Eugene Jones, "Gustav Stresemann and the Crisis of German Liberalism," *European Studies Review* 4, no. 2 (Apr. 1974): 141–63.

4. Hellpach and Bäumer frequently expressed this wish, and so did many others, more indirectly. See the remarks of Hellmuth Jaeger, a Young Democratic leader, in the PA, 28 April 1929, NSDAP *Hauptarchiv*, 38/750. Albertin, ed., *Führungsgremien*, p. 501; Koch-Weser to Hans Muhle, 17 April 1930, NL KW, no. 101, p. 142.

5. Friedensburg to Adam Barteld (prominent in the DDP in the Prussian *Landtag*), 23 May 1928, NL Friedensburg, no. 25.

6. Erkelenz to Frankfurter, 2 May 1928, NL Erkelenz, no. 48, p. 193.

7. August Weber to Jaenicke, 1 Nov. 1929, NL Jaenicke, no. 18; *Geschäftsausschuss*, 23 Jan. 1930, NSDAP *Hauptarchiv*, 36/724; Goetz to Stolper, 30 Jan. 1930, NL Stolper, no. 44; NL KW, no. 101.

8. *Vorstand* meeting, 25 July 1930, NSDAP *Hauptarchiv*, 37/732. Albertin, ed., *Führungsgremien*, pp. 556–61; FZ, nos. 548 and 549 (25–26 July 1930); KW to Julius Curtius, 28 July 1930, NL KW, no. 105, pp. 45 and 111; FZ, nos. 560–561 (30 July 1930); *Vorwärts* (10 Aug. 1930).

9. KW Diary, 23 Aug. 1928, NL KW, no. 32, p. 205; Erich Eggeling, *Partei oder Bewegung. Der jungdeutsche Kampf und die Staatspartei* (Berlin, 1930); Karl-Hermann Beeck, "Die Gründung der Deutschen Staatspartei im Jahre 1930 . . ." inaug. diss. (Cologne, 1957); Klaus Hornung, *Der Jungdeutsche Orden* (Düsseldorf, 1958); Alexander Kessler, *Der Jungdeutsche Orden in den Jahren der Entscheidung*, (1928–1930), 2 vols. (Munich,

1974, 1976); *Der Jungdeutsche Orden auf dem Wege zur Deutschen Staatspartei* (Munich, 1980).

10. Arnold Paucker, *Der jüdische Abwehrkampf gegen Anti-Semitismus und Nationalsozialismus* (Hamburg, 1969), pp. 94 and 268.

11. Jaenicke, Friedensburg, and Stolper have valuable sets of private papers at the BA Koblenz, while Weber deposited an unpublished autobiography there. Weber, "Lebenserinnerungen 1871–1945," BA, no. 384.

12. Lemmer, *Manches war doch anders*, pp.149–68, provides no clues as to his behavior.

13. Stephan, "Zur Soziologie der Nationalsozialistischen Deutschen Arbeiterpartei," *Zeitschrift für Politik* 20 (March 1931): 794–804; "Grenzen des nationalsozialistische Vormarsches," ibid. 21 (Dec. 1931): 571–78.

14. Meyer, *Von Bismarck zu Hitler: Erinnerungen und Betrachtungen* (New York, 1944).

15. Hellpach to Jaenicke, 28 March 1930, NL Jaenicke, no. 56; Hellpach, *Erinnerungen* 2:113. See the account of his speech, "Jugend und Staatsbürgerliche Wiedergeburt," *KZ*, no. 304 (4 June 1930).

16. See Hermann Dietrich's reaction to the character of the Nazi Reichstag *Fraktion* following the 1930 election. He saw the Nazis as "people without property who have no understanding of the private sector and private economic interests." Dietrich to Frau Agnes Schmidt (his sister-in-law), Kehl, 18 Oct. 1930, NL Dietrich, no. 125.

17. *BT*, no. 199 (28 April 1930).

18. Lange was a Hirsch-Duncker trade unionist and an old friend of Erkelenz who served as DDP party secretary in Düsseldorf-West. His correspondence with Erkelenz for many years is a valuable source for the study of DDP organizational problems at the *Wahlkreis* level.

19. Pois, *Bourgeois Democrats*, pp. 62–64.

20. Lemmer was highly emotional in his speeches, but a more sober state of mind and concern for material interests and party reform may be found in a letter he wrote to Schücking, 30 April 1930, NL Schücking, no. 50.

21. NL Stolper, no. 44; on Heuss's political values, see Hess, *Theodor Heuss vor 1933* and Pois, *Bourgeois Democrats*. Pois describes Heuss's *Staat und Volk* (Berlin, 1926) as "the greatest single effort on behalf of the republic," p. 55.

22. Bäumer in the C.V. *Zeitung* 9, no. 32 (8 Aug. 1930): 42.

23. See the section "Everybody Knew, Nobody Knew" in Milton Mayer, *They Thought They Were Free*, pp. 125–35; Lüders to Koch-Weser, 29 July 1930, NL Lüders, no. 109.

24. Koch-Weser to Scheidemantel, 11 Oct. 1930, NL KW, no. 110, pp. 29–41.

25. *Vorstand* meeting, 5 May 1930, NSDAP *Hauptarchiv* 37/732. Albertin, ed., *Führungsgremien*, pp. 529–33; *FZ*, no. 335 (6 May 1930); *Der Demokrat*, no. 10 (20 May 1930): 227–28, 230–32; Erkelenz to Lange, 23 May 1930, NL Erkelenz, no. 58, p. 183; PA meeting, 25 May 1930, NSDAP *Hauptarchiv*, 38/750. Albertin, ed., *Führungsgremien*, pp. 533–53; *FZ*, no. 386 (27 May 1930); Lemmer in the *BT*, no. 276 (14 June 1930). See the analysis of the popular mood at this time by the prominent Rhineland Democrat Gustav Dechamps. Dechamps to Erkelenz, 10 May 1930, NL Erkelenz, no. 58, p. 65.

26. Erkelenz to Bäumer, 9 June 1930, NL Erkelenz, no. 58, p. 227; Erkelenz to Lange, 30 June 1930, ibid., p. 350.

27. The need for an emergency levy led to the resignation of Paul Moldenhauer as finance minister when the DVP opposed his policies. Dietrich replaced him, which placed the DDP in a difficult position; it, too, initially opposed the Brüning tax program and the use of article 48 to implement the government's program. *FZ*, nos. 450, 461, 467, (19, 24, 26 June 1930); DDP *Geschäftsstelle, Rundschreiben*, 4 July 1930, NSDAP *Hauptarchiv*, 39/771; Stolper to Oscar Meyer, 17 July 1930, NL Stolper, no. 44.

28. *FZ*, no. 519 (15 July 1930); no. 530 (19 July 1930).

29. For a DDP report on the NSDAP see Hugo Pulvermacher, Bürscheid-Düsseldorf, to Erkelenz, 25 May 1930, NL Erkelenz, no. 58, p. 174; *FZ*, no. 455 (21 June 1930); *FZ*, no. 459 (23 June 1930). The DDP received about 83,000 votes, compared to 115,000 in the previous election; the DVP 227,000 versus 363,000; the NSDAP 376,000 compared to 133,000. The VR (*Jungdo*) received nearly 40,000 votes.

30. PA meeting, 30 July 1930, NSDAP *Hauptarchiv*, 38/750. Albertin, ed., *Führungsgremien*, pp. 562–78; Külz to Stephan, 20 July 1930, NL Külz, no. 132.

31. *FZ*, no. 532 (19 July 1930), for the text of the *Aufruf*. Stephan, *Linksliberalismus*, pp. 441–44, discusses the secret negotiations; Bäumer to Erkelenz, 5 July 1930, NL Erkelenz, no. 58, p. 228.

32. *FZ*, no. 546 (25 July 1930).

33. *Vorstand* meeting, 25 July 1930, NSDAP *Hauptarchiv*, 37/732. Albertin, ed., *Führungsgremien*, pp. 556–61.

34. Stephan, *Linksliberalismus*, pp. 446–48; DDP *Geschäftsstelle*, 27 July 1930, NSDAP *Hauptarchiv* 39/771; NL KW, no. 106, pp. 37–39; *BT*, no. 352 (29 July 1930); *FZ*, no. 556 (29 July 1930); *Der Jungdeutsche* (Journal of the *Jungdo*, 29 July 1930). Koch-Weser's *Nachlass* is brimming with letters on the launching of the DStP. Erkelenz announced his resignation at this time. Erkelenz to KW, 29 July 1930, NL KW, no. 105, p. 61; Heuss to Koch-Weser, 1 Aug. 1930, NL Heuss, no. 58; NL Dietrich, no. 222.

35. PA meeting, 30 July 1930, NSDAP *Hauptarchiv*, 38/750. Albertin, ed., *Führungsgremien*, pp. 562–78. Reaction to the new party varied considerably. The *BZM*, no. 203 (28 July 1930), voiced skepticism about the new party along with many Berlin Democrats. In the provinces, the DDP organizations were more supportive of efforts to renew German party life and to join with rightist parties. Georg Freck, Donaueschingen, to Dietrich, 28 July 1930, NL Dietrich, no. 120.

36. Stephan, *Linksliberalismus*, p. 448.

37. Rabbi Vogelstein to Jaenicke, 10 Oct. 1930, NL Jaenicke, no. 25. Heuss had fought his way up the list until, in 1930, he finally managed to move Wieland out of the top position. Heuss to Goetz, 31 July 1930, Heuss NL, no. 56.

38. *FZ*, no. 583 (7 Aug. 1930); ibid., no. 671 (9 Sept. 1930).

39. *FZ*, no. 559 (30 July 1930); *BT*, no. 362 (8 Aug. 1930); *FZ*, no. 685 (14 Sept. 1930); Schwarz, *Wolff*, p. 229; Wolff to Stolper, 13 Sept. 1930, NL Stolper, no. 44. Wolff advised his readers to "vote for the left" and his children ended up voting for the SPD, while his wife was apparently the only

family member who voted for the DStP. Koch-Weser's children also voted SPD in this election.

40. A messy and confused lawsuit destroyed Bernhard professionally, and he resigned in June 1930, although he always contended he was removed as editor because of the rightist shift in the Ullstein family. Kosyk, *Geschichte der deutschen Presse* 3:251–57; Rosie Goldschmidt, *Prelude to the Past*, pp. 275–78, 347, 372–73.

41. Dönhoff to Rexrodt, 28 July 1930, NL Lüders, no. 109; Lüders to Koch-Weser, 29 July 1930, ibid. According to Lüders, "dirty tricks" had been used against Ulich-Beil in Saxony to deny her a suitable list position. Bäumer tried to reassure Dönhoff that their "new friends" were not antifeminist, although the *Jungdo* was. Bäumer to Dönhoff, 11 Aug. 1930, ibid. (Copies of correspondence in Lüders' NL.) Lüders to a "very honored colleague" (probably Höpker-Aschoff or Dietrich), 3 Sept. 1930, ibid. According to Lüders, "our new friends" were worthless for political work and were anti-Semitic. It became the unenviable task of Meyer and Höpker-Aschoff to explain to disappointed and angry Democrats why they were being asked to sacrifice themselves for DStP unity. Koch-Weser to Bruckmann, 31 July 1930, NL KW, no. 105, p. 117; Meyer to Rönneburg, 27 Aug. 1930, NL Dietrich, no. 246, p. 471; Höpker-Aschoff to Lüders, 27 Aug. 1930, NL Lüders, no. 109; Lüders to Höpker-Aschoff, 1 Sept. 1930, ibid.

42. Stephan, *Linksliberalismus*, pp. 456–62.

43. Heuss to Petersen, 15 Aug. 1930, NL Stolper, no. 44; Stolper to Wolff, 12 Sept. 1930, ibid.; Goetz to Stolper, 22 July 1930, ibid.; Heuss to Hieber, 31 July 1930, NL Heuss, no. 82; Heuss to Goetz, 31 July 1930, ibid., no. 56; Heuss to Petersen, 1 Aug. 1930, ibid., no. 59; Weber to Jaenicke, 31 July 1930, NL Jaenicke, no. 56; Weber to Jaenicke, 22 Aug. 1930, ibid., no. 18. There are several letters concerning Friedenburg's aborted attempt to secure a high list position in East Prussia in NL Friedensburg, no. 25.

44. See Büll's angry reaction to his replacement by Stolper. Büll to Stolper, 23 Aug. 1930, NL Stolper, no. 44.

45. Stolper to Ernst Brauweiler, 5 Aug. 1930, NL Stolper, no. 44; Stolper to Wolff, 12 Sept. 1930, ibid.; Wolff to Stolper, 13 Sept. 1930, ibid.; Stolper to Friedensburg, 13 Sept. 1930, ibid.

46. Lüders to Höpker-Aschoff, 1 Sept. 1930, NL Lüders, no. 109. A secretary of Höpker-Aschoff told Lüders that she had been in politics so long that she had assumed she could secure a position without working for it, which quite naturally angered her. Fischer early received word that he would not receive a high list position because of his extensive business connections. Külz had to take a second position and was not reelected, while in Berlin the local DDP organization denied Koch-Weser the top position although he was elected on the *Reichslist*. Fourteen of the "top-of-the-list" candidates were new to partisan politics.

47. Peter M. Bowers, "The Failure of the German Democratic Party, 1918–1930," unpub. diss. (Univ. of Michigan, 1974), p. 219.

48. *Der Illustrierte Beobachter*, no. 5, *Folge*, 32 (9 Aug. 1930); *Folge* 36 (6 Sept. 1930); *Folge* 42 (18 Oct. 1930).

49. *Der Demokrat* 11, no. 17 (5 Sept. 1930); *FZ*, no. 556 (29 July 1930; KW's

statement on the DStP and the DVP, 30 July 1930, in Dietrich NL, no. 222; KW to Oscar Meyer, n.d., written in a sleeping car, in NL Stolper, no. 44.

50. SP German materials at the Hoover Institution (Stanford Univ.); Young Democratic propaganda statement, NL Dietrich, 30 Aug. 1930, no. 123.

51. For examples of Dietrich's speeches, see the text of a radio speech, 1 Sept. 1930, ibid., no. 306 and the Baden "common list" *Manifesto*, ibid., no. 222. Creating a "workable Reichstag" was often stressed as well as producing a *Sammlung* of "free citizens." *FZ*, no. 682 (13 Sept. 1930), published a speech which Dietrich delivered to 15,000 people in the *Sportspalast* in Berlin. For an example of a Höpker-Aschoff speech, see *Der Demokrat* 11, no. 17 (18 Aug. 1930).

52. *FZ*, no. 579 (6 Aug. 1930); ibid., no. 583, editorial (7 Aug. 1930). The Young Democrats were also alarmed about the anti-Semitic program of the NSDAP. "Are your Aryan roots to the 14th century so secure that you won't be worried when the *Hakenkreuzler* come to power?" Jaeger and others to party members, 30 Aug. 1930, in NL Dietrich, no. 123. Feder Diary, 18 Sept. 1930, p. 268; *Breslauer BZ* (25 Aug. 1930), in NL Jaenicke, no. 56. All during the period 1918–1930, the DDP had been attacked as a Jewish party and its Jewish candidates were often abused. There is a description of a 1924 "confrontation" between Bernhard and various right-wing groups— *Stahlhelm*, *Wehrwolf*, and other organizations in the Halle-Merseburg district (Eisleben). Among other things, he was assailed as a "damned black-red-gold Jew," a "dirty fink." In spite of the heckling, he spoke for one and one-half hours on the DDP program and in defense of the "policy of understanding." Hummel Folder, 1924 *Reichstagwahl*, in Hesse-Darmstadt *Staatsarchiv*. See the description of a Bernhard rally in 1928 in Linke, *Restless Days*, p. 353, in which Bernhard was attacked and heckled by both Nazis and Communists. Also see the description of a talk to a student group which Bernhard gave in Göttingen. In this meeting, the Nazis used tear gas and stink bombs to try to break it up, although in time the *Reichsbanner* restored order. *CVZ*, 8, no. 28 (12 July 1929): 356–66.

53. The photograph is among the campaign materials in the SP Germany Collection at the Hoover Institution.

54. *Der Demokrat* 11, no. 18 (20 Sept. 1930). Also see Bowers, "The Failure of the German Democratic Party," pp. 221–25. Only in two districts, Dresden-Bautzen and East Hannover, where the VR was strong, did the DStP show an improvement over 1928 DDP figures.

55. Stolper to Wimbauer, 17 Sept. 1930, NL Stolper, no. 44; *Beamten-Ausschuss* Report, 19 Sept. 1930, NSDAP *Hauptarchiv* 39/772. The DDP members of the Prussian *Landtag*, resentful of the DStP alliance and its results, refused to coalesce with the VR members who had been elected on the DStP ticket. *Vorwärts*, no. 450 (25 Sept. 1930). See the heated recriminations voiced at the *Vorstand* meeting, 29 Sept. 1930, NSDAP *Hauptarchiv*, 37/732. Albertin, ed., *Führungsgremien*, pp. 581–97. Bernhard's remarks seemed particularly telling.

56. *Der Meister* 6, no. 1 (Oct. 1930).

57. She was supported by Koch-Weser, Hieber, and Wachhorst de Wente. *Vorstand* meeting, 27 Sept. 1930, NSDAP *Hauptarchiv*, 37/732. Albertin, ed.,

Führungsgremien, pp. 581–87. Also see Bäumer's articles in *Die Hilfe* 36, no. 41 (11 Oct. 1930): 1009–10, and ibid., no. 44 (1 Nov. 1930): 1081–84; Huber, "Gertrud Bäumer," pp. 160–70; Koch-Weser to Schücking, 11 Oct. 1930, NL Schücking, no. 50. Koch-Weser contended that the VR had honored its pledges to the DDP and had not been anti-Semitic. He anticipated an attack on himself by the "Berlin *Richtung*."

58. Stolper to Landahl, 16 Sept. 1930, NL Stolper, no. 44; Stolper, *Ein Leben*, pp. 262–64.

59. Max Nolte, Hagen, to Dietrich, 26 Sept. 1930, NL Dietrich, no. 256, pp. 25–26; DDP *Ortsverein*, Pforzheim, to Deitrich, ibid., p. 38.

60. Külz in *Der Demokrat* 11, no. 19 (10 Oct. 1930): 439–41.

61. Stolper to von Eckhardt, 17 Sept. 1930, NL Stolper, no. 44. In anticipation of a large vote from the traditional non-voters, the DStP prepared special electoral appeals to them. *Rundschreiben*, no. 16, 3 Sept. 1930, NSDAP *Hauptarchiv*, 39/772. One of Bäumer's arguments for the formation of the DStP was that the non-voters refused to vote for any traditional party but might vote for a new party.

62. *Vorstand*, 27 Sept. 1930 and 16 Oct. 1930, NSDAP *Hauptarchiv* 37/732. Albertin, ed., *Führungsgremien*, pp. 597–612.

63. NL Jaenicke, no. 56.

64. Jaenicke to Rabbi Vogelstein, 11 Oct. 1930, NL Jaenicke, no. 25.

65. Cohnstaedt's changing position may be seen in the meeting of the *Vorstand*, 27 Sept. 1930, NSDAP *Hauptarchiv*, 37/732. Albertin, ed., *Führungsgremien*, p. 590; Stephan, *Linksliberalismus*, p. 472. On the economic plight of the FZ see Werner Wirthle, *Frankfurter Zeitung und Frankfurter Societäts Druckerei GMBH. Die wirtschaftlichen Verhältnisse 1927–1939* (Frankfurt a/M, 1977). Ernst Feder also lost his position about this time. Feder to Friedensburg, 24 March 1931, NL Friedensburg, no. 21.

66. BBZ, no. 469 (8 Oct. 1930); ibid., no. 482 (15 Oct. 1930); *Der Demokrat* 11, no. 20 (21 Oct. 1930); FZ, no. 750 (8 Oct. 1930).

67. Feder Diary, 7 Oct. 1930, p. 272.

68. Koch-Weser's attempt to retain his Reichstag seat was not the most attractive chapter of his career, in part because he defamed Winschuh in his attempt to save his seat in the Reichstag. KW to Max Wiessner, 10 Oct. 1930, NL KW, no. 110, pp. 58–59; Feder Diary, 13 Oct. 1930, p. 272; Petersen to KW, 13 Oct. 1930, NL KW, no. 110, p. 75; Scheidemantel to KW, 14 Oct. 1930, ibid., pp. 43–45; Ehlermann to KW, 14 Oct. 1930, ibid., p. 81; Winschuh to Eduard Dingeldey, n.d. Oct., 1930, NL Dingeldey, no. 30. Dingeldey succeeded Scholz as chairman of the DVP.

69. Heuss, interestingly, felt in 1924 that Koch-Weser had the technical skills to be a good leader, but that he lacked sympathetic human qualities. Heuss to Albert Hopf, 30 Jan. 1924, NL Heuss, no. 57. Feder had a discussion about Koch-Weser with a wealthy Jewish industrialist, Julius Berger, who told him that he was a friend of Koch-Weser "as much as he has friends." Feder Diary, 21 June 1931, p. 298.

70. *Vorstand* meeting, 8 Nov. 1930, NSDAP *Hauptarchiv*, 37/732. Albertin, ed., *Führungsgremien*, pp. 612–14. The protocol of the first DStP PT is in 37/732. See Feder's article on the dissolution of the DDP in the BT, "Die Auflö-

sung der Demokratischen Partei," no. 529 (8 Nov. 1930); "Die Demokraten-Tagung in Hannover," *VZ*, no. 268 (9 Nov. 1930); *Der Demokrat* 11, no. 22 (20 Nov. 1930): 514–15; *FZ*, no. 838 (9 Nov. 1930).

9. Left Liberals after 1930

1. Issberner was one of the unsung figures of German left liberalism from Richter to the end of the DStP. He apparently attended most meetings, edited the DDP newsletters and publications when asked to do so, and also worked on *die Hilfe* when the party's funds began to dry up. His work goes unmentioned and unrecognized in the DDP memoirs literature and receives only a trifling notice in Stephan's *Linksliberalismus*.

2. Hopf to Dietrich, 25 Sept. 1932, NL Dietrich, no. 224, p. 297; Nuschke to Külz, 10 Oct. 1932, NL Külz, no. 18.

3. Heuss to Mück, 28 Jan. 1932, NL Heuss, no. 269; Heuss to Külz, 15 June 1932, NL Külz, no. 17; Lüders to Dietrich, 1 Sept. 1932, NL Lüders, no. 100; Dietrich admitted that he lacked the energy and health to lead the party. Dietrich to Höpker-Aschoff, 15 June 1932, NL Dietrich, no. 223, p. 53.

4. Reinhold Maier, *Ende und Wende. Das schwäbische Schicksal. 1944–1946. Briefe und Tagebuchaufzeichnungen* (Stuttgart, 1948); *Erinnerungen 1948–1953* (Tübingen, 1966). Maier strongly advocated a rightist course for the Württemberg DDP in 1930, which angered the DDP's left wing and drove the Payer family from the DDP. For a good guide to his political thinking in 1933 see the speech he delivered to the DStP PT in Württemberg in January 1933. NL Dietrich, no. 265, p. 4.

5. NSDAP, nos. 39/40, folders 775-780.

6. Paul Helbich to the DStP *Zentrale* 6 April 1931, NL Dietrich, no. 243. Dietrich's papers contain many of the letters and documents sent to Nuschke.

7. There is much material on this *Sammlung* effort in both the NL Wildemuth and the NL Dietrich. Also see Jones, "Sammlung oder Zersplitterung? Bei Bestrebungen zur Bildung einer Neuen Mittelpartei in der Endphase der Weimarer Republik 1930–1933," *VZG* 25, no. 3 (July 1977): 265–304.

8. *Gesamtvorstand*, 7 July 1932, NSDAP 39/777. Albertin, ed., *Führungsgremien*, pp. 731–39; *Geschäftsführender Vorstand*, 7 July 1932, 39/778. Albertin, ed., *Führungsgremien*, pp. 727–30.

9. Mosich to Gessler, 24 June 1932, NL Gessler, no. 19.

10. *FZ*, no. 504 (8 July 1932); KW to the *Hauptvorstand* (Sic!) 9 July 1932, NL KW, no. 40, p. 309; Rönneburg to Lüders, 13 July 1932, NL Lüders, no. 99.

11. Lüders to Dietrich, 15 July 1932, NL Dietrich, no. 223, p. 203. Dietrich's secretary wrote her soon, asking for her "*Ruhe*" and to stop her divisive actions. Dietrich (secretary) to Lüders, 20 July 1932, NL Lüders, no. 100. Dietrich to Lüders, 1 Sept. 1930, NL Lüders, no. 100. Lüders to August Weber, 22 Oct. 1932, ibid. Külz and Wieland were also removed from the *Reichslist*.

12. Theodor Heuss, *Hitlers Weg. Eine historisch-politische Studie über den Nationalsozialismus* (Stuttgart, 1932). New edition ed. by Eberhard Jäckel (Tübingen, 1968); Pois, *Bourgeois Democrats*, pp. 92–97; Hess, *Theodor Heuss vor 1933*, pp. 115–33.

13. KW Diary, 24 Oct. 1932, NL KW, no. 40, p. 323. Paul Liebig to Gessler, 5 Aug. 1932, NL Gessler, no. 19. Also KW to Gessler, 16 Sept. 1932, ibid.

14. *Geschäftsführender Vorstand*, 2 Sept. 1932, NSDAP 39/744. Albertin, ed., *Führungsgremien*, pp. 739–50.

15. *Gesamtvorstand*, 11 Sept. 1932, ibid., 39/778. Albertin, ed., *Führungsgremien*, pp. 741–49; *BT*, no. 433 (12 Sept. 1932); Anna Misch to Lüders, 15 Sept. 1932, NL Lüders, no. 100.

16. Dietrich to *Oberschulrat* Bauser of the *Volksrechtspartei*, 10 Oct. 1932, NL Dietrich, no. 224, p. 335.

17. Baumgarten (*Landesverband* Schleswig-Holstein) to the DStP *Zentrale*, 17 Oct. 1932, NL Dietrich, no. 234, p. 351.

18. Frieda Wunderlich to Lüders, 20 Oct. 1932, NL Lüders, no. 100; Lüders to Johanna Haescher, Kassel, 29 Nov. 1932, ibid.

19. Heuss to Landahl, 20 Oct. 1932, NL Heuss, no. 58.

20. A copy of this issue was in the SP Germany materials in the Hoover Institution. Dietrich's papers and the NSDAP collection also contain examples of electoral propaganda for the November 1932 election.

21. August Weber to Jaenicke, 21 Nov. 1932, NL Jaenicke, no. 59. Maier to the *Arbeitsausschuss*, 9 Nov. 1932, in Erich Matthias and Rudolf Morsey, eds., *Das Ende der Parteien* (Düsseldorf, 1960), pp. 87–88.

22. NL Külz, no. 18.

23. Heuss to Goetz, 31 Dec. 1932, NL Heuss, no. 80. *Gesamtvorstand*, 8 Jan. 1933, NSDAP 38/770. Albertin, ed., *Führungsgremien*, pp. 752–63; *BT*, No. 14 (9 Jan. 1933); *FZ*, nos. 24–25 (10 Jan. 1933).

24. Stolper to Nuschke, 11 Jan. 1933, NL Stolper, no. 44.

25. Pro and con opinions can be found in the following: Nuschke to Dietrich, 2 Feb. 1933, NL Dietrich, no. 265, p. 15; Ortsgruppe Dresden to Külz, 7 Feb. 1933, NL Külz, no. 19; Dietrich to Tantzen, 8 Feb. 1933; Matthias and Morsey, eds., *Das Ende der Parteien 1933*, pp. 90–91; NSDAP, 40/791, document dated 11 Feb. 1933; *FZ*, nos. 112–113 (11 Feb. 1933); Heuss-Knapp to Gertrud Stetinner-Fuhrmann, 12 Feb. 1933, *Bürgerin zweier Welten*, pp. 215–16; Goetz to Külz, 10 Feb. 1933, in Matthias and Morsey, eds., *Das Ende der Parteien 1933*, p. 88–90. DStP (Mannheim) to Dietrich, 13 Feb. 1933, NL Dietrich, no. 265, p. 18; Dietrich to Vögeler, Mannheim, 16 Feb. 1933, ibid., p. 21.

26. Dietrich to Adolf Mast, 16 Feb. 1933, NL Dietrich, no. 265, p. 24.

27. *Der Beobachter* (Stuttgart, 22 March 1933), in the Baden-Württemberg *Staatsarchiv* clipping file, (E 132 #122).

28. Matthias and Morsey, eds., *Das Ende der Parteien 1933*, p. 90; NSDAP 40/791.

29. Georg Borkmann to the Hamburg DStP, 23 Feb. 1933; Borkmann to Dietrich, 2 March 1933, in NL Dietrich, no. 143, pp. 214 and 216. On Maier's willingness to work with the Nazis see Pois, *Bourgeois Democrats*, p. 91.

30. Matthias and Morsey, eds., *Das Ende der Parteien 1933*, pp. 68–72 and 93–94; Lemmer, *Manches war doch anders*, pp. 170–77; Lüders, *Fürchte dich nicht*, p. 129n; Eksteins, *Theodor Heuss*, pp. 117–18, 190–92.

31. Dietrich to Ablass, 28 March 1933, NL Dietrich, no. 142, p. 4. Bäumer,

"Unsere nationale Bewegung und der Nationalsozialismus," *Die Hilfe* 39, no. 6 (18 March 1933): 162–63.

32. *Reichstag Verhandlungen* 457 (23 March 1933): 38.
33. NL Goetz, no. 56.
34. Matthias and Morsey, eds., *Das Ende der Parteien 1933*, pp. 91–92.
35. Ibid., pp. 93–95.
36. Jann Berghaus to Dietrich, 15 May 1933, NL Dietrich, no. 143, p. 81; Külz to Dietrich, 8 June 1933, ibid., no. 149, p. 226.
37. Paul Hestwig, Nuschke, and Schreiber to the president of the Prussian *Landtag*, Hermann Göring, 27 June 1933 and Göring's reply, NSDAP 40/790.
38. Dietrich, Heuss, and Lemmer to the Reich minister of the interior, Wilhelm Frick, 10 July 1933. NSDAP 40/790; Matthias and Morsey, eds., *Das Ende der Parteien 1933*, pp. 96–97; *BT*, no. 296 (27 June 1933).
39. Rudolf Diels, *Lucifer ante portas. Es spricht der erste Chef der Gestapo* (Stuttgart, 1950); Friedensburg, *Lebenserinnerungen*, pp. 245–61.
40. NL Höpker-Aschoff, nos. 5, 49.
41. Lüders, *Fürchte dich nicht*, pp. 140–41; von Velsen, *Im Alter die Fülle*, p. 354; Huber, *Gertrud Bäumer*, pp. 286–87, 375, 391; Pois, *Bourgeois Democrats*, p. 38; Evans, *The Feminist Movement in Germany*, pp. 260–61.
42. Lemmer, *Manches war doch anders*, pp. 184–218; Walter Laqueur, *The Terrible Secret. Suppression of the Truth about Hitler's 'Final Solution,'* (Boston, 1981), pp. 211–12.
43. Ulich-Beil, *Ich ging meinen Weg*, pp. 149–64.
44. Luppe, *Mein Leben*, pp. 289–326.
45. See Stolper's books, *This Age of Fables* (London, 1943) and *German Realities* (New York, 1948).
46. Karl Lowenstein, a DDP member who aspired to a political career in Bavaria, became a distinguished professor of political science at Amherst, Bonn joined the faculty at the University of California, while Fritz Epstein had a unique career as a bibliographer, archivist, and historian. Hajo Holborn was another DDP gift to America. Among the children who achieved distinction, one should include the late Klaus Epstein, Fritz Stern, Gerhard L. Weinberg, and Hannah Holborn Gray.
47. Heinz Ullstein, *Spielplatz meines Lebens. Erinnerungen.* (Munich, 1961).
48. On Hamm, see Georg Hohmann, "Dr. Hamm zum Gedächtnis. Ein historisch-politisches Zeitbild," *Süddeutsche Zeitung* (13 Aug. 1946); Georg Hohmann, *Ein Arzt erlebt seine Zeit* (Munich, 1954), pp. 175–79; Hans Luther, *Politiker ohne Partei* (Stuttgart, 1960), p. 94.

Conclusion

1. Among the most important analyses of the DDP's failure are the following: KW Diary, 5 July 1929, NL KW, no. 39, p. 57. In this entry, Koch-Weser describes the condition of the DDP and the alternatives that were available to it. Also see the *Vorstand* meetings, 14–15 June 1928, NSDAP 37/730. Albertin, ed., *Führungsgremien*, pp. 452–69; Memorandum of Lüders, 6 June 1928, NL Lüders, no. 109; Jaenicke to August Weber, 30 May 1928, NL Jaenicke, no. 18; Frankfurter to Erkelenz, 27 April 1927, NL Erkelenz,

no. 44, pp. 155–57; Carl von Voss, "Kann die Deutsche Demokratische Partei eine Partei der Masse werden?" 31-page memorandum (Spring 1930). There are copies of this in several *Nachlässe*, including NL Heile, no. 23, Erkelenz to Hofheinz, 27 Jan. 1930, NL Erkelenz, no. 56, pp. 160–61; Erkelenz to Voss, 7 May 1930, NL Erkelenz, no. 58, pp. 33–36. Bonn, "Bricht die Brücke?" *BT*, no. 208 (4 May 1930); Feder, "Die Auflösung der Demokratischen Partei," *BT*, no. 529 (8 Nov. 1930); Erkelenz, "Das Ende der Staatspartei," *Vorwärts*, no. 501 (25 Oct. 1930); Erkelenz to Dönhoff, 28 Nov. 1930, NL Erkelenz, no. 59; Friedensburg to Voss, 5 May 1930, NL Friedensburg, no. 25; Höpker-Aschoff in *Der Demokrat* 11, no. 21 (15 Nov. 1930); Bachrach to Friedensburg, 30 Oct. 1932, NL Friedensburg, no. 25; Erkelenz to Bäumer, 3 Feb. 1934, copy in NL Heuss, no. 77; Schiffer to Gerland, 31 Oct. 1940, NL Gerland, no. 21. Koch-Weser and Erkelenz were obsessed with the DDP's decline and the Republic's failure, and there are hundreds of references to this topic in their correspondence and in KW's diary. As early as April 1921, Koch-Weser seemed to realize that democracy in Germany was floundering because it had not taken root among the mass of nominal supporters of the Republic. He despaired of the inadequate local leadership of the DDP which he found in Darmstadt and Karlsruhe—"little people who don't understand why democratic ideas are dying in southern Germany." Diary, 16 April 1921, NL KW, no. 16, p. 453. Despite the general pessimism about the future of the DDP and the Republic, some Democrats refused to wilt. See, for example, Petersen's explanation of why he remained a Democrat. Petersen to Gessler, 17 July 1926, NL Gessler, no. 18. The memoirs literature of the DDP abounds in analyses of the DDP's failure. For example, Willy Hellpach, *Erinnerungen* 2:133 and *passim*; Hellpach in the *Neue Zürcher Zeitung*, no. 1551 (10 Aug. 1930); Hermann Dietrich, *Auf dem Weg zum neuen Staat. Die deutsche Aufgabe*, p. 18 and *passim*; Koch-Weser, *Und dennoch aufwärts! Eine deutsche Nachkriegsbilanz*, p. 180 and *passim*; NL Külz, no. 11 (Külz's unpublished autobiography), pp. 252–54; Stephan, *Linksliberalismus*, pp. 491–505. All of the secondary accounts of the DDP/DStP also have reflections on the party's failure. For example, Schneider, *Die Deutsche Demokratische Partei*, pp. 264–72; Jürgen C. Hess, "Gab es eine Alternative? Zum Scheitern des Linksliberalismus in der Weimarer Republik," *HZ* 22, no. 3: 638–54; Frye, "The German Democratic Party 1918–1930," *The Western Political Quarterly* 26, no. 1 (March 1964): 176–79; ibid., Yearbook of the Leobaeck Institute, 21 (1976), 143–172.

2. The DDP was always reluctant to use its political position to advance its members in the bureaucracy or government employment. Koch-Weser, for example, while minister of justice for nine months, appointed only one known Republican in that department but did appoint one DNVP member and several right-wing DVP members. This not only demonstrated a lack of will to power but also a lack of commitment to the democratic Republic and a desire to curry the favor of professional civil servants. Erkelenz to Hofheinz, 27 Jan. 1930, NL Erkelenz, no. 56, pp. 160–61.

Appendix A

1. Material on the DDP/DStP organization is scattered throughout the party records and private papers and has been synthesized in several secondary accounts. Stephan's *Linksliberalismus* is a unique and valuable source on the organization. The *Nachlässe* of Koch-Weser, Erkelenz, Heuss, and Dietrich are particularly valuable on organization questions. The Bad Eilsen meeting on party organization in 1925 and the *Organisationshandbuch* which Stephan compiled for that meeting and which was published in 1926 have provided much of the detailed information which secondary sources have employed. It is available in the NSDAP 39/770 as well as in the published version, *Organisationshandbuch der Deutschen Demokratischen Partei* (Berlin, 1926). Also see Stephan, "Die Organisation der Demokratischen Partei," in Erkelenz, ed., *Zehn Jahre*, pp. 543–48. Stephan attempted without much success to continue the organizational impetus built up at Bad Eilsen. See, for example, *Geschäftsstelle, Rundschreiben*, no. 17, 14 Oct. 1927, NSDAP 39/763. Dietrich's papers have much organizational information for the period 1929–1933. See NL 243, in particular. Albertin, ed., *Führungsgremien*, pp. XX–XXXVIII for a survey of the organization. *Fraktion* records were lost in 1933 and never recovered. Heuss, who was the *Fraktion*'s last business manager, sought to locate them in 1933 but was unsuccessful. Records of the Prussian *Landtag Fraktion* are stored in the BA Koblenz, but on the three occasions I attempted to see them over a period of several years, I was told they were not yet ready to be utilized by researchers. The best guide to the formal organization of the party are the four statutes (*Satzungen*) approved in 1919, 1925, 1929, and 1930. They are conveniently printed in parallel columns in Albertin, ed., *Führungsgremien*, pp. 810–19. They show the relatively few changes which were made in the organization.
2. Stephan, *Linksliberalismus*, pp. 307–8.
3. The business wing tried desperately to block the election of Erkelenz. Cohnstaedt to Payer, 23 Nov. 1921, NL Payer, no. 14, p. 105. The left wing of the party, with the exception of Preuss and Frankfurter, who tended to be centrists on economic and social issues, backed Erkelenz. Cohnstaedt to Erkelenz, 7 Nov. 1921, NL Erkelenz, no. 17, p. 121, and ibid., 28 Nov. 1921, p. 171. Much of the struggle occurred against a background of a battle over tax policy in the DDP and in the Reichstag. PA meeting, 4 Dec. 1921, NSDAP 38/748. Albertin, ed., *Führungsgremien*, pp. 231–33. Cohnstaedt to Erkelenz, 6 Dec. 1921, NL Erkelenz, no. 17, p. 200.
4. Frankfurter to Gerland, 30 April 1920, NL Gerland, no. 7.
5. Stephan, *Linksliberalismus*, p. 112.
6. PA meeting, 8 Oct. 1922, NSDAP 38/756. Albertin, ed., *Führungsgremien*, pp. 275–79.
7. By 1930, the *Kieler Zeitung* supported the NSDAP.
8. The information is in the organizational report of 1925.
9. There is a pamphlet on the history of the Democratic Club up to 1921 in the NL Haussmann, no. 105, and there are frequent references to the club in the early years of the Republic in the Gerland papers. Also see Johann Heinrich von Bernstorff, *Memoirs of Count Bernstorff*, trans. from the German (New

York, 1931), p. 271. After the formation of the DStP, the party offices were moved to the club.

10. There is a description of DDP social life at a Bavarian PT attended by reprcsentatives of the national women's committee which recreates the light-hearted mood of the meeting and the enjoyable time which the members had. Marianne Weber, *Lebenserinnerungen*, pp. 424–25. There is a graphic and amusing description of a Young Democrats' meeting by Heuss. Heuss to Koch-Weser, 18 Dec. 1924, NL Heuss, no. 58.

11. Fischer to Dietrich, 9 April 1932, NL Dietrich, no. 254, p. 79.

12. Feder Diary, 29 Oct. 1932, p. 321.

Appendix B

1. The official election statistics are in the appropriate volumes of the *Statistisches Jahrbuch für das Deutsche Reich*. I have relied heavily on Alfred Milatz, *Wähler und Wahlen in der Weimarer Republik*. Bowers, "The Failure of the German Democratic Party," has much useful material on elections.

2. For contemporary press reaction, see *FZ*, no. 412 (7 June 1920); *BT*, no. 263 (7 June 1920); U.S. State Department, Decimal File, Clipping Collection, 336/441. Hartenstein, *Die Anfänge der Deutschen Volkspartei 1918–1920*, pp. 200–37.

3. KW Diary, 7 June 1920, NL KW, no. 27, p. 117. See Ernst Feder's post mortem in the *BT*, no. 264 (8 June 1920).

4. *Im Deutschen Reich* 26, nos. 7/8 (July–Aug. 1920): 233.

5. *MNN*, no. 227 (8 June 1920).

6. *FZ*, no. 412 (7 June 1920).

7. *BT*, no. 274 (13 June 1920).

8. *Die Hilfe*, no. 25 (17 June 1920): 376–78.

9. Ernst Müller-Meiningen, *Aus Bayerns schwersten Tagen. Erinnerungen und Betrachtungen aus der Revolutionszeit* (Berlin, 1924), p. 284; Reimann, *Müller-Meiningen*, pp. 254–55.

10. *Die Hilfe*, no. 27 (5 July 1920): 406–7; no. 28 (15 July 1920): 414–15; no. 29 (25 July 1920): 437–38.

11. *Vorstand*, 10 June 1920, NSDAP 36/736. Albertin, ed., *Führungsgremien*, pp. 129–31; PA meeting, 22 June 1920, NSDAP 38/746. Albertin, ed., *Führungsgremien*, pp. 132–33; *BT*, no. 290 (23 June 1920); PA meeting, 27 Nov. 1920, NSDAP 38/746. Albertin, ed., *Führungsgremien*, pp. 141–48.

12. Payer to Peter Bruckmann, 7 March 1924, NL Payer, no. 14, p. 177; Milatz, *Wähler und Wahlen*, pp. 116–17; Bowers, "The Failure of the German Democratic Party," pp. 119–24, 133–39.

13. *Die Hilfe*, no. 10 (15 May 1924): 153; for Koch's analysis, see *Der Demokrat* 5, no. 12: 149–56.

14. *Vorstand*, 21 May 1924, NSDAP 36/729. Albertin, ed., *Führungsgremien*, pp. 317–22.

15. *CVZ* 2, no. 2 (11 Jan. 1923): 9; ibid., no. 5 (1 Feb. 1923): 33; 3, ibid., no. 1 (27 March 1924): 1–4; ibid., no. 45 (7 Nov. 1924): 677. The CVZ reproduced posters and cartoons which showed how the rightist parties were linking the DDP to "bloated Jewish capitalists," ibid., no. 50 (12 Dec. 1924):

796. There are several examples of DNVP anti-Semitic materials used in the 1924 election in the *Nachlass* Hummel (Folder, 1924 Election), in the Hesse-Darmstadt *Staatsarchiv* in Darmstadt.

16. Erkelenz to Tantzen, 16 Oct. 1924, NL Erkelenz, no. 33, p. 67; *Vorstand*, 21 Oct. 1924, NSDAP 36/729. Albertin, ed., *Führungsgremien*, pp. 329–32; *FZ*, no. 791 (22 Oct. 1924); *Der Demokrat* 5 (23 Oct. 1924): 284–85.

17. Gerland to his sister, Cornelia, 24 Oct. 1924, NL Gerland, no. 45; Heuss to Koch-Weser, 29 Oct. 1924, NL Heuss, no. 58; Cohnstaedt to Erkelenz, 23 Oct. 1924, NL Erkelenz, no. 33, p. 121; Stephan, *Linksliberalismus*, pp. 275–77.

18. Second special party congress (PT), Berlin, Nov. 1924, NSDAP 37/738; *Der Demokrat* 5, nos. 36/37: 297–302.

19. Koch to his wife, 13 Nov. 1924, NL KW, no. 31. Bowers, "The Failure of the German Democratic Party," pp. 141–50.

20. *Der Demokrat* 5, nos. 42/3: 357–58. An old trade union colleague wrote to Erkelenz after the election from Breslau that the DDP there was in terrible shape. It had lost its worker supporters, its leadership was poor, and its financial condition desperate. Moreover, there was great friction between Jews and non-Jews in the local organization, which damaged the party there. Kotbue to Erkelenz, 20 Dec. 1924, NL Erkelenz, no. 90.

21. See Stürmer, *Koalition und Opposition in der Weimarer Republik. 1924–1928*; "Parliamentary Government in Weimar Germany, 1924–1928," in Anthony Nicholls and Erich Mattias, eds., *German Democracy and the Triumph of Hitler* (London, 1971), pp. 59–77; Schneider, *Die Deutsche Demokratische Partei*.

22. NSDAP 37/739.

23. NSDAP 37/740.

24. Hellpach wrote many newspaper articles on this theme as well as a book, *Politische Prognose für Deutschland*, (Berlin, 1928), and a pamphlet, *Die Krise des deutschen Parlamentarismus* (Karlsruhe, 1927); Robert A. Pois, *Friedrich Meinecke and German Politics in the Twentieth Century* (Berkeley, 1972); Alfred Weber, "Zur Platform der Deutschen Staatspartei," *FZ*, no. 594 (12 Aug. 1930); *Das Ende der Demokratie?* (Berlin, 1931).

25. U.S. State Department, 862.00/2391-2482, doc. no. 2422.

26. *FZ*, no. 366 (16 May 1928).

27. NSDAP 37/730. Albertin, ed., *Führungsgremien*, pp. 452–63.

28. NSDAP 37/739. Albertin, ed., *Führungsgremien*, pp. 464–69.

29. NSDAP 39/766; Schücking to the DDP party secretary in Frankfurt a/M, Wolff, 22 May 1928, NL Schücking, no. 50; U.S. State Department, No. 336, roll 27, docs. 2415 and 2422.

30. PA, 20–21 Oct. 1928. NSDAP 37/731. Albertin, ed., *Führungsgremien*, pp. 471–78.

Note on Sources

The primary sources for a history of the German Democratic party and the German State party are rich and voluminous. The national party leaders were habitual preservers of letters and documents, and their families respected their wishes to have their papers turned over to the archives. Most of the sets of private papers (*Nachlässe*) are at the *Bundesarchiv* Koblenz. In addition, quite by chance, a portion of the party's archive escaped the Nazi shredding machines, although the protocols of the *Fraktion* meetings (meetings of the parliamentary delegations) disappeared. These documents are preserved in five reels of the NSDAP *Hauptarchiv* (Reels 36–40) and in the *Bestandsgruppe* R 45, III, in the BA Koblenz. Recently, the notes of the major party committees in this collection along with much other valuable information about the party have been published, edited by Lothar Albertin and Konstanze Wegner, *Die Führungsgremien der Deutschen Demokratischen Partei und der Deutschen Staatspartei 1918–1933*. The official party documents have been supplemented by a large number of party publications, campaign literature, and materials from state and local party organizations. The great bulk of party documents, however, pertain to the national party organization, as do the *Nachlässe*. The nature of the available documents shapes the focus of the book. It concentrates on national problems, the national party, and the leaders who were prominent at the national level of party work rather than local or state party organizations.

The party documents are supplemented by a large number of party publications: *Das demokratische Deutschland, Der Demokrat, Deutsche Einheit, Deutscher Aufstieg*, and *Blätter der Deutschen Staatspartei*. The Naumannite journal *Die Hilfe*, though never an official DDP publication, contains much news about the party and articles by party members. Several major newspapers generally supported the DDP and were usually edited by active Democrats. They included the *Berliner Tageblatt*, the *Frankfurter Zeitung*, and the *Vossische Zeitung*. Clippings from other newspapers "close" to the DDP/DStP supplemented the materials in these newspapers. The clipping files of the *Hauptsstaatsarchiv* (Stuttgart), the

Institut für Weltwirtschaft (Kiel), and the U.S. State Department Decimal File for Germany, 1919–1929, proved especially valuable. I also worked in several libraries and archives which contained additional specialized materials on the DDP/DStP: the Hoover Institution (Stanford, California); the Leo Baeck Institute (London); the *Institut für Zeitgeschichte* (Munich); the BA Koblenz; the *Staatsarchiv* Darmstadt; the *Staatsarchiv* Stuttgart.

In addition to the party documents and press materials, there is a rich store of government documents available to the historian of the Weimar period. Aside from the Reichstag debates and the debates of the National Assembly (*Verhandlungen des Reichstages*; Eduard Heilfron, ed., *Die deutsche Nationalversammlung*), and various handbooks and statistical collections, there are several document collections and monograph series of great importance to German party history: Karl Dietrich Erdmann et al., *Akten der Reichskanzlei. Weimarer Republik*; *Beiträge zur Geschichte des Parlamentarismus und der politischen Parteien*; *Quellen zur Geschichte des Parlamentarismus und der politischen Parteien*.

The most important sources for this study were the private papers of the DDP/DStP leaders. The papers illuminate many of the dark corners of the party's history, often left purposely in shadows in the bland protocols of the party records and the deceptive autobiographies and official biographies. I worked in thirty-seven sets of private papers, most of them at the BA Koblenz, others in state and local archives in Stuttgart, Berlin, Hamburg, and Darmstadt, and in the Hoover Institution. In addition, I utilized the papers of the DVP members Gustav Stresemann and Eduard Dingeldey and of the Centrists Wilhelm Marx and Karl Bachem. Although every *Nachlass* contributed to my knowledge and understanding, the most important papers for this study proved to be those of Erich Koch-Weser, Anton Erkelenz, Hermann Dietrich, and Theodor Heuss. Koch-Weser's diary and the correspondence of Erkelenz and Heuss proved especially revealing. Erkelenz's correspondence with Adolf Lange, the DDP party secretary in Düsseldorf-West, and Heuss's correspondence with Friedrich Mück and Albert Hopf, important figures in the Württemberg organization, did much to clarify for me the problems of local DDP organizations. The letters of Heinrich Gerland and Richard Frankfurter in the NL Gerland revealed much about the subtle differences between Right and Left in the party in the early years of the Republic, while the papers of Hermann Dietrich, Marie-Elisabeth Lüders, Ferdinand Friedensburg, Wolfgang Jaenicke, and Gustav Stolper were invaluable for the last years of the DDP and the formation of the DStP. Others whose papers made important contributions to various stages of the party's history include: Otto Gessler, Walter Goetz, Georg Gothein, Conrad Haussmann, Wilhelm Heile, Hermann Luppe, Wilhelm Külz, Friedrich von Payer, Carl Petersen, Hartmann von Richthofen, Walther Schücking, and Eberhard Wildemuth. Less important for my purposes, either because they contained only copies of published works or materials of lesser importance, were the papers of Moritz Julius Bonn, Elisabeth Brönner-Höpfner, Bernhard Dernburg, Hermann Höpker-Aschoff, Hermann Hummel, Hans-Albert Kluthe, Adolf Korell, Friedrich Meinecke, Eugen Schiffer, Theodor Wolff, and Arthur Feiler. In addition to the sets of private papers, DDP/DStP members published fifty autobiographical works, which contain information about the party's history and/or biographical material. There are several unpublished autobiographies in the BA Koblenz, most notably those of Bernhard Falk, Georg Gothein, Wilhelm Külz, and August Weber.

Because of the DDP/DStP's valuable primary sources, the party has attracted a number of historians. Several books and dissertations have been written on limited chronological phases of the party's history or on specialized topics. Yet only Werner Stephans's *Aufstieg und Verfall des Linksliberalismus 1918–1933* has attempted to survey the entire period, but his book lacks footnotes and scholarly objectivity. He was the general secretary and business manager of the party for several years, and his work has insights and information about the history of the organization which are extremely valuable. Space limitations have forced me to delete many references to secondary literature and discussions of secondary works, but I would be remiss if I did not at least acknowledge the names of authors whose studies have aided my work: Lothar Albertin, Werner Becker, Peter M. Bowers, Rennie W. Brantz, Attila Chanady, Modris Eksteins, Ludwig Elm, Erich Eyck, Lothar Gall, Regina Gottschalk, Jürgen C. Hess, Wolfgang Hartenstein, Karl Holl, Larry Eugene Jones, Wolfgang J. Mommsen, Arnold Paucker, Robert A. Pois, Ernst Portner, Joachim Reimann, Stuart T. Robson, Werner Schneider, Hartmut Schustereit, Gotthart Schwarz, Gustav Seeber, Henry Ashby Turner Jr., Konstanze Wegner.

Archival Sources

Bundesarchiv Koblenz

NL Moritz Julius Bonn
NL Elisabeth Brönner-Höpfner
NL Bernhard Dernburg
NL Hermann Dietrich
NL Eduard Dingeldey
NL Anton Erkelenz
NL Ferdinand Friedensburg
NL Heinrich Gerland
NL Otto Gessler
NL Walter Goetz
NL Georg Gothein
NL Wilhelm Heile

Note on Sources

NL Theodor Heuss
NL Hermann Höpker-Aschoff
NL Wolfgang Jaenicke
NL Hans-Albert Kluthe
NL Erich Koch-Weser
NL Wilhelm Külz
NL Marie-Elisabeth Lüders
NL Hermann Luppe
NL Bruno Marwitz
NL Friedrich von Payer
NL Hartmann von Richthofen
NL Eugen Schiffer
NL Walther Schücking
NL Gustav Stresemann
NL Alfred Weber
NL Eberhard Wildemuth
NL Theodor Wolff
Bernhard Falk, "*Lebenserinnerungen* 1867–1944" BA
no. 385
August Weber, "*Lebenserinnerungen* 1871–1956" BA
no. 384

Staatsarchiv Darmstadt

NL Hermann Hummel (Fragment)
NL Adolf Korell

Stadtarchiv Cologne

NL Karl Bachem
NL Wilhelm Marx

Preussisches Geheimes Staatsarchiv (Berlin-Dahlem)

NL Friedrich Meinecke

Staatsarchiv Hamburg/Petersen Family Archive, Ham-
burg-Wentorf

NL Carl Wilhelm Petersen

Hauptstaatsarchiv Stuttgart

NL Conrad Haussmann

Hoover Institution Archive

Note on Sources

Arthur Feiler Papers

Unpublished party documents

Akten of the DDP/DStP, BA Koblenz, *Bestandsgruppe* R 45–111. *Liberale Partei*. NSDAP *Hauptarchiv*, rolls 36–41.

Other unpublished materials

Letter from Eduard Rosenbaum to the author, 14 Oct. 1967

Returns from questionnaire framed by the author and sent to surviving DDP figures in 1963–1964. Answers provided by Emmy Beckmann, Ernst Lemmer, Marie Elisabeth Lüders, Reinhold Maier, Werner Stephan, and Josef Winschuh.

U.S. Department of State, records of the Department of State relating to the internal affairs of Germany, 1910–1939. 862.9111/101–170. Microfilm copy 336, rolls 141, 142, 144.

DDP/DStP Document Collections and Uncatalogued Materials

Bundesarchiv Koblenz
Hauptstaatsarchiv Stuttgart
Hoover Institution, Stanford California
Institut für Zeitgeschichte, Munich
Institut für Weltwirtschaft an der Universität Kiel.
Preussisches Geheimes Staatsarchiv, Berlin-Dahlem

Index